Instructor's Manual

to accompany

International Business
The Challenge of
Global Competition

Eighth Edition

Donald A. Ball

Wendell H. McCulloch, Jr.
California State University, Long Beach

Paul Frantz
California State University, Long Beach

J. Michael Geringer
California Polytechnic State University

Michael S. Minor
The University of Texas Pan American

Boston   Burr Ridge, IL   Dubuque, IA   Madison, WI   New York   San Francisco   St. Louis
Bangkok   Bogotá   Caracas   Kuala Lumpur   Lisbon   London   Madrid   Mexico City
Milan   Montreal   New Delhi   Santiago   Seoul   Singapore   Sydney   Taipei   Toronto

McGraw-Hill Higher Education

A Division of The McGraw-Hill Companies

Instructor's Manual to accompany
INTERNATIONAL BUSINESS: THE CHALLENGE OF GLOBAL COMPETITION, EIGHTH EDITION
Ball, McCulloch, Frantz, Geringer, Minor

1 2 3 4 5 6 7 8 9 0 1BKM/1BKM 0 9 8 7 6 5 4 3 2 1

ISBN 0-07-245408-3

www.mhhe.com

TABLE OF CONTENTS

Part I—The Nature of International Business

Chapter 1: The Rapid Change of Global Business 1
Chapter 2: Trading and Investing in International Business 16
Chapter 3: Economic Theories of International Business 35

Part II—The International Environment

Chapter 4: The Dynamics of International Organizations 50
Chapter 5: Understanding the International Monetary System 68

Part III—The Foreign Environmental Forces

Chapter 6: Financial Forces: Influencing International Business 84
Chapter 7: Economic and Socioeconomic Forces 99
Chapter 8 : Physical and Environmental Forces 116
Chapter 9 : Sociocultural Forces 133
Chapter 10 : Political Forces 154
Chapter 11 : Legal Forces 170
Chapter 12 : Labor Forces 184
Chapter 13 : Competitive Forces 197

Part IV—The Organizational Environment

Chapter 14 : Strategic Planning, Organization Design and Control of the Firm 227
Chapter 15 : Assessing and Analyzing Markets 247
Chapter 16 : Marketing Internationally 255
Chapter 17 : Export and Import Practices 268
Chapter 18 : Human Resource Management 285
Chapter 19 : Financial Management 297
Chapter 20 : Global Operations Management: The Third Industrial Revolution 312

VIDEO CASES 327

INTERNATIONAL BUSINESS: DIVERSE, COMPETITIVE AND SUBJECT TO RAPID TECHNOLOGICAL CHANGE

Learning Objectives

1. Heighten the students' interest in international business by showing them why its study is important to them even though they may not be planning for an overseas career.

2. Encourage the students to tie in what they have learned in the functional areas to international business by pointing out that many of the concepts and business techniques as practiced domestically can be applied elsewhere.

3. Point out that international managers must study and compare the various forces in the domestic, international and foreign environments so that they will know when a concept or technique: (1) may be used as is, (2) must be modified or (3) must even be discarded.

Overview

Competition from global competitors is mounting. The huge increase in import penetration plus the massive amounts of overseas investment mean that firms of all sizes face competitors from everywhere in the world. The increasing internationalization of business is requiring managers to have a global business perspective gained through experience, education or both.

International business differs from its domestic counterpart in that it involves three environments–domestic, foreign, and international–instead of one. Although the kinds of forces are the same in the domestic and foreign environments, their values often differ and changes in the foreign force values are at times more difficult to assess.

While international businesspeople must have a solid understanding of business concepts and techniques used in the industrialized nations, they must also know enough about the differences in the environmental forces of the markets in which they operate to be able to decide if a concept or a technique (1) can be transferred to another country as is, (2) must be adapted to local conditions or (3) cannot be used elsewhere.

Suggestions and Comments

We have found that students generally are unaware of their dependence on international business. To arouse their early interest in the course (especially at schools where international business is a required course in compliance with AACSB requirements), we use one or more of the student involvement exercises listed in the following section.

Student Involvement Exercises

1. Hold up a common object such as a lead pencil. Where do the materials come from? Rubber comes from the Far East, the copper and tin from which the brass ferrule is made may come from Chile and Malaysia respectively, etc.

2. Ask if anyone in class is involved in international business. The response is usually negative, although in this edition we do have the discussion about how the students began their day so they may be ready for this one. This can open up a discussion to show our dependence on imports (VCRs, TVs, cars, etc.)

3. We get a good response from the class when we show a transparency that has the 16 companies from page 5. We ask the students to pick out the brands or companies that are American–owned. Usually, they pick the wrong ones and we have a lively discussion.

You can start the class off on an international business project here or wait until the class begins to study the section on forces. If you start now, here is an example of a handout (condensed):]

International Business Project

Objective: To create a business opportunity for an American consumer product in a foreign country.

Project Outline

1. Size of market (demographics, socioeconomic state, urban/rural).
2. Sociocultural acceptance of product–adaptation necessary?
3. Legal/bureaucratic environment (imports, local manufacture, taxation).
4. Competition in market.
5. Economic and political climate for foreign business.
6. Methods for marketing and distribution.
7. Managerial and labor climate.
8. Financial viability (profit margin, currency translation, profit repatriation).

Project Report

The report will essential cover all topics in the outline plus an executive summary, introduction (country and product) and recommendations. The report will be typewritten, about 20 pages (double-spaced) and will have an appendix that contains exhibits. Examples are maps of the country, tables and charts.

Project Presentation

The project will be presented to the class in the week prior to the exam week. Fifteen minutes will be allotted to each team. Each member will participate in the presentation. Develop appropriate visuals to aid your oral presentation.

Guest Lecturers

Any of the following business people should present an interesting talk:

1. Executives from a local international or multinational firm.
2. People from export or import companies.

3. personnel managers who staff the overseas subsidiaries and international divisions for a local firm to talk about job possibilities.

4. Retired executives who have worked overseas.

5. Bankers from the International Division of a local bank. Often, they can give you leads to firms in your area that is engaged in international business.

Lecture Outline

I. Opening Section
The chapter begins with a section , Why You Need International Business Experience and How to Get It." Executives of two Fortune 500 companies are quoted as saying that international experience is necessary for employees to become executives in their firms. Unfortunately, frequently, there are more candidates for the overseas positions than there are vacancies. What can the employee do in that situation? The section contains some suggestions.

We also quote from our study of multinational CEOs: 79% believed *all* business graduates they hire should take an international business course and 70% felt that business graduates' education in foreign languages and the international aspects of the functional areas of business is important. The top executives want their employees to have a global business perspective to help them be alert for overseas business opportunities as well as threats from foreign competitors preparing to invade their domestic market. Table 1.1 shows that import penetration has increased for three out the five largest importing nations. Japan and Germany are the exceptions.

We begin the chapter with a list of 16 brand or company names and we ask the reader which of them is foreign-owned. Only Scott Paper and Godiva Chocolate are American-owned.

II. International Business Terminology
A. Multinational, Global, International, Transnational
   1. Some people use the terms world and global interchangeably with multinational to describe a business with international operations.
   2. Others define a global firm as one that attempts to standardize operations in all functional areas, but that responds to national market differences when necessary. They define a multinational as a kind of holding company with a number of overseas operations, each of which is left to adapt its products and marketing strategy according to the local markets.
   3. For decades, the United Nations and governments of most developing nations have been using *transnational* instead of multinational to describe a firm doing business in more than one country.
   4. More recently, some writers are using the term transnational for a firm that is both (1) striving to standardize its functions worldwide and (2) being highly responsive to local environments. Since this is similar to the common definition of global, the writers have redefined a global firm as one that responds weakly to local environments.
   5. Businesspeople usually define a transnational as a company formed by a merger of two firms approximately the same size that are from two different countries. The text describes the organization of two large transnational firms, Unilever and Shell.
B. Definitions Used in This Text
   1. *International business* is business whose activities are carried out across national borders.

2. *Foreign business* denotes the domestic operations within a foreign country.

3. *Multidomestic company* (MDC) is an organization with multicountry affiliates, each of which formulates its own business strategy based on perceived market differences.

4. *Global company* (GC) is an organization that attempts to standardize and integrate operations worldwide in all functional areas.

5. *International company (IC)* refers to both global and multidomestic companies.

III. History of International Business

A. International trade and the international firm are not new aspects of business.

1. East India Company (1600) established foreign branches.

2. Colt Fire Arms had an English plant before the Civil War.

3. By 1914, there were 37 American companies with production facilities in two or more overseas locations. At that time, American foreign direct investment was $2.53 billion, which amounted to 7% of nation's GNP.

4. National Cash Register, Burroughs, Parke-Davis, and Ford were some of the first companies to have overseas plants.

5. European firms were going overseas at the same time.

6. International firms have become the objects of much discussion especially the increasing globalization of their production and their markets. What are the reasons for globalization?

B. Globalization

What is it?

Although there are many definitions of globalization, such as political, technical, social, etc., the most common definition is the one used in international business that of economic globalization—the international integration of goods, technology, labor, and capital; that is, firms implement global strategies which link and coordinate their international activities on a worldwide basis. Globalization is the name of the process and now a new word, globality, has been introduced to designate the results of this process.

C. Globalization Forces

There are five major kinds of drivers: (1) political, (2) technology, (3) market, (4) cost, (5) competitive.

1. Political-there is a trend toward unification and socialization of the global community. The reduction of barriers to trade and foreign investment and the privatization of industry are hastening the opening of new markets by international firms.

2. Technology-advances in computers and communications technology are permitting an increased flow of ideas and information across borders. This enables small firms to compete globally.

3. Market-As companies globalize, they also become global customers.

4. Cost-Globalizing product lines help to achieve economies of scale, which reduce development, production, and inventory costs. Company can also locate where the costs of factors of production are lower.

5. Competitive-One of the competitive driving forces for globalization is the fact that companies are defending their home markets from foreign competitors by entering the competitors' home markets to distract them.

D. Explosive Growth

There has been an explosive growth in the size and number of U. S. and foreign international concerns. One variable used to measure this growth is the increase in total foreign direct investment (FDI).

a. Foreign Direct Investment

1. The world stock of FDI is estimated to have risen from $510 billion in 1980 to $4.12 *trillion* in 1998—an eightfold increase in just 18 years.

2. Total FDI rose by nearly 40 percent to $644 billion, while total assets of multinational foreign affiliates grew by 19.7 percent in 1998 to reach $14.62 trillion.

3. Majority-owned cross-border mergers and acquisitions (M&As) registered a 1998 growth of $411 billion, up almost 75 percent over 1997's increase of 45 percent. Preliminary 1999 results show that cross-border M&As ($720 billion) are still the driving force behind the growth of FDI flows ($827 billion in 1999).

4. Firms in the U.K. were the largest acquirers of foreign countries. U.S. firms were in second place. The two countries also represented to each other the principal home country as well as host country.

b. Number of International Companies

1. According to UNCTAD, in 1999, there were over 60,000 companies with a half million foreign affiliates that accounted for 25 percent of global output and two-thirds of world trade. Foreign affiliates' sales ($11 trillion) are far in excess of global trade ($7 trillion).

2. The world's largest 100 transnational corporations, measured in terms of foreign assets, account for US$trillion in total sales and hold a stock of total assets over US$4.3 trillion. General Electric is the largest, followed by Ford and Royal Dutch Shell.

3. Since the 1980s, there has been a marked liberalization of government policies and attitudes toward foreign investment in both developed and developing nations.

4. Critics of large global firms cite such statistics as the following to "prove" that host governments are powerless before them:

   a. In 1998, only 23 nations had GNPs greater than the total annual sales of General Motors, the world's largest international company.

   b. Also in 1998, the total annual sum of money spent in Wal-Mart worldwide surpassed the sum of the GNPs of over 100 nations.

5. However, regardless of the parent firm's size, each subsidiary is a local company that must comply with the local laws or be subject to legal action or even seizure. Today, most differences are settled by arbitration.

E. Recent Developments

1. Lessening of American dominance? Note that there are more Asian and European international firms than there are American in Table 1.3 but Fortune's 500 list for 1999 ranked by sales shows 167 American firms, 111 Japanese, 43 U.K., 32 German, and 29 French. Compared with 1989, only the British and the Japanese had fewer companies on the 1999 list.

2. Market value comparison shows that in 1999, among the top 100 firms, 62 were American, 32 W. European, Japanese, 1 Canadian, and 1 Australian.

IV.   Why in International Business Different?

    A. International business managers must deal with forces from three environments instead of one, (1) domestic, (2) international and (3) foreign.

    B. Forces in the Environments

        1. External (uncontrollable)

a. Competitive	f. Physical
b. Distributive	g. Political
c. Economic	h. Sociocultural
d. Financial	i. Labor
e. Legal	j. Technological

        2. Internal (controllable)

| a. Personnel | c. Production |
| b. Finance | d. Marketing |

    C. Domestic Environment

    D. Foreign Environments

        1. Composes of all the uncontrollable forces originating outside of home country that surround and influence the firm.

        2. Forces in these environments are the same as for domestic environment.

        3. Force values are different.

        4. The force values are difficult to assess, especially the legal and political elements.

        5. Forces are interrelated, but in ways different from interrelatedness of domestic forces.

    E. International Environment

        1. The interaction between (1) the domestic environmental forces and the foreign environmental forces and (2) the foreign environmental forces of one country and those of another country.

        2. Headquarters managers work in this environment but personnel in a foreign subsidiary do not unless they are engaged in international trade. International organizations also included in international environment–World Bank, regional groupings (EU) and organizations of nations bound by industry agreements (OPEC).

    F. Decision Making More Complex

        1. Multiple forces make decision making more complex.

        2. Not only are they're many sets of forces, but the differences among them sometimes are extreme.

        3. Managers are frequently unfamiliar with other cultures. Moreover, many have the tendency to refer unconsciously to their own cultural values. Self-reference criterion, as this is called, is probably the biggest cause of international business blunders.

V.   International Business Model

Figure 1.2, p. 23, is a model of the domestic, international, and foreign environments showing the controllable and uncontrollable forces.

VI.   Relevance for Business People

A solid understanding of business and its concepts is necessary for success in international business, but in addition, international managers must study and compare the environmental forces of the many sets of foreign forces.

Although they can take as given many of the domestic forces, when managers enter the international business scene, they must be on the lookout for important differences.

Answers to Questions

1. A global company attempts to standardize and integrate operations worldwide, whereas a multidomestic is an organization with multi-country affiliates, each of which formulates its own business strategy based on perceived market differences. An international company refers to both global and multinational companies.

2. The students will come up with any number of examples such as:
   a. If a law is passed limiting the number of foreigners who may be employed in the firm (legal force), management will have to make the appropriate changes in the company's personnel (controllable force).
   b. If a new highway is built (physical force), the manager may have to make changes in the firm's physical distribution system (controllable force) to reach the new market created by the highway.

3. The comparison of total sales to GNP is similar to comparing apples with oranges. The subsidiary must obey a nation's laws or run the risk of legal action or even expropriation. Admittedly, a global or multinational firm does have some bargaining power in some instances that a purely local firm would not have. It can threaten to leave the country which will reduce the number of jobs available and the earning of foreign exchange if it is exporting from that country. The important factor is that a firm with operations in various countries permits management to be flexible in choosing where it wants to produce and supply other subsidiaries and markets. Sales of the subsidiary, not the entire firm, could have some bearing if they indicate that the affiliate is significant within the local economy.

4. There are five major kinds of drivers that are leading international firms to the globalization of their operations: (1) political, (2) technology, (3) market, (4) cost, and (5) competitive.

5. Some techniques and concepts can be applied to operations in other nations. However, the differences among the environmental forces often require that these techniques are altered and in some cases, they cannot be used at all.

6. Because international business managers must operate in three environments instead of one, they have to contend with many more forces than they would if they were doing business within only one country. In addition, the values of these forces vary greatly and may even be in conflict with one another.

7. International firms have grown in size and number. As a result, they have become increasingly significant in the economies of many nations. Governments have found that important segments of their industry have come under the control of foreigners whereas previously local citizens were the principal owners. This has led to a fear the absentee owners may follow policies, which are in conflict with government objectives. This fear is heightened by the knowledge that headquarters can and does control their affiliates much more closely than previously.

8. When a situation familiar to the manager arises, there is a tendency to respond without analyzing the reasons from another cultural viewpoint, especially if it is something he or she has dealt with successfully before. The nearly automatic response is conditioned by the manager's experience in his or her own culture. Thus the manager would give the local personnel director a list of job descriptions for which the firm needs to fill and let the director do the job. The manager probably would not stop to think that the personnel

director's extended family needs work and as a result, these people may be hired even over others whose skills better match the job descriptions. Rick's *International Business Blunders* is full of examples. Many of the famous "horror" stories overseas business failures are directly attributable to a failure to analyze the situation from the point of view of the local culture.

9. No matter where a person is, he or she cannot be entirely free from the impact of international business. Foreign firms can create competition for your hometown company. Exchange rates can cause local prices for imported goods to become more or less competitive. Ask a salesperson who works for a local Toyota dealer if he or she felt the impact of the more expensive yen. If the hometown firm cannot compete with imports, you can lose your job. What you learn in the international business course will make you a more knowledgeable citizen.

10. The kinds of forces in the two environments are identical, but they operate differently because:

    1. Their values frequently differ widely and sometimes are diametrically opposed.
    2. Changes are often difficult to assess. A manager from a country where laws are vigorously enforced may take literally a new law passed where law enforcement is less rigorous.
    3. Many times, forces are interrelated so that even though the values of a force may be the same in two markets, values of other forces may be different. The resulting interactions, then would not be similar.

Answers to Internet Problems

1. We all know, course, that globalization is a very controversial subject, and, as we stated in the text, it has various definitions. For this question, we are using "economic globalization."

    a. According to the article, Globalization Myths, the OECD Commission questions the demands by employers for wage restraints to avoid delocalizations to low-wage countries, asserting that "there are no signs that the foreign transfers of production is predominantly determined on wage-cost grounds, even if this might be the case for some labor-intensive sectors such as clothing, footwear, and toys."

    The IMF staff paper asks "How real is the perceived threat that competition from 'low-wage economies' displaces workers from high-wage jobs and decreases the demand for less skilled workers?" The writer then says that as industrial economies mature, they are becoming more service-oriented to meet the changing demands of their profession. Another trend is the shift toward more highly skilled jobs. The article states all the evidence is that these changes would be taking place with or without globalization and, in fact, globalization makes this process easier and less costly to the economy by bringing benefits of capital flows, technological innovations, and lower import prices. Economic growth, employment, and living standards are all higher than they would be in a closed economy. However, gains are not evenly distributed among groups within countries, ex., workers in declining older industries may not be able to transfer easily to new industries. Governments should focus on (1) education and vocational training and (2) social safety nets to assist people who are displaced.

    The Economist article, One World, discusses the pros and cons of globalization. A positive view is that globalization is an unmixed blessing because a globally integrated economy can lead to a better division of labor between nations. Low wage countries will specialize in labor-intensive tasks, but high-wage countries will use workers in more productive ways. Critics say that competition from low-wage developing nations will destroy jobs and push down wages in the rich economies. In the 4th article, Trade Winds, the writer states that the threat to rich-country workers from developing country competition is often overstated. One reason is that countries with cheap labor don't always have lower costs. Wage differences generally reflect differences in productivity and firms in low-wage countries often need more labor to produce a given amount of output. Communications and transportation are less efficient. In most cases, hourly wages are not decisive in determining where a product is made. In the 6th Economist article, Worldbeater, Inc., the writers discuss a common criticism that multinationals are exporting jobs to low-wage nations. This may be true in some industries, such as textiles and electronics, but in most cases, it is exaggerated. Labor costs now make up only 5-10 percent of production costs in OECD countries, down from 25 percent in the 1970s.

The 8th Economist article, Bearing the Weight of the Market, also discusses the possible impact of global economic integration on the power of the government to govern. "The view that globalization makes it harder for governments to govern has come to be widely accepted. The basic idea is globalization adds to the reach and power of the market: now even governments, not just firms and people, must bow down before the new master of worldwide competition. A government might want to prohibit dangerous or undesirable work practices, for instance. But if it did, the affected industries might move abroad or shut down because the new regulation would put domestic firms at a disadvantage in competition with foreign producers. Governments don't have their former freedom to design their own social policies. If the financial markets deem that a new national health-care scheme or a massive education reform will prove too costly, they will punish the country with higher interest rates or a collapsing currency." The authors claim that if this thinking were correct, there would be good reason to oppose further globalization. However, it is not correct. Governments have learned from experience: evidence down the years suggested that ambitious economic intervention was often unsuccessful. Politicians in rich and poor countries alike, regardless of whether they were of "the left" or "the right," began calling for lower taxes and public spending, for lighter regulation of industry, for privatization of state-owned enterprises, and in general for their economies to be given greater "flexibility." In other words, governments have freely chosen to give market forces more sway, in the hope that this will raise living standards. As for the argument that the new global economy makes it impossible for governments to mandate social protection, such as minimum wage laws, rules for working hours, health-and-safety standards in the workplace, and so forth, the popular view is that if governments grant such protection, they will make firms uncompetitive and put workers on the dole. The writers say "there is no reason why this should be true." Social protection does carry economic costs, reducing the amount of output that can be squeezed from any given amount of capital, labor, and other resources. Citizens may decide that the cost is worth paying. The question is how must the cost be borne? In an economy closed or open to flows of trade and finance, the cost will take the form of lower incomes. The only difference is that open economies with floating currencies may experience the fall in income through currency depreciation—thus higher prices for consumer goods—while a closed economy will suffer a decline in local wages expressed in local currency. Social protection rules are as feasible and cost no more in a globalized economy than they do in a closed economy.

Various studies and the controversy over how globalization affects productivity and the real wages and real incomes of workers are discussed in Futurework. In 1995, the percentage of developing countries' exports to the U.S. had risen to 33.6 percent, up from 18 percent in 1973. As one writer discloses, the average wages paid to production workers in countries trading with the U.S. increased from 38 percent of U.S. wages in 1960 to 85 percent in 1992. This demonstrates that the U.S. is not trading more with countries paying relatively lower wages.

The A.T. Kearney Co. in its paper, Globalization Ledger, reports that between 1978 and 1997, rapidly globalizing countries significantly expanded political and civil liberties as measured by Freedom House, a leading nongovernmental organization. During this period, aggressive globalizers raised their scores by 10.5 percent, while strong globalizers raised their scores by 12 percent. But scores of countries at the other end of the globalization spectrum fell by over 11 percent in the passive globalizers and 17.3 percent for the stalled globalizers. At a minimum, these findings suggest that economic integration across national borders has not hindered the gradual expansion of political and civil rights.

b. In the briefing paper, What is Globalization?, the writers point out that firms based in one country increasingly make investments to establish and run business operations in other countries. Although, from 1988 to 1998, world FDI flows more than tripled and the share of FDI to GDP is rising in both developed and developing nations, developed nations received three-quarters of the total FDI, leaving only one-quarter for the lower-wage developing nations.

In Globalization Myths, author Robert Went claims that a study by Ruigrok and Van Tulder showed convincingly that the often repeated story that employers can take their capital and leave, to invest and move activities to low-wage countries is a myth. Of the one hundred largest multinationals in the world, not one is really footloose. They also pointed out that the world economy at the end of the last century was at least as internationalized as it is today. Hirst and Thompson developed the same argument in their study. Oman, the globalization expert of the OECD observed that the relocation of production for OECD markets to low-wage production sites in other regions has not accelerated overall, but has actually decelerated since the early to mid 1980s.

The authors of the paper published in the Urban Institute's Futurework, maintain that the overwhelming amount of business investment and financial investment occurs between industrial nations, not between industrial and developing nations. They also showed that foreigners actually invested more in the United States than American firms were investing abroad. The Wade study, p. 8 of Futurework, suggests that multinationals move only their most routinized operations abroad and that changes such as "just-in-time" inventory management and increased specialization weakens the incentives to disperse production globally and encourage location near final markets.

c. Wentz, the author of Globalization Myths declares that "we see an increase in problems of governance or regulation on a global level. This is a consequence of the fact that national states are becoming and making themselves less effective, while the strengthening and legitimacy of supranational institutions, which play an increasing role, is lagging behind the speed with which the global economy is developing." He also believes that "the internationalization of production leads to changed relations between the industrialized countries and the countries of the Third World: 'leveling down' of wages, conditions of work and social security." Wentz quotes the authors of In States of Markets, who declare that "national states have no space left to maneuver in the globalized economy, that they are unable to take alternative choices and policies, that they are in fact superfluous and therefore doomed to disappear. They see important changes in the role of states, leading among other things to less social policy and more investments and deregulation to make countries attractive for capital."

The IMF in Globalization: Threat or Opportunity? claims that globalization does not reduce national sovereignty. The writers say that "it creates a strong incentive for governments to pursue sound economic policies." Some critics are concerned that globalization leads to the abolition of rules or constraints on business activities. The IMF, however, claims that, to the contrary, that "one of the key goals on the international financial architecture is to develop standards and codes that are based on internationally accepted principles that can be implemented in many different national settings." The writers also state "that the income gap between high-income and low-income countries has grown is a matter of concern. But it is wrong to jump to the conclusion that globalization has caused the divergence, or that nothing can be done to improve the situation. To the contrary, low-income countries have not been able to integrate with the global economy as quickly as others, partly because of their chosen policies and partly because of factors outside of their control. No country, least of all the poorest, can afford to remain isolated from the world economy. The international community should endeavor—by strengthening the international financial system through trade and aid—to help the poorest countries integrate into the world economy, grow more rapidly, and reduce poverty."

The World Bank in the first briefing of the series entitled Assessing Globalization, reminds us that "it is important to recognize that economic globalization is not a wholly new trend. It has been an aspect of the human story from earliest times, as widely scattered populations gradually became involved in more extensive economic relations. In the modern era, globalization saw an early flowering towards the end of the 19th century, mainly among the rich nations. Its early peak was reversed in the first half of the 20th century, a period of growing protectionism, but in the last 50 years, the trend has been toward greater globalization. The pace accelerated in the 1980s and 1990s as governments reduced policy barriers that hampered international trade and investment. There has been a general shift towards greater reliance on markets and private enterprise, especially in developing former communist nations that have seen the failure of high levels of government planning and intervention to deliver the desired development results.

The writers of the Economist's 6th brief, Worldbeater, Inc. say, that although the multinationals' growth is fairly benign, it is not always so. "For one thing, multinationals' size and scale can make it possible for them to exert power in an exploitative way. A company whose facilities are located in a single country has no alternative but to comply with the country's laws and social norms. A multinational, however, can move production to another country. It can also lower its tax bill by using internal pricing to shift profits from high-tax to low-tax nations." This flexibility may make it harder for governments to raise revenue, protect the environment, and promote worker safety. Critics fear an undesirable "race to the bottom" with government reducing desirable social protection in order to attract multinational investment. Others believe that the race can be healthy insofar it forces governments to be careful before imposing costly regulations and taxes.

The authors of the Globalization Ledger state that "as countries globalize, citizens often call upon their governments to mitigate the painful social and economic dislocation that international exposure may bring." The growth of social expenditures in aggressive and strong globalizers suggests that governments have responded with increased funding for social safety nets, worker training, and small business loan guarantees among other similar programs aimed at easing the economic transition. Rising levels of economic growth permit additional leeway for budget increases in rapidly globalizing countries. Findings show that government social spending was reduced or remained flat in passive and stalled globalizers, but expanded significantly in aggressive and strong globalizers. Between 1978 and 1997, strong globalizers more than doubled their public contributions for health, housing, social security, education, and other social concerns. In contrast, public spending on these items fell by over one-half for passive globalizers during the same period.

d. Wentz in Globalization Myths says that the often repeated myth that globalization is the automatic and therefore unstoppable consequence of the emergence of new technologies, is laid to rest by Professor Helleiner, who shows that such a claim cannot even be maintained for the most globalized markets, the financial markets: institutional changes and political decisions are necessary to allow enabling technologies to be used and developed.

Professor Lubbers in The Globalization of Economy and Society, writes that "the development of technology is relevant both to the economic world and to the process of globalization. There has always been interaction between the two. The improvement of communication has made a direct contribution to 'becoming worldwide' and assisted in the globalization of the economy. In fact, technology is the driving force behind all progress in the economy, politics, and even culture. The rebirth of physics after the Middle Ages is a case in point, and in historical descriptions of earlier developments in the economy and in the formation of states, one can always give a parallel description of technological development."

e. There is an extensive ongoing debate about whether globalization is really a new phenomenon. For example, one of the many definitions from the Fred Riggs, article, Globalization is a Fuzzy Term (click on "Globalization" at end of article) is submitted by Professor Tehranian of the U. of Hawaii. "Globalization is a process that has been going on for the past 5000 years, but it has significantly accelerated the demise of the Soviet Union in 1991."

The authors of the IMF article, Globalization: Threat or Opportunity?, states that globalization is not just a recent phenomenon. Some analysts have argued that "the world economy was just as globalized 100 years ago as it is today." Although the 20th century saw unparallelled economic growth—with global per capita GDP increasing almost five-fold, the growth was not steady—the strongest expansion came during the second half of the century.

f. Worldbeater, Inc., the 6th brief in the Economist's series on globalization, examines the multinational companies' role in integrating the world's economies. The writers say that "there is no doubting that multinationals matter. They are one of the main conduits through which globalization takes place. In 1995, multinationals sold $7 trillion through their foreign affiliates—more than the world's total exports. Multinational's sales outside their home countries are growing 20-30 percent faster than exports. They also have an important role in global investment. At the end of 1996, the total stock of foreign direct investment (FDI) totaled over $3 trillion. The UN World Investment Report estimates that that 70 percent of all international royalties on technology involve payments between parent firms and their foreign affiliates, proving their importance in disseminating technology globally. Even though most multinationals are not global firms, they are the main force behind worldwide flows of capital, goods, and services.

2. This is another exercise to give students practice in doing research on the Internet. Students can call up the conditions of the treaty establishing the Binational Company by using the URL in the endnote cited in the text. The answers are (a) no, (b) no, (c) no, and (d) there are no tariff nor non-tariff barriers to their importation. See page 1, 1st paragraph, for answers to a, b and c. See 1st paragraph, page 2, for answer to d.

Discussion of Minicase 1-1, Key Differences Between the Global and the Multinational Corporation

The characteristics are global (G), multinational (M), or neither as follows:

1.	G	8.	G	15.	neither
2.	M	9.	G	16.	M
3.	G	10.	M	17.	G
4.	G	11.	G	18.	G
5.	G	12.	M	19.	M
6.	M	13	M	20.	neither
7.	neither	14.	G		

Explanation of neither

6. There is no international law by which a multinational or global can be formed and have legal existence in several countries. Companies can be formed only under national law and they acquire the nationality of the country under whose law they are incorporated. The parent company has the nationality of the home country and the subsidiaries have the nationality of the host nations in which they are formed.
   Nations that have adopted the worldwide taxation principle, tax the home-based parent on its global earnings. However, they tax only the local earnings of local subsidiaries of foreign-based companies. The earnings of the parent and subsidiaries in other nations do not belong to the local subsidiary because it is not the owner of the parent and foreign affiliates.

15. A company's sales is an unsatisfactory indicator of whether a firm is global or multinational. A small company may be obtaining over 50 percent of its sales by exporting. What if the firm's foreign sales exceed 50 percent of total sales? Foreign sales may still not be regarded as important as domestic sales by top management because they are divided among a number of overseas markets. The sales of any individual nation are less important than home country sales.

20. This is related to point 7. A global corporation is generally made up of a parent company located in the home country and subsidiaries in host nations. Ownership and control of the parent company remain national and not multinational. There are multinational firms whose stock is listed on foreign exchanges so that non-home nationals can own shares in the parent firm. However, the majority of the shares is usually owned by people in the home nation. The exceptions are the few binational companies such as Shell, Lever, or multinationals from small countries such as Nestlé. Professor Yao-Su-Nu points out that although 95 percent of Nestlé's assets are outside Switzerland, the Swill law permits its firms to exclude foreigners from holding shares with voting rights. Since Nestlé limits non-Swiss voting rights to 3 percent of the total, effectively it is a national and not a global firm with respect to ownership.

TM 1.1
Figure 1.1   **Overseas Locations of an International Service Company, McDonald's (Countries/-Number of Stores)**

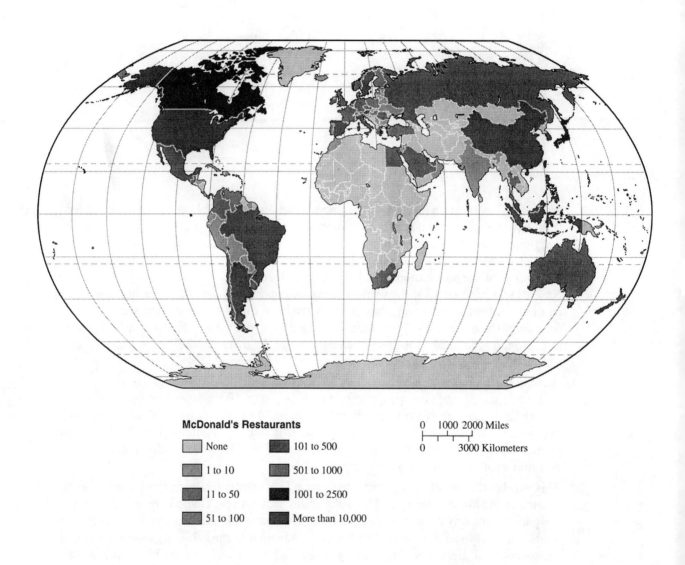

McDonald's Restaurants

None		101 to 500	
1 to 10		501 to 1000	
11 to 50		1001 to 2500	
51 to 100		More than 10,000	

0   1000 2000 Miles
0   3000 Kilometers

Source: McDonald's Corporation.

TM 1.2
Figure 1.2   **International Business Environments**

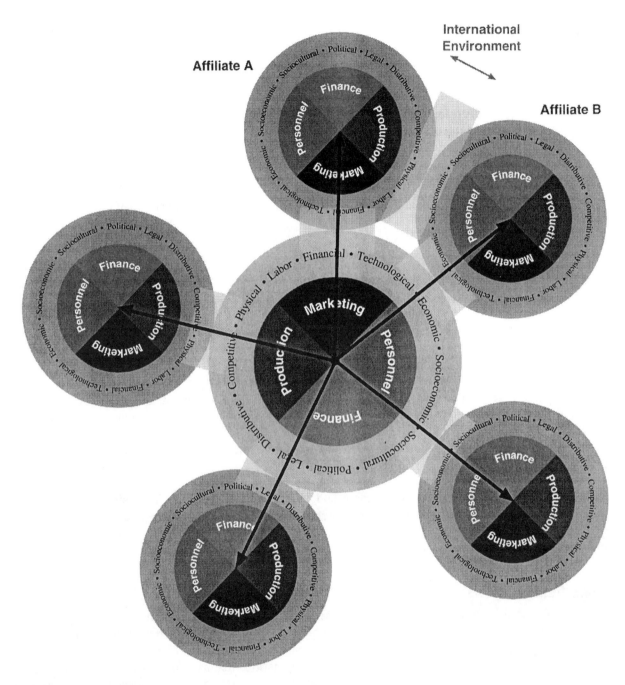

- **Domestic environment**
  (Includes socioeconomic, sociocultural, political, legal, distributive, competitive, physical, labor, financial, technological, and economic environments)

- **Foreign environment**
  (Includes socioeconomic, sociocultural, political, legal, distributive, competitive, physical, labor, financial, technological, and economic environments)

CHAPTER 2
TRADING AND INVESTING IN INTERNATIONAL BUSINESS

Learning Objectives

1. Familiarize students with the growth, size and direction of international trade.

2. Show the students the practical benefits of analyzing trade statistics.

3. Give the students an idea of the growth, magnitude and direction of foreign investment, the other aspect of international business.

4. Teach the students *why* firms engage in international business.

5. Show the students how firms enter the international market (market entry methods.)

6. Inform the students about the channel of distribution members that are available.

Overview

Both aspects of international business, international trade and foreign investment, have grown dramatically over the last three decades. Although new trading and investment patterns have emerged, developed nations still trade with and invest primarily in other developed nations.

The reasons why a firm goes abroad are linked to the desire to either increase profits and sales or protect them from being eroded by competition. Some companies begin their foreign entry by first exporting, then setting up foreign sales companies and finally, where the sales volume warrants, establishing foreign production facilities. There are times when they will bypass exporting and become involved in foreign manufacturing. Five distinct alternatives are available—wholly owned subsidiaries, joint ventures, licensing agreements, franchising and contract manufacturing. A sixth arrangement, the management contract, is used by manufacturing and service companies to earn income by providing management expertise for a fee. Commonly, global and multinational companies are involved in all of the market entry methods mentioned.

Channels of distribution are both controllable and uncontrollable variables. To assist a firm to export indirectly, directly, or distribute in a foreign market, various kinds of channel members are available. The wholesaling and retailing structures vary among nations. An unauthorized wholesaler, the parallel importer, costs authorized importers billions of dollars in lost sales annually.

Suggestions and Comments

1. We usually find that students are unaware of the rapid growth of international trade so we discuss Tables 2.2 and 2.3 in class. We point out that there have been numerous changes in trade relationships as Tables 2.4 and 2.5 illustrate. Most students believe that the major trade direction is between developed and developing nations (exchanging raw materials for finished goods). Table 2.4 shows that developed nations continue to trade with other developed nations (73% of their total exports), but the increase in industrialization of developing nations is resulting in greater trade among them (39.2% in 1970 to 39.2% in 1999).

2. Generally students are surprised to learn that the United States' share in total foreign investment is still as large as it is (Table 2.6). They also believe that Japan's share is largest. Do you want to see how many read the assignment? Ask them which country has the largest share of foreign direct investment (U.S.).

3. Table 2.10 gives your student an opportunity to see the great disparity between the top and bottom nations with respect to GNP and GNP growth—a dim picture for developing nations. Compare the two groups' population growth rates. Only Hong Kong and Singapore have population growth rates close to bottom ranking nations.

4. Inasmuch as there is a rather common misconception that firms have a choice between exporting and foreign production, we show that this choice often is unavailable when we cover the reasons for going abroad. The How to Enter section enables you to cover a lot of ground concerning the various methods of entry.

5. You may be interested in discussing the topic, "Does trade lead to FDI or does FDI lead to trade? This illustrates how closely trade and FDI are interlinked.

6. This probably would be a good time to introduce the 7 global dimensions because various aspects of this topic come up later in a number of places.

7. The students who have studied Principles of Marketing will not find the section on channel members difficult because of their similarity to channel members in this country. The trading companies are a new concept, however.

Student Involvement Exercises

1. Ask the students to check advertisements in *The Wall Street Journal*, New York Times, and other big city newspapers for ads in which investment inducements are offered by foreign governments. Similar ads also appear in *Business Week*, the *Economist* and *Fortune*. What kinds of inducements are offered? Does your city and state offer foreign firms inducements to invest in your area?

2. We state in the text that one reason for going overseas is to protect the firm's foreign markets. In many countries, the major U. S. competitors are competing as they do here. The students might take an industry and see in how many countries the top two or three industry leaders are present. For example, in how many markets do Colgate-Palmolive and Procter & Gamble compete with local production facilities? The annual reports of these firms will tell where production facilities are.

Guest Lecturers

Some businesspeople, if available locally, who could contribute to the material in this chapter would be:

1. Someone in the technical department of a multinational to talk about licensing and contract manufacturing arrangements that firm has with overseas licensees.

2. Product manager of the international division of a multinational who should be knowledgeable about licensing and all the means for entering a market. Can also explain why firm went overseas.

3. Financial person in the international division who can discuss the points mentioned in questions 1 and 2 plus the return obtained from these arrangements.

4. Someone from an export management company.

5. Representatives from a foreign-owned subsidiary in your area. Ask them to tell the class what motivated them to come to the United States and your area.

6. If you have an economic development department in your state that is active in attracting foreign investors, you may be able to get a representative to tell the class what it does to attract foreign investors and what foreign investors are looking for. Your chamber of commerce'

director of economic development may have had visits from foreign company representatives which he or she is willing to share.

7. Someone from the kinds of companies listed in the section, International Channel of Distribution Members, can also talk on these subjects.

Lecture Outline

I. The Opening Section
Data in the opening section demonstrate that large international firms both export and invest overseas. Foreign direct investment by American firms increased to $151 billion in 1999 (versus $84 billion in 19996 and an average of $41 billion annually from 1985-1995). American exports of goods and services increased 78 percent in the 1990–1999 period, rising from $537 billion in 1990 to $956 billion in 1999. For the largest 28 U.S. multinationals (Table 2.1), the ratio of foreign sales to total sales ranged from 77.1 percent for Texaco to 13.8 percent for Wal-Mart Stores. For 17 of the 28 companies (61 percent), more than 40 percent of net profits were from foreign sales. The two means of supplying overseas markets—*exporting* to and *production* in those markets—are not confined to large manufacturing concerns. Of the *Forbes* list of the 100 largest U.S. multinationals, 21 are service companies. Small and medium-sized international firms comprise 20.8 percent of the total 3,470 U.S. international corporations and they also have an important role in generating exports (see SME insert on page 64).

II. International Trade
A. Volume of Trade
1. The volume of international trade in goods and services is approaching $7 trillion. Merchandise exports account for $5.5 trillion, 17 times their 1970 value (Table 2.2). In constant dollars, trade volume in 1999 was nearly 4 times the 1970 value (Figure 2.1).
2. While smaller in absolute terms at over $1.3 trillion, trade in services grew faster in the 1990s than did merchandise trade (Table 2.3). See Relevance for Businesspeople on page 63.
3. One-fourth of everything grown or made in the world is now exported
B. Direction of Trade
1. Developed nations trade primarily with other developed nations (Table 2.4).
2. Developing nations also trade primarily with developed nations, although this proportion is declining.
3. The Three Exceptions – Japan, the U.S., and Australia/New Zealand. Nearly three-quarters of exports from developed countries go to other industrialized nations, not to developed nations. Japan, the U.S., and Australia/New Zealand are exceptions, with each sending a larger portion of their exports to developing nations than do developed nations as a whole. The U.S., Japan, and Australia, but not Europe, are approaching a 50–50 split in exports to developing and developed nations.
4. The changing direction of trade. The direction of trade frequently changes over time among nations or regions (Table 2.4). Regional trade agreements can alter the level and proportion of trade flows within and across regions. The share of world trade accounted for by members of regional trade agreements increased from 37.3% in 1980 to 70.7% in 1999.
C. Major Trading Partners: Their Relevance for Businesspeople
1. Advantages of focusing attention on a nation that is already a sizable purchaser of goods from the would-be exporter's country include:

a. Business climate in the importing nation is relatively favorable.

b. Export and import regulations are not insurmountable.

c. There should be no strong cultural objections to buying that nation's goods.

d. Satisfactory transportation facilities have already been established.

e. Import channel members are experienced in handling import shipments from the exporter's area.

f. Foreign exchange to pay for the exports is available.

g. The trading partner's government may be applying pressure on importers to buy from countries that are good customers for that nation's exports.

2. Major trading partners of the United States.

   a. Table 2.5 shows the major trading partners of the United States. Mexico and Canada are major trading partners because of their geographic proximity. Now, as members of NAFTA, their importance is growing.

   b. Rankings of America's trading partners have changed markedly in 30 years. Asian nations have become increasingly important trade partners for both exports and imports. The trade deficit with China has grown rapidly. Between 1991 and 1999, China moved from 6th to 4th in exports (from $19 to $82 billion, a 331 percent increase in 8 years), but it was only in 13th place as an importer ($13 billion).

3. Relevance for Businesspeople

   For a company starting to search for new international business opportunities, the preliminary steps of (1) studying the general growth and direction of trade (Table 2.4) and (2) analyzing major trading partners (Table 2.5) would provide an idea of where the trading activity is.

III. Foreign Investment

Foreign investment is usually divided into two components: portfolio investment and direct investment. The distinction between these two has begun to blur, particularly with growing size and number of international mergers, acquisitions, and alliances.

A. Portfolio Investment

   1. Not directly concerned with the control of a firm

   2. Nonresidents owned American stock and bonds with a value of $2,509 billion in 1999 (including $1,446 billion in corporate stocks), a 59 percent increase versus 1997. Americans own $2,583 billion in foreign securities, of which $2,027 billion is in corporate stocks, an increase of 68 percent since 1997.

B. Foreign Direct Investment (FDI)

   1. Volume.

      a. The book value of all foreign investments is over $4.7 trillion (Table 2.6).

      b. The U.S. is the largest investor nation, with 1.7 times the FDI of the U.K. (#2) and 2.7 times Germany (#3).

      c. The proportion of FDI by the U.S. declined from 35.5% to 23.8% between 1985 and 1999.

   2. Direction. Table 2.7 indicates that the industrialized nations invest primarily in one another just as they trade more with one another.

   3. Trade leads to FDI.

      Historically, foreign direct investment has followed foreign trade because:

      a. Foreign trade is less costly and less risky.

        b. Management can expand the business in small increments rather than in the greater investment and market size that a foreign production facility requires.

    4. Does trade lead FDI or does FDI lead trade?

        a. New business environment of fewer government barriers to trade, increased competition from globalizing firms, and new production and communications technology is causing international firms to locate their production systems close to available resources.

        b. Where to locate may be either an FDI or a trade decision.

  C. U.S. Foreign Direct Investment

    1. Table 2.6 showed that the U.S. is the world's largest foreign investor.

    2. American firms have invested more in developed than developing nations (Table 2.8).

    3. U.S. investment to Europe and Asia is increasing, but to Canada is declining.

    4. Table 2.7 shows that developing countries as a whole received increased worldwide FDI between 1996 and 1999. African nations participated relatively little in the flow, while FDI to Asia and Latin America increased.

  D. Foreign Direct Investment in the United States

    1. Rapid increase. FDI in the U.S. rose from $185 billion in 1985 to $989 billion in 1999 (Table 2.9). Nearly three-quarters was from 6 nations: (1) United Kingdom, (2) Japan, (3) Netherlands, (4) Germany, (5) Canada, and (6) France.

    2. Acquire going companies or build new ones? Of FDI in the U.S., most has been spent to acquire going companies rather than to establish new ones

IV.   Why Enter Foreign Markets?

  A. Increase Profits and Sales

    1. Enter new markets. Managers find that markets with rising GNP per capita and population growth appear to be attractive for doing business.

        a. New market creation. Table 2.10 shows growth rates among the top and bottom countries ranked by GNP per capita. Care must be taken in comparing markets on the basis of GSN/capita: reliability of data is questionable, exchange rates do not reflect the relative domestic purchasing powers of currencies, and GNP per capita is an arithmetic mean but incomes are not equally divided among a nation's people.

        b. Preferential trading arrangements. For many products, preferential trading arrangements (European Union, NAFTA) have created new, larger markets.

        c. Faster-growing markets. Many foreign markets are growing faster than the home market.

        d. Improved communications.

            i. the ability to communicate with customers and employees by e-mail and videoconferencing has given managers confidence in their ability to control foreign operations.

          ii. Inexpensive international communication enables service companies, such as banking, insurance, and software firms to "body shop."

    2. Obtain greater profits.

        a. Greater revenue. Where there is less competition, the firm may get a better price.

        b. Lower cost of goods sold. Reduce R&D costs per unit, permit manufacturing economies of scale, access government inducements.

      c.   Higher overseas profits as an investment motive. Greater profits on overseas investments were a strong motive for going abroad in the 1970s, 1980s, early 1990s, but cost and competition drivers to globalization are reducing differences between overseas and home country profits.

      d.   Test market. Opportunity to make changes to any part of the marketing mix based on results, but danger that a market test will give competitors an early warning.

B. Protect Markets, Profits, and Sales

   1. Protect domestic market

      a.   by following domestic accounts overseas.

      b.   Attack in competitor's home market to keep it occupied defending that market

      c.   Using foreign production to lower costs. Firms move production overseas to lower manufacturing costs and protect their domestic markets from lower-priced imports.

      d.   In-bond plant concept. American firms have established in-bond plants (production facilities mainly on the Mexican-American border and in the Caribbean Basin to take advantage of lower-cost labor for labor-intensive processes. The Andean Trade Preference Act is similar to the Caribbean Basin Initiative. Asian growth triangles and other export processing zones also offer production cost savings similar to in-bond plants. See the Worldview, "Reverse Maquila, a New Concept."

   2. Protect foreign markets

      a.   Lack of foreign exchange–Firms produce in countries where foreign exchange for buying their exports is scarce.

      b.   Local production by competitors–Firms follow competitors who invest in their export markets.

      c.   Downstream markets–Some OPEC nations have invested in refining and marketing outlets to guarantee market for their crude oil. Citgo owned by Petroleos de Venezuela.

      d.   Protectionism–Firms go abroad when governments erect import barriers to their exports.

      e.   Guarantee supply of raw materials.

      f.   Acquire technology and management know-how.

      g.   Geographic diversification.

      h.   Satisfy management's desire for expansion.

V.   How to Enter Foreign Markets

All the means for involvement in overseas markets may be subsumed in (1) exporting to them and (2) manufacturing in them.

A. Exporting

   1. Indirect exporting–Selling to others who export. But this is costly and indirect exporter has no direct contact with overseas customers.

   2. Direct exporting–Company does own exporting. May set up sales company in overseas markets and do own importing.

B. Foreign Manufacturing

   1. Wholly owned subsidiary–Company may build a new plant, acquire a going concern or purchase its own distributor.

2. Joint venture–May be formed between an international firm and a local partner, two or more international firms, or a cooperative undertaking to handle a limited-duration project such as construction of a highway. There may be tax benefits from having a local partner or the international firm may wish to limit involvement to reduce risk.

   a. Disadvantages of joint ventures–shared profits, lack of control.

   b. Control by minority owners–control of a joint venture even with minority ownership is possible when the majority partner does not want control or the minority partner has a management contract.

3. Management contract–A firm provides managerial know-how in one or more functional areas to another party for a fee. International firms earn commissions acting as purchasing agents for overseas joint ventures and wholly owned subsidiaries.

4. Licensing–The licensor grants to the licensee the right to use any kind of its expertise for a fee. Licensing has become a major source of income for many multinationals. U. S. firms received $36.5 billion in fees and royalties in 1999.

5. Franchising–A special kind of licensing which permits the franchises to sell products or services under a highly publicized brand name and well-proven set of procedures with a carefully developed marketing strategy. Fast-food operations are the most numerous worldwide.

6. Contract manufacturing–The firm contracts with a local manufacturer (1) to produce products for it according to its own specifications, (2) to assemble products or (3) to produce parts.

7. Strategic alliances–cooperation between competitors, customers, or suppliers that may take a number of forms. Partners wanting to share technology may cross license. If they want to pool R&D resources, they will form an R & D partnership. Some may form joint ventures in manufacturing and marketing. Alliances may be mergers or acquisitions.

VI. Multidomestic or Global Strategy?
Many multinationals begin their foreign operations by first exporting and then manufacturing overseas, but they also enter some markets by manufacturing. They employ all the methods we have discussed to reach their worldwide markets.

A. The World Environment is Changing

   1. Although the linear relationship of first exporting and then manufacturing overseas still holds for many firms, manufacturing overseas still hold for many firms, changes in the world environment are affecting trade and foreign investment-(1) governments have liberalized flow of factors of production, (2) improvements in information technology enable managers to direct company activities over long distances in diverse areas. As a result, global competition has increased.

   2. Which strategy will the company follow- multinational or global; that is what can the company standardize worldwide?

B. Seven Global Dimensions

   1. There at least seven dimensions along which management's can standardize: (1) product, (2) markets, (3) promotion (4) where value is added to product, (5) competitive strategy, (6) use of non-home-country personnel, (7) extent of global ownership in the company.

   2. Possibilities range from the standardization of 0 (multidomestic) to all seven dimensions (completely global). Management must decide how far the firm should go along each dimension.

VII. Channels of Distribution

Channels of distribution are both controllable and uncontrollable. They are controllable to the extent that channel captains are free to choose from those available, but the agencies themselves are generally beyond the marketer's control and are therefore uncontrollable.

VIII. International Channel of Distribution Members

The selection of these members will depend on the method of entry into the market. If the decision is to export, the firm may do so directly or indirectly. Figure 2.8 shows that management has considerable latitude in forming the channels.

A. Indirect Exporting

1. Exporters that sell for the manufacturer.

    a. Manufacturers' export agents.

    b. Export management companies.

    c. International trading companies – similar to EMCs in that they also act as agents for some companies and as merchant wholesalers for others. They also generally export as well as import, own transportation facilities, and provide financing. The most diversified and the largest are the Japanese sogo shosha.

        i. Sogo shosha – general trading companies originally established by zaibatsu (centralized, family-dominated economic groups). Mitsui is an example.

        ii. Korean general trading companies – similar in scope to the Japanese sogo shosha, they are responsible for a major part of Korea's exports and are also the country's principal importers of key products. Many are owned by the huge Korean diversified conglomerates called chaebols.

        iii. Export trading companies – Export Trading Company Act passed by U.S. to permit businesses to join together to export goods and services without fear of violating U.S. antitrust laws. Bank holding companies may participate in ETCs.

2. Exporters that buy for overseas customers – export commission agents represent overseas purchasers, such as import firms and large industrial users. They are paid a commission by the purchaser for acting as resident buyers.

3. Exporters that buy and sell for their own account.

    a. Export merchants (export distributors) – buy and sell in their own names.

    b. Cooperative exporters (piggyback or mother hen) – established multinationals who also handle products of other firms.

    c. Webb-Pomerene Associations – organizations of competing firms joined together to export. Are exempt from antitrust laws generally.

4. Exporters that purchase for foreign users and middlemen.

    a. Large foreign users.

    b. Export resident buyers.

B. Direct Exporting

A firm which does its own exporting has 4 types of overseas middlemen available.

1. Manufacturers' agents – residents in foreign markets who take orders in companies name. Work on commission.

2. Distributors – wholesale importers who buy for their own account. May have exclusive representation.

3. Retailers – frequently are direct importers.

4. Trading companies – importers of wide range of goods. Also export raw materials. State trading companies in communist bloc and in nations where the state has a monopoly.

C. Foreign Production

When selling from local production, firm's concern is with internal channels. Generally same types of middlemen are available in these markets as in the U.S. Their manner of operating may be different because of differences in the environmental forces.

1. Wholesale institutions.

    a. In other developed nations, generally there are the same kinds of middlemen as in the U.S.

    b. Just as in the U.S., as retailers have become larger, they have sought to bypass the wholesalers and buy directly from the manufacturer.

    c. Diversity of wholesaling structures. In the developing nations that depend on imports to supply the market, importing wholesalers are large and few in number and the channels are long. As countries industrialize, there are more wholesalers who are smaller and more specialized.

    d. Parallel importers and gray market goods – parallel importers are wholesalers that import products independently of the manufacturer-authorized importer or that buy products for export and then sell them in the domestic market. These gray market sales are estimated to total more than $10 billion annually.

2. Retail institutions.

    a. Generally, the less developed the country, the more numerous, more specialized, and smaller the retailers.

    b. In going up the scale from developing to developed nations, one encounters more mass merchandising; more self-service, large-sized units; and a trend toward retailer concentration.

Answers to Questions

1. False, Table 2.4, p. 65, shows that about 73 percent of the developed nations' exports go to other developed nations. It's true that 56 percent of developing nations' exports go to industrial nations as compared to the 39 percent that goes to other developing nations. However, the volume of developing nations' exports is only about 40% of what the developed nations export (Table 2.2, p. 62).

2. False. Table 2.5 p. 68, shows that the relative importance of U. S. trading partners changes over time. The Asian NIEs are new to the list of U. S. major markets. Venezuela still exports crude oil to the United States, but it is relatively less important. The "Relevance for Businesspeople." on page 68 gives the reasons why this information is relevant for a businessperson.

3. The analysis of foreign trade data is preliminary for anyone starting to search outside the home market for new business opportunities. This provides an idea of where the major markets for the home country products are. The fact that exports have quadrupled in a relatively short time indicates that the export market continues to grow and therefore there are opportunities for firms to export. Businesspeople should interpret this to mean that this a business opportunity for them, but it does also indicate that they can be facing increased foreign competition.

4. Knowing that a country is a major trading partner tells the analyst that:

    a. the business climate in the partner is favorable.

    b. export and import regulations are not insurmountable.

c. no strong cultural objections to buying the nation's goods.

d. there is satisfactory transportation between the exporting nation and the partner.

e. import channel members (banks, customs, brokers, and importers) are experienced in handling shipments from the exporter.

f. foreign exchange is available.

g. government of the partner may be pressuring its businesses to buy from the exporters nation, especially if it is running a trade surplus with it.

5. Establishing a market presence in a foreign market by exporting is much less costly, and thus less risky, than entering with a large investment to establish local production without first accumulating this experience. Exporting allows the firm to expand its business in a market in small increments. It can always pull back with little loss. The new international business environment of fewer governmental barriers to trade, increased competition from globalizing firms, and new production and communications technology are causing many firms to invest first and then export (components to affiliates in other countries and finished products when foreign affiliates are assigned production responsibility for certain product groups.

6. Service companies such as banks and ad agencies follow their clients overseas because they do not want the foreign affiliates of a home competitor to service their client's overseas subsidiary. They fear that a relationship established overseas may lead to the competitor's taking all or part of the client's business in the home country. Firms selling to original equipment manufacturers (tires to auto makers) have the same fear. Companies also go abroad to lower production costs and thus be able to compete with lower-prices foreign exports. This is the purpose of in-bond plants, CBI and Singapore's growth triangle. (p. 80–81).

7. The dimensions are independent of each other and a firm can be anywhere on a continuum between multidomestic and global on any one dimension. We gave the example of a company using a global approach to its promotion, but using the multidomestic strategy for producing the physical product.

8. At times, management has no choice but to enter a market with a joint venture because the host government may require local participation in the company. Even when this is not required by law, the firm may still center into a joint venture if there is strong nationalistic sentiment. Often a country will extend tax benefits to foreign firms that accept local partners. A joint venture also lowers the investment risk for the foreign partner. Some management's feel that a local partner lessens the risk of expropriation.

9. a. The management contract is a source of extra income for the foreign partner and it also enables the foreign partner to control certain aspects of the joint venture if it has a contract to supply key personnel such as the technical and production managers. These people will insist that imported inputs produced by the foreign partner that are usually more vertically integrated will be purchased from it and not from its competitors; in other words, the joint venture will be a captive customer for the foreign partner.

   b. Management contract fees are usually a tax deductible expense for the foreign subsidiary so they are a tax-free payment to the global firm. Furthermore, if foreign exchange is scarce, the host government. may not permit the headquarters to expatriate dividends. However, governments recognize that management contracts are necessary if the local company (subsidiary) is to have the needed management expertise and it will usually provide foreign exchange to pay management contract fees.

10. a. In-bond plants are production facilities in Mexico that temporarily import raw materials, components or parts duty-free to be processed with less expensive local labor. The finished product is required to be exported.

   b. If Congress were to repeal the law that permits American importers to bring in finished products from Mexico containing American-made parts and materials (806.30 and 807) and pay import duties only on the value added in Mexico, the in-bond plants would probably be out of business. If it were not for this law, importers would have to pay import duty on the whole finished article with no allowance made for American parts or materials. Under NAFTA, import duties will be phased out in any case.

11. A sogo shosha is one of the very large and diversified Japanese general trading companies that facilitate and develop trade flows both internationally and domestically. Its principal activity is to import and export goods on behalf of manufacturers and buyers of commodities in other nations. The U.S. answer is the export trading company which resembles the sogo shosha but is much smaller. The export trading company does not form part of large industrial groups, as the sogo shosha do. Also, they are more restricted by law in their activities than are the sogo shosha.

Answer to Internet Problems

1. Note to Professor, students can get the names of the top exporters to and importers from the United States from Table 2.5, "Major Trading Partners of the United States," on page 68. Then the students can go to the Office of Trade and Economic Analysis website mentioned in the "Relevance for Businesspeople" section of the "Major Trading Partners" section. In this website, the students can look at the "U.S. Foreign Trade Highlights" for over 100 tables of goods and services, including one that provides data on the top U.S. exports and imports from its 80 largest trading partners. At a 1-digit SITC commodity level, monthly and yearly data are available from the website www.census.gov/foreign-trade/sitc1/1999/c1220.html which will allow students to identify the primary areas of trade between the U.S. and her main trading partners. You can ask students to obtain results for the most recent month (or year), if you wish.

2. For 1999, the following data were available, with figures in millions of U.S. dollars:

	Exports	Imports	Balance
Telecom equipment	$26,623	$23,939	$2,684
Semiconductors	46,962	37,627	9,335
Computers	10,034	10,807	(773)
Wine and related products	766	4,162	(3,396)
Lumber (logs & lumber for exports)	4,158	8,015	(3,857)
Records, tapes, and disks	3,875	1,259	2,616
Autos, vehicles, parts & engines	75,756	179,393	(103,637)

Discussion of Minicase 2–1: Method of Entry for Local Manufacturing–The McGrew Company

Beal's list should include

A. Wholly Owned Company
1. Start from ground up and build a factory.
2. Buy a company making products, which use about the same processes. Such a plant can be readily converted with a minimum amount of labor training.
3. Purchase the Brazilian distributor and expand his facilities. The distributor already repairs the combines so he must have a sizable machine shop and he certainly has the marketing expertise.

B. A Joint Venture
1. With the distributor.
2. With a company making similar products.

C. Licensing Agreement

D. Contract Manufacturing

She probably will recommend either A3 or B1 because McGrew lacks marketing expertise in Brazil. Beal must check Brazilian laws to see if 100 percent foreign ownership is permitted (it is) and if there are any tax incentives given to joint ventures when one partner is Brazilian (none at this time).If the university library where McGrew is located subscribes to Business International or receives the Ernst and Ernst country reports, she can find this out easily. If not, she can call the nearest Brazilian Consulate or the Brazilian Embassy in Washington. Probably the president made his calculations based on McGrew's exports and possibly on total U. S. exports that he got from the U. S. Department of Commerce. You will want to learn if other countries also export to Brazil. The quickest way is to ask your Brazilian distributor to get these data from the Brazilian government. The distributor should be able to find out from what countries Brazil imports peanut combines, how many from each country and the quantity imported over the years. Is it growing or diminishing?

The distributor can also give an estimation of the quality of competitive machines, their prices and acceptance in the Brazilian market. Is the crop size growing, remaining stable or diminishing? If McGrew doesn't know, Beal should ask how the local growers pay for the machines. Are they dependent on government credit? It would be useful to know if Brazil offers any investment incentives. Does it require a local subsidiary to export? This could cut into McGrew-U. S. exports. What are labor costs? Are there any requirements for local partners in the venture? Probably you would do your analysis in steps. First, see what the total market appears to be and then if it looks satisfactory, proceed to obtain data on the cost of setting up a production facility, the Brazilian government's requirements and the costs of production.

World Trade in Merchandise Exports (FOB Values; in Billions of Current U.S. Dollars)

	1970	1980	1990	1995	1999
Total world exports	$314	$2,001	$3,436	$5,004	$5,478
Developed countries	225	1,269	2,449	3,435	3,690
Germany[a]	35	193	423	508	541
United States	43	217	394	585	702
Japan	19	130	288	443	418
France	18	111	210	287	300
United Kingdom	19	110	185	242	268
Italy	13	78	170	234	230
Developing countries[b]	56	587	806	1,384	1,586
EU	88[c]	690[d]	1,477[e]	2,038	2,166
EFTA	5[f]	112	99[g]	122	123
LAIA	3	80	113	173	209

Notes: EU = European Union.

EFTA = European Free Trade Association.

LAIA = Latin American Integration Association (formerly Latin America Free Trade Association).

[a] Includes exports to East Germany before reunification.

[b] Defined by the World Bank as low- and middle-level-income nations as indicated by GNP/capita.

[c] Original six members only (Belgium, Luxembourg, France, West Germany, Italy, and the Netherlands).

[d] Includes original six members plus Denmark, Ireland, and the United Kingdom.

[e] Includes Greece, Spain, and Portugal and excludes Austria, Finland, and Sweden before 1995.

[f] Includes Finland as associate member with the original seven states: Austria, Denmark, Norway, Portugal, Sweden, United Kingdom, and Switzerland.

[g] Includes Iceland, Austria, Finland, and Sweden before 1995 and excludes the United Kingdom and Denmark.

Sources: *Monthly Bulletin of Statistics* (New York: United Nations, June 1997), pp. 92–102, 266–71; and *Monthly Bulletin of Statistics* (New York: United Nations, August 2000), pp. 92–111, 122.

World Trade in Services Exports (FOB Values; in Billions of Current U.S. Dollars and in Percentage Share)

	1990	1995	1999	Percentage Share of Worldwide Exports
World	$782.0	$1,187.0	$1,339.2	100.0%
United States	132.2	197.2	251.7	18.8
Japan	41.4	64.0	59.8	4.5
European Union	369.9	506.1	565.8	42.2
France	66.3	83.1	79.3	5.9
Germany	51.6	75.2	76.8	5.7
Italy	48.6	61.2	64.5	4.8
Netherlands	29.6	46.8	53.1	4.0
United Kingdom	53.2	74.6	101.4	7.6
East Asia	68.1	160.3	161.2	12.0
Korea	46.9	101.1	98.1	7.3
Taiwan	6.9	14.9	14.8	1.1
Hong Kong	18.1	34.3	35.4	2.6
Singapore	12.7	29.7	22.9	1.7
Thailand	6.3	14.7	14.1	1.1
Malaysia	3.8	11.4	10.8	0.8
China	5.7	18.4	26.6	2.0
Latin America	29.7	44.5	53.5	4.0
Middle East	n.a.	n.a.	n.a.	n.a.
Africa	18.6	25.2	28.4	2.1
Russia and Central and Eastern Europe	n.a.	n.a.	n.a.	n.a.

Note: n.a. = not available.

Source: Excerpted from *JETRO White Paper on Foreign Direct Investment 2000* (Tokyo: Japan External Trade Organization, 2000), p. 5. based on World Trade Organization data.

Stocks of Outward Foreign Direct Investment, Selected Countries, 1985, 1990, 1995, and 1999 ($ billions)

Country	1985 Amount	1985 Share	1990 Amount	1990 Share	1995 Amount	1995 Share	1999 Amount	1999 Share
United States	$251.0	35.5%	$430.5	25.1%	$699.0	24.4%	$1,131.5	23.8%
United Kingdom	100.3	14.2	229.3	13.4	304.9	10.6	664.1	14.0
Japan	44.0	6.2	201.4	11.7	238.5	8.3	292.8	6.2
Germany	59.9	8.5	151.6	8.8	268.4	9.3	420.9	8.8
France	37.1	5.2	110.1	6.4	184.4	6.4	298.0	6.3
Netherlands	47.8	6.8	109.0	6.4	179.6	6.3	306.4	6.4
Belgium and Luxembourg	9.6	1.4	40.6	2.4	88.5	3.1	159.5	3.4
Switzerland	25.1	3.5	66.1	3.9	142.5	5.0	199.5	4.2
Italy	16.6	2.3	57.3	3.3	109.2	3.8	168.4	3.5
Canada	43.1	6.1	84.8	4.9	118.1	4.1	178.3	3.7
Developing countries	32.4	4.6	81.9	4.8	258.3	9.0	468.7	9.8
Other	40.2	5.7	153.8	8.9	279.2	9.7	471.2	9.9
World total	707.1	100.0%	1,716.4	100.0%	2,870.6	100.0%	4,759.3	100.0%

Source: Various "Country Fact Sheets," *World Investment Report 2000*, United Nations Conference on Trade and Development, Geneva, October 2000.

McGraw-Hill/Irwin

TM 2.4
Figure 2.1

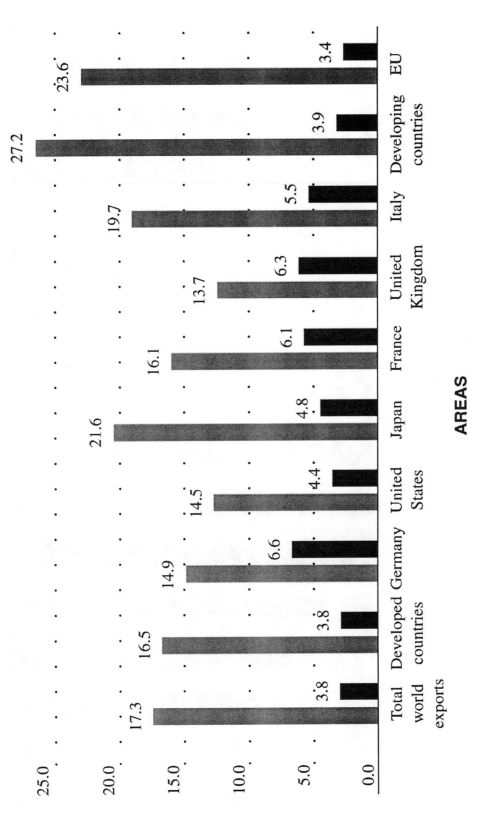

AREAS

● Current dollars ratios, 1996/1970   ● Quantum index ratios, 1996/1970

McGraw-Hill/Irwin

TM 2.5
Figure 2.2

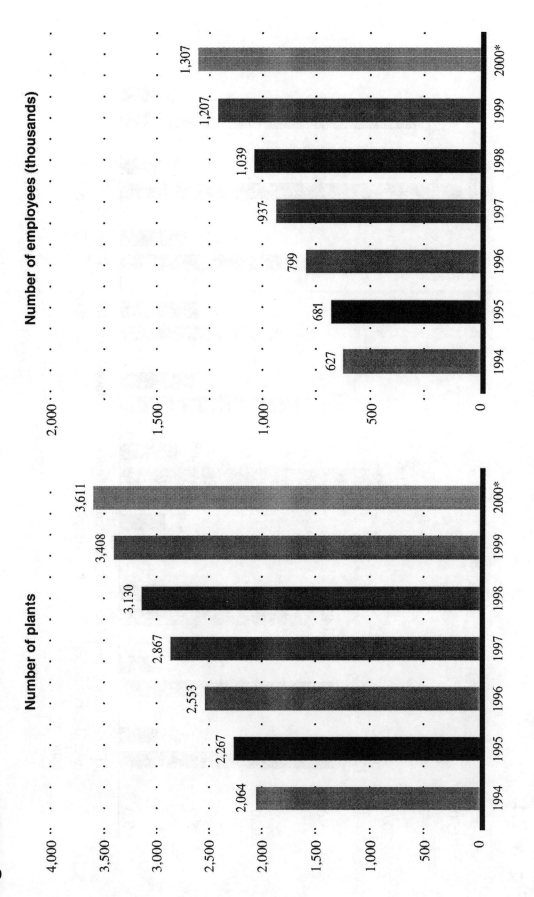

Number of plants

Number of employees (thousands)

McGraw-Hill/Irwin

TM 2.6
Figure 2.3

Investment outlays ($ millions)

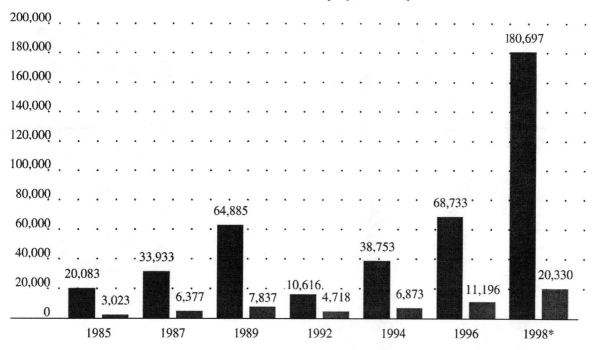

Number of investments

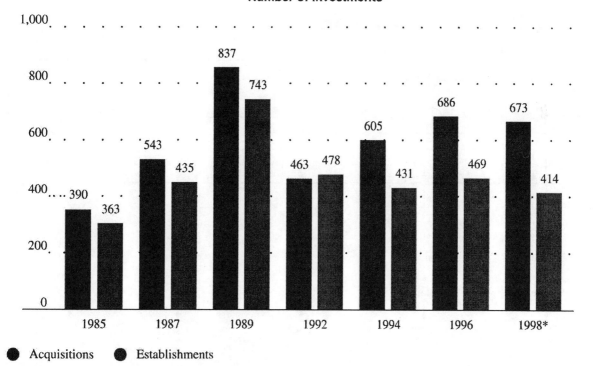

● Acquisitions   ● Establishments

TM 2.7
Figure 2.4

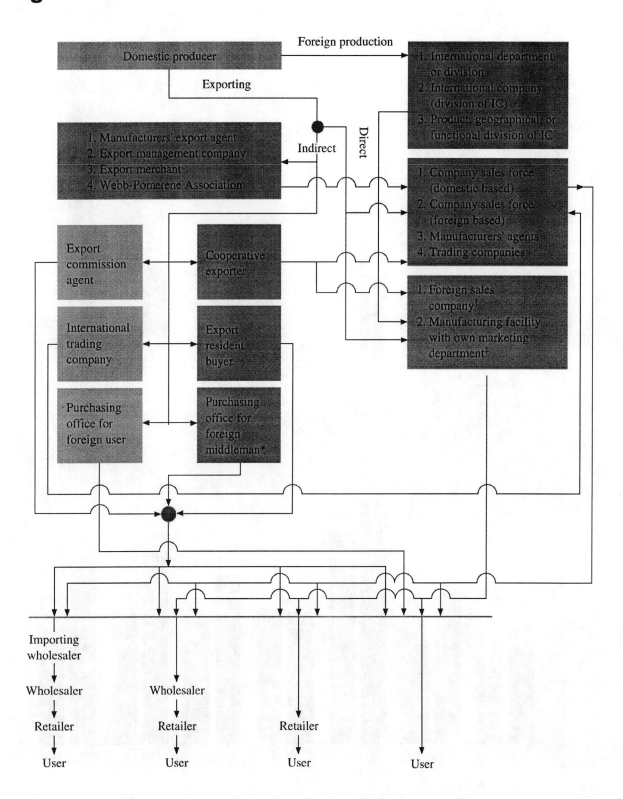

CHAPTER 3
ECONOMIC THEORIES ON INTERNATIONAL TRADE, DEVELOPMENT AND INVESTMENT

Learning Objectives

1. Introduce some of the more well known theories of trade such as mercantilism, theory of comparative advantage. Heckscher-Ohlin's theory of factor endowments and the international product life cycle and show that they have practical applications. Also Linder's theory and Porter's analysis.

2. Discuss the arguments commonly given for imposing trade restrictions.

3. Describe the various tariff and nontariff barriers to trade.

4. Introduce a number of theories concerning economic development and show that they have practical applications.

5. Present contemporary theories of foreign direct investment and Dunning's Eclectic Theory of International Production.

6. Discuss how the reduction of import duties and the elimination or weakening of import barriers as a consequence of the Uruguay Round is opening foreign markets to international business firms and is making it easier to source world wide.

Overview

Because many business decisions and governmental actions are both explained and influenced by economic concepts, international business managers must have a basic knowledge of the most popular theories in both areas.

Trade theories attempt to explain why nations trade with each other. Mercantilists (1550 to 1800) believed that trade should be a vehicle for accumulating gold. Adam Smith, displeased with mercantilist ideas, showed that a nation could acquire what it does not produce by means of free unregulated trade. A nation could gain most by producing only goods which it could produce with less labor than other nations. Ricardo carried Smith's argument a step farther by proving that a country that was less efficient in the production of all goods could still gain from trade by exporting those products in which it was more efficient. Heckscher and Ohlin claimed that a nation would export those goods that required a relatively large amount of the amount of the production factors with which it was endowed.

The international product life cycle theory states that products first produced in developed nations later are produced in the LDCs for local consumption and eventually become their exports to the developed countries where their production first began.

Although these theories argue for free trade among nations, tariff and non-tariff barriers to trade still exist. Various arguments are given for their existence such as the necessity to protect local industry from cheap foreign labor, to protect new industries until they are mature and to ensure that a country will have the needed defense industries.

Because many decisions and governmental actions are both explained and influenced by the economic theories of international trade, development and foreign investment, international business managers must have a basic knowledge of the most popular theories in all three areas.

Since the 1970s, economists have come to realize that economic development encompasses more than economic growth and so a new, more comprehensive definition of economic development has evolved. The human-needs approach defines economic development as the reduction of poverty, unemployment and inequality of income distribution. The reduction of poverty now includes less illiteracy, less malnutrition, less disease and so forth.

However, there is no one accepted general theory. The unbalanced growth theory has some followers but there is a growing belief that investment in human capital is required. Also more governments are changing to a production strategy of export promotion from one of import substitution because of the disadvantages of the latter.

International investment theory attempts to explain why foreign direct investment occurs. Product and factor market imperfections provide firms primarily from oligopolistic industries with advantages not open to indigenous companies. The international product life cycle helps explain the direction of international investment as well as international trade. Some companies follow the industry leader overseas and the tendency for European firms to invest in the United States and vice versa seems to indicate that this cross investment is done for defensive reasons. The internalization theory states that international firms will seek to invest in a foreign subsidiary rather than license their superior knowledge to receive a better return on investment used to produce the knowledge. Two financially based explanations for foreign direct investment are: (1) foreign exchange market imperfections resulting in overvalued and undervalued currencies may attract investors from nations with overvalued currency to countries with undervalued currency, and (2) the portfolio theory which postulates that international operations are made for risk diversification. There is a brief description of the Eclectic Theory of International Production.

Suggestions and Comments

1. This material is somewhat difficult for many students and it is easy to lose their interest when discussing theories from the 17th century. We emphasize in class that there are good, practical reasons for knowing the essentials as we have also emphasized in the text. The Student Involvement Exercises should help to arouse their interest. We recommend that you go slowly in discussing comparative advantage. If you whip through it, you will probably lose most of the class. We commonly ask a student to come to the board and create a table to explain the theory and we give him or her all of the help required.

2. We find it advantageous to follow the discussion of comparative advantage with the example in which we introduce money because the students learn quickly about the importance of exchange rates and they are better prepared when we examine the financial markets.

3. The section on Arguments for Protection is usually well received because of the publicity that these arguments receive. Everybody knows about the automobile industry's problems. The students are often surprised to learn that in many countries, there is a call for protection from U.S. imports.

4. For gaining interest in the discussion of theories on economic development, we again stress their practical applications. It seems to help when we give examples of nations whose policies indicate that its leaders are believers in one or more of the theories. Export promotion (NIEs) vs. import substitution is a good current topic.

Student Involvement Exercises

1. Ask the students what arguments for protecting U.S. industry from imports reflect present day mercantilist thinking. Why is Japan called the Fortress of Mercantilism?

2.   This is the output of cigars and calculators for countries A and B.

Output/Man-Day

	A	B
Calculators	6	2
Cigars	20	10

a.   Would it be advantageous for B and A to trade?

b.   What would be the trading limits of cigars for calculators? (3 1/3 cigars/calculator to 5 cigars/calculator).

c.   Total production costs per day are $30 in A and 120 pesos in B. If the exchange rate is 10 pesos in B = $1 in A, will trade still place in the same direction as for part a?

<u>A</u>

Calculators	$\dfrac{\$30}{6\ \text{calculators}}$	=	$5/calculator
Cigars	$\dfrac{\$30}{20\ \text{cigars}}$	=	$1.50/cigar

<u>B</u>

Calculators	$\dfrac{120\ \text{pesos}}{2}$	=	60 pesos/calculator
Cigars	$\dfrac{120\ \text{pesos}}{10}$	=	12 pesos/cigar

Converting to dollars

	A	B
Calculators	$5/Calculator	$6/calculator
Cigars	$1.50/cigar	$1.20/cigar

d.   What change must be made in the exchange rate to change the flow of trade?
Answer:

(1) If rate goes to 12 pesos = $1, calculator will cost $5 in B, which is the same price as in A, so based on price alone, B will not import from A. B can still sell cigars to A because their price has improved and gives them a greater price advantage.

(2) If the rate goes to 8 pesos = $1, then B's cigars will cost A $1.50 and B will lose its price advantage. Calculators in B will cost $7.50 to produce.

e.   If rate goes to 8 pesos or even 7 pesos = $1, will B sell any cigars to A?
Answer:

(1) They probably will if their cigars taste better or are handmade, if A's are machine made. Cigars, like most products, are not bought purely on the basis of price.

3.   a.   Ask the students what kinds of automobiles we would be driving today if duties on imported cars had been so high over the last 10 years that none would have come into this country. Would prices of U.S. cars have been any different?

b.   If steel imports in the U. S. were stopped, would there be as much pressure on the American steel industry to modernize their production facilities?

4.   According to Table 3.3, page 144 in the text, each job saved in the clothing industry costs American consumers $340,727. Should the American consumer be expected to pay such a high price to protect the clothing industry?

Guest Lecturers

1. Institutions in areas having foreign consuls can invite a member of the consulate to discuss his or her government's policy with respect to trade restrictions and economic development especially as it affects foreign investment in that country. The representative could also be asked about that government's efforts to promote foreign trade.

2. Invite someone from a local multinational company to discuss the procedure which the company followed to obtain governmental permission to set up a foreign production facility. This person can be asked (you'd better check with him or her before class) if a knowledge of economic development and international trade theories has been useful.

Lecture Outline

I.   The Opening Section
        The opening section provides a practical application of the law of comparative advantage in Chile. It illustrates how anyone with a basic knowledge of trade and development theory could have predicted what the government was going to do.

II.   International Trade Theory
        International trade theory attempts to answer the question, "Why do nations trade?"
        A. Mercantilism
            1. One of the first economic doctrines (1550 to 1800).
            2. Central idea–countries having no gold sources could accumulate gold by exporting more goods than they import.
            3. Governments should control foreign trade because individuals might trade gold for imports. Only the government was in a position to assure that only local products were purchased.
            4. France's high-tech mercantilism.
            5. Japan, the "Fortress of Mercantilism?"
        B. Theory of Absolute Advantage
            1. Dissatisfaction with excessive government controls prompted many writers to advocate less government control of foreign trade.
            2. Adam Smith (*The Wealth of Nations*–1776) attacked mercantilism and said that to trade in order to accumulate gold was foolish. By means of free, unregulated trade, a nation could acquire what it did not produce.
            3. He stated that a nation should produce only those goods in which it was most efficient. The surplus could be traded to obtain the products which could not be produced advantageously.
            4. The question was then asked, would it be advantageous for a nation to trade if it were not as efficient as another in the production of any product?
        C. Theory of Comparative Advantage
            1. Ricardo in 1817 showed that if a nation were less efficient in the production of two products, it could still gain from international trade if it were not equally less efficient in the production of both goods.

2. Smith's and Ricardo's theories considered labor as the only important factor in calculating production costs and no thought was given to the possibility of producing the same goods with different combinations of factors until the the Heckscher-Ohlin theory in 1933.

3. We can also illustrate the gains from trade graphically using production possibility curves. See Figure 3.1, page 127.

D. Heckscher -Ohlin Theory of Factor Endowment

1. Trade between countries is caused by a difference in the endowments of their production factors.

2. Each country should concentrate on producing the goods which require a large amount of the most abundant factor. (Taiwan, labor-intensive goods; Germany, capital-intensive goods).

3. Leontief, an economist, found in a study that the U.S., one of the most capital-intensive countries in the world, was exporting labor-intensive products. Economists have speculated that this happened because the U.S. exports technology-intensive products produced by highly-skilled labor requiring a large capital investment to educate and import goods made with mature technology requiring capital-intensive mass production processes operated by unskilled labor.

4. There are exceptions to this theory in the world because they ignored transportation costs, ignored taste preferences and assumed that the same technology is available to all nations.

E. Introducing Money
When money is added to the example of comparative advantage, depending on the exchange rate, the price of one currency stated in the terms of the other, the actual direction of trade may be different from that predicted by the theory.

F. International Product Life Cycle (See Figure 3.2, page 130)

1. This new concept was offered in the 1960s and is related to the product life cycle.

2. It is helpful in the analysis of a product's export potential and may help to predict which products are in danger from import competition.

3. Under IPLC concept, many products pass through four stages:

   a. Developed nation's exports.

   b. Beginning of foreign production.

   c. Foreign competition in export markets.

   d. Import competition in home markets.

G. Some explanations for the Direction of Trade

1. Economies of Scale and the Experience Curve affect international trade because they permit a nation's industries to become low-cost producers without having an abundance of a certain class of production factors.

2. First Mover Theory. Although some management theorists argue that firms entering the market first (first mover's) will soon dominate it, new research indicates that previous studies were flawed because they were based on surveys about surviving firms and did not include a large number of the true pioneers.

3. The Linder Theory of Overlapping Demand
   Linder, a Swedish economist, realized the Heckscher-Ohlin theory was satisfactory for
   explaining international trade in primary products, but not for the trade in manufactured
   goods. His theory deduces that international trade in manufactured goods will be greater
   between nations with similar levels of per capita income than between those with
   dissimilar per capita income levels. The goods that are traded are those for which there is
   an overlapping demand (consumers in both countries demand the good). Unlike the
   theory of comparative advantage, this theory does not specify the direction of trade.

4. Porter's Competitive Advantage of Nations
   Porter, an economist, studied 100 firms to learn if a nation's prominence in an industry
   can be explained better by variables other than the factors of production used in the
   theories of comparative advantage and factor endowment. Porter claims there are four
   kinds of variables that have an impact on the ability of local firms to utilize a country's
   resources to gain a competitive advantage: (1) demand conditions, (2) factor conditions,
   (3) related and supporting industries, and (4) firm strategy, structure, and rivalry-extent of
   domestic competition, existence of barriers to entry, and the firm's management style and
   organization. His work complements the theories of Ricardo and Heckscher-Ohlin, but,
   as one scholar stated, there is nothing new in Porter's analysis. Also, Porter's evidence is
   anecdotal, not empirical.

H. Summary of International Trade Theory
   We can say that international trade occurs primarily because of relative price differences
   among nations. The differences stem from differences in production costs which are the result
   of differences in the endowment of factors of production and the level of efficiency at which
   they are utilized. The demand variable, taste differences, can reverse the direction of trade
   predicted by the theory (Italian cars to U.S.).

III. Trade Restrictions
Although international trade theory provides strong arguments for free trade, every country in the
world employs trade restrictions to protect local industry.

A. Arguments for Trade Restrictions and Their Rebuttal
   1. National defense
      a. Which industries are vital?
      b. Better to subsidize so that taxpayers know what the protection costs.
   2. Infant Industry
      a. Tariffs to protect new industry until it can compete against imports.
      b. Problem is, no firm wants to admit that it has come of age.
      c. Argument accepted and used by developing country governments.
   3. Protect domestic jobs from cheap foreign labor.
      a. Wage costs not production costs.
      b. Government-imposed fringes are often higher elsewhere.
      c. Import protection can affect exports.
      d. Scientific tariff or "fair competition"—Some want duties "only" equal to difference
         between domestic and foreign production costs. This, however, will protect
         inefficient producers and give a bonanza to the efficient ones.
   4. Retaliation—Industries whose exports have had import restrictions placed on them may
      request their government to retaliate with similar restrictions. E.U.-U.S. example.

5. Dumping—Selling abroad for less than the cost of production or the price to third countries less than the home market price. If exporter expects to raise prices in the foreign market after forcing local producers out of business, it is called predatory dumping.

6. New types of dumping.
   There are at least four new kinds of dumping for which fair-trade lobbies want sanctions. They are:
   a. Social dumping—unfair competition by firms in developing nations that have lower labor costs and poorer working conditions.
   b. Environmental dumping—unfair competition caused by a country's lax environmental standards.
   c. Financial services dumping—unfair competition caused by a nation's low requirements for bank capital/asset ratios.
   d. Cultural dumping—unfair competition caused by cultural barriers aiding local firms.

7. Export subsidies—When governments offer various kinds of export subsidies to encourage firms to export, importing nation may levy countervailing duties.

B. Kinds of Restrictions—See Table 3.1, page 137, for tabulation of all kinds of restrictions.
   1. Tariffs
      a. Ad valorem—percentage of invoice value.
      b. Specific—fixed sum per physical unit.
      c. Compound—ad valorem and specific charged on product.
      d. Variable levy—used by E.U. to guarantee that market prices of imported grains will be the same as support prices grains produced in E.U.
   2. Nontariff barriers—all forms of import discrimination except import duties.
      a. Quantitative—quotas, orderly marketing arrangements, countertrade
      b. Nonquantitative nontariff barriers—government participation (subsidies), customs and other administrative procedures, and standards. Figure 3.3, p. 142, shows the value of farm subsidies and their percentage of total farm output.

C. Costs of Barriers to Trade—Table 3.3, p. 144, illustrates the tremendous cost to the consumer for import protection.

IV. Economic Development
   A. Categories Based on Levels of Economic Development
      1. *Developed* is the name given to the industrialized nations of Western Europe, Japan, Australia, New Zealand, Canada, Israel, and the United States.
      2. *Developing* is a classification for the world's lower-income countries, which are less technically developed.
      3. *Newly industrialized* economies (NIEs) refer to the four Asian tigers.
      4. International agencies employ various classification systems. The World Bank uses a system based on GNP/Capita (see p. 145).
   B. GNP/Capita as an Indicator
      Although GNP/capita is widely used to compare nations, there are some problems.
      1. Values are only estimated.
      2. GNP earned in underground economy goes unreported. See Figure 3.4, page 146.
      3. In many nations, much internal trade by barter. These figures not included in GNP.

4. Official exchange rates used to convert local currencies to dollars usually underestimate country's level of living. To overcome this problem, World Bank and UN also use purchasing power parity. See discussion on page 147 and Table 3.4, page 148.

C. More than GNP/Capita Is Required
1. Assumes equal distribution of income.
2. Various attempts to include nonmonetary indicators to compare nations' living levels.

D. Common Characteristics of Developing Nations
1. GNP/Capita less than $9,265 (World Bank criterion)
2. Unequal distribution of income, with a very small middle class.
3. *Technological dualism*– a mix of firms employing the latest technology and companies using very primitive methods.
4. *Regional dualism*–high productivity and incomes in some regions and little economic development in others.
5. A preponderance (80 to 85 percent) of the population earning its living in a relatively unproductive agricultural sector.
6. Disguised unemployment or underemployment–two people doing a job that one person can do.
7. High population growth (2.5 to 4 percent annually)
8. High rate of illiteracy and insufficient educational facilities.
9. Widespread malnutrition and a wide range of health problems.
10. Political instability
11. High dependence of a few products for export, generally agricultural products or minerals.
12. Inhabitable topography, such as deserts, mountains, and tropical forests.
13. Low savings rates and inadequate banking facilities.

E. Human Needs Approach to Economic Development
Economists and governments now realize that economic development includes more than economic growth. The human-needs approach defines economic development as the reduction of poverty, unemployment and inequality of income distribution. Definition of poverty has also been broadened to include reduction in illiteracy, malnutrition and disease.
1. No accepted general theory–Even though the experts don't agree on a general theory, businesspeople should know something about the following theories.
2. *Investment in human capital*–This development in the theory recognizes that there must be investment in human capital to ensure that the capital invested is productive. Managements of multinationals must emphasize this aspect of their investment.
3. *Import substitution vs. export promotion*–Developing nations are realizing that the industrial strategy of import substitution is not reducing their dependence on the developed nations and so are turning to the promotion of exports. Multinationals must be prepared for demands to export from host country officials.

V. International Investment Theories
A. Contemporary Theories of Foreign Direct Investment
1. Monopolistic Advantage Theory
Foreign direct investment occurs largely in oligopolistic competition which means that these companies possess advantages not available to local firms such as economies of scale, superior technology, etc.

2. Product and Factor Market Imperfections
   Caves expanded on Hymer's work to show that superior knowledge permitted investing firm to produce differentiated products which consumers would prefer to similar locally made goods.

3. International Product Life Cycle
   Theory explains that foreign direct investment is a natural stage in the life of the product.

4. Other Theories

   a.. Follow-the-leader.

   b. Cross-investment--Europeans tend to invest in U.S. and vice versa. Permits retaliation in each other's home market.

   c. Internalization theory–Extension of market imperfection theory. By investing overseas instead of licensing, firm keeps knowledge within company and earns a better ROI.

   d. Aliber believes imperfection in foreign exchange markets may be responsible for foreign direct investment.

   e. One commonality to nearly all theories--major part of F.D.I. made by large, research-intensive, oligopolistic industries.

   f. Eclectic theory of international production states that for a firm to invest overseas, it must have 3 kinds of advantages: ownership-specific, internalization, and location-specific.

Answers to Questions

1. a. According to the theory of absolute advantage, each nation should specialize in producing the goods it can produce most efficiently. Some of them can be exported to pay for imports of goods that can be produced more efficiently elsewhere.

   b. Ricardo showed that even though a nation did not hold an absolute advantage in producing any good, it could still trade with another country with advantages for each as long as the less efficient nation was not equally less efficient in producing both goods.

2. The factor endowment theory explains that a nation will export the products which require a large amount of the relatively abundant, thus less costly, factor of production with which a nation is endowed. This gives it a cost advantage, which is the absolute or comparative advantage of Adam Smith's and Ricardo's theories.

3. TVs, sewing machines, appliances. Look at what the NICs are producing–cars, ships, steel and now computer chips are entering the fourth stage of the IPLC.

4. Trade restrictions are imposed at the request of special interest groups, not the public. Defense departments of developed nations urge restrictions to protect "vital" industries, labor unions and local communities to avoid losing a plant, etc.

5. Unfortunately, we still live in a world where military preparedness is necessary, but the problem is that the military has the same needs as the general public (shoes for the military in the text). At any rate, if a nation subsidizes these necessary industries instead of erecting trade barriers to protect them, then it will be clear to the public what the cost of preparedness really is.

6. Wage costs are only part of labor costs which are only part of production costs.

7. a. ad valorem, specific and compound duties

   b. quotas, orderly marketing arrangements, countertrade, government subsidies, customs and administrative procedures, standards.

8.   To know that a nation is a developing nation indicates to the marketer that the consumer's ability to purchase is limited, although, because of the skewed distribution of income, there is usually a small group capable of buying large ticket items. It tells marketers something about the educational and technological levels about which they must know to design promotional programs and product mixes. Lack of good roads can cause distribution costs to be high and so forth.

9.   Import substitution has not lessened the dependence of developing nations on imports from the industrialized nations–it has merely changed the composition of their imports. In fact, dependency has increased. Import substitution has also brought protection from imports to the developed nations which has kept pressure for reducing costs and improving product quality from local manufacturers.

10.   False. Tellis and Golder in their Sloan Management Review article showed that the previous studies claiming that first movers held a 30 percent of the market and that 70 percent of the market leaders were first movers were flawed because they were based on surveys of the surviving firms and failed to include a large number of the true pioneers. They gave the example of Ampex, maker of the first VCRs. It sold very few at a $50,000 price. Sony and Matshushita worked for 20 years to make one to sell for $500 and cornered the market. The authors argued that early success in the market went to the companies that entered the market an average of 13 years after the "first movers."

Answers to Internet Problems

1.   This is from "The Agreement on Textiles and Clothing at the WTO web site. www.wto.org/wto/goods/textiles.htm, which appears in footnote 30 and is also in the Internet directory under the World Trade Organization.

   a.   The integration process is being carried out in three stages. The first stage began January 1, 1995 with the integration of products representing at least 16 percent of a country's total 1990 imports. At stage 2 on January 1, 1998, at least another 18 percent was integrated, and on January 1, 2005, all remaining products (amounting to up to 49 percent of 1990 imports) will be integrated.

   b.   The Textiles Monitoring Body is monitoring the application of the Agreement. Members represent (1) ASEAN countries, (2) Canada and Switzerland (first year), (3) Pakistan and China (after accession), (4) EU, (5) Hong Knog and Korea, (6) India and Egypt/Morocco/Tunisia, (7) Japan, (8) Latin American and Caribbean Members, (9) Turkey, Czech Republic/Hungary/Poland/Romania, Slovak Republic.

   c.   These offenses require cooperation and full cooperation in the investigation by member nations concerned. When sufficient evidence is available, recourse might include the denial of entry of goods. Member nations should establish the necessary legal provisions to address and take action against these offenses.

   d.   The four members were required to undertake the integration process and notify the Textile Monitoring Body of the first phase of their integration programs by October 1, 1994.

2   a.   Import duties once as high as 140% of invoice value have been brought down to between 1% and 17% for most products; surcharges, customs administrative charges, and consular fees have been abolished; and the country has done away with most non-tariff barriers to trade, including import license requirements. In 1999, the importation of plastics, electrical equipment, textiles transportation equipment, and food products rose by more than 30% over 1997 levels.

   b.   The United States accounts for 50% of Honduran foreign trade, followed by (2) Central American Common Market, and (3) Mexico.

c. Capital goods pay 1% of invoice value, including transportation costs. (CIF)

d. The market for construction machinery was $94.2 million in 1999, $103.6 million in 2000, and is estimated to reach $116.0 million in 2001.

e. The U.S. embassy ranks the construction machinery sector in second place after textiles. The Honduran government has begun a US$1 billion infrastructure rehabilitation program, which includes rehabilitation of existing roads, highways, bridges, urban road maintenance and repair to city streets damaged by Hurricane Mitch. The hurricane also increased the nation's housing deficit by 83,000 houses that must be rebuilt.

f. The Honduran market is highly receptive to U.S. construction equipment because of its good reputation for quality and availability of spare parts. Faster and cheaper delivery because of U.S. proximity are other favorable factors.

g. Until the mid-1980s, Honduran development strategy was based on the import substitution model. After 1990, Honduras moved towards a more liberalized international trade regime aimed at eliminating trade barriers and strengthening commercial relations with the rest of the world.

h. It will not because there is no local production available. (See p. 4 of chapter V).

i. Foreigners exporting to Honduras are not required by law to sell to customers directly nor through distributors.

j. The U.S. embassy says, "To market aggressively, U.S. exporters should establish local representation or a local sales office. Independent intermediaries are especially important for smaller companies as their knowledge of the market and of the relevant business customs and practices add to the strength of the U.S. exporter."

k. Contact the Commercial section of the U.S. embassy in Honduras who can locate interested, qualified representatives through its Agent/Distributor Service, a low-cost, highly effective program.

Discussion of Minicase 3-1: Taurus Manufacturing

This is an exercise in handling specific and ad valorem duties as well as exchange rates. The reduction in the amount of duties when local content is added is typical of many countries, developed and less developed. The calculations are as follows:

Imported Quarts

Invoice price	$1.60
Import duties	
40% ad valorem	.64
60 pesos specific	.10
Total..	$2.34

Imported 55-gallon Drum–Cost per Quart

Invoice price	$1.40
Import Duties	
30% ad valorem	.42
6,600 pesos/drum specific duty	.05*
Cost of can, labels and labor...........................	.30
Total..	$2.17

$$\text{*Specific duty (cents/qt.)} = \frac{6600 \text{ pesos}}{600 \text{ pesos}/\$1} = \frac{\$11/\text{drum}}{220 \text{ qt}/\text{drum}} = \$0.05/\text{qt.}$$

TM 3.1
Figure 3.1   Production and consumption possibility frontiers before and after trade

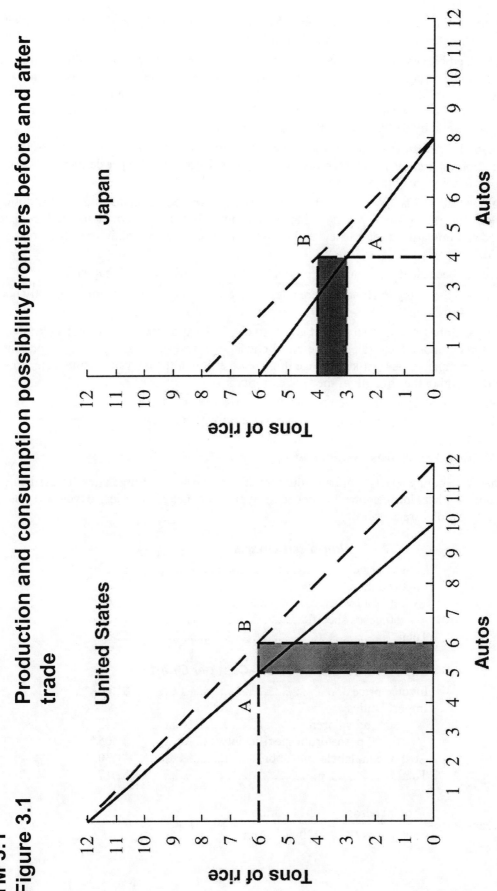

McGraw-Hill/Irwin

International Product Life Cycle

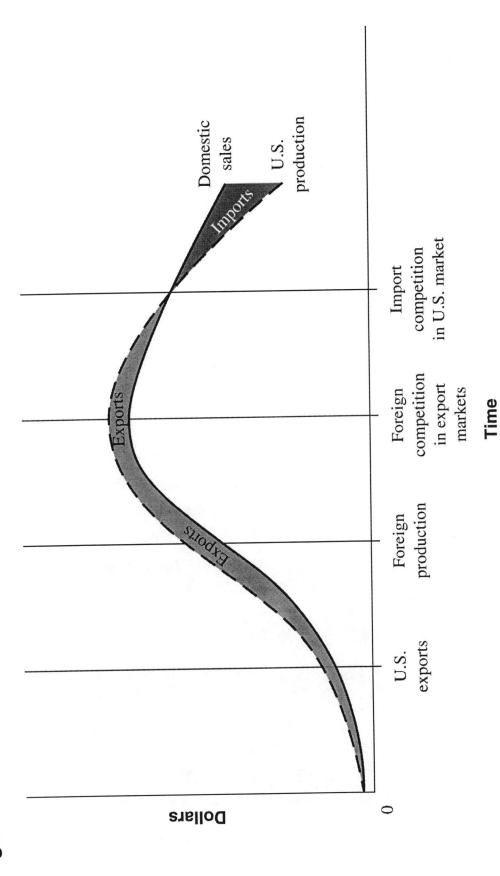

McGraw-Hill/Irwin

TM 3.3
Figure 3.3   Value of OECD Member Farm Subsidies ($billions)

Percent of value of production

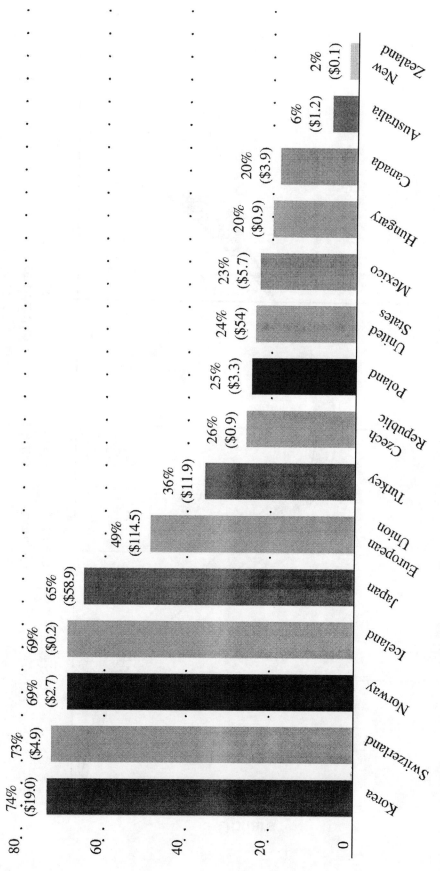

Source: "Producer Subsidy Equivalents," OECD in Figures (Paris: OECD, 1996), Table Agriculture II.

McGraw-Hill/Irwin

TM 3.4
Figure 3.4

Underground Economies (percentage of GDP, 1998)

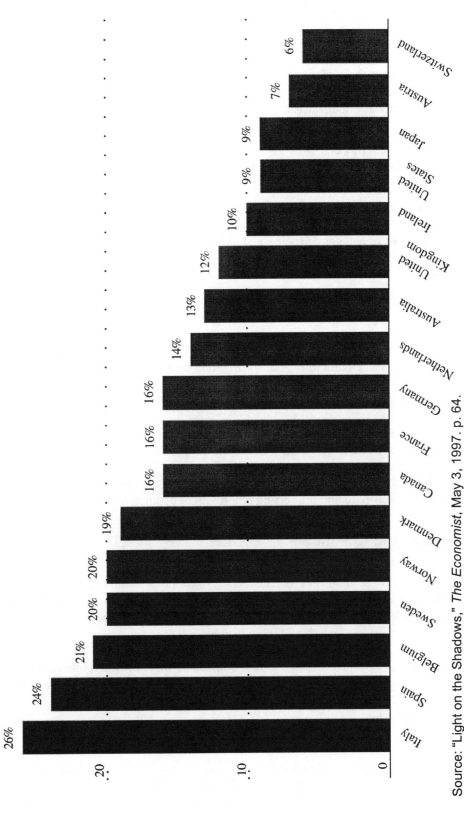

Country	Percentage
Italy	26%
Spain	24%
Belgium	21%
Sweden	20%
Norway	20%
Denmark	19%
Canada	16%
France	16%
Germany	16%
Netherlands	14%
Australia	13%
United Kingdom	12%
Ireland	10%
United States	9%
Japan	9%
Austria	7%
Switzerland	6%

Source: "Light on the Shadows," *The Economist*, May 3, 1997. p. 64.

McGraw-Hill/Irwin

CHAPTER 4
INTERNATIONAL ORGANIZATIONS

Learning Objectives

1. Point out to the students that business must deal with governments at the local level, the state level and the national level. International business must do all that and deal with the international organizations.

2. Differentiate the types of international organizations. Some have powers similar to the government powers. Others study and disseminate information about subjects such as health, meteorology, telecommunications and many more. Still others are sources of money and information.

3. Clarify for the students the uses of the international organizations to businesses. If management is alert and knowledgeable, the company can make sales to the organizations or their member countries or can get financing and valuable information from them.

Overview

No other textbook with which we are familiar gives as much information about as many international organizations as we present here. While international organizations are mentioned in other texts and in other chapters of this book, we felt it highly desirable to devote an entire chapter to their study.

These organizations are numerous and are of great and growing importance to international business. They operate in many fields, a few of which are labor conditions, agriculture, international company behavior, transportation, patent and trademark protection and postal system operations.

Thus, our purpose is to introduce the students to many of the international organizations with which businesses must cope and from which businesses can get information and financing.

Moreover, the students when they are job hunting should try the international organizations. They offer many well-paid and interesting employment opportunities.

Suggestions and Comments

All the students should have had civics or government courses in high school, political science courses as college freshmen or sophomores or business law courses which dealt with government control of business. Introduce the students to international organizations by pointing out that they are similar on an international scale to many government functions on the national, state, and local levels. Both the similarities and the differences should be indicated.

Throughout the chapter, the professor should emphasize ways in which international organizations can be helpful to the business managers who know how to use them. Companies can get financing, beneficial information and sometimes contracts from the various organizations. Some of the students may very well get jobs with them.

The growth in numbers and importance of developing countries is affecting most international organizations. That fact and its important ramification should be brought to the students' attention. Doubtless, many of them, when they take jobs with business or government, will confront the problems and opportunities posed by dealing with developing countries or by the influence of the developing countries on international organizations.

Student Involvement Exercises

All the organizations dealt with put out several publications. Professors may wish to have students order some of the publications in order to sample their contents and quality.

Call your students' attention to the Internet Directory addresses of the international organizations dealt with in this chapter. You might want to assign specific organizations to individual students or groups to research the history, purposes, activities, successes or failures, or forecast future of the organization.

Despite much opposition from protectionists, organized labor and environmentalists, the North American Free Trade Agreement (NAFTA) came into effect in 1994. For years, trade between Mexico and the U. S. has grown as exports from both countries increased substantially. The feared exodus of jobs from the U. S. to low-wage Mexico did not occur. Congress approved NAFTA at the request of President Clinton under the so-called fast-track authority that Congress had granted him and the recent presidents preceding him. Fast- track permits the president to negotiate trade agreements with other countries and submit them for congressional approval or disapproval by an up or down vote with no amendments permitted. Other countries are reluctant to negotiate agreements with the U. S. if they are subject to congressional amendments, but the fast-track provision expired in 1996. President Clinton wanted to negotiate expansion of NAFTA and other trade agreements, and he asked Congress to renew the fast track authority in 1997. Congress refused to do so.

Have your students study why fast track is necessary for successful trade agreement negotiations and why Congress refused President Clinton's request for its renewal. What are the results in terms of trade and jobs for American workers? Will Congress grant fast-track to President Bush?

Since most organizations discussed in this chapter are in fact organizations of governments, it is important to understand how and when these organizations speak for their members government and the impact their power has. Recent meetings of international organizations have made the news not necessarily because of the discussions going on in the meeting, but often because of the protestors outside of the meetings. A discussion about protests in Seattle in 1999 during the World Trade Organization meeting and in Quebec City in 2001 during the meeting of the western hemisphere leaders discussing the proposed Free Trade Area of the Americas should engender lively classroom debate.

The European Union (EU) is encountering difficulties in its pursuit of economic and monetary union (EMU). Have your students explain EMU and describe the difficulties. How have the twelve Euroland countries changed with the adoption of the euro?

Guest Lecturers and Film

If your school is near New York or Washington, D. C., you could probably get individuals from the international organizations to speak to the classes. In other areas there may be consular offices of various countries and international banks or businesses from which representatives could be found who are knowledgeable about international organizations. Sometimes other members of your school's faculty may have had experiences with the organizations which they would share with your classes.

A film, *Europe United*, can be obtained for the EU office in Washington. It gives the history of the EU formation and can be quite helpful.

Lecture Outline

I.   Opening Discussion

It is important for people involved in international business to understand the impact international organizations have on businesses and business people throughout the world. The text introduces the students to many of these international organizations. Since most of the organizations discussed in this chapter are in fact organizations of governments, it is important to understand how and when these organizations speak for their member governments and the impact their power has.

II.   The United Nations (UN)

A. The UN, formed at the end of World War II (WWII) disappointed many of its supporters when it failed in its mission to keep peace in the world It was hoped that the disintegration of the Union of Soviet Socialist Republics (USSR) in the 1990s, the end of the Cold War, and the succession of Russia to the UN seat of the USSR would lead to improvement in this area, but it continues to disappoint. The UN has peace keeping forces on the scene in numerous spots around the world, including Cambodia, Cypress, Haiti, and Lebanon, but fighting and unrest continues. The UN troops in the former Yugoslavia were replaced by forces of the North Atlantic Treaty Organization (NATO).

B. The UN is quite decentralized (see Table 4.1) but its potential value to business makes it worth the time to familiarize oneself with it.

C. The UN has grown tremendously since its establishment in 1945 and new nations continue to join as they gain independence. Developing countries now constitute a majority of the UN membership, and more and more UN effort is directed to aid these developing countries.

D. UN Specialized Agencies

1. United Nations Conference on Trade and Development (UNCTAD) was created because of demand for an agency to further interests of developing countries. UNCTAD has helped developing countries in several ways, including:

a. influencing the International Monetary Fund (IMF) to liberalize financing for developing countries.

b. getting IMF financing for commodities from developing countries.

c. getting developed countries to grant easier loans or grants to developing countries.

2. United Nations Industrial Development Organization (UNIDO) is another which was established to aid developing countries. UNIDO gives technical assistance, does in-plant training and feasibility studies and coordinates UN activities in the industrial development of developing countries. UNIDO has several publications of interest to business.

3. United Nations Children's Fund (UNICEF) aids developing countries with:

a. maternal and child health

b. child nutrition

c. disease control

d. education

UNICEF issues several publications of value to business,

4. World Health Organization (WHO) assists member countries:

a. improve health services

b. eradicate mass disease

c. stimulate medical research

WHO operates an international warning system to alert the world to the outbreak and spread of disease from any part of the world. It publishes monographs, reference works, technical reports and health statistics which can be of interest to business.

5. Food and Agriculture Organization (FAO) work includes:

a. encouragement of investments in developing countries agriculture

b. battles against insects and rodents

c. breeding disease-resistant grains, fruits and vegetables

d. improving range and pasture

e. combating animal diseases

f. improving commercial fish farming

FAO offers a wide variety of publications.

6. International labor Organization (ILO). The ILO objectives are to better the conditions of labor. Each member country sends four delegates of whom, in theory, two represent the government, one labor and one the business employers. American business and labor leaders complained that theory was impossible with communist governments which control all labor unions and own all business. The United States quit the ILO in 1977 but rejoined in 1980. There are several ILO publications of potential use to business.

7. There are a number of other UN specialized agencies. Their names usually indicate their areas of activities, for example:

a. International Telecommunication Union

b. World Meteorological Organization.

E. Every country that is a UN member belongs to the General Assembly and has one vote there regardless of size, population, or wealth. Inasmuch as there are far more poor developing countries than there are wealthy ones, the developing countries control the General Assembly.

F. The Security Council has 15 member countries of which five are permanent members. They are the countries that were victorious in the second world war: the People's Republic of China, France, Russia (which inherited the seat from the Soviet Union), the United Kingdom, and the United States. These five have veto power. Thus, a motion fails if any one of the five votes against it. The other 10 Security Council members are selected by the General Assembly for two-year terms.

Because other countries are larger, wealthier, or more populous than some of the permanent members, there are demands that the Security Council be enlarged. some countries that argue they should be permanent members are Germany, Italy, and Japan. Another argument for larger membership is geographic fairness; there are no permanent members from Africa, Latin America, or Southeast Asia. On that basis, Egypt, Nigeria, Argentina, Brazil, India, and Indonesia have put themselves forward.

It is a contentious issue. Existing permanent members are loathe to share their power and argue that a larger Security Council would be unwieldy, and that more countries with the veto would make it more difficult or impossible to get measures approved.

Membership in the United Nations (UN) Security Council is highly prized, and there is frequently fierce competition for the nonpermanent seats. There are two seats reserved for Western Europe and North America, and for membership beginning in 1999, Canada, Greece, and the Netherlands were the contestants. Canada invited members of the General Assembly, which elects the nonpermanent Security Council members, to a performance of Cirque du Soleil. Greece hosted more than 100 UN delegates and their spouses on a cruise of the Aegean, while the Netherlands treated its guests to a moonlight boat ride around New York City. In the voting, Canada and the Netherlands won. The other three seats, beginning in 1999, were won by Argentina, Malaysia, and Namibia.

G. The International Court of Justice (ICJ) is also called the World Court. The ICJ renders legal decisions involving disputes between national governments because it was established to resolve disputes between sovereign states and not between individuals. As a result, only nations may be parties to litigation before the court. Governments can, and often do, intervene on behalf of private parties such as corporations and individuals in the country. Even though the court has worldwide jurisdiction to hear disputes between governments, it hears relatively few cases - usually less than ten a year. The ICJ has fifteen judges who must be from fifteen different countries. The judges serve nine-year terms. To be elected, a majority of the General Assembly and a majority of the Security Council must support candidates. Activities of the ICJ are explored more fully in Chapter 11.

H. Career Opportunities

Thousands of people are hired by the UN and its specialized agencies. Many of the available jobs are well paid and frequently carry tax, travel and prestige perquisites. When you are job hunting you should investigate those opportunities.

III. Multilateral Development Bank

There are five multilateral development banks (MDBs). Listed alphabetically, they are: African Development Bank, Asian Development Bank, European Bank for Reconstruction and Development, Inter-American Development Bank, and the World Bank. As their names indicate, they are all regional except the World Bank.

See the text for information about opportunities for businesses and consultants. Consultants may be hired by a borrowing country or by one of the MDBs.

The largest of the MDBs is the World Bank, and we shall deal with it first.

The International Bank for Reconstruction and Development is usually referred to–including in its own publications–as the World Bank. You are reminded to re-read the two articles and accompanying commentary with which this chapter opened.

A. The World Bank is important to business because

1. Many companies are suppliers to borrowers and billions of dollars (and other currencies) are borrowed and spent each year.

2. The development finance institutions can help companies.

3. The Bank's center for arbitration can help resolve a company's difficulties with foreign customers.

4. Information gathered by the Bank tends to be more complete and accurate than might be available to a private bank or business.

5. In 1986 the United States joined the new Multilateral Investment Guarantee Agency of the Bank. This insures investors in foreign countries from loss due to numerous risks.

B. Hard loans are loans made in hard, convertible currencies and repayable in those currencies at full market interest rates. This is the kind of loan made by the *World Bank proper* and it has operated at a profit in every year since 1947. The Bank borrows money in the world's capital markets and its bonds carry the highest quality rating available, AAA.

C. Soft loans are made by a part of the World Bank, called the International Development Association (IDA). These loans are made to the extent practicable in soft, non-convertible currencies. They are made for longer periods (for example, up to 40 years) than are Bank loans (15-25 years) and carry no interest burden. IDA loans are called "credits" and IDA credits go to the poorest of the poor countries. Money for IDA credits comes from member country donations and from part of the World Bank profits. By 1996, the IDA had become the world's largest multilateral aid program.

D. Although no Bank loans have thus far been declared in default, the current world debt situation has forced rescheduling of some loans. It is not unlikely that some will be written off in the near future.

E. The International Finance Corporation (IFC) is another part of the World Bank group, IFC is called the group's investment banker as its objectives are to encourage private investments in developing countries. It also encourages local investment to the maximum extent feasible and attempts to create and expand local capital markets in the developing countries. Another task of IFC is to help create local development finance companies. By 1997, the IFC was reaching out to small and medium-size businesses. It reduced the minimum of projects it would finance from $5 million to $250,000 and simplified the procedures for approval of the smaller projects.

F. The World Bank group publishes a great deal of information which can be helpful to business.

G. Under the leadership of its president, James Wolfensohn, who was reelected in 2000 to a second five-year term, the World Bank has changed its emphasis. It has shifted from projects, such as infrastructure and energy, which promote industrial developments to programs, such as health and education, that foster social advancement.

In the first quarter of 1998 it raised a record $14.9 billion in 17 currencies at low financing costs, frequently at interest rates below the benchmark London Interbank Offered Rate. At that time the World Bank had $107 billion in loans outstanding.

IV. Regional MDBs. There are four:

A. African Development Bank (AFDB)

1. In 1997 the AFDB capital was increased from $6.9 billion to $22 billion.

2. Its African Development Fund was doubled to $3 billion. This fund is for loans to the poorest of the poor as is the IDA of the World Banks.

3. Due to governments' mismanagement of finances, the AFDB is moving to make more loans to private companies.

4. In the 1990's, the AFDB began channeling money to two of Africa's most vital resources which had been ignored. They are rural women who produce more than two-thirds of Africa's food and small businesses.

5. Nevertheless, by 1994 the AFDB was in trouble. A report by external consultants found a chaotic, top-heavy bureaucracy, riddled with political intrigue and suspicion. The consultants could not assess the quality of AFDB loans because of unreliable and insufficient data. They could not find a central file on any project.

B. Asian Development Bank (ADB)

1. The ADB management is dominated by Japanese.

2. There is disagreement between the Japanese and the Americans who want more loans made to private companies and fewer to inefficient governments.

3. Some perceive the Japanese running the ADB as a source of capital to finance Japanese exports.

4. In a move to direct more money to the private sector, the ADB established a separate bank in 1989 of which it owns 30 percent. The name is Asian Finance and Investment Corp., and the other 70 percent is owned by commercial banks and securities companies.

5. The ADB raises money by selling bonds in Australia, New Zealand, Europe, Japan, and North America. The bonds it sells in Hong Kong, Singapore, and Taipei are called dragon bonds.

C. European Bank for Reconstruction and Development (EBRD)
   The EBRD was created in 1990 to assist the countries of the ex-Soviet Union and the eastern European countries which had been USSR satellites. It is headquartered in London and had an initial capitalization of $13 billion. After a rocky start with its first president, Jacques Attali whose personal tastes in travel and office decorations were lavish, the EBRD has turned around and begun performing its assigned tasks. These are financing projects in Eastern Europe and the former Soviet Union, and it is co-financing with private banks to provide some of the money and with local banks to act as agents.

D. Inter-American Development Bank
   In 1994, IDB held its 35th annual meeting in Guadalajara, Mexico. One author characterized this meeting as having had "a touch of history."
   1. It was the first IDB meeting with NAFTA in force.
   2. The bank's capital was increased from $61 billion to over $100 billion.
   3. Latin American countries gave up their majority voting power, the U. S. reduced its power from 34.7 percent to 30 percent, and Europe and Japan got larger stakes.
   4. A priority is poverty reduction.

E. The U. S. Department of Commerce has assigned liaison officers to each of the MDBs for the convenience of businesses wishing to tap their resources.

V. International Monetary Fund (IMF)

A. The IMF was created to foster orderly foreign currency exchange arrangements at fixed exchange rates, convertible currencies, and shorter duration and lesser degree of balance of payments disequilibria.

B. The late 1970s and the early 1980s saw some fundamental changes to the IMF.
   1. The fixed exchange rate goal of the IMF was dropped.
   2. The IMF was given power to exercise "firm surveillance" over member countries' exchange rate polices.
   3. Longer term development loans were authorized to be made by the IMF. Prior to that, it limited itself to short-term loans to help a country overcome a temporary balance of payments difficulty.
   4. The IMF sold part of its gold and put part of the proceeds in a trust fund for the benefit of developing countries.
   5. In 1986, these monies were turned over to the new Structural Adjustment Facility (SAF) which also received IDA funds from the World Bank. SAF marks the first formal collaboration between the Bank and IMF.
   6. The SAF, which is called an enhanced structural adjustment facility if the developing countries problems are great, applies conditionality. The developing country submits a development plan which when approved by the Bank and the Fund, must be put into effect and followed by the developing countries. Money for the developing country from the SAF (or ESAF) is forthcoming only on condition that the developing country is successfully applying the plan.

C. Beginning in 1982, the IMF commenced new activities. As the gravity of developing country debt problems became clear, the IMF gave forceful leadership as it:
   1. pushed banks to give new loans to the capital starved developing countries.

2. pushed the debtor developing countries into austerity programs which might enable them to repay loans and restore economic health.

3. cooperated with the banks and developing countries as they renegotiated the old, nonperforming loans.

4. As time went on and the banks and developing countries gained experience dealing with their loan problems, the IMF stepped back and ceased taking leading roles.

D. In 1998 there were 179 IMF member countries.

E. In 1995, the IMF with the U. S. came to the assistance of Mexico whose faulty fiscal and monetary policies caused it to devalue its peso. That panicked foreign short-term investors who withdrew billions of dollars from Mexican banks, bonds, and stocks. Mexico recovered and repaid the loans.
Beginning in 1997, several Asian countries found themselves in need of similar help.

F. In 1998 there were calls to abolish the International Monetary Fund (IMF). One proposal would replace it with three small multilateral institutions. One institution would provide timely, uncensored information on countries' financial health. The second would help prevent crisis by playing an active role in the world's financial system rather than a reactive one, as the IMF currently does. The third would be in charge of "cleanup" and would deal with countries that in spite of all efforts go into a crisis. Under strict conditionality, it would provide funds and help them restructure their debts.

G. There are many useful IMF publications.

VI. Bank for International Settlements (BIS)

BIS, located in Basel, Switzerland, is a central banker's bank. Representatives of the U. S. Federal Reserve and the central banks of other major countries meet periodically to discuss mutual problems. BIS also cooperates with the IMF in achieving its goals. In 1981, the BIS embarked on a new sort of activity. Because of the growing debt crises of developing countries, the BIS made the first of several "bridge" loans to bridge the debtor countries over the time gap between their immediate lack of cash to service their loans and the IMF/commercial banks/central banks time-consuming measures to solve the debt problem. The four main BIS functions are listed on pages 159–160.

1. provide a forum for central bankers' meeting and provide cover when a member country wants to deal anonymously in the currency or gold markets.

2. do economic research

3. make bridge and other loans to countries.

4. be a clearing and settlement agent for Eurobonds.

In addition, it has begun workshops to train bankers from eastern European and Former USSR countries how to run banks in market economies and democracies.
When the BIS was founded in 1930, the U. S. declined membership but changed its mind in 1994. Since then, the U. S. Federal Reserve chairman has been an active participant.

In 1998 the Bank for International Settlements (BIS) opened its first overseas office in Hong Kong. As you remember, its headquarters are in Basel, Switzerland. The Hong Kong office comes as part of efforts by the BIS to strengthen financial sector supervision in the wake of the Asian financial crisis.

VII. World Trade Organization (WTO) which was preceded by the General Agreement on Tariffs and Trade (GATT)

At the conclusion of WWII the UN was formed to safeguard peace and it was hoped that another organization, the International Trade Organization (ITO) would function in the trade areas, encouraging free trade. By the time the ITO charter was ready for ratification by member country governments , the UN experience had begun to sour and ITO was not ratified. GATT had been set up as a temporary organization until ITO was ratified, and when it became clear ITO would not be ratified, GATT simply continued to operate.

A. WTO benefits to business

1. The WTO and the GATT had considerable success lowering tariffs and discouraging quotas, establishing fairer customs evaluation methods, standardizing import documentation and settling disputes between exporting and importing countries.

B. In 1986, a new round of GATT negotiations began in Uruguay and is referred to as the Uruguay Round. It was hoped this round would deal with protectionism in areas not previously dealt with by GATT such as services, government procurement, intellectual properties and agriculture.

C. After extremely difficult negotiations and several missed deadlines, the Uruguay Round finally ended in December, 1993. The WTO, the organization charged with resolving them, came into being on January 1, 1994.

D. One WTO feature is more dispute resolution power than the GATT had. Disputes involving dumping and Japan–U.S./Europe trade are prominent.

E. WTO members include 140 countries.

F. Some worry that regional trade agreements (RTAs) such as EU, Mercosur, and NAFTA may weaken the WTO by discriminating against non members. There is evidence that trade among member countries is growing faster than trade with other countries.

G. The World Trade Organization (WTO) disputes panel has begun action at a faster pace than was achieved by its predecessor, GATT. In just 3 years the WTO dealt with 132 complaints; over its 47-year existence, GATT heard only 300. More than 30 countries, including China and Russia, are lining up to join WTO, the membership of which had grown to 132 countries by mid-1998.

However, the WTO is not without critics. Many argue it is not responsive to labor and environmental issues.

H. Helpful WTO publications include:

1. *Manual of Export Promotion Techniques*

2. *Market Studies*

3. *International Trade*

4. *Forum*

VIII. Organization of Petroleum Exporting Countries (OPEC)

A. Creation of OPEC. OPEC was formed in 1960 when oil companies decreased the price of petroleum without consulting the countries in which the petroleum was produced. This angered the countries and increased their anxieties about control and conservation of their natural resources.

B. Stages of OPEC. From its inception in 1960 until 1973, many did not take OPEC seriously. Then at the end of 1973 and 1974, OPEC approximately quadrupled the price of its oil and the Arab members of OPEC embargoed shipments to the Netherlands and the United States. The embargo stemmed from those countries' support of Israel in the Arab-Israeli war.

C. OPEC imposed another major oil price increase in 1979, but by then new sources of oil had come into production and consumers had learned to conserve oil and use substitute energy sources. For those reasons and a worldwide economic recession, demand for oil slumped and there was an oversupply in the market. OPEC members began to squabble up to and including war against each other. Nevertheless, OPEC continues as an organization despite wars and oversupply of oil in the world.

D. The oversupply of oil caused prices to weaken. As a result, conservation efforts lagged along with exploration for new sources and research for alternate energy. Some fear that if those trends continue, OPEC may again become the powerful controller of world's energy.

E. Table 4.3 shows demand for petroleum by countries and country groups for the years 1974 to 2001. Notable is the big consumption growth in Asia.

F. In 1998 the Organization of Petroleum Exporting Countries (OPEC) was supplying only 40 percent of the world's oil, but it sits on 75 percent of the world's proven reserves, and its oil is much cheaper to exploit than that in fields in the North Sea and Alaska. The center for Global Energy Studies, a London-based think tank, predicts that non-OPEC oil supplies will begin to run out around 2005.

Growth in demand in the Asian region has resumed since the Asian crisis. Putting these factors together makes it clear that OPEC will be in a powerful position in the not distant future.

IX. European Union (EU)

The EU joins most of the economic and industrial might of Western Europe. For information on trade and foreign investment between the EU and the United States see Table 4.4 and Figure 4.2.

A. The Marshall Plan, under which the United States provided billions of dollars and the European countries worked together to invest them in the post-WWII reconstruction of Europe, was the seed for the EU which was created in the 1950s.

B. There are 15 members: Austria, Belgium, Denmark, Finland, France, Germany, Greece, Ireland, Italy, Luxembourg, the Netherlands, Portugal, Spain, Sweden and the United Kingdom.

C. There are four main institutions of EU.

1. The Council of Ministers which establishes policy.

2. The Commission which suggests and executes policies.

3. European Parliament which is popularly elected and which in 1987, was given powers to amend legislation drafted by the Commission. Some European countries, notably Germany, want to increase Parliament's power to the point where it inaugurates and makes all EU law. That is stoutly resisted by other countries, notably the U. K.

4. Court of Justice decides all cases arising from the Treaty of Rome which is a very broad document sometimes called the constitution of the EU. The Court's decisions can overrule those of the courts of any member nation.

D. The 1991 Maastricht Treaty committed the EU to an economic and monetary union (EMU) which would include a European central bank and a single currency, the euro. A number of influential people and organizations are opposed to EMU. The euro is now the official currency in 12 EU countries.

E. A United States of Europe is a political goal of many Europeans, but a fortress Europe is a fear of outsiders.

F. Fraud is a major EU problem costing at least $7 billion a year, and some say "tens of billions of dollars" from the agriculture budget and through customs, export subsidies and tax fraud.

G. Although the economic and monetary union has brought nations together with the European Central Bank and the euro (both discussed elsewhere), one important business, remains national: domestic financial services. A country imposes its own conduct of business rules on banks operating in its territory and can block certain services in the name of the "general good." This is a "gaping loophole" that allows the protection of domestic financial services.

X.   Other Regional Groupings of Nations

The success of the EU has led several other groups of nations to join with similar but usually more limited objectives. Discussed briefly, are the European Free Trade Association (EFTA), the Association of Southeast Asian Nations(ASEAN), the North America Free Trade Agreement NAFTA), and the Free Trade Agreement of the Americas (FTAA). Other important groupings are the Asia-Pacific Economic Cooperation, Andean Group, Australia-New Zealand Closer Economic Relations, Caribbean Community and Common Market, Central American Common Market, Southern African Development Community, and Southern (American) Common Market (Mercosur).

Despite fierce opposition, the U. S. Congress passed the NAFTA agreement thanks to the so-called fast-track authority it had granted the Clinton administration. All presidents since the second world war have had the authority, but it lapsed, and neither the administration nor congressional leaders pushed for its renewal until 1997. By that time, a majority of Democrats and some Republicans in Congress were fearful of organized labor opposition and voted against renewal so that it failed. Fast track requires Congress to vote yes or no on a trade treaty negotiated by the president without any amendments, and without it other countries will not engage in negotiations with the U. S. The U. S. could not fulfill its usual role as a leader in the movements toward free trade. A vacuum ensued–nature and politics abhor a vacuum–and into it stepped Brazil as the biggest country in Mercosur.

Mercosur, whose members were Argentina, Brazil, Paraguay, and Uruguay, is considering expanding. Negotiations are under way with other South and Central American countries and Mexico, and discussions have begun with the EU.

The 18 months leading into 1999 was a difficult period for the Association of South East Asian Nations (ASEAN). It was unable to stem the region's financial crisis. Of its nine members, seven went through a change of leader or regime. A prospective tenth member, Cambodia, fell victim to a coup. Some countries, most notably the Philippines and Thailand, are calling for ASEAN to modify some of its most cherished principles. They suggest that ASEAN address difficult regional and domestic issues, but the response from Burma, Laos, Malaysia, and Vietnam has been swift and negative.

On the positive side, the ASEAN members agreed to speed up tariff cuts to achieve a regional free trade area. It is thought that increasing trade would help overcome the negative impact of currency devaluations in ASEAN countries.

Not wanting to be left out, Canada is entering trade agreements with other Western Hemisphere countries, potentially leaving the U. S. behind.

There are four major forms of economic– and finally political–integration. They are: 1) Free trade area, 2) customs union, 3) common market, and 4) complete economic integration which involves surrender of sovereignty by member countries.

In the decade to 1999, trade among Mercosur members has grown fivefold, and it is now the world's third largest economic bloc after the North American Free Trade Agreement countries and the European Union. The members are now discussing a monetary union similar to the European economic and monetary union.

Figure 4.3 is a map of ASEAN members; Figure 4.4 is a map of African trade agreement members, Figure 4.5 is a map of Central and South American trade agreement members.

XI.   Organization for Economic Cooperation and Development (OECD)

OECD members are the noncommunist developed countries. Headquarters are in Paris and it produces extensive research and statistics on numerous international business and economic subjects. It also produced a declaration of guidelines of good business practices for international companies OECD publications have been extremely useful to college and university students and to international business managers. Students can use them as research material for term papers, thesis, or dissertations. They are helpful to executives with international business opportunities or problems. Information about how to contact OECD's Washington, D. C. publications office including its homepage is given in the text.

XIII   Summary

As mentioned at the beginning of the chapter, an understanding of international organizations is important for anyone in international business. As the world becomes more interrelated, the importance of international organizations will only increase. Probably every student reading the text will have had some exposure to international organizations. Everyone certainly will have heard of the United Nations. Most probably will be familiar with the World Trade Organization, or at least with the protestors at the WTO meeting in Seattle in 1999.

This chapter seeks to expose the reader to the wide range of international organizations and the amount of information available on the organizations. Some of the organizations have experienced great successes while others have not. The text looks at organizations in which the United States is a member as well as organizations in which the U.S. is not a member, but whose activities affect the United States. In addition to the UN, the text looks at financial institutions including the multilateral development banks and the IMF and the BIS. The chapter examines the EU and other regional groupings. The chapter looks at the WTO, which grew out of the GATT. The OECD, which is an excellent source of research on many subjects, is examined. It has also issued guidelines for good international business practices.

Answers to Questions

1. Business and students of business should be aware of international organizations because those organizations spend billions of dollars (and other currencies) every year for goods and services which can be sold to them by the alert business management. The UN and the World Bank provide arbitration opportunities for international commercial disputes. Information gathered by the UN or the Bank from member countries is apt to be more complete and accurate than a private company could obtain on its own.

2. The United Nations is an organization with 189 member countries, all agreeing to abide by the Charter of the United Nations. The UN operates through its principle organs and various programs and agencies. The Security Council is the organ in which important decisions are made. There fifteen member nations serving on the Security Council, with five of them (including the United States) having permanent status. All member countries are members of the General Assembly. The other organs and agencies serve specific functions.

3. It depends on the type of loan. The World Bank, and all other Multilateral Development Banks (MDBs), provides financing for development activities through several types of financial facilities:

    1) Long term loans, which are based on market interest rates. The Banks borrow on the international capital markets to fund these loans and re-lend to borrowing governments in developing countries.

    2) Very long term loans (often termed credits), which are loans with interest well below market interest rates. These facilities are funded through direct contributions from governments in donor countries.

    3) Grant financing is also a part of the financing offered by some MDBs, mostly for technical assistance, advisory services or project preparation.

4. a.   The International Finance Corporation (IFC).
    b.   Because it invests in and seeks investments for new and expanding private businesses, the IFC seeks private capital in the host developing countries to invest in

61

local private business and tries to create a capital market in the developing countries in which capital can be raised and stocks or bonds of local companies can be bought and sold.

5. Multilateral Development Banks are international lending institutions owned by member nations. They work primarily with developing countries, as their objective is promotion of economic and social progress in developing member nations by providing loans, technical assistance, capital investment, and help with economic development plans.

6. The International Monetary Fund's objectives are to foster (1) orderly foreign exchange arrangements, (2) convertible currencies, and (3) a shorter duration and lesser degree of balance of payments disequalibria.

7. The World Trade Organization (WTO) came into existence as a result of the Uruguay Round of the General Agreement on Tariffs and Trade. The WTO is a multinational organization designed to deal with rules of trade between nations. The WTO works with its core agreements, which were negotiated and signed and ratified by the bulk of the world's trading nations. The goal is to help producers of goods and services, exporters, and importers conduct their business by reducing or eliminating trade barriers and restrictions worldwide.

8. The four main institutions of the European Union are the Council, Commission, Parliament, and the Court. All four have specific duties outlined in the text. The Council is the main policy setting institution. The Commission is the administrative arm of the EU, ensuring that provisions of the founding documents are followed. The Parliament is an elected body representing individual citizens in the EU member states. While its powers have been increased, the main policy setting institution remains the Council. The European Court of Justice is a court with authority over EU matters.

9. NAFTA was and remains a political issue. Organized labor opposed NAFTA because it feared a loss of jobs to Mexico. Many argue today that NAFTA has been successful in raising the standard of living in Mexico. Mexico is the second largest trading partner of the United States and all three countries (Canada, Mexico, and the United States) enjoy increased trade with each other.

10. Neither the Clinton administration nor the Congress followed through on the momentum created by the approval of NAFTA and the enthusiasm for its expansion. The fast track authority, without which successful trade treaty negotiation is virtually impossible, elapsed. The administration did not campaign for its renewal by educating the American people how free trade could benefit them. In the meanwhile, organized labor, which is strongly opposed to free trade, showed strength in the 1996 election so that when the administration finally requested fast track renewal in 1997, a majority of Democrat and some Republican members of Congress turned it down under labor union pressure
A number of other countries had wanted to joint NAFTA, but in the absence of fast track authority in the U. S., they were unwilling to negotiate trade treaties which could then be amended by the U. S. Congress. At the same time, Mercousur, which includes Brazil, Argentina, Paraguay, and Uraguay, established a free trade area.

11. The Organization for Economic Cooperation and Development (OECD) is the source of extensive research and statistics about its member countries and the world. If has issued a series of guidelines for good business practices by multinational enterprises.

Answers to Internet Problems

1.   (a) Economic and monetary union.

(b) Fair trade in a single market.

(c) Govern, protect and oversee activities by member countries. The Council coordinates national policies and coordinates these policies as they are set into effect. The European Commission initiates proposals for legislation, act as a guardian of treaties, and manages Union policies and international trade relationships.

(d) Private citizens can apply if victimized by any EU Institutions for the position of a European Ombudsman.

One of the many similarities is a body of representatives from member states gathered under one roof to collectively pass laws governing all member states.

The EU Web site is http://europa.eu.int

2. (a) The International Bank for Reconstruction and Development
        The International Development Association
        The International Finance Cooperation
        The International Center for Settlement of Investment Disputes
        The Multilateral Investment Guarantee Agency
        A common goal – to improve living standard by promoting economic growth.

    (b) The World Bank is the world's largest source of development assistance, providing nearly $16 billion in loans annually to its client countries. It uses its financial resources, highly trained staff, and extensive knowledge base to help each developing country onto a path of stable, sustainable, and equitable growth in the fight against poverty. It has a large number of programs and projects, which are outlined on the Web site.

    (c) The annual report, which is quite detailed, outlines activities of the World Bank for the previous year.

    (d) The World Banks works in more than 100 developing economies, bringing a mix of finance and ideas to improve living standards and eliminate the worst forms of poverty. It works with government agencies, nongovernmental organizations, and the private sector to formulate assistance strategies.

    The World Bank's site is http://www.worldbank,org.

Discussion of Minicase 4-1: Use of International Organizations–Setting up a 100% Owned Subsidiary

One possible source of money or assistance in obtaining financing would be the IFC. Of course, the IFC favors some or all ownership to be local–in this case, Guatemalan–so you might suggest to your client that it consider agreeing to divest itself or at least part ownership in the future.

Another possible source of financing is the Inter-American Development Bank. If your client can demonstrate its hotel will create jobs for Guatemalans and tourist income for the country, the IADB could be interested.

For the information about the client's likelihood of being able to convert profits to U. S. dollars and remit them to the United States, either of the above two organizations could provide information and options.

The IMF issues an annual report on exchange restrictions. Individuals at the Fund might be willing to provide up-to-date information before it is published in the annual report.

The Bank for International Settlements keeps information on exchange restrictions. While the IMF is probably the best source, a request to BIS might turn up something interesting.

Figure 4.2   Sources of Foreign Direct Investment in the United States by Region

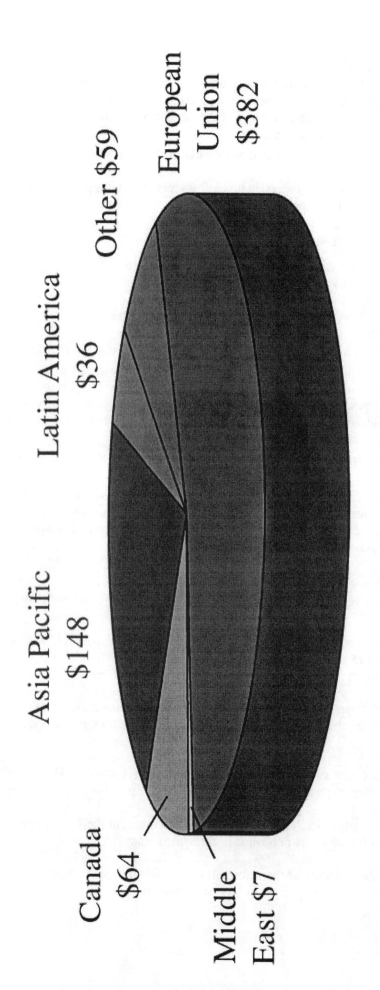

Canada
$64

Middle
East $7

Asia Pacific
$148

Latin America
$36

Other $59

European
Union
$382

1998 ($US BILLIONS)
TOTAL FOREIGN INVESTMENT IN THE UNITED STATES: $812 BILION
Source: U.S. Department of Commerce, Bureau of Economic Analysis, 1998.

Map of ASEAN Members

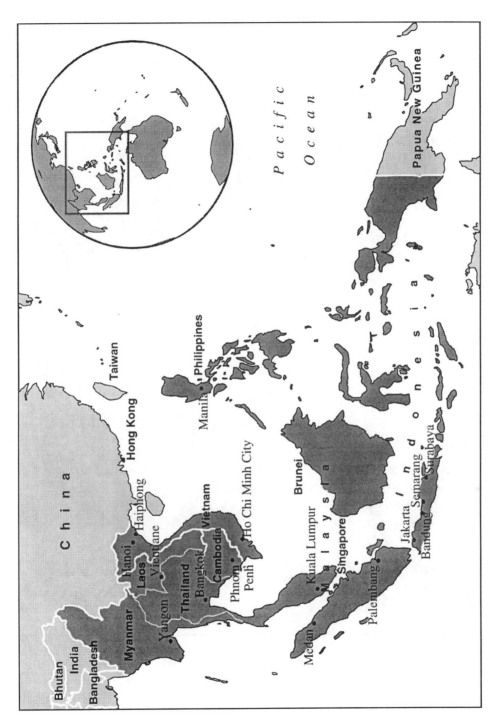

● Members of the Association of Southeast Asian Nations (ASEAN) as of October 2000

McGraw-Hill/Irwin

TM 4.3

Figure 4.4　　　　**African Trade Agreements**

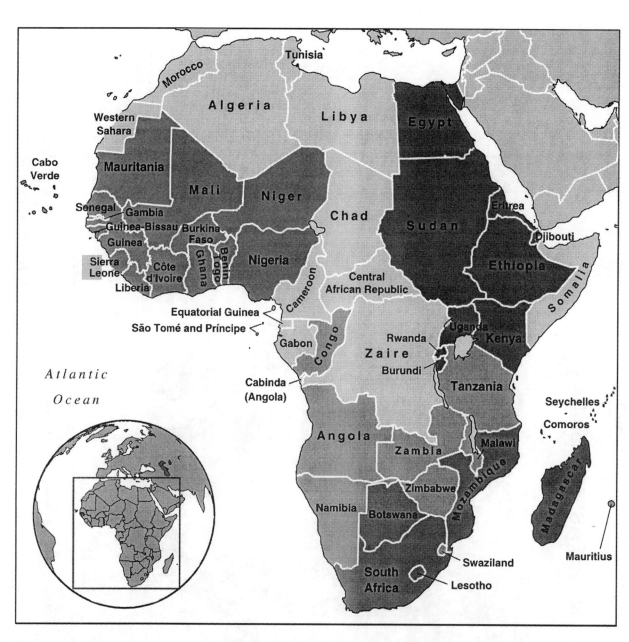

● ECOWAS: Economic Community Of West African States

● SADC: Southern African Development Community

● COMESA

● Both SADC and COMESA as of October 2000

TM 4.4

Figure 4.5   **Regional Trade Agreements in Central and South America**

Regional Trade Agreements in Central America and South America as of October 2000

● Andean Community   ● Central American Free Trade Zone   ● Mercosur   ● None

CHAPTER 5
INTERNATIONAL MONETARY SYSTEM AND BALANCE OF PAYMENTS

Learning Objectives

1. Students should be introduced to the fact that almost every country has its own currency. Each has a name such as dollar, franc. lira, peso, or mark and each has a value in terms of other currencies. For example, one dollar may cost four francs. These values fluctuate as the currencies are traded.

2. Some currencies are said to be hard in that they are freely convertible to other currencies. Others are soft and are not freely convertible; in many instances conversion is illegal without government approval.

3. Show the students the historical role of gold as money and explain why some economists now advocate a return to a gold standard.

4. Explain national balance of payments (BOP) and the role of the IMF in helping countries correct their BOP deficits.

5. Introduce the students to capital or money markets and the recent growth in their number.

6. Foreign currencies as reserve assets should be explained followed by introduction of special drawing rights (SDRs) which are also reserve assets.

7. The difference between fixed currency exchange rates and floating rates should be explained. Then the European Monetary System should be introduced as an important move back to fixed rates.

8. The European Currency Unit (ECU) should be explained along with the reasons why it uses exceeded those of the SDR. In 1999, the ECU was supplanted by the euro.

9. By the terms of the Maastricht Treaty, most EU countries agreed to create a new currency called the euro that came into use on January 1, 1999. Over a phase-in period, the euro is to supplant the national currencies of the agreeing countries.

10. There is strong opposition to the euro. It should be explained that a major basis for the opposition is the euro's companion, the European Central Bank, which will take over monetary authority from the central banks of the agreeing countries. Thus, the EU will have a powerful central banks without a powerful central government. The U. S., is used as an example where the Federal Reserve is a powerful central bank, which is counterbalanced by a powerful central government.

Overview

The International currency markets are now the world's largest in terms of amounts of money involved. They are bigger than securities or commodity markets and bigger than the total world trade. Of course, currency exchange markets are used in connection with the other markets and world trade, but a large part of the currency markets is simply for other currencies. The holder of a "weak" currency whose value is expected to decline may want to exchange it for a "strong" currency whose value is expected to at least maintain its value.

Some history of the gold standard is presented. Until recently most economists regarded the gold standard as a relic of history and many still consider it unworkable. But, a growing number of economists now advocate some form of gold standard.

Until late in the 20th century, most economists and many businesses and other people believed gold to be a safe haven that would continue to increase or at least hold its value. By the 1980s, doubts about gold's value had spread. Other non-currency commodities such as diamonds and platinum enjoy much larger marketing budgets and more concentrated support. However, it is too soon to write off gold as an important element in the financial system; many people still prize and hold it, efforts are being made to increase its marketing budgets, and the world gold trading markets are much larger and more liquid than are those of diamonds and platinum.

The international monetary instituted at Bretton Woods and based on the gold exchange standard with fixed currency exchange rates is covered. Like the gold standard, this is now history, but one of the world's most powerful economic blocs established fixed exchange rates for all its currencies. That was the European Monetary System (EMS),and it is well to understand what happened to the Bretton Woods fixed rate system. In addition, economists and politicians periodically advocate a return to the "Bretton Woods System."

The IMF was discussed in Chapter 4, but it is so important in the international monetary system operation that it is brought into this chapter also.

Balance of payments (BOP) is explained together with the IMF role in its attempts to correct BOP disequilibria. The U. S. BOP deficit has been the biggest and many results have flowed from that. Among them were collapse of the gold exchange standard, end of fixed currency exchange rates and encouragement of the Eurocurrency and Eurobond markets.

Fixed and floating currency exchange rates are compared, and the EMS return to a fixed rate system is discussed.

As of January 1, 1999, most EU countries will begin using the euro and will substitute if for their own currencies over a phase-in period.

At the beginning, eleven of the 15 EU countries adopted the euro and surrendered their monetary policy powers to the European Central Bank. They are referred to as the Eurozone, and were joined in 2001 by Greece. The three EU countries not yet in the Eurozone are Denmark, Sweden, and the United Kingdom.

Money or capital markets of the world are introduced. We cover the growth and spread of such markets and their uses.

Foreign exchange (FX) markets around the world grew rapidly from the 1950's, well into the 1990's, but growth then slowed. One reason for the slowing is the coming of the euro, which is supposed to replace several European currencies. Markets for Asian currencies continue to grow, as do the markets for derivatives, hedges, and swaps.

The traditional FX markets, dominated by big banks, are meeting increasing competition from electronic brokers, which will put brokering machines in the offices of international business managers. They can then trade currencies without using–or paying–any bank or live broker.

Nations frequently hold strong foreign currencies as part of their reserve assets. For years the U. S. dollar was almost the exclusive currency so held by other countries, but the loss of gold by the

United States and the weakening of the dollar caused countries to look elsewhere. Now other strong currencies such as the West German mark, the Japanese yen and the Swiss franc have joined the dollar. They have all been joined by an IMF creation, the special drawing right (SDR) which is dealt with in this chapter. Of course, gold is also a national reserve asset.

Suggestion and Comments

1. Although an increasing number of students now have traveled or lived outside the United States, and thus been exposed to money other than the U. S. dollar, very few have thought or been taught about a worldwide system underlying all the monies, their relative values and their exchange. Explain the big picture to the students.

2. The relevance of the gold standard history to the present, in the eyes of some influential economists, can be explained. The pros and cons can be discussed.

3. Lessons learned from the Bretton Woods gold exchange standard, fixed currency rates, should be discussed. The effects of the loss of U. S. gold on confidence in the U. S. dollar should be pointed out. Connect that loss of confidence to subsequent occurrences such as use of other currencies and SDRs as central reserve assets.

4. Make the students aware of the effects of BOP deficits or surpluses on the value of the countries currencies.

5. Explain floating and fixed currency exchange rates. Give the arguments on both sides of that issue as some economists favor fixed while others prefer floating rates.

6. Introduce the students to the European Central Bank and euro. Why is support for and opposition to those developments so strong?

Student Involvement Exercises

1. In this chapter there are several matters which are the subjects of current disagreements among economists. You can divide the class into teams and have them study and debate the pros and cons of the subjects.

2. One is the gold standard. Should the major world trading countries adopt a gold standard? If so, why and how? If not, why not? Should the United States go it alone and adopt a gold standard even though its major trading partners do not?

3. Another subject is the U. S.. policy toward its BOP deficits and loss of gold during the 1950s and 60s. Was the United States correct in what it did and did not do? If not, what changes should have been made?

4. Still a third discussion could compare fixed with floating currency exchange rates. Which is better? Why?

5. New developments are the coming of the European Central Bank and the euro. What are the arguments pro and con?

Guest Lecturers

1. Banks near your school may have international officers who are familiar with the financial system.

2. Such officers sometimes leave the bank to become executives of international businesses and inquiry could be made if the school is near such businesses.

3. The faculty at your school or another in the area may have someone knowledgeable in the subject.

Lecture Outline

I. Introduction

A. Within one country the people and businesses use almost exclusively the currency of that country, e. g., the dollar in the United States.

B. As soon as business or travelers go outside the one country, it is almost surely necessary to deal with at least one more currency, e.g., the peso and the dollar if you go to Mexico.

C. The trading (exchange) between currencies and their relative values are no haphazard matters. They are governed by an operating international monetary system.

II. The Gold Standard

A. From about 1200 A. D. to the present the direction of gold prices has been generally up.

1. The price rise was not straight up.

2. In the period between 1971 and the present the price has fluctuated between $35 per ounce and a high in January 1980 of about $850 per ounce.

B. Americans were forbidden by law to own gold bullion between 1933 and 1976.

C. In the 18th century England was one of the world's great powers and London was the center of International finance.

1. In 1717, Sir Isaac Newton, Master of the Mint, established the price of gold at 3 pounds, 17 shillings, 10.5 pence per ounce. England was then on the gold standard and stood ready to buy or sell gold at the established price.

2. The other trading nations followed suit. Each set the price of gold at a fixed number of units of their own currency.

D. Gold or gold-backed notes constituted the money of the countries on the gold standard.

1. If a country bought more abroad than it sold, part of its money would go abroad to pay for the excess. Thus the amount of money left at home would decrease.

2. The decrease in the amount of money would cause prices to fall so that the home country's products would become less expensive and thus more competitive on the world markets.

3. The opposite would occur in the country which exported more than it imported. It would receive money to pay for the excess and its money supply would increase.

4. The increases amount of money would cause prices to rise so that this country's products would become more expensive and thus less competitive on the world markets.

5. As those processes continued, the volume of exports and imports of the two countries would reverse and the money would flow back to the original home country.

6. Thus the gold standard tended to be self-operating and automatic.

E. The gold standard operated until the First World War, and There were attempts to revive it between that war and the Second World War. They were not very successful, and by the end of WW II most people thought the gold standard was a dead subject.

F. Some economists and politicians, of whom a leader was the French economist Jacques Rueff, continued to advocate the gold standard. They maintained it to be desirable because it prevents inflation by imposing discipline on the politicians. It limits the amount of paper they can print.

G. Wayne Angell, a former Federal Reserve Board governor, suggests that Russia should tie its ruble to gold.

H. Figure 5.1 is an advertisement by a dealer in gold bullion and coins.

III. Bretton Woods and the gold Exchange Standard

A. Representatives of the allied powers met at the New Hampshire resort, Bretton Woods, before the end of WW II to agree on the postwar monetary system. The system they settled upon is called the Bretton Woods system. They agreed:

1. Fixed, stable currency exchange rates are desirable although experience may force adjustments.

2. Floating or fluctuating ranges are unsatisfactory although the reasons may force adjustments.

B. The IMF, which we have discussed before, was established to encourage and help member countries keep their exchange rates fixed.

C. The U. S. dollar (US$) was agreed to be the only currency directly convertible into gold. An ounce of gold was agreed to be worth $35 and other currencies were assigned par values in US$ terms, for example:

1. The British pound was set at US$2.40.

2. The French franc was US$.18

3. The German mark was US$.2732

D. Whenever a foreign country had more US$s than it wanted to hold or invest it would turn them to the U. S. Federal Reserve at $35 per ounce in exchange for gold. This is why that part of the system was called a gold exchange standard. It should not be confused with the gold standard.

E. Balance of payments (BOP) deficits result when a country spend more money abroad than it is able to earn through the sale of its products or services. If the deficit is large or continuous, foreigners get more of the country's money than they want and the value of that money tends to decline. The value of that money cannot decline without *breaking* the fixed exchange rates with other countries. Thus, the IMF steps in whether the BOP is *temporary* or *fundamental*.

1. A temporary deficit may be caused by a crop failure, labor unrest or a natural disaster which can be corrected fairly quickly with a good crop, labor peace or reconstruction. Or the temporary deficit may be caused by inflation which the country corrects by monetary and fiscal policies. In these instance the IMF can make money and expert advisors available to help the country.

2. Fundamental deficits are those which the country cannot or will not correct. Then IMF rules permitted the country to devalue its currency (change the fixed exchange rate) in relation to the US$. Thus, if the exchange rate were 2 francs per US$1, a devalued franc might be 3 per US$1. It takes more francs to buy the same amount of US$s.

3. Each country's BOP is presented as a double-entry accounting statement in which total credits and debits are always equal. The statement is divided into several accounts which are:

a. current account

b. capital account

c. official reserves account

d. net statistical discrepancy

F. Although there were many devaluations between 1946 and 1971, none led to international financial crises such as followed the devaluations of 1931. Credit must be given to the IMF for being an important force preventing the competitive devaluations which proved so futile and destructive during the 1930s.

G. The IMF was also instrumental in getting all the major trading nations to eliminate their currency to exchange controls (these are discussed in Chapter 6) on trade.

H. The biggest and longest running BOP deficit is the American one. Classical methods to correct a BOP deficit include *deflation* of the economy and *devaluation* of the currency.

   1. The United States did not deflate the economy because U. S. leaders had vivid recollections of the hunger and hardships of the 1930s depression. They saw deflation as the great danger, not inflation.

   2. The U. S. did not devalue the US$ and its allies and trading partners liked it that way because:

      a. that made their products less expensive in terms of competing American products, and

      b. other countries held US$ as part of the national reserve assets and were reluctant to see them lose value.

IV. The inherent contradiction of the gold exchange standard followed from the contradictory needs and attitudes of the post-WW II world. The other countries needed US$ for several purposes:

   1. To finance the growth of trade and investments. Vehicle currency

   2. To build their central reserve assets. Reserve currency.

   3. To support the value of their currencies. Intervention currency

   4. As a safe haven. This is a political concept. Since WWII, the world has perceived the U.S. as being less likely than other countries to be successfully invaded or the subject of a military or political coup.

   5. To buy gold. From 1958 through 1971, the U. S. gold reserves fell from $24.8 billion to $12.2 billion at $35 per ounce. Foreign government had exchanged US$s they did not use otherwise for that much gold. During the same 1958-71 period the number of US$s in foreign hand increased from $13.6 billion to $62.2 billion.

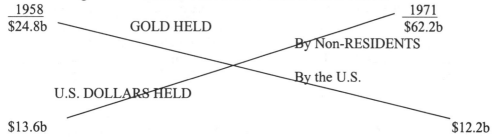

At about 1963 there was just enough gold held by the United States to cover every US$ in foreign hands. From that time on there was not enough gold to cover every US$ and at $35 per ounce and the dollar was no longer as good as gold. by 1971 there was only US$.22 worth of gold for every US$$1.00 held by foreign central banks. Foreigners still *wanted and could use US$s but worried that they could not all get gold with them.* They had exchanged so many US$ for gold there was not enough gold left. That was the *inherent contradiction of the gold exchange standard.*

V. Balance of Payment (BOP)

A. A nation's BOP compares the amount of money coming in from abroad with the amount going out. If more is coming in, the country is running a surplus. The opposite is a deficit.

B. There are two types of methods a country can utilize to try to correct a deficit.

    1. Market methods are to devalue the currency or deflate the economy.

    2. Nonmarket methods include tariffs, quotas or currency exchange controls.

C. There are debits and credits in international transaction. Money coming in is recorded as credit; going out as debit in double-entry accounting.

D. The BOP accounts are:

    1. Current

    2. Capital

    3. Official reserves

    4. Net Statistical discrepancy

E. The United States has run a BOP deficit for years but only infrequently tried to market methods to correct it.

VI. August 15, 1971, and the Next Two Years

A. On August 15, 1971, President Nixon ended the gold exchange standard abruptly when he ordered the close of the "gold window." The gold window was the office at the New York Federal Reserve where foreign central banks presented their US$s to exchange them for gold. The United States would no longer give gold for US$s.

B. With the gold exchange standard there also ended the fixed currency exchange rates, and relative currency values began to "float" according to market supply and demand.

C. Between 1971 and 1973 two attempts were made to establish new fixed rates, but both times banks, businesses and individuals (collectively referred to as "speculators" by unhappy politicians) felt the government had fixed the rates incorrectly. The "speculators" put billions of US$s and other currencies into the currencies they felt to be strong and sold the currencies they felt to be weak. The market forces were too immense and in march 1973, the governments gave up, and currencies floated freely.

VII. 1973 to the Present

A. There are two kinds of currency floats, which are called free (clean) or managed (dirty).

    1. Free float is the condition in which market forces operate *without government intervention*. For the major currencies there are *thousands of buyers and sellers* all around the world every day and there are *billions of the product* (money in different currencies) being traded. Thus, free float is one of the rare examples of *perfect competition* in the economist's sense.

    2. Manages float, which is the usual situation, occurs when governments intervene. They say they are "smoothing" the market or "assuring orderly markets." They may instead be trying to support their weak currency or to prevent it appreciating too far or too fast.

B. Experience with floating exchange rates has surprised many observers. Efforts to maintain fixed rates ended in 1973. In 1974 came the large increase in oil prices by OPEC, and there were fears the banking and monetary systems could not handle the resulting changes in amounts and directions of currency flows.

    1. However, the systems did not collapse.

    2. After a period of uncertainty, the costs of undertaking foreign exchange transactions had leveled out by 1977 at no higher than they had been with the Bretton Woods fixed rates.

    3. Advocates of the floating thought it would end BOP disequilibria. They were proved wrong, too, at least in part because governments intervened and would not permit their currency values to go up or down enough to clear the market at prices where demand would equal supply.

C. Forecasting foreign currency exchange rates is necessary for international banks and businesses. Relative inflation rats and differing costs of living from country to country give indications as to whether currencies will strengthen or weaken. The purchasing power parity (PPP) is a measuring device, and to illustrate PPP. *The Economist* has established the hamburger standard. A McDonald's Big Mac is sold in cities around the world, and is supposed to be identical wherever you bite it. The hamburger standard compares Big Mac prices in the currencies of the countries where it is sold.

D. Probably the major reasons for the floating rate system working as well as it has are the efforts by the major banks around the world to make the currency markets required by businesses, individuals and governments.

   1. By the end of a typical trading day the equivalent of more than US$1.2 trillion may have changed hands.

   2. Financial centers and capital markets have sprung up around the world and are growing. In addition to the traditional ones in London, Paris and Zurich, centers and markets are thriving in Asia, the Middle East, the Caribbean and Latin America. Tokyo has become the third largest trading center after London and New York. Now one can trade 24 hours a day. Figure 5.5 is a map showing trading hours of the world's major financial centers.

   3. Growth of foreign exchange (FX) currency trading grew rapidly from the 1950's into the 1990's, but then slowed for two reasons. In Europe, the euro replaced several national currencies. Electronic currency brokering began to empower international business managers to trade currencies without recourse to their traditional bank brokers. In Asia, FX activity continues to grow and worldwide markets for derivatives, hedges, and swaps are becoming more active.

   4. In the current system, currency areas have formed and they are similar to the currency blocs during the 1930s. A number of LDCs have pegged the value of their currencies to a major currency such as the US$, the French franc or the British pound. Others have tied themselves to SDRs (discussed below). See Figure 5.3.

   5. The "snake" was one currency area. It was an effort of several European countries to tie their currencies to each other's and let them float against other major currencies such as the yen, the US$ and the Canadian $. See the graph in the text subsection headed Snake.

   6. The descendant of the snake was the European Monetary System (EMS) under the terms of which European countries agreed to limit exchange rate fluctuations of their currencies within agreed upon limits. At the end of 1991, the EU countries held a summit meeting in Maastricht in the Netherlands, at which it was agreed that beginning in 1999 most of them would commence phasing out their national currencies which would be replaced in 2002 by a new currency, the euro. The countries adopting the euro, agreed also to surrender their monetary policy powers to the European Central Bank. Those countries constituted what came to be called the Eurozone.

E. Beginning in 1997 several Asian countries suffered falling stock and property values, and investors, local and foreign, withdrew money, converting local currencies to dollars. It was called the Asian financial crisis. It began in Thailand and spread to India, South Korea, the Philippines, and Indonesia whose rupiah lost 70 percent of its value in dollar terms. By 2000, most of those countries had regained strength and their currencies' value had risen although political unrest made for fragility, particularly in Indonesia and the Philippines.

F. Troubles with the gold exchange standard were foreseen and before its demise in 1971, the IMF created *special drawing rights (SDRs)*. One purpose of SDRs was to replace US$s as central reserve assets as concern about the US$ increased due to the loss by America of its gold.

1. The SDR is a bookkeeping entry at the IMF. Each member's account was credited with SDRs in amounts depending on the size of the member's account. America was credited with more than other countries because it has previously deposited more money and gold than they at IMF.

2. The SDR's value is based on a "basket" of five currencies which are the following with percentage weightings in parentheses US$ (41.3), German mark (19), Japanese yen (17), British pound (12.4), and French franc (10.3).

3. The SDR's value tends to fluctuate less than that of any one currency because as the value of one goes up, the value of another may be going down.

4. SDRs may be held only by the IMF, member central banks and 16 official institutions such as regional development banks approved by the IMF. This may change if SDRs' stability make them attractive for use by private parties, for example, as value standards in long-term contracts.

5. The SDR has not replaced the US$ as the major reserve asset. Higher interest can be earned holding hard national currencies and those currencies are more flexible, e.g., SDRs can be held by only a limited number of holders.

G. The European Currency Unit (ECU) was created by the EMS for official use purposes very similar to those foreseen for the special drawing rights (SDRs) created by the IMF. The ECU was replaced by the euro, and the EMS by the Eurozone.

H. The euro and the European Central Bank (ECB) were agreed to in the Masstricht Treaty by the terms of which most EU countries agreed that on January 1, 1999, the ECB would take control of their monetary policies from their national banks and that the euro would, over a phase-in period, supplant their national currencies. Despite strong opposition, The Eurozone mentioned above, came into being on schedule, and euro notes and coins are replacing the national currencies of the 12 member countries on January 1, 2002. At the core of the opposition is the fear that the ECB will be a powerful but unaccountable central bank with no powerful EU government to counter it. An example is given of the U. S. Federal Reserve that is a powerful central bank that faces an at least equally powerful central government.

I. If the euro, is a success, it will be the currency of the most EU countries, a formidable force, and the euro can be expected to replace the U. S. dollar for many uses.

J. The US$ is still the most used value as countries central reserve asset although other hard currencies, gold and SDRs are now held. There is inherent conflict when a national currency is an important reserve asset of other countries. The other countries need a steady growth in the asset to finance investment and trade. But it may not be in the national interest of the country whose currency is being used to run the continuing BOP deficit needed to supply the asset growth.

ANSWERS TO QUESTIONS

1. Jacques Rueff held that basing the amount of paper money a nation can print on the amount of gold it holds imposes discipline on the politicians. They cannot print money in order to do favors for supporters before an election without regard for the inflation that will cause after the election. If the country loses gold, it must reduce the amount of currency in circulation.

2. Some reasons for currencies to strengthen or weaken in Fx markets are: inflation (relative to other countries), confidence in government policies and stability, size of budget deficits, and size of trade deficits or surpluses.

3. SDRs were created when the inherent contradiction of the gold exchange standard recognized. The idea was to substitute SDRs for US$s as the world's central currency. So far it has not worked, The special drawing right (SDR) is a creation of the International Monetary Fund (IMF). By agreement, the IMF management credits various numbers of SDRs to member countries and the SDRs are counted as a part of each country's central reserve assets. The value of the SDR is based on a "basket" of five currencies of the world's most important trading nations. As indicated above, the SDR is accepted by the countries as a central reserve asset along with gold and convertible currencies. Many want to expand that role and phase out gold and currencies. It is argued that gold is supplied in uncertain amounts by the USSR and South Africa and the supply is static. As to currencies, the argument is that they are creations of individual countries and each must serve the needs of its country which may be contrary to the needs of the international monetary system. SDRS, on the other hand, can be controlled as to numbers, original distribution, and transfer by the IMF members. Thus, the amount and growth of liquidity is within control of that international organization rather than of individual countries.
    It is further pointed out that the value of the SDR will fluctuate less than that of gold and individual currencies. Being based on the values of five major currencies, increases in values of some would usually be offset by decreases in values of others.

4. The European Central Bank (ECB) will be a powerful institution running the monetary policy of the most powerful EU countries and others. The EU lacks a powerful central government to counterbalance the ECB. It is argued that monetary union needs to come after, not before, political union. One commentator says, "major European governments seem fecklessly ready today to commit their nations' future to a committee of bankers." Others say that transition to the euro from several national currencies will be complicated, confusing and difficult. It is forecast to be a "fiendishly complex transition period."

5. National economic needs such as inflation control may conflict with world needs for more of the nation's currency for growth or investment purposes.

6. The Masstricht summit was a meeting during December 1991, of the heads of state of the EU counties in Maastricht, The Netherlands. They agreed to economic and monetary union for the EU, and EU-wide currency and an EU central bank, all to be accomplished by 1999. Much opposition has developed in Europe for the surrender of sovereignty called for by the economic and monetary union (EMU) agreed to in the Maastricht Treaty.

7. The EMS was unable to prevent wide fluctuations in the currency exchange rates among the European country members. The reasons were that the economy of each country was unique and different from the others, and each country had its own fiscal and monetary policy. There was no coordination among them. This disarray pushed a majority of the EU member countries to join the economic and monetary union (EMU) in which they agreed to surrender their monetary policy powers to the European Central Band and trade in their national currencies for the new euro. They created the Eurozone.

8. Managers should be particularly wary when the BOP is in deficit. For one thing. a deficit BOP is frequently accompanies by inflation, and businesses must adjust their accounting, inventory, pricing and investment plans and practices differently to account for inflation. For another, management can expect the government to take steps to correct the deficit. Such steps may include higher taxes, more restrictive monetary policies, tariffs, quotas or currency exchange controls.

Answers to the Internet Problems

1.   (a) 3 Quarter: Current Accounts shows negative 42,156 million dollars, Goods and Services show negative 29,631 million dollars.

       (b) No, the deficit has decreased from 1996 to 1997.

           The Balance of Payment Accounts can be found at the Internet Web site for the Bureau of Economic Administration in the United States Department of Commerce, which is http://www.bea.doc.gov.

2.   (a) Promote international monetary cooperation.

       (b) In order to apply for loans a country must be unable to pay back imported goods.

       (c) Annual bilateral article IV consultations, Multilateral Surveillance, Program Monitoring.

       (d) The bank is a development institution, IMF promotes trade.

           The IMF's Web site is http://www.imf.org.

Discussion of Minicase 5-1: SDR Exchange Risk

SDR 8 million		
	DM	4,216,000
	Ff	8,160,000
	¥	267,200,000
	£	714,000
	US$	3,616,000

MINICASE 5-2

Payment Terms for an International Contract

Your are the financial executive of an American construction company. Your company is about to contract for a multiphase project in Italy. Progress payments will be made, but most of the money will not be due until near the end of the project, eight or nine years in the future.

Your company wants to be paid in US$s. The Italian customer wants to make payments in Italian Lira (Il) You fear devaluation of the Il in terms of the US$ over the term of the contract. Draft a contract payment clause to be used as a compromise. Use an IMF developed value discussed in this chapter.

Discussion of Minicase 5-2: Use of Special Drawing Rights (SDRs)

On each payment date established by this contract, the U. S. dollar (US$) value of a special drawing right (SDR) shall be determined using the formulae and procedures used by the International Money (IMF) as of the date of this contract. On each such payment date the Italian lira (Il) value of an SDR shall be determined by the same formulae and procedures.

The US$ value of an SDR shall be divided into the total US$ payment due on each payment due to determine an SDR amount as if payment were to be made in SDRs. Thus, if the SDR value is US$s were 1.25 and the payment due were US$1 million, the resulting SDR amount would be 800,000.

Italian Co. hereby agrees to pay American Co. on each payment date that number of Ils which would be equivalent to the SDR value of that payment. If the SDR value in Ils on payment date were IL 1,250 = SDR 1, then the payment for the SDR 800,000 amount would be I billion (Il 1,000,000,000).

Baird & Co. Ltd.

Bullion Merchants. Precious Metal Refiners & Fabricators

BULLION GOLD COINS & BARS

AVAILABLE NOW

EXEMPT FROM VAT

1 oz - 1/2 oz - 1/4 oz - 1/10 oz

S.A. KRUGERRAND.   US. EAGLE.   CAN. MAPLE LEAF.

AUST. NUGGET.   CHINA. PANDA.   G.B. BRITANNIA.

we have many other gold coins in stock including

G.B. SOVEREIGNS.   HALF SOVEREIGNS.

MEX. 50 PESOS.   AUS. 100 CORONAS.   1 DUCAT.   4 DUCATS.

SWISS. 20 FR.   FRANCE 20 FR.   NAPS. ANGELS.   ROOSTERS.

LIMITED QUANTITY SPECIAL OFFER

VICTORIA JUBILEE HEAD 1887 FIVE & TWO POUND PIECES.

BULLION BARS AVAILABLE

2.5gr - 5gr - 10gr - 20gr - 50gr - 100gr - 1000gr - 1oz - 10 TOLA

FOR THE LATEST PRICES OR TO ORDER BY TELEPHONE CALL

020 8555 5217

OR ORDER DIRECT ON THE INTERNET

HTTP://WWW.GOLDLINE.CO.UK

Daily Gold & Silver Fixing prices. Graphs. Bullion Coin prices. Rare Coins.

Baird & Co. Ltd. 137 High Street London E15 2RB. Tel: 020 8555 5217

Source: *Financial Times*, June 28, 2000, p. Survey IV.

TM 5.2
Figure 5.2

Accumulation of US$s in non-U.S. resident hands and loss of U.S. gold

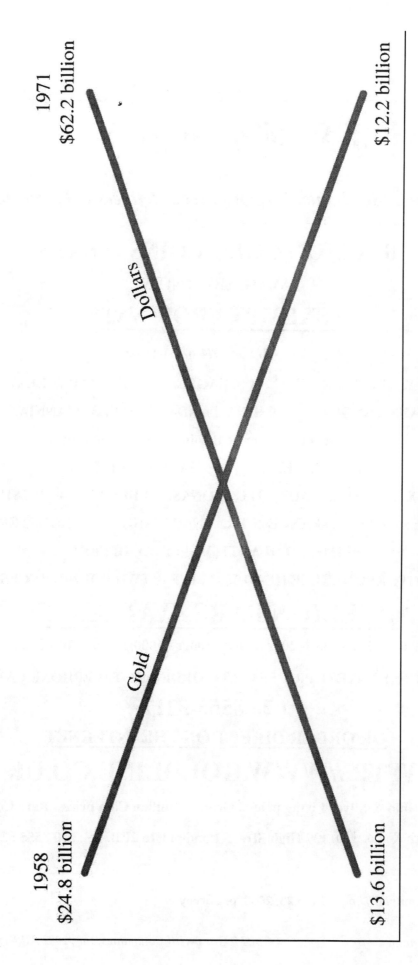

1958
$24.8 billion

1971
$62.2 billion

$12.2 billion

$13.6 billion

Dollars

Gold

The gold value was set at $35/ounce

McGraw-Hill/Irwin

TM 5.3

Figure 5.3   Pegged LDC currencies

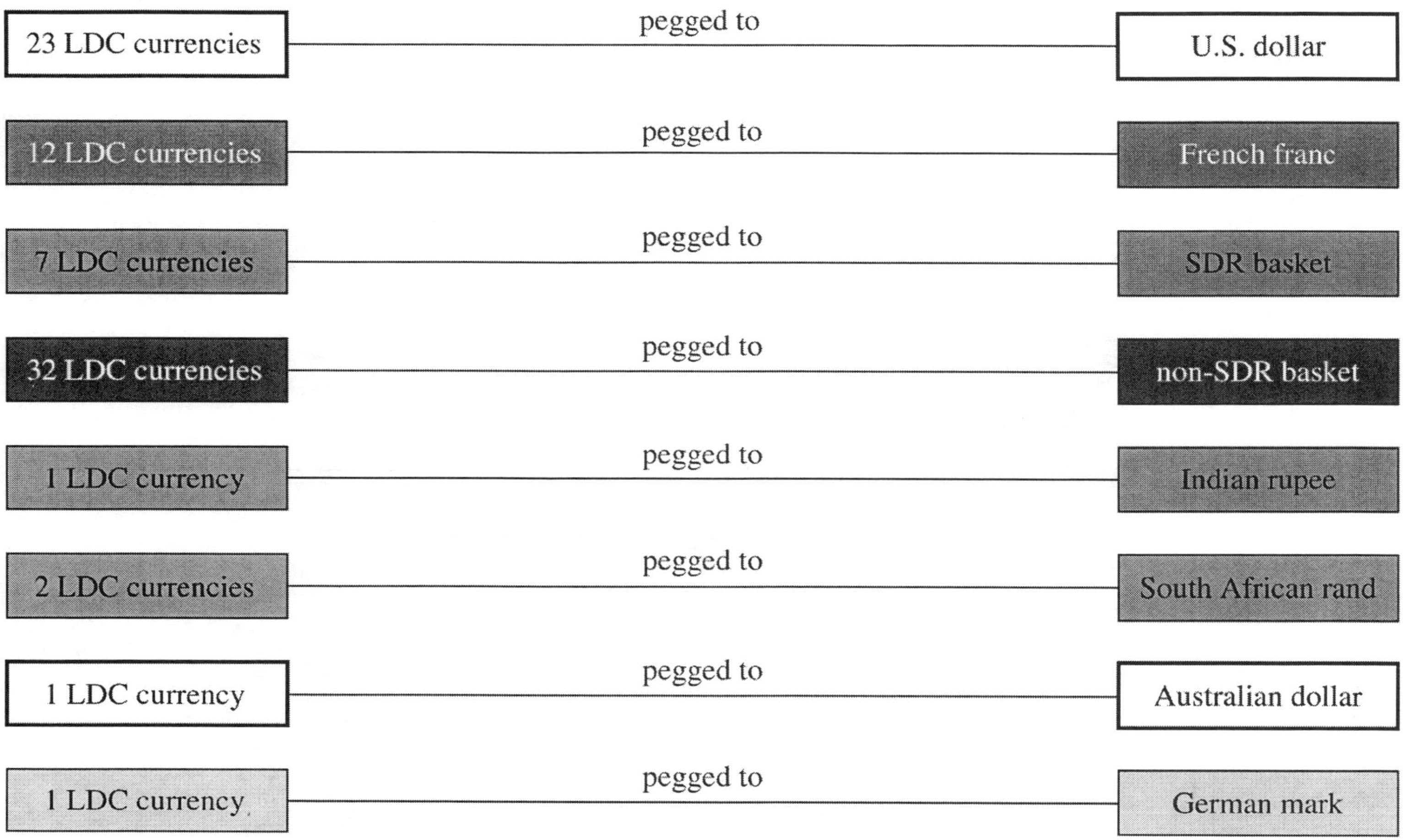

U.S. dollar	pegged to	23 LDC currencies
French franc	pegged to	12 LDC currencies
SDR basket	pegged to	7 LDC currencies
non-SDR basket	pegged to	32 LDC currencies
Indian rupee	pegged to	1 LDC currency
South African rand	pegged to	2 LDC currencies
Australian dollar	pegged to	1 LDC currency
German mark	pegged to	1 LDC currency

Source: *IMF Survey,* July 17, 2000, p. 235

McGraw-Hill/Irwin

TM 5.4
Figure 5.4

Trading hours of the world's major financial centers

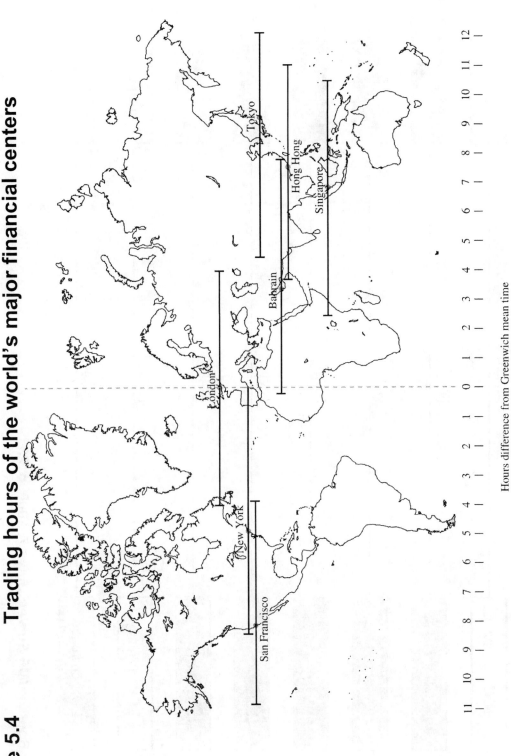

Hours difference from Greenwich mean time

Source: *Bank for International Settlements, 63rd Annual Report, June 14, 1993, p. 194*

McGraw-Hill/Irwin

TM 5.5

Figure 5.6 **One of the earliest capital market offerings denominated in Euros**

CHAPTER 6
FINANCIAL FORCES

Learning Objectives

Teach students or have them learn in group learning exercises:

1. How to read and understand foreign currency exchange quotations.

2. The differences between spot and forward rates.

3. Some causes of exchange rate changes.

4. About government intervention in exchange markets.

5. How to recognize an exchange risk.

6. About government currency controls

7. Some effects of inflation on business.

8. About monetary and fiscal policies that cause or combat inflation.

9. Why business must watch BOP developments, exchange rate forecasts and comparative inflation rates.

10. About the developing country debt crisis and some possible solutions.

11. That the United States has the largest net negative international investment position in the world.

Overview

Trading in the foreign exchange (FX) currency markets can be for investment, or, if you prefer, speculative purposes. For example, if you believe that the Japanese yen (¥) will weaken in terms of the U.S. dollar (U.S.$) over the next six months, you might sell the (¥) short in the six months forward market. You are obliged to deliver the agreed-upon number of yen in return for the agreed-upon number of U. S. $s in six months at the exchange rate at the date of the agreement. If your are correct, and the (¥) is weaker in six months it will cost you less in U.S.$s to buy the agreed upon number of (¥) than it would have cost you at the agreement date. The difference is your profit. Of course, as with any investment there is some risk. The (¥) and U.S.$ exchange rate may not change or even worse from your point of view, the (¥) may strengthen the vis-à-vis the U.S.$. The "One Big Mac, Hold the Fluctuations," story is an illustration of a use of the FX markets by McDonald's to protect itself against adverse FX movements. Of course, it is fundamental that the students should be able to read and understand foreign exchange quotations, spot and future. Managers must recognize and understand currency exchange risks.

Tariffs, customs and duties are financial forces with which management must contend. The different and complex classifications of goods for customs purposes can make the difference between profit or loss. Income, value added tax (VAT) and other taxes are costs of doing business.

Inflation has become a worldwide problem. Costs increase and business must try to pass them along in prices. The accounting treatment of inflation can make major changes in reported earnings and taxes paid. Developing country debt, not to mention the huge American debt, has caused and will cause major changes in trade, investment and lending worldwide.

Suggestions and Comments

1. You can illustrate the changes of currency exchange rates over time by comparing the rates in Figure 6.1 with the rates reported on the day of this lesson

2. Use Figure 6.3 to illustrate currency exchange risk and which party bears the risk.

3. The force of inflation can be brought home with simple comparison of common consumer products prices today with prices last year, five, ten years ago.

4. Methods governments use to encourage exports should be discussed.

5. Reasons for the central position of the US$ in foreign exchange transactions should be explained.

Student Involvement Exercises

1. Have your students do research to locate examples of the effects fluctuating currency exchange rates have on costs of importers.

2. When the students understand foreign exchange quotations, divide them into teams and assign each team the same amount of money. Have them trade the currencies reported in the foreign exchange column of *The Wall Street Journal* or your local paper once or twice a week and see which team has the most money at the end of the term.

3. Have students research the different tariff charges which can follow from customs classification of imports.

4. Students might enjoy studying two countries which have very different inflation rates and explaining the reasons.

Guest Lecturers

1. If a nearby bank has an international department, an officer of the bank could expand on currency trading and risks.

2. Several commodity traders and brokers deal in currency. Their insights could be interesting.

3. A U.S. Commerce Department officer might speak on BOP problems and adjustments.

4. Someone from your economics department could expand on monetary and fiscal policies and their effects on BOP. This could also be a source for discussion of inflation, cause and effect.

5. An export/import company officer or a customs official could explain tariffs.

6. Accountants or lawyers who specialize in taxes would be helpful for the tax material.

Lecture Outline

I. Opening Section
There are two lessons in the McDonald's story. The one applying to international business is how the company needs to import into Japan ingredients for its restaurant, paying for them with the yen it earns in Japan, protecting itself from higher costs due to the yen's fall in value in relation to the U. S. dollar. The yen fell from less than 100 to a dollar to 122, but McDonald's had protected itself by use of a forward currency agreement with its bank in terms of which it could buy dollars at the rate of 103 to 1. That is just less than 16 percent saving from 122 to 1 cost McDonald's would incur without the forward agreement. That would be a tremendous advantage in the competitive fast-food market.

The second lesson comes in two parts, neither of which is peculiar to international business. The older part is the strength of volume buying with a purchasing system that buys for more than 19,500 McDonald's shops in 101 countries. The newer part is the software McDonald's has developed to find the least expensive suppliers.

II.   Fluctuating Currency Values

Values of currencies in terms of each other do not remain fixed by change sometimes rapidly, as they are traded in the world's financial centers. An international business or traveler will need currencies other than that of the home country. Reference may be made to the foreign exchange column of a newspaper. See Figure 6.1.

A. There you see, among others, the quote:

	Wed.	Tues.
Britain (pound)	1.4250	1.4343

That means at 3 p.m. on Wednesday the pound cost in United States dollars (US$) 1.4250: At the same time Tuesday the pound had cost US$ 1.4343.

III.   Foreign Exchange Quotations

A. Although other currencies such as the Yen (¥) and the deutsche mark (DM) or most recently the Euro (€)have become very important in international transactions, the U. S. dollar remains the most used currency. It is used as a:

1. Central reserve asset
2. Vehicle currency
3. Intervention currency
4. Safe haven currency

B. Most large foreign exchange transactions go through the U. S. dollar even though the U. S. dollar is not the needed currency. It is, however, possible to trade other currencies directly, and the quotes for those exchanges are called cross rates. See Figure 6.2.

C. The usual currency exchange quotes show the U. S. dollar value in relation to other currencies. See Figure 6.1. There are four columns.

1. The left two columns indicate the amount in U. S. dollars needed to buy one unit of the other currency at the end of two consecutive trading days.

2. The right two columns indicate the amount in the other currency needed to buy one U. S. dollar.

D. The quotes on the same line as the name of the country and its currency are spot rates. These are for delivery of the traded currencies within two business days.

E. Note that for a few more heavily traded currencies, Britain (pound), Canada (dollar), France (franc), Japan (yen), Switzerland (franc) and Germany (mark), quotes are given for 1-month forward, 3 months forward, and 6-months forward. These are forward rates for delivery of the traded currencies on the agreed day in the future.

1. If the forward rates are higher than spot, the currency is said to be trading at a premium
2. The opposite is called trading at a discount.

IV.   Fluctuating exchange rates create risks which are unique to international transactions.

A. The person who is obliged to make a foreign currency payment in the future or who is entitled to receive payment in a foreign currency in the future bears the risk of value change in that currency.

B. See Figure 6.3.

V. Currency Exchange Controls

These laws and regulations limit or prohibit the legal use of a currency in international transactions.

A. The government sets the value of its currency at an arbitrary level regardless of its market value.

1. The arbitrary value is higher than the market value, and

2. A black market springs up but is rarely of any use to a legitimate business.

B. Any resident who wants foreign currency must request it from the government and justify the request with good reasons.

C. If the resident cannot get government permission to transfer funds out of the country, they must be spent or invested in the country.

D. Table 6.1 is a comparative table of exchange controls in selected countries.

VI. Balance of Payments (BOP)

BOP is important to business management, which should foresee and adjust to government measures to correct a BOP disequilibirium, particularly if it is a deficit.

A. Governments may use market methods such as devaluation of the currency and deflation of the economy.

B. Non-market methods include tariffs, quotas and currency exchange controls.

C. Governments frequently encourage exports with various export incentives, e.g., low financing costs or tax rebates.

VII. Tariffs, Customs or Import Duties

These are costs to an importing company and, of course, management strives to minimize them.

A. The amount paid depends on how customs classifies the goods. Until 1988, the United States used a classification system different from the system followed by most other major trading countries. After years of work a new system became effective January 1, 1988; it is called the Harmonized Commodity Description and Coding System and is observed by all the important trading countries.

B. Some groups of countries notably the EU, have taken steps to lower or abolish tariffs on trade among them.

VIII. Taxation

Taxes are levies under each country's tax laws and are dealt with as legal forces in Chapter 10. Taxes are also financial forces. Remember:

A. Different countries have different types of taxes, such as income, VAT, sales or capital gains.

B. Different countries levy their taxes at different rates from over 100 percent to zero.

C. Different countries enforce their tax laws more or less strictly and

D. There are other differences in tax laws, for example, as to credits, depreciation, deductions and many others.

IX. Inflation

Contagious inflation was probably the major cause of the end of the world's unprecedented economic boom which lasted from the end of WW II until 1973.

A. National Monetary and Fiscal Policies. Monetary policies deal with the amount of money in circulation and whether and how fast the amount grows. Fiscal policies deal with the collecting of money (taxes) and the spending of money by governments.

1. Since WW II several countries have, at certain times, stopped inflation.
2. They were Germany in 1948, the United States in 1953 and in 1981-1986 and Britain in 1983-87. In each case they removed wage, price and other economic controls and applied fiscal and monetary restraint.
   a. Fiscal policy included lower taxes.
   b. Monetary policy was slow, steady growth of supply.

B. Importance of Inflation for Business.
1. High inflation rates may encourage borrowing as borrowers hope to repay the loan with cheaper money.
2. For the same reason such rates discourage lending. The moneyholder tends to buy something expected to increase in value rather than lending or investing the money in business.
3. High inflation makes capital expenditure spending planning more difficult.
4. Nominal interest rates may be higher in one country than another while real interest rates are lower. One computes real interest rates by subtracting the country's inflation rate from the nominal interest rate. Compare a country with a nominal interest rate of 14 percent and inflation of nine percent. This leaves a real interest rate of five percent with that country. Another example where the nominal rate is 13 percent but lower inflation of seven percent leaves a better real interest rate of six percent. Lenders seek the highest real, not nominal, interest. Figure 6.4 shows real rate computations for the year 1996.
5. International business must deal with inflation rates in more than one country and they usually differ.
   a. The country(ies) with higher rates may see their currencies decrease in value, their goods and services become more expensive and may impose currency or other controls or tighten their monetary and fiscal policies.
   b. Business in countries with lower inflation rates may look for the opposite effects.
   c. Countries where an IC raises and invests capital are affected by relative inflation rates.
6. Figure 6.5 shows inflation rates in OECD countries.
7. When you add a country's inflation rate to its unemployment rate, the total has been called a misery index. Figure 6.6 compares the misery index of several countries.

X.   Accounting Practices

Both inflation and currency exchange value fluctuations cause companies' financial and earning statements to differ widely depending, in part, on accounting practices.

A. Inflation and Accounting Practices, Price-Level Accounting

Accounting practices vary widely from country to country, so a firm with operations in several countries must devise methods to translate to a common standard. The standard usually chosen is that of the home country of the parent company. U. S. firms cannot use price-level accounting which permits depreciation for tax purposes of an item at is replacement cost rather than its historic cost. Many feel some sort of inflation-adjusted accounting would yield more realistic results.

XI. Household savings. The amount of savings is important because it allows creation of capital for new investment. The United States, which is a consumer driven economy, has a low savings rate while Japan, which has a culture encouraging savings, has a high savings rate. Many argue that the high savings rate in Japan has helped boost Japan's economy by allowing capital investment sufficient to build Japan's manufacturing base. Figure 6.7 shows dramatically the differences between the United States and Japan in their rates of savings.

XII. Countries Went Bust

Contrary to the confident forecasts of some prominent bankers, it became obvious in 1981 and 1982 that the governments of a number of countries would not be able to repay their loans when due. The causes of their debt problems were several.

A. Rapid inflation during the 1970s had two effects.

  1. By 1973 it ended the worldwide economic boom which had begun after WW II.

  2. It encouraged borrowing because borrowers thought they could repay debts with inflation depreciated money.

B. The OPEC price increases in oil in 1973-74 and 1979-80 worsened the inflation and pushed the world more deeply into recession which drove down the prices of and demand for the debtor country exports.

C. In 1980, industrial countries, and notably the U. S., adopted anti-inflation policies which had two effects:

  1. U. S. inflation was reduced significantly which prevented the U. S. dollar (US$)–in which most of the loans are denominated–from deteriorating in value as rapidly as the debtors had planned when they took the loans.

  2. U. S. interest rates increased, which added billions more to the debts, most of which are subject to variable interest rates.

D. The solutions to the debt problem are numerous. They are short term and long term:

  1. Short term, the loans are being rescheduled with payment being stretched over more years.

  2. There are number of longer-term solutions. They are listed and discussed in the text.

E. In 1996, the World Bank, the IMF, and the Paris Club (a group of private creditor banks) approved a plan to relieve the massive debt load of some of the world's most heavily indebted poor countries (HIPCs). Figure 6.9 gives the numbers of the external debt of all HIPCs.

F. Banks and other developing country creditors have unloaded some of their developing country debts by selling them to other investors at discounts-some quite large-from the face amount of the debt market has developed. Table 6.1 gives numbers of secondary market transactions in debt instruments of developing countries and countries in transition.

G. There is one type of third world debt that is almost always paid in full. That is the low amount loan to small businesses trying to get started or expand. See the Worldview on this subject.

XIII. The United States Net Negative International Investment Position
   A. The United States has a net negative international investment position which means nonresidents of the United States own more American assets than Americans own abroad.
   B. The United States position differs from developing country debt.
      1. Much of it is in U. S. government or corporate bonds which fluctuate in value.
      2. U. S. foreign assets are often valued at book value which is usually lower than current value.
      3. United States assets abroad earn more than foreign holdings in the United States.
      4. As a percentage of GNP, the U. S. debts are smaller than those of the developing countries.
      5. The U. S. debt is denominated in its own currency.

Answers to Questions

1. With U.S. money (US$), in order to buy one Norwegian krone, you must pay .1478 cents.

2. The spot market is for the immediate (within two business days) exchange of one currency for another. For example, if you were buying US$ with Norwegian krone, you would pay the krone and at the same time receive the US$. In the forward market, you contract to buy or sell at an agreed exchange rate an amount of one currency for another at a date in the future. For example, a holder of US$s could agree to see US$1,000,000 for Norwegian krone at krone 5.10 for US$1.00 the currencies to be exchanged in 30 days or six months or at whatever date is set or agreed upon.

3. The forward market allows for the purchase of a currency at a quoted price for delivery at a determined date in the future. When the currency is trading at a premium it means it costs more to buy it for a later date than to buy it for immediate delivery. A premium happens when it is felt the currency will gain value in relation to the US$ over the period specified.

4. You bear the risk. If the value of your currency declines in terms of foreign currency, you will have to spend more of your currency to buy the agreed-upon amount of foreign currency.

5. Currency controls are laws and regulations imposed by a government because it has too little convertible foreign currency. All foreign currency dealings must be done through a government agency and many requests for foreign currency are refused.

6. When management of an IC realizes that the balance of payments of a country where it is doing business is in deficit they should be alert for government measures to correct the deficit. There are a number of those measures which could affect the company's operations. some of them are currency controls, export stimuli, currency devaluation or restrictive monetary or fiscal policies.

7. Inflation may encourage borrowing because loans will be repaid later when the money is worth less. On the other hand, lenders are aware of the falling value of the money and charge higher interest rates to compensate, or, if inflation is at a very high rate, they may refuse to lend. Inflation makes planning more difficult because the rate of future inflation is an unknown. For international business, management must consider and compare two or more inflation rates in the different countries where they do business. The currencies of countries with lower inflation rates tend to be stronger than those with higher rates, and management will try to maximize holdings of stronger currencies.

8. The nominal interest rate charge and the inflation rate.

9. Bank creditors of developing countries have sold part or all their developing country debts at discounts to investors, and a market has developed in which those debts are bought and sold. Reasons for the market include desires of creditor banks to get non-performing loans off their books plus willingness of some investors to hold debt if they can buy them at what they judge to be an adequate discount. Sometimes the investors will exchange the debt of a developing country with the country for a tangible asset in the country, e.g. land or ownership of a business. On other occasions, developing countries have bought their own debt thereby retiring it.

10. First, over $300 million of U. S. foreign-owned assets are U. S. Treasury or corporation obligations that are traded daily and are subject constant change unlike the face value of developing country debt.
Second, U. S.-owned foreign assets are often stated at book value less depreciation. Replacement costs would be much higher.
Third, U. S.-owned foreign assets reportedly earn more in interest and dividends than foreign holdings earn in America.
Fourth, U. S. net liabilities are relatively small as a percentage of GDP.
Fifth, U. S. liabilities are denominated in its own currency while developing countries liabilities are not denominated in their own currencies but in the hard currency of some developed countries, usually the U. S. dollar.

Answers to Internet Problems

1. As of 4/24/01
   a. French Franc 7.3332
   b. Japanese Yen 122.1700
   c. Thai Baht 45.5300
   d. Portuguese Escudo 224.1274
   e. Cyprus Pound 0.6450
   f. Jordanian Dinar 0.7100
   g. Kenyan Schilling 77.2500

   These are many sources for financial information and one example in CNNfn's Web site http://www.cnnfn.com

2. As of 4/24/2001
   Dow Jones Industrial Average 10454.34
   NYSE Composite 613.97
   Hang Seng 13328.28 (Hong Kong)
   IGPA 4976.16 (Santiago)
   DAX 6139.38 (Frankfurt)

   The Internet Directory in this text contains many Web sites for specific countries and regions of the world. One of these sites is http://nordicforecasts.com offering a detailed analysis and research on the long-term economic, political and business outlook for the four main Nordic countries.

Discussion of Minicase 6-1: Management Faces a BOP Deficit.

The host government might use market methods of deflating the economy or devaluing the currency. Deflation can cause recession while devaluation will increase the cost of imports.

Of course devaluation will also make host country products, including yours cheaper for foreigners with their currencies relatively stronger. You should make concerted efforts to develop export markets for your product, and to that end, your parent company and other subsidiaries might be of great assistance.

If you can develop export markets, you will be popular with the host government because you are combating the BOP deficit and bringing in foreign currency. Being on the government's good side will help if it decided on non-market methods such as currency exchange controls, tariffs or quotas.

Regardless of your popularity, in case you see non-market methods coming, you should get any surplus cash out of the country and stockpile needed import parts or components. And once the non-market methods are imposed, you will have much easier relations with the government if you can sell in export.

TM 6.1

Figure 6.3   **Currency Exchange Risk**

	August 1	Payment date exchange rate
February 1	Goods delivery date exchange rate	
Suppose:	US$1 = 1.78 Swiss francs	US$1 = 1.78 Swiss francs
	Whichever party bore the currency exchange risk, neither gained or lost.	
Suppose:	US$1 = 1.78 Swiss francs	US$1 = 1.80 Swiss francs
	Whichever party bore the currency exchange risk lost. It now requires 1.80 Swiss francs to buy the US$1, which could have been bought for 1.78 Swiss francs at the time the goods were delivered.	
Suppose:	US$1 = 1.78 Swiss francs	US$1 = 1.76 Swiss francs
	Whichever party bore the currency exchange risk gained. It now requires only 1.76 Swiss francs to buy the US$1, which would have cost 1.78 Swiss francs at the time the goods were delivered.	

Note: Parties agree to payment in US$.

Source: *The Wall Street Journal*, November 9, 2000.

McGraw-Hill/Irwin

TM 6.2
Figure 6.4   Nominal and Real Interest Rates (1992-2000)

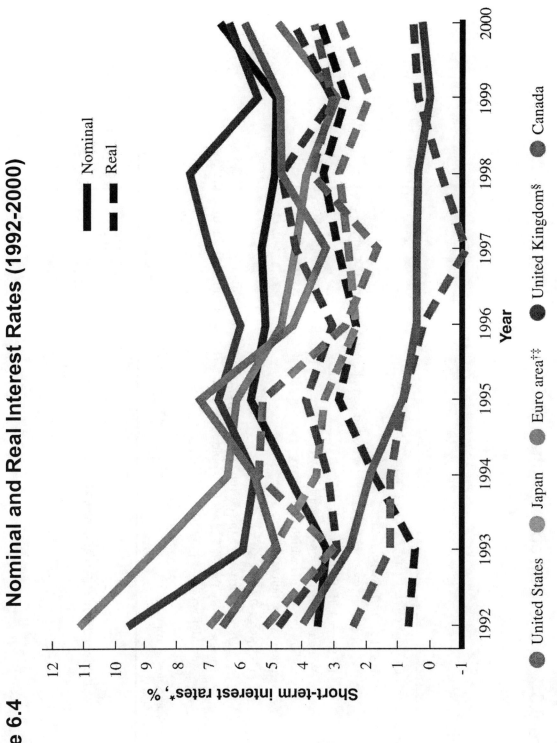

Nominal

Real

Short-term interest rates*, %

Year

1992 1993 1994 1995 1996 1997 1998 1999 2000

● United States   ● Japan   ● Euro area†‡   ● United Kingdom§   ● Canada

McGraw-Hill/Irwin

TM 6.3
Figure 6.5

Inflation Rates in OECD Countries

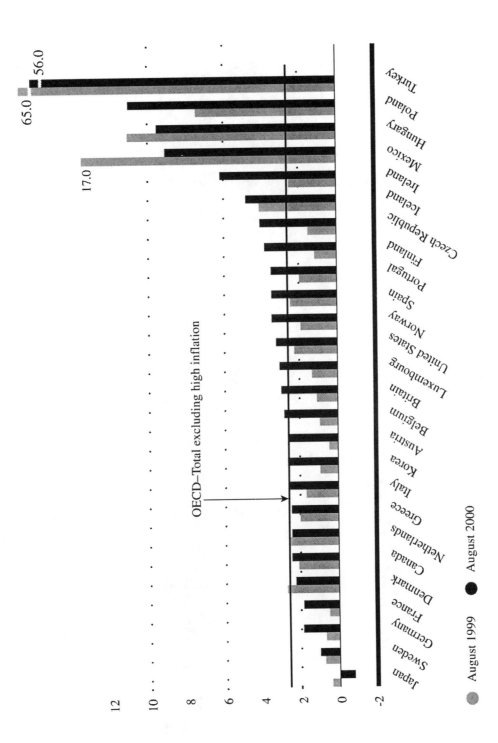

● August 1999   ● August 2000

Source: *The Economist*, April 6, 1996, p. 108

McGraw-Hill/Irwin

TM 6.4

Figure 6.6   **Misery Index**

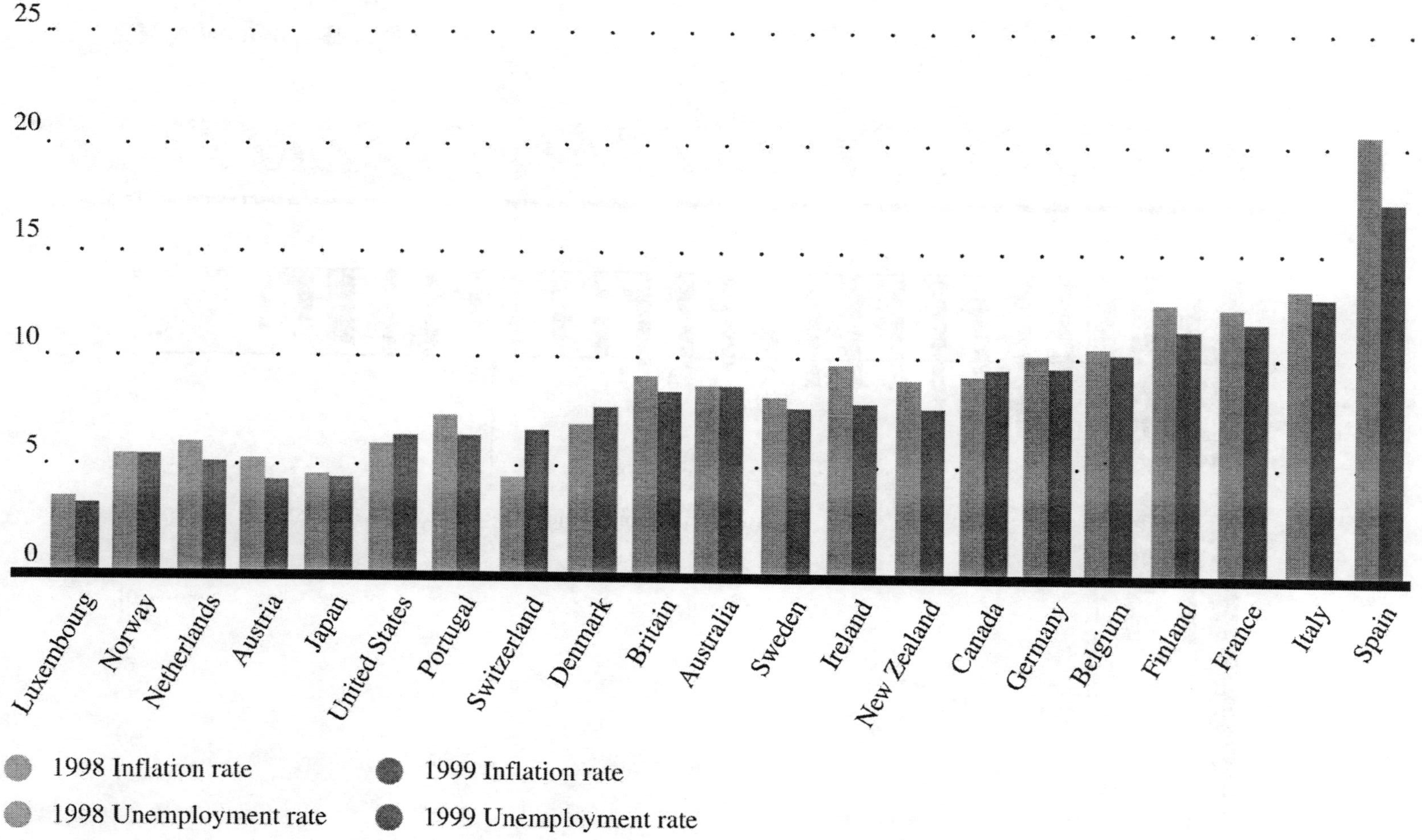

Legend:
- 1998 Inflation rate (●)
- 1999 Inflation rate (●)
- 1998 Unemployment rate (●)
- 1999 Unemployment rate (●)

Countries (from top): Spain, Italy, France, Finland, Belgium, Germany, Canada, New Zealand, Ireland, Sweden, Australia, Britain, Denmark, Switzerland, Portugal, United States, Japan, Austria, Netherlands, Norway, Luxembourg

Vertical axis scale: 0, 5, 10, 15, 20, 25

Sources: *The Economist*, October 25, 1997, p. 114, IMF, *World Economic Outlook Database*, September 2000

McGraw-Hill/Irwin

Figure 6.9   **Debt of all HIPCs (1992-2001)**

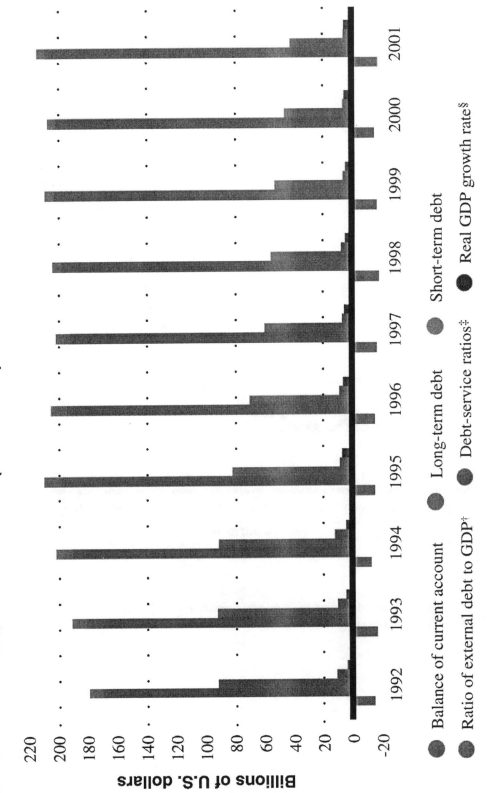

● Balance of current account   ● Long-term debt   ● Short-term debt

● Ratio of external debt to GDP†   ● Debt-service ratios‡   ● Real GDP growth rate§

Source: *World Economic Outlook*, IMF, September 2000.

McGraw-Hill/Irwin

TM 6.6

Figure 6.10   **Foreign Holdings as a Percent of Total Privately Held Public Debt***

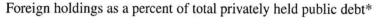

Foreign holdings as a percent of total privately held public debt*

*Privately held debt excludes holdings of the Federal Reserve.
Source: U.S. Department of Treasury, 2000, www.treas.gov/domfin/foreign.htm

CHAPTER 7
ECONOMIC AND SOCIOECONOMIC FORCES

Learning Objectives

1. Learn the purpose of an economic analysis and the kind of information it provides.

2. Present the important economic and socioeconomic dimensions that managements use to compare markets.

Overview

The assessment and forecasting of economic conditions is a regular activity for most firms. When a firm enters foreign markets, the task is more complex because of the number of economies involved.

Managers of all the functional areas in the firm are interested in the size and rate of change of various economic and socioeconomic factors. Some of the economic dimensions are GNP, GNP/capita, income distribution, personal consumption expenditures, and amount of private investment and unit labor costs. The principal socioeconomic dimensions are total population, population density, and age distribution and population distribution. Publications of the international agencies, governments, banks, as well as business publications are all sources of this kind of information.

The national economic plans formulated by many nations provide insight as to government expectations.

Suggest and Comments

1. To help explain the economic and socioeconomic dimensions, we show on the board that there are comparable dimensions in each category: Total Population–GNP, GNP/Capita–Population Density, Income Distribution–Population Distribution, etc.

2. The analysis in the opening section on India's market potential is straightforward and you might assign some similar research to your class. Let them choose the countries if you want.

Student Involvement Exercises

1. We have had good response from students when we have asked them to choose a country and become a specialist on it. You can assign this as a term project and also ask for short periodic verbal reports during the term. Chapter 7 is a good place to start. You may prefer to assign them countries.

2. Assign various kinds of changes in the economic and socioeconomic dimensions (similar to Figure 7.1) and ask the students to prepare a report to top management as to the expected effects of these changes on all the functional areas of the firm. To add realism, you may prefer to assign this exercise as a continuation of Exercise 1.

Guest Lecturers

1. Someone involved in planning or economic analysis in a multinational should prove interesting.

2. The international trade specialist from your U. S. Department of Commerce office will have economic data available and should be able to show how firms use it. You may want to save this person for the chapter on exporting, however.

3. If you don't send your class to take a guided tour with the reference librarian, you might ask him/her to give a short presentation to the class about the resources available. Usually they will since the students will be better prepared when they go to the library.

4. If you have a friend in the economics department who does economic studies as a consultant, that person can describe to the class the kinds of data and sources that he/she uses.

Lecture Outline

I.   Opening Sections

The opening section explains why a nation with a GNP/capita of only $430 is attracting the attention of multinationals. Of the over 1 billion people, there appears to be a bonafide middle class of up to 494 million. Notice the purchasing power of the fourth and fifth quintiles. There does appear to be a market in India for refrigerators, TV sets, and automibles.

II. International Economic Analyses

Economic analyses for multinationals are more complex than those for a purely domestic firm because there are many economies to consider instead of just one, there are interactions between them, and values are highly divergent. International economic analyses should cover both actual and prospective markets. In addition, they are helpful when done for countries where their major competitors are operating. The responsibility for controlling the collection of data should rest with the home office, not the foreign subsidiaries that may do much of the actual work.

A.   Dimensions of the Economy

Management requires socioeconomic data (information on the number of people) and economic data (information related to their purchasing power).

1.   Economic dimensions

a.   GNP

b.   GNP/capita

c.   Income distribution (Table 7.2, page 243).Data from income distribution studies provide useful insights for business people:

(1) Generally, income is distributed more evenly in developed nations.

(2) Income redistribution proceeds slowly so that older data are still useful.

(3) Income inequality increases in the early stages of development and reverses this tendency in later stages. Depending on the type of product and the total population, relatively even or uneven income distribution may represent a viable market segment. Notice the calculation for Costa Rica in the text on page 244.

d.   Private consumption (Tables 7.3, page 245 and 7.4, page 246). Data follow Engle's law–as income increases, the percentage of income spend on food decreases. There is a calculation to show students the importance of a small difference in consumption expenditures.

e.   See Growth Rates of Consumption and Investment, Table 7.5, page 247.

f.   Labor compensations costs (Table 7.6, page 250.) Stated in dollars, the average hourly rates of 10 nations are higher than those of the United States. Note how the rankings have changed over the years.

g.   Other economic dimensions–interest rates, balance of payments, inflation rates are just a few. Note major changes in inflation rates in Table 7.1. See the large international debts of the major international debts of the major international debtors in Table 7.7 on page 251, an important problem for international firms. There are some interesting examples of debt for equity swaps on page 252.

    2. Socioeconomic Dimensions

        a. Total population–population alone not good indicator of economic strength and market potential. Switzerland, with only 7.0 million people, is far more important economically than Bangladesh with 160 million.

        b. Age distribution–useful to marketers for market segmentation and to human resource managers as information on labor force. Decreasing birthrates are a worldwide phenomenon. Developing nations have a more youthful population than do developed nations. See Figure 7.4, page 253. This means that firms selling to youth markets must look to developing nations for expanding markets. Declining birthrates in industrialized nations are causing concern. Pension and hospitalization costs are increasing, for example. EU governments are concerned because for over a decade, European birthrates have been below the replacement rate of 2.1 children per woman. Japan's rate of 1.50 children is more serious. The labor shortage has raised average manufacturing pay in Japan to \$20.89 compared to \$19.20 in the United States. Mandatory retirement age in Japan has been raised from 55 to 60. See the dependency ratios, actual and projected, for numerous countries in Figure 7.8, page 257.

        c. Population density and distribution–densely populated nations make product distribution and communication simpler and less costly. However, population density figures suffer from same drawback as GNP/capita–they're only arithmetic means. In a country with low density, there may be concentrations of population (Brazil and Canada). Important is rural–urban shift, especially in developing nations, See Table 7.8, page 258.

        d. Other socioeconomic dimensions–women entering work force population of ethnic groups, divorce rate. See Figure 7.10, page 260. Significant to marketers and human resource managers.

B. National Economic Plans

    1. These can be an important source of data to marketers. They range from annual to five-year plans and are used as production control instruments in some nations or as indicative plans in others.

    2. By studying these plans, the analyst obtains an idea of which of the industries are receiving governmental priority.

C. Industry Dimensions

    1. Certain factors are more significant to a given industry or to a specific functional area of the firm.

    2. Examples are growth trend of automobiles in a market to OEM and aftermarket suppliers (tires, batteries). The number of machine operators being graduated by the technical schools is interesting to human resource and production managers.

    3. The industry section of the analysis should provide information on competing firms, suppliers of inputs, and purchasers of company's outputs.

    4. Industry studies are generally made by the firm's economists or its trade association. Studies can be purchased from independent research organizations such as the Economist Intelligence Unit. International banks publish free newsletters containing useful economic data. Many sources are listed in the Appendix at the end of Chapter 15.

Answers to Questions

1. Marketers–a general 10% increase in wage rates will provide consumers with more disposable income and will probably enable a new group of customers to buy their products. Many marketers will revise their sales forecasts upwards.

   Production–will have to increase output. More workers, raw materials and possibly machinery will be needed.

   Human resources manager–will have to hire more workers.

   Purchasing–will have to increase the amounts of raw materials, components and suppliers they buy and perhaps have to locate new sources if supplies are tight.

   Financial officer–may have to obtain loans if more working capital or production equipment is needed.

2. International dollars refer to GNP/capita estimates based on the relative purchasing power of the various currencies instead of being based on market exchange rates. As you saw in Table 7.3, private consumption in terms of the 'international dollar is, on the average, 4 to 5 times as large as it is when measured in dollars based on market exchange rates. This can indicate a market for goods that appear to be out of reach of most of the population when only the GNP/capita converted by the market rate of exchange is considered.

3. Both are arithmetic means and may conceal important concentrations of populations and fail to disclose the presence of a sizable segment with high incomes. We need to investigate the distribution of both income and population.

4. TOTAL GNP= GNP/capita x population

   Canada: $19,320 x 31 million = $ 598.9 billion

   Netherlands: $24,320 x 16 million = $ 389.1 billion

   GNP of top 20% = total GNP x percentage in Table 7.2.

   Canada: $598.9 billion x 0.393 = $235.4 billion

   Netherlands: $389.1 billion x 0.401 = $156.0 billion

   $$\text{GNP/capita of top 20\%} = \frac{\text{GNP of top 20\%}}{\text{pop. of top 20\%}}$$

   $$\text{Canada}: \frac{\$235.4\,\text{billion}}{6.2\,\text{million}} = \$37,967$$

   $$\text{Netherlands}: \frac{\$156.0\,\text{billion}}{3.2\,\text{million}} = \$48,750$$

5. Use Table 2.10 for population and Table 7.3 for consumption expenditures/capita

   One percent increase in total clothing and footwear expenditures – private consumption expenditures/capita x population x 0.01.

   For Switzerland: $15,536 x 7 million x 0.01 = $1.87 billion

	1995	1996
6. Italian hourly rates in U. S. $:	$16.52	$18.08
Italian hourly rates in lira	26,911	27,894

   $$\text{Percentage increase in US\$} \frac{\$18.08}{\$16.52} = 1.094(9.4\%)$$

   $$\text{Percentage increase in It. lira} = \frac{27894}{26911} = 1.037(23.7\%)$$

The rate of increase in lira is 3.7%. Therefore, $\dfrac{(9.4 - 3.7)}{9.4} = 60.6$ percent of the apparent increase in the dollar hourly cost is due to an increase in the dollar value of the lira from 1995 to 1996.

7. The CFO would be very concerned that the total external debt has risen by a factor of more than 5 in the last 20 years.

    This could mean that the country will suffer a shortage of foreign exchange causing the government to impose exchange controls. This could impact the firm in various ways. The government may not have foreign currency to sell to the company to pay for imports of machinery and raw materials. There also may be no foreign exchange that the Argentine subsidiary can buy to remit profits to the home office.

8. High inflation rates are an ongoing problem in many developing nations. All the countries in Table 7.1, page 241, may merit the attention of the firm's CFO. He or she cannot permit the firm's subsidiaries in these countries to accumulate cash not to take out loans in foreign currency. The CFO will continue to pressure them to delay payment of invoices while trying to accelerate payments of their receivables.

9. The falling birthrates in Europe are causing numerous disruptions. Governments are laying off public school teachers, cutting university subsidies and extending the draft period for the armed forces. They fear serious labor shortages, fewer working taxpayers to support the retirees and greatly increased retirement and medical costs.

10. You might prefer to assign a product and country to everyone and spend a class period during which the students compare results. We have done it both ways and the results, as in so many of these exercises, depend on the enthusiasm and initiative of the students.

    The student who chooses a low-priced, mass-produced product will concentrate on total population size and growth. If a high-priced luxury good is chosen, income distribution and per capita income assume importance. There is a practical reason for this exercise. At times, management will ask for some quick research, which will be limited by time constraints to a study of these two classes of dimensions. For some products, some kind of a chain ratio will be used such as a market potential for sulfuric acid in the automotive industry–number of automobiles produced x the square feet of steel per automobile x the quantity of sulfuric acid to needed per square foot of steel.

Answers to Internet Problems

1. "Relative Social Indicators, LAC Countries Compared to the Industrialized World," at www.lanic,utexas.edu/la/region/aid/aid94/Social/COMPARE1.html is the source for the answers to these questions.
    (a) Bolivia, (b) Haiti, (c) Haiti, (d) Paraguay, (e) Haiti

2. OECD in Figures-Demography at www.oecd.org/publications/figures/2000/english/demography.pdf the source of the answers to these questions.

    (a) Canada, United States

    (b) United States, Japan

    (c) Korea, Netherlands

    (d) Mexico, Luxembourg

    (e) Mexico, Sweden

Discussion of Minicase 7.1: World Laboratories

Private expenditures on pharmaceuticals–GNP x % GNP that is private consumption x % private consumption spent on health care x % of health care spent on pharmaceuticals. Ex. Brazil: $425.4 bill x 0.60 x .03 x .02 = $2,552 million.

Government expenditures on pharmaceuticals–GNP x percentage of GNP that is government expenditures x percentage of government expenditures spent on health care x percentage of health care spent on pharmaceuticals. Ex. Brazil: $425.4 billion x 0.131 x 0.03 x 0.2 = $334.4million.

	Pharm. 1992	Expend. on ($million) 1989	Priv. Exp. on Pharm./Cap 1992	1989	1992/1989 change (%)	Gov. Exp. on Pharm. ($mil) 1992	1989
Argentina	$ 950.0	$ 222.0	$28.70	$ 6.96	312.0%	$ 157.4	$ 42.0
Brazil	2,552.0	2,074.0	16.58	14.08	17.8	1,502.9	1,400.3
Chile	196.0	133.2	14.20	10.25	38.5	182.0	87.8
Paraguay	16.0	13.0	3.55	3.10	14.5	4.9	2.3
Peru	94.0	116.8	4.20	5.51	-23.8	29.8	29.3
Uruguay	68.0	51.8	22.04	16.71	31.9	29.8	18.8

	Gov. Exp. on Pharm./Capita 1992	1989	1992-1989 change (percent)	Govt. Exp. on Pharm. Cap. Priv. Exp. on Pharm./Cap.	
Argentina	$4.76	$1.32	260.6%	0.17	0.19
Brazil	9.77	9.51	2.7	0.59	0.68
Chile	13.19	6.75	95.4	0.93	0.66
Paraguay	1.09	0.55	98.2	0.31	0.18
Peru	1.33	1.38	-3.6	0.32	0.25
Uruguay	9.61	6.06	58.6	0.44	0.36

Total expenditures/capita

	1992	1989	1992/1989 % Increase
Argentina	$33.46	$ 8.28	304.0%
Brazil	26.35	23.59	11.7
Chile	27.39	17.00	61.1
Paraguay	4.64	3.65	27.1
Peru	5.53	6.89	-19.7
Uruguay	31.65	22.77	39.0

In every country except Peru, the government per capita expenditure on pharmaceuticals has risen substantially in just three years. Also, the per capita expenditure on pharmaceuticals has risen in the private sector in every country except Peru. Notice that even though government expenditures on pharmaceuticals per capita have increased, with the exception of Peru, the ratios of government to private expenditures on pharmaceuticals per capital have not moved in the same direction in three of the six countries. It should be clear to the vice president that his subsidiaries should obtain sales increases in all markets except, perhaps, Peru. He should expect greater increases in the private sectors of Argentina and Brazil and in the government sectors of Chile, Paraguay, and Uruguay. The affiliates seem to be covering the market well. Sales by product category follow closely each country's population distribution.

Figure 7.1   Impact of Economic Forecast on Firm's Functional Areas

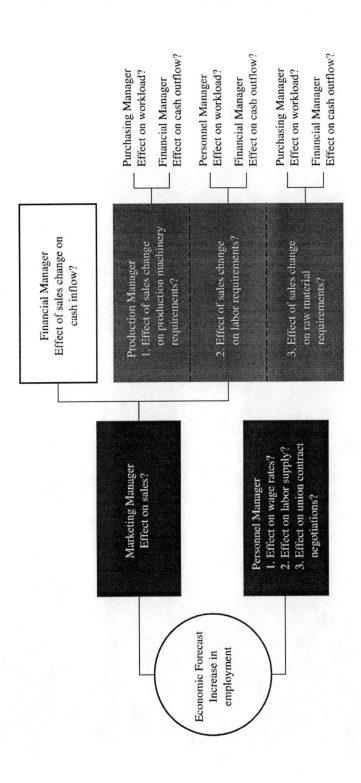

Annual Rates of Inflation for Selected Countries

Annual Rates of Inflation for Selected Countries

Country	1995	1999
Georgia	2,280%	19%
Turkmenistan	1,167	30
Ukraine	1,041	20
Brazil	965	5
Angola	775	270
Russian Federation	517	86
Zambia	108	27
Nicaragua	98	12
Peru	62	5
Uruguay	56	4

Source: *World Development Indicators 1997* (Washington, DC: World Bank, 1997), pp. 206–08; and www.cia.gov/publications/factbook/docs/guide.html, various country pages.

McGraw-Hill/Irwin

TM 7.3

Figure 7.3   **Comparison of Labor Costs for Selected Countries**

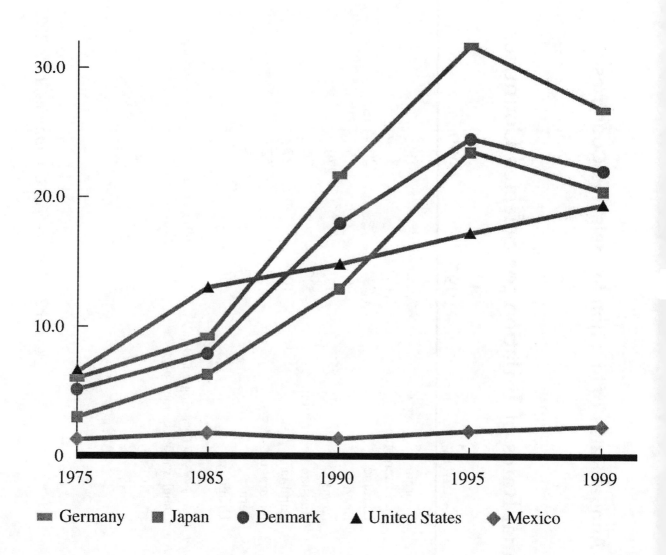

Population by Age and Sex— 1996 and 2020 (millions)

Developed nations (1996: 1.17 billion   2020: 1.25 billion)

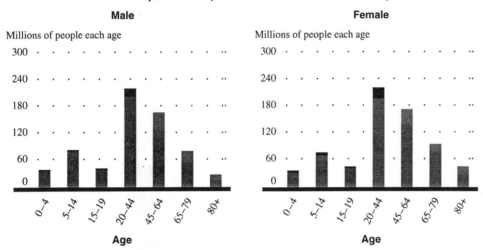

Developing nations (1996: 4.60 billion   2020: 6.35 billion)

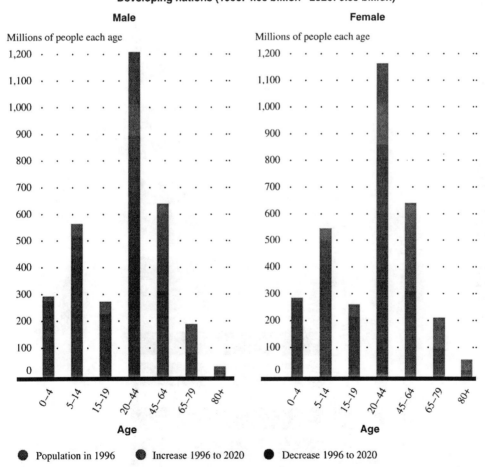

● Population in 1996   ● Increase 1996 to 2020   ● Decrease 1996 to 2020

Source: Based on U.S. Bureau of Census projections, www. Census.gov/ipc/pred/wp96/wp96a1.pdf (December 7. 1997)

McGraw-Hill/Irwin

Population Growth of Countries with Over 100 Million Inhabitants in the Year 2010 (Millions of Inhabitants)

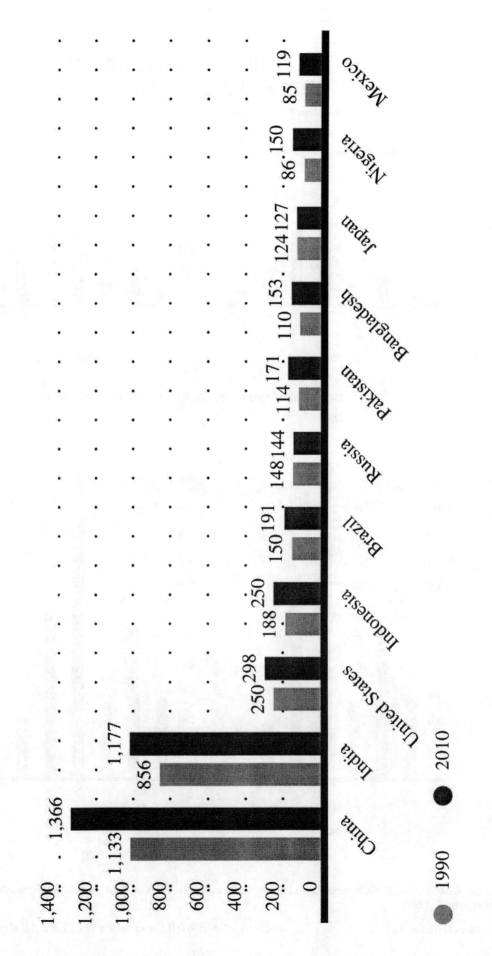

McGraw-Hill/Irwin

1990   2010

TM 7.6

Figure 7.6a **Contraceptive Prevalence Rate for Selected Countries by Rural/Urban Residence: mid-1990s**

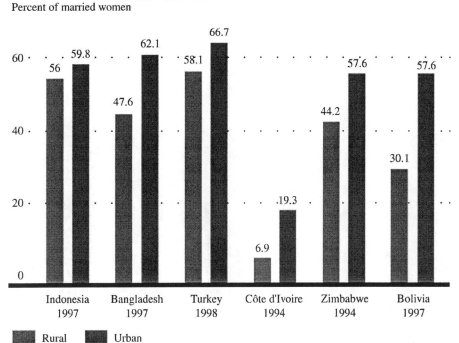

Figure 7.6b **Contraceptive Prevalence Rate for Selected Countries by Level of Education: mid-1990s**

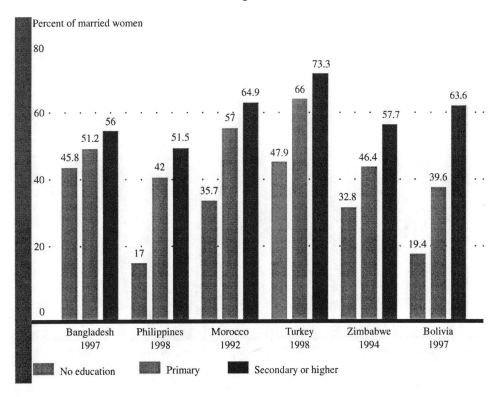

Figure 7.7   **Percentages of Elderly (Over 65) in Population**

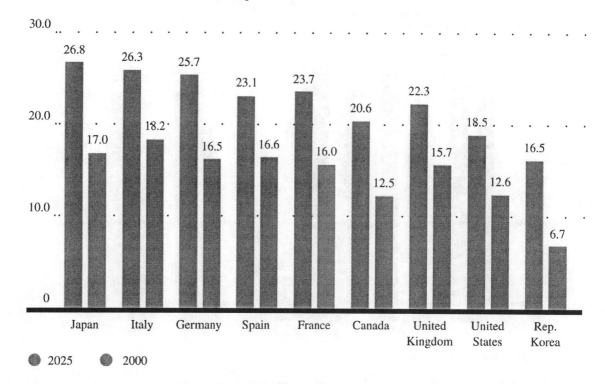

Figure 7.8   **Dependency Ratio Per 100 People of Working Age**

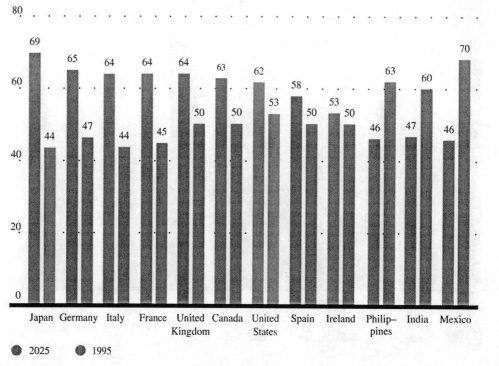

25 Megacities 1970—2015 (millions)

Beijing	Calcutta	Greater Bombay	Karachi	Los Angeles	Moscow	Paris	Seoul	Tokyo
1970: 8.3	1970: 7.1	1970: 6.0	1970: 3.1	1970: 8.4	1970: 7.1	1970: 8.3	1970: 4.5	1970: 14.9
2015: 19.4	2015: 17.6	2015: 27.4	2015: 20.6	2015: 14.3	2015: 9.3	2015: 9.6	2015: 13.1	2015: 28.7

Buenos Aires	Dhaka	Istanbul	Lagos	Manila	New York	Rio de Janeiro	Shanghai
1970: 8.6	1970: 4.3	1970: 1.8	1970: 1.51	1970: 3.6	1970: 16.3	1970: 7.2	1970: 11.4
2015: 12.1	2015: 19.0	2015: 12.3	2015: 24.4	2015: 14.7	2015: 17.6	2015: 11.6	2015: 23.4

Cairo	Delhi	Jakarta	London	Mexico City	Osaka	São Paulo	Tianjin
1970: 5.7	1970: 3.6	1970: 4.5	1970: 10.6	1970: 9.1	1970: 7.6	1970: 8.2	1970: 6.9
2015: 14.5	2015: 17.6	2015: 21.2	2015: 7.1	2015: 18.8	2015: 10.7	2015: 20.8	2015: 17.0

Changing Divorce Rates in Selected Countries

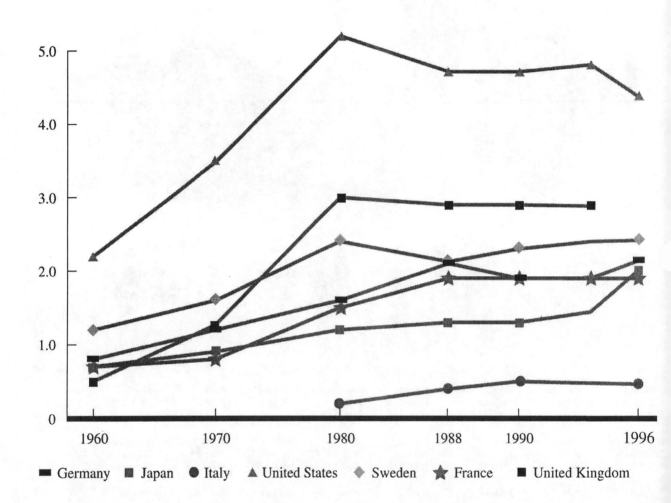

■ Germany ■ Japan ● Italy ▲ United States ◆ Sweden ★ France ■ United Kingdom

TM 7.10

Telephones per 1,000 people in selected countries

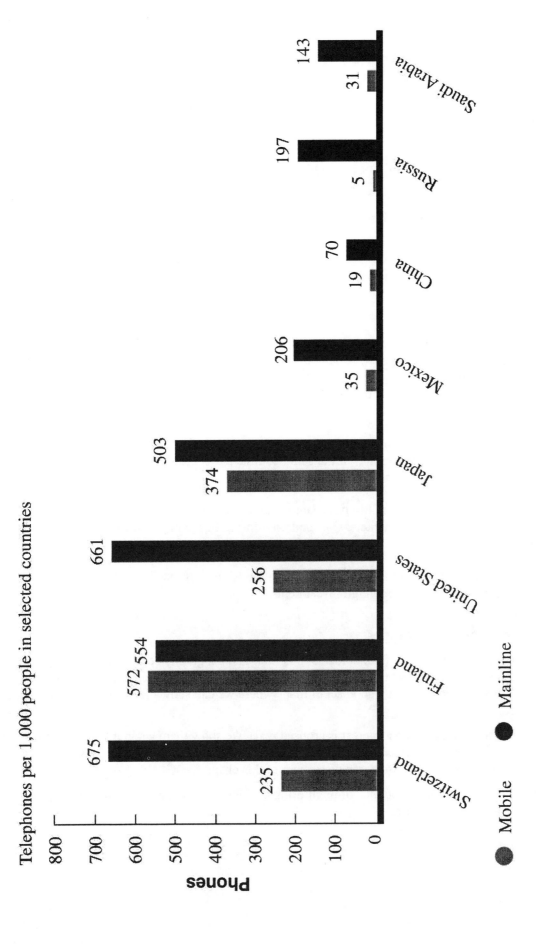

McGraw-Hill/Irwin

CHAPTER 8
PHYSICAL AND ENVIRONMENTAL FORCES

Learning Objectives

1. Show students that the physical forces exert an important influence on the other forces.

2. Illustrate the importance of location, topography and climate.

3. Discuss the reasons why an international manager must be concerned with natural resources.

4. Explain how recent industrial accidents are affecting all multinational firms.

Overview

The physical forces are significant because they affect many of the other forces. The international manager should, at a minimum, be familiar with the location of countries, their size, topography and climate.

A nation's location often explains trading relationships and political alliances. Its topography may affect physical distribution and the product. Mountains can divide a nation into various cultures and climates. They can also create concentrations of populations. Deserts and tropical forests also separate markets, make distribution more difficult and create concentrations of populations. Bodies of water usually have the opposite effect.

A nation's climate can set the limits of what people can do physically and economically. Similar climates tend to exist in the same latitudes and in the same continental position. Climatic conditions can affect a firm's product mix, packaging and inventory costs.

Natural resources are important not only because they are essential to manufacturing, but also because their discovery can create new markets. Constant monitoring of the physical forces is necessary because they are constantly changing.

The industrial accidents at Bhopal, in Alaska, and on the Rhine River will have long-term effects on the way multinationals manage their foreign investments.

Suggestions and Comments

1. Unfortunately, most of our students took their last geography course in junior high school and they are not receptive to our suggestion that they study economic geography in college. However, we find that a good set of maps where we can show the examples from the text does catch their interest.

2. We also find that their interest is aroused when we show them geography's influence on the other forces. A discussion of the effects of geography on the Swiss economy (Opening Section) might be a good way to begin discussion of this chapter.

3. To illustrate the importance of monitoring developments in natural resources, try question 3 from the text in class.

Student Involvement Exercises

1. Hand out a copy of a South American or Far Eastern map with only the geographic borders traced at the beginning of class. Ask students to fill in country and capital names as thought it were a quiz. Great way to start class.

2. Ask the students to give a concrete examples of geography's influence on the other uncontrollable variables.

3. Discuss question 3 from the text.

4. If your students started country projects in Chapter 6 or 7, they'll have plenty to do for this chapter.

Guest Lecturers

1. If you know someone from the geography department who is a good speaker, ask him or her to talk on the subject. If that department is looking for students, someone may be convinced to address your class.

2. A marketing executive who has worked in such countries as Colombia, Brazil, Spain or Switzerland will be able to tell the class a number of interesting experiences based on the country's geography.

Lecture Outline

I. Opening Section

The Opening Section examines the impact of the physical forces on Swiss industry and agriculture. They are even responsible for lacemaking and woodcarving. It illustrates what one writer wrote: "the physical character of a nation is perhaps the principal and broadest determinant of both the society found there and the means by which the society undertakes to supply its needs.

Some of the elements of geography that are particularly significant for the businessperson: location, topography, climate, and natural resources.

II. Location

Location explains many of a nation's trade and political relationships. Austria's locations on the borders of the European Union is the reason why its trading links have been so close with EU members. Because it is also located on the borders of former communist nations Czechoslovakia and Hungary, Austrians have captured an important share of western nations' exports to Eastern Europe.

III. Topography

A. The surface features of a country–mountains, plains, deserts and bodies of water–contribute greatly to differences in a country's economy, culture, politics and social structure.

B. Mountains and Plains

1. Mountains can divide a market into a number of small ones–Colombia, Spain, Switzerland

2. Temperatures and humidity vary widely in the Tropics because of large differences in elevation.

3. Mountains create concentrations of people that often have their own culture, including language. The Basques, for example, have their own language and they want more autonomy, not total separation, from Spain. Figures 8.2, page 272, and 8.3, page 273, show how mountains separate Switzerland and Colombia into separate cultural regions.

C. Deserts, Topical Forests and Bodies of Water

Deserts and tropical forests are like mountains in that they divide markets, create concentrations of population and make transportation difficult.

1. Deserts

   a. Australia) see map in text, Figure 8.4, page 275) is world's driest continent. As a result, more than ½ of the population is concentrated in 1/5 of the land area. Australia has one of the highest percentages of people living in cities.

   b. Because 2/3 of the population is concentrated on the coast away from the major desert area in the center of the country, most goods are moved by coastal shipping. Transportation adds as much as 30% to the final cost of the product. This is three times as expensive as in the U. S. and Europe.

   c. There are also parts of Australia that receive up to 100 inches of rainfall annually.

2. Tropical Rain Forest

   a. These are sometimes called deserts because of their low population density.

   b. Although the Brazilian Amazon occupies ½ of Brazil, it contains only 4% of the country's population.

   c. Canadian Shield–is neither a desert nor a tropical forest, but its forbidding characteristics make its population very low. The Canadian Shield is ½ of Canada's landmass, but it has only 10% of the country's population.

   d. Relevance for businesspeople–Unless they are aware that some markets such as Brazil and Canada have geographical conditions which create concentrations of population, businesspeople may think that these markets with low population densities may be difficult and costly to service as compared with those having much higher densities.

3. Bodies of Water

   a. Bodies of water attract people because river valleys are low, there is fertile soil, water for irrigation and inexpensive transportation.

   b. Rhine waterway (Figure 8.5, page 277), main transportation artery in Europe, provides a pathway for goods to Germany, French Rhone area, Switzerland, Australia, Czech Danube region, and the Black Sea.

   c. Extensive use is made of navigable waterways in every continent except Australia.

   d. Outlets to the sea have been subject of political differences (Bolivia, Paraguay). Bolivia's export corridor and the Paraná Paraguay rivers trade corridor provide outlets to the sea for both nations (Figures 8.7, p. 280 and 8.6, p. 278).

   e. Fourteen of the world's 20 landlocked nations are in Africa. This requires them to construct expensive highways to connect to countries with coastlines. Governments of nations with coastlines through which the exports and imports of landlocked nations must pass are in a position to exert considerable political influence over them.

IV. Climate

A. Climate can set the limits of what people can do both physically and economically. Similar climates occur in similar latitudes and continental positions and the more water-dominated an area, the more moderate is its climate. Kansas and Central Asia are both far from the sea and at the same latitude. They are both dry and have cold winters and hot summers.

B. Climate and Development

   1. Numerous experts have tried to show that differences in economic development, human temperament and ability are caused by dissimilar climates. They claim that development in the tropics has been slower than in the temperate zone because the climate limits human energy and mental power.

   2. Studies by the World Bank show that pests and parasites are responsible for many of the problems in the tropics. However, as they come under control, the characteristics will give them advantages in agriculture.

   3. International managers who are aware of these problems and thus understand that workers in the tropics are not inherently inferior, can improve their workers' performance with subsidized lunches and health care.

C. Climate Implications for International Business

   1. Climate conditions can affect a firm's product mix.

   2. They can add to production and inventory costs.

V. Natural Resources

We define natural resources as anything supplied by nature on which people depend. Some of the principal types of natural resources important to businesspeople are energy and non-fuel minerals.

A. Energy

   1. Petroleum-the Iraqi invasion of Kuwait and the Gulf War reminded industry and government officials that it was necessary to continue searching for new sources of petroleum, both conventional and unconventional.

      a. Conventional sources-analysts do not agree on the quantity of reserves. Reserve estimates change because of new discoveries and new techniques for its extraction.

      b. Unconventional sources-among the many unconventional sources are oil sands, oil shale, natural gas, and coal.

      c. Sources of renewable energy-at least 8 types: hydroelectric, solar, wind, geothermal, waves, tides, biomass, and ocean thermal energy conversion.
      Global sales of photovoltaic cells for capturing solar energy increased by five times from 1988-1998. Developing countries are using them for rural electrification in isolated communities with small electricity requirements. Figure 8.8, page 285, compares the percentages of each energy type for the United States and the world.

B. Alternate Energy Sources

   1. Oil Sands and Shale

      a. Tar sands in Athabasca, Canada used to produce synthetic crude.

      b. An estimated 600 billion barrels U. S. shale oil reserves.

      c. Recovery expensive and there are environmental problems.

C. Non-Fuel Minerals

   1. Figure 8.9, page 287, illustrates the minerals that are a source of apprehension for governments and industry in the U. S.

   2. United States is dependent on South Africa for much of its platinum, chromium, manganese and vanadium.

   3. Bleak Situation?

      a. Only small areas in the world have been explored adequately–5% in Mexico and 10% in Bolivia, for example.

      b. Satellite mapping discovering new sources.

4. Ocean Mining-the Last Frontier?
    a. In 1997, a mining company filed a claim to mine the world's richest underseas deposit of gold, silver, copper, and zinc. The deposit, located a mile below the surface in Papua New Guinea, has about 10 times the gold and 5 times as much copper found in land-based mines. Temperatures as high as 800 degrees F. caused by underwater volcanic activity make the minerals separate from rocks deep in the earth and form chimney-like towers, which are crushed, scooped up, and sent to the surface through piping.
    b. The Worldview, p. 288, describes the U.N. Law of the Sea Treaty that governs the underwater mining of nodules and underwater black smokers (see picture on p. 288).

D. Changes Make Monitoring Necessary
  1. Mineral Resources
    a. discoveries of new sources, especially in the seabeds–nodules and seafloor crusts.
    b. Discoveries of how to use less of the imported strategic minerals.
    c. A fascinating discovery is the fuel cell that converts fuel directly to electricity without having to burn it. Unlike Japanese hybrid cars, fuel-cell-driven cars need no battery.
  2. Other Changing Physical Forces
    a. Changes in infrastructure, especially highways, can create new markets.
    b. New infrastructure is responsible for economic development in developed nations as well as in developing nations-the Channel Tunnel connecting England and France and the Oresund Bridge, the first land link between Denmark and Sweden.

VI. Destruction of Natural Resources
  A. Pollution control has been considered a luxury by many governments. Tragedies such as Bhopal disaster and Chernobyl are awakening government officials.
  B. Bhopal Disaster
    1. 7,000 killed by a leak of methyl isocyanate gas used in pesticide production from storage tanks at Union Carbide (India).
    2. Union Carbide reached an out-of-court settlement with the Indian court under which it would pay $470 million to victims of the Bhopal disaster. The court did not assign blame for the accident.
  C. Chernobyl
    1. The UN called the nuclear explosion at Chernobyl in the Soviet Union the world's worst human-made disaster. It caused the population of the Republic of Belarus to be exposed to radioactivity 90 times greater than that released at Hiroshima.
    2. A UN report in 1995 claimed that at least 9 million people in Belarus, Ukraine, and Russia were affected.
  D. Alaskan Oil Spill–called America's Chernobyl. It was the worst oil spill in U. S. history. Exxon, owner of the tanker that spilled the oil, spent over $2.5 billion for the cleanup involving 11,000 people, 1,200 vessels, and 80 aircraft.
  E. Eco-terrorism in the Gulf War. Before retreating from Kuwait, the Iraqi army caused an ecological disaster far worse than the Alaskan oil spill. 75 million barrels of oil spilled out over the desert.

F. The biggest ecological disaster since Chernobyl ocurred in January, 30, 2000 when 100,000 cubic meters of water mixed with cyanide spilled from a mine into the Tisa river, a tributary of the Danube. The Serbian environment minister estimated it would take 5 years for life in the Tisa to recover.

G. Relevance for Businesspeople

1. Governments strengthening pollution laws, controls and inspections.

2. Multinationals in hazardous industries may resist taking minority positions if this causes them to lose control on questions of plant design and safety.

Answers to Questions

1. The lack of a seacoast is probably a contributing factor to lack of development. The distance from a seaport increases the cost of transporting exports and imports to the landlocked country. Most of the transit states for developing landlocked nations are poor and do not have adequate port facilities for themselves, let alone for their landlocked neighbors. Usually there are delays in delivering transit traffic to landlocked states because of cumbersome customs procedures, incompetent staff and inadequate communication. These delays increase costs because there are losses, damage, pilferage, higher insurance rates and demurrage charges. Transit traffic may be delayed because of strikes, civil unrest or even war in the transit countries. These difficulties discourage potential exporters thus making it difficult for landlocked nations to increase their export trade.

2. Currently, 20 percent of Canada's petroleum comes from the Athabasca oil sands, but thirteen oil companies have announced investment plans that could increase the amount to 25 percent by the year 2010. It is estimated that 300 billion barrels of petroleum can be recovered economically from these sands, exceeding the reserves of Saudi Arabia, the world's largest producer of conventional crude.

    Oil-bearing shale. The largest source of oil shale is the three-state area of Utah, Colorado, and Wyoming, which has remained undeveloped because less expensive conventional oil is available, there are environmental problems with waste rock disposal, and great quantities of water are needed for processing.

    A new technology which minimizes danger to the environment is being tested in Australia. No chemicals are required, only a small amount of energy is needed, and there is no contaminated waste. The production cost should compete with the US$25/barrel for conventional crude.

3. This is a good question for a group of students to role-play. The production, finance, and marketing functions should be represented. The ramification are extensive, but the committee might wish to discuss the possible loss of Middle East markets because of lower export earnings, new markets in oil-poor developing countries (no foreign exchange would have to be spent on petroleum imports) or the possibility of their own firm being able to compete (because of lower energy costs) in areas from which they had been shut out because of higher costs. If their finished products require hydrocarbons as inputs, this new process might permit the firm to set up in countries, which presently have no crude oil production. Production processes geared to energy saving will need to be changed to take advantage of lower cost energy.

4. a. Except in the tropics, the population density decreases as the elevation increases because dense population requires commerce, manufacturing, and agriculture to support it and all of these depend on good transportation and ease of communication obtainable on plains. Furthermore, agriculture requires large areas of level ground if growers are to use efficient machinery.

b. People were settling in the tropics before air conditioning and they could find a pleasant climate only at high altitudes.

5. False. New discoveries may create markets in countries where none existed previously or may increase dramatically a nation's purchasing power. all of the OPEC countries are much more important markets now than they once were. North Sea oil has improved measurably the economic conditions in Norway and Great Britain. Mineral finds in Australia in the 1960s accounted for a large influx of foreign investment in both the extractive and supporting industries. Keeping current on this subject may enable them to detect instances where a nation may lose purchasing power as would happen if less expensive sources found (an inexpensive method processing oil-bearing shale) or if more economical substitutes were discovered.

6. Mountains, deserts and tropical rain forests are generally cultural barriers. People on one side of the barrier frequently differ in language, economy, religion and race from those on the other side. The east-west highland system of Europe separates Mediterranean culture from that of northern Europe. The cordilleras of the Andes form culture pockets in Colombia, and the Pyrenees permit the Basques to maintain their old cultural differences in the northwest corner of Spain and the southwest part of France. In Africa, the Sahara is a barrier between the Mediterranean and African cultures. When these differences in topography and landforms surround a nation as in the case of Egypt, they isolate its culture from others, and if there is an appreciable variation within the country as in Colombia, and Spain, smaller pockets of culture tend to exist.

7. Bodies of water attract people for various reasons. Growers in arid regions live near water which they use for irrigation. Businesspeople live in seaports that are centers of commerce receiving goods for export and import. Rivers are arteries of low-cost transportation that receive minerals, manufactured goods and agricultural products to be carried to markets. These require businesses and people to run them.

8. Governments have already begun to strengthen their pollution laws, controls and inspection. Multinational firms are examining their foreign investments in hazardous industries to see if the risk is worth taking. Joint ventures in which the multinational has a minority interest may be shunned because it wants to control over production processes, machinery and plant safety which generally require majority ownership.

9. Numerous kinds of products are sensitive to climatic differences. Internal combustion engines require extra cooling capacity and special lubrication to be able to withstand the high tropical temperatures. Electrical motors may need extra insulation to resist the humidity in highly humid places. Special, more expensive packing and packaging may be required for humidity-sensitive products sold in the tropics. Where winters are severe of there is a heavy rainy season, a firm may have to warehouse a large inventory to compensate for delays in delivery from the factory.

10. Because Australia's coastline is humid and fertile, whereas the huge center of the country is mainly a desert, 85% of the total population is urban. The long distances between the cities result in transportation costs amounting to as much as 30% of the product cost, compared with the usual 10% in the United States and Europe.

Answers to Internet Problems

1. Students can use a search engine to find the URL for the Department of Energy's International Energy outlook 2001. The URL is ftp://ftp.eia.doe.gov/pub/pdf/ international/0484(2001).pdf. At the time of working this problem, the DOE's WWW site was not functioning.

2. a. Mexico: 3.2% (page 175)

   b. natural gas: 3.2% (page 177)

   c. India: 5.4% (page 179)

   d. China: 4.3% (page 181)

   e. Industrialized: -0.3%; Developing: + 4.9% (page 182)

   f. China: 11.8% (page 182)

   g. S. Korea: 7.9% (page 183)

   h. China: 4.7% (page 191)

   i. This information helps to distinguish markets for manufacturers of equipment for power plants and distribution systems. Special attention should be paid to production of gas-fired equipment and relatively less to coal in industrialized countries (pages 176-177). Note the shrinkage of the nuclear market in the industrialized countries, although there is strong growth projected for the developing countries.

Discussion of Minicase 8.1: Bhopal Fallout

I. What to Do Now

    A. VP Manufacturing

       1. We are bringing production managers to the home plant to discuss their training of production personnel, their plant safety inspection procedures and their emergency plans. They have been requested to bring all their documentation with them. After a seminar for the group, each manager will review his written procedures with home office safety personnel.

       2. An inspection team consisting of a process engineer, safety engineer and a maintenance specialist will visit every one of our plants overseas. We shall require annual inspections.

    B. VP Legal

       1. Where we have joint ventures overseas, we shall work with our local partners to change our contracts so that we either have control of equipment design, training and maintenance procedures or a new contract will be drawn up that clearly limits our responsibility. If we cannot come to a satisfactory arrangement in situations where the local governments has insisted that we produce the ingredients locally, we shall request the government to rescind that requirement. Should it not agree, it will be the Legal Department's recommendation that the company withdraw from the joint venture.

       2. We shall work jointly with the VP for Health, Safety, and Environment to persuade local governments to clear the area around the local plant of all residences and to draw up plans for emergency evacuation.

    C. VP Health, Safety and Environment

       1. Besides working with the Legal Department, we shall personally check jointly with the Production people each plant's provisions for training workers, issuing safety equipment to workers, providing maintenance and periodic safety inspections during which the backup systems are tried out.

2. We shall work with each plant to see that each has an emergency committee and emergency plans. My staff will revise each plant's emergency plan annually. If you agree, I shall require any plant with an emergency involving possible loss of life due to toxic materials to call me immediately.

3. We shall maintain a list of medical experts on whom we can call for assistance in case of an emergency. We also shall see that the company's medical staff are trained to handle injuries from contact with all of the dangerous chemicals with which our plants work.

4. We shall provide the general manager and the head of the plant security at every domestic and overseas plant with the home telephone numbers of all members of this permanent committee with orders to call me first in case an emergency occurs outside of our normal working hours. If I can't be reached, the caller is to keep calling other members until he reaches one of us.

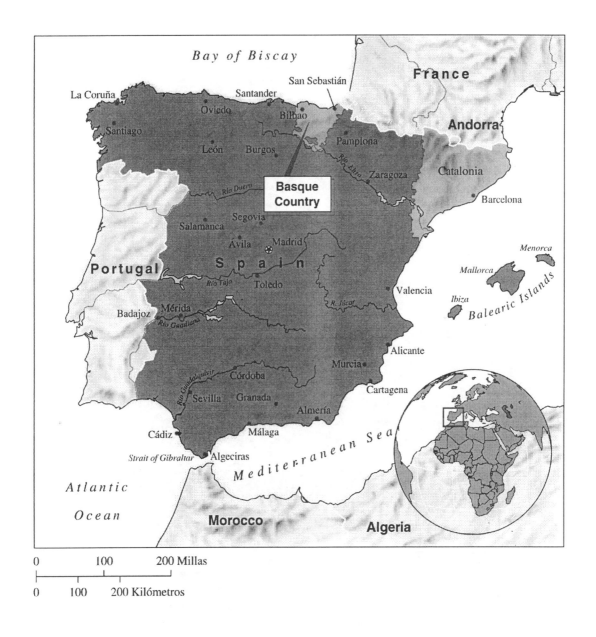

TM 8.2
Figure 8.2   The Cantons and Major Language Areas of Switzerland

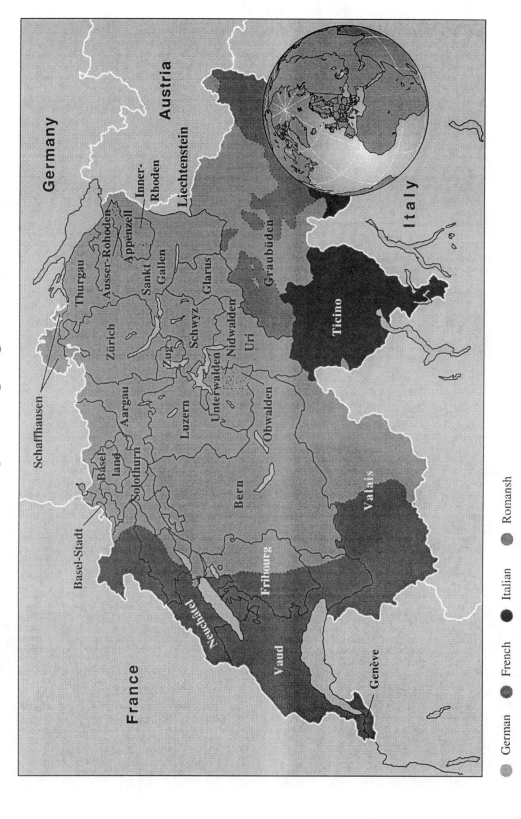

● German   ● French   ● Italian   ● Romansh

McGraw-Hill/Irwin

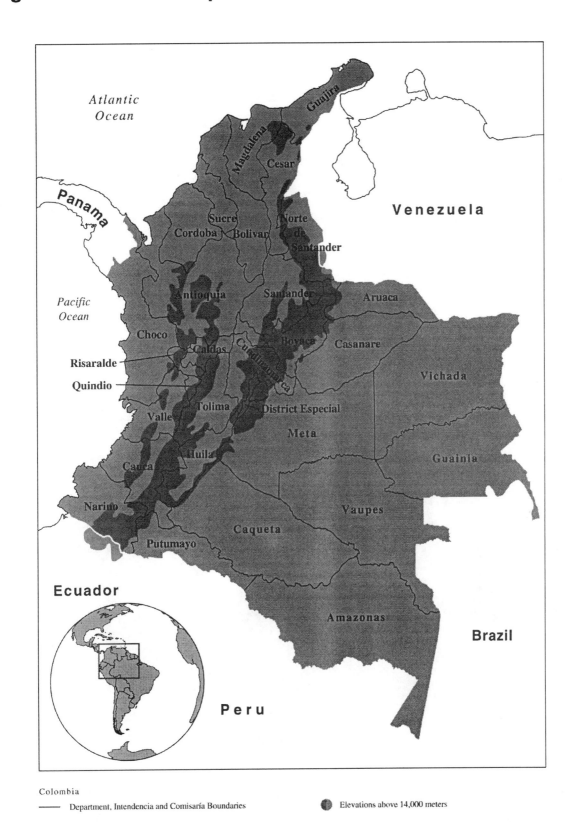

Colombia

——— Department, Intendencia and Comisaría Boundaries   ● Elevations above 14,000 meters

TM 8.4
Figure 8.4   **Map of Australia**

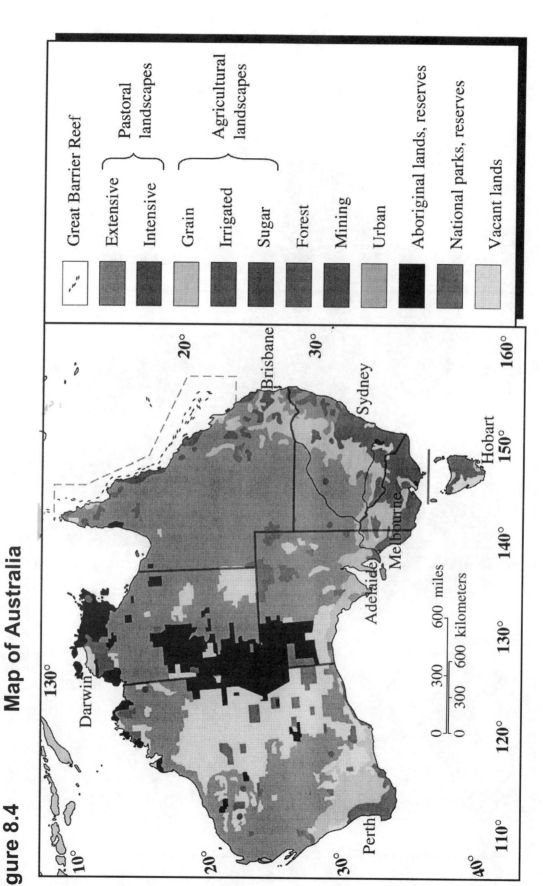

McGraw-Hill/Irwin

European Waterway System

McGraw-Hill/Irwin

Paraná -Paraguay Rivers Trade Corridor

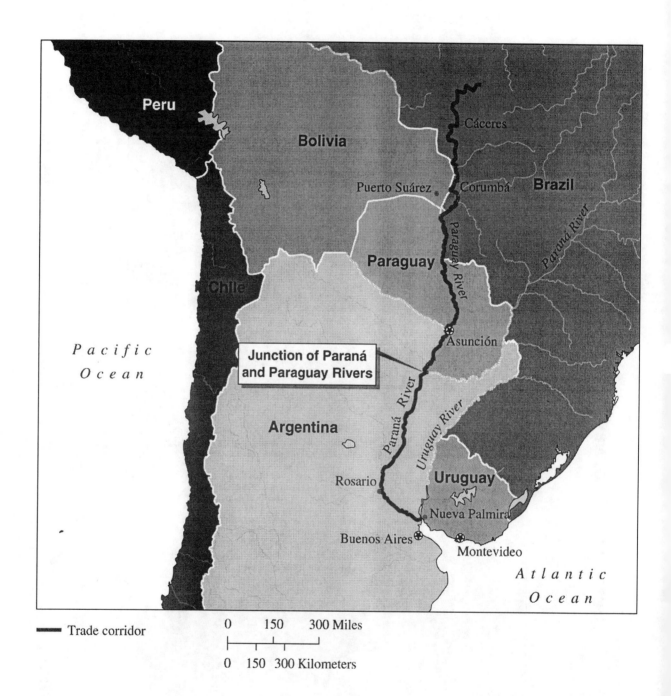

Trade corridor

0   150   300 Miles

0   150   300 Kilometers

TM 8.7
Figure 8.7

Bolivia's Export Corridor

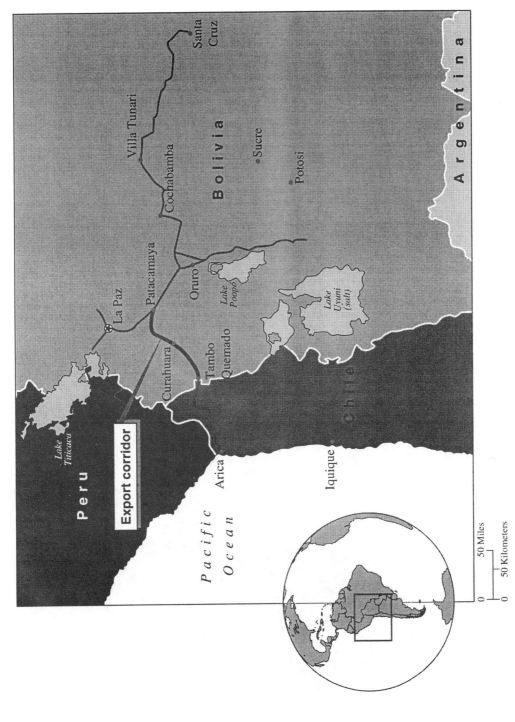

McGraw-Hill/Irwin

U.S. and World Energy Supplies by Source

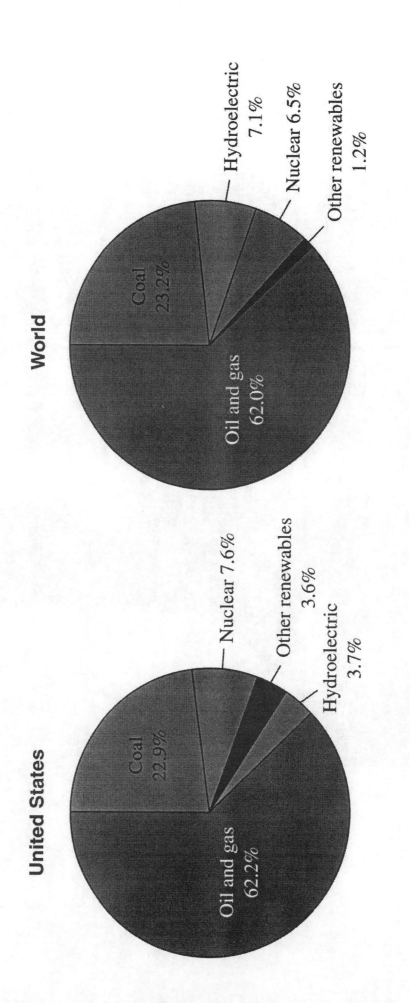

United States

Nuclear 7.6%

Other renewables
3.6%

Hydroelectric
3.7%

Coal
22.9%

Oil and gas
62.2%

World

Hydroelectric
7.1%

Nuclear 6.5%

Other renewables
1.2%

Coal
23.2%

Oil and gas
62.0%

McGraw-Hill/Irwin

CHAPTER 9
SOCIOCULTURAL FORCES

Learning Objectives

1. Make students aware of the cultural differences among the general, business and corporate cultures.

2. Show students that these differences exert an influence on all of the functions in the firm.

3. Present the major cultural components which can serve as a guide when analyzing a problem from the sociocultural viewpoint.

4. Illustrate some of the cultural differences with practical examples.

5. Explain the pervasiveness of the Information Technology Era.

Overview

Culture, the sum total of beliefs, rules, techniques, institutions and artifacts that characterize human populations, is learned and shared. Its various aspects are interrelated and it defines the boundaries of different groups. The study of culture is essential to international business executives who must operate in cultures different from their own.

Opinions vary as to the components of culture. In the text, the following are included: (1) aesthetics, (2) attitudes and beliefs. (3) religion, (4) material culture, (5) education, (6) language, (7) societal organization, (8) legal characteristics, and (9) political structures.

Suggestions and Comments

1. A number of professors tell us they use the quiz in Minicase 9-1 as an icebreaker to start the discussion of this chapter.

2. It is not easy to cover such a vast subject as this in the short time available. Our aim is to make the class realize that there are cultural differences and that international business executives must be on the lookout for them. They must have their radar working at all times. We emphasize that business plans must be examined from a cultural point of view.

3. We believe that, as a minimum, the nine elements should be mentioned with an example of a difference between "their and our" cultures given for each one. We have attempted to give examples of how the various functional areas are affected so that the students will understand that it is not only the marketers who must be concerned.

Student Involvement Exercises

1. Have the students prepare a cultural analysis for a product to be introduced in a specific country. This can be part of the continuing exercise which was begun in Chapter 6 or 7.

2. Have the students discuss how the different religions might affect the work of (1) the marketing manager, (2) the production manager, and (3) the human resource manager of foreign subsidiaries in a Latin American country, a Mideast country, and a European country. If a person were to be transferred from one subsidiary to another, what changes would need to be made in the way that person handled the work? This is a very real problem for people who are transferred every few years to a different culture.

3. Discuss the constraints that a nation's low level of education puts on marketing and human resource managers in foreign subsidiaries.

4. Ask the students what kinds of preparation they would want to have with respect to a nation's culture if they were told that in six months they would be transferred overseas.

5. Ask students from other countries if they suffered cultural shock when they first arrived in your state. The discussion is a good way to open the eyes of local students.

Guest Lecturers

1. Someone from the anthropology department, especially if he or she has traveled or lived in other countries, can present some interesting aspects of cultural differences.

2. A marketer or personnel manager with overseas experience may be willing to address the class. They should be able to recount some interesting experiences in coping with the local culture.

3. A retired Department of State employee who worked overseas is a possibility.

4. A student who served in the Peace Corps might also have interesting observations.

Lecture Outline

I.   Opening Section

    The Opening Section presents six useful rules for Americans going to other countries to sell and in doing so, points out some cultural differences.

II.   What Is Culture?

    A. Culture is the sum total of beliefs, rules, techniques, institutions, and artifacts that characterize human populations.

    B. Culture is learned and shared, its various aspects are interrelated and it defines the boundaries of different groups.

    C. Anthropologists often combine the words **social** and **cultural** into one word, **sociocultural**. This is the term we use because the variables in which businesspeople are interested are both social and cultural.

III.   Significance of Culture for International Business

    A. The first step in learning to live with other cultures is to realize that there are cultures different from our own. Then we must go on to learn the characteristics of these cultures so that we may adapt to them.

B. Hall, a noted anthropologist, says there are only two ways to do this: (1) spend a lifetime in a country or (2) undergo an extensive training program that covers the main characteristics of a culture, including the language.

C. Culture impacts all business functions. Note the problems of Procter and Gamble in Japan and Walt Disney in Paris and how they were able to reduce them after acquiring knowledge of the local culture and applying it to their situations.

IV. Sociocultural Components

A. The concept of culture is so broad that ethnologists break subject matter down into topics to facilitate study.

B. The components of culture listed in this text are: (1) aesthetics, (2) attitudes and beliefs, (3) religion, (4) material culture, (5) education, (6) language, (7) societal organization, (8) legal characteristics, and (9) political structures. Items 8 and 9 will be discussed in later chapters.

1. Aesthetics pertains to a culture's sense of beauty and good taste and is expressed in the arts, drama, music, folklore and dances. You may want to tell your students that an extensive list of colors and their meanings for a number of regions is shown at webofculture.com/worldsmart/design_colors.html.

2. Attitudes and Beliefs

   a. Every culture has a set of attitudes and beliefs which influence human behavior and bring order to a society.

   b. The more one can learn about them, the easier it is to understand why people behave as they do.

   c. Attitudes which are of special importance to the international executive are attitudes towards time, achievement, work and change.

      (1) Attitude towards time

         (a) Americans, can be prompt-hora Brasileira

         (b) Mañana

         (c) Directness and drive–American trait considered to be brash and rude by many foreigners.

         (d) Deadlines–American emphasis often against them when negotiating in other countries.

      (2) Attitudes toward achievement and work. "Germans put leisure first and work second" Mexicans say, "You Americans live to work; we work to live." Prestigious jobs-disdain for physical labor in many countries results in an overabundance of attorneys and stockbrokers and a lack of welders and toolmakers. In Japan there is a dislike of "3D" work-dirty, dangerous and difficult.

      (3) Attitude towards change

         (a) The new idea–relate it to traditional one for easier acceptance.

         (b) Economic motivation–economic motives are a strong influence for accepting change.

3. Religion
Religion is responsible for many of the attitudes and beliefs affecting human behavior. See Figure 9.1, page 313 for a world map showing the major religions of the world.

a. Protestant ethic–work is a moral virtue; called Confucian work ethic in Asian countries or Shinto work ethic in Japan.

b. Asian Religions–In Asia, the ideas of reality are different, especially in India. There is a notion that this world is an illusion because nothing is permanent. All living things are in a constant process of birth, death and reincarnation. The goal of salvation is to escape from this cycle and move into a state of eternal bliss–nirvana. Of the seven best-known religions originating in Asia, four came from India (Hinduism, Buddhism, Jainism, and Sikhism), two from China (Confucianism and Taoism) and one from Japan (Shinto).

   (1) Hinduism–A conglomeration of religions with no single founder or central authority.

      (a) Caste system–entire society divided into four castes and the dalits. An individual's position in the caste system is inherited.

      (b) Managers must be cautious when placing a member of a lower caste in charge of people from a higher caste.

   (2) Buddhism–Founder, Guatama, after six years of experimenting with yoga, suddenly understood how to break the laws of karma and the endless cycle of rebirth. Guatama emerged as the Buddha (the Enlightened One). Buddhists and Hindus teach that if the followers have no desires, they will not suffer. Having no desires adversely affects motives for achievement.

   (3) Jainism–founded by a contemporary of Buddha. The Jain doctrine teaches that there is no creator, no god, nor an absolute principle.

   (4) Sikhism–not only a religion, but also an Indian ethnic group, a military brotherhood and a political movement. Most Sikhs live in the Punjab region.

   (5) Confucianism–less a religion and more philosophy of conduct embodying Chinese norms of social and personal morality. PRONUNCIATION NOTE; "jen" (the principle of unselfish love for others) is pronounced like "run," that is, the "j" is actually an "r."

   (6) Taoism–A mystical philosophy possibly founded by a contemporary of Confucius. Taoism means "the way." PRONUNCIATION NOTE; pronounced "dowism" as in "Dow Jones." The primary text of Taoism, the *Tao Te Ching*, is actually pronounced *Daodejing*.

   (7) Feng Shui–(literally, "wind and water") has roots in Taoism and nature worship. Based on a simple concept: If buildings, furniture, roads and other manmade objects are placed in harmony with nature, they can bring good fortune. If not, they will cause a disaster. Note that feng shui now is fashionable in the West, and there is a Feng Shui Institute in California. Sometimes known as neomancy.

   (8) Shintoism–indigenous religion of Japan, perhaps 2,500 years old. There is no founder or sacred text. Natural objects or elements which inspire a sense of awe are worshipped at the more than 110,000 temples and shrines in Japan. One element of Shintoism was the belief that the Emperor held divine status.

c. Islam

   (1) Islam means to submit in Arabic and Muslim means "submitting." The Koran, a collection of Allah's (God's) revelations to Muhammad, the founder, is accepted as God's eternal word.

      (2) In Muslim nations there is no separation of church and state.

      (3) The basic spiritual duties for all Muslims consist of the five pillars of faith.

      (4) Split between Sunnis and Shiites. Much of what occurs in the Mideast is the result of this split. Most Muslim countries are Sunni-governed, but many have substantial Shia populations. The great majority of Muslims—perhaps 90%—are Sunni.

  d. Animism–spirit worship including magic and witchcraft.

  e. Importance of religion to management–religious holidays and rituals can affect employee performance and work scheduling. When members of different religious groups work together, there may be strife, division and instability within the work force. Table 9.1 lists the religious populations of the world.

4. Material Culture
Material culture refers to man-made objects. Its study is concerned with how man makes things (technology) and who makes what and why (economics).

  a. The technology of a society is the mix of the usable knowledge that the society applies and directs toward the attainment of cultural and economic objectives.

  b. Technological superiority is especially important to international firms. It enables firms to be competitive or attain leadership in world markets.

  c. Technology's cultural aspects are important to international managers because new methods and products require people to change their beliefs and ways.

  d. Generally, the greater the difference between the old and the new method or product, the more difficult it is for the firm to institute change.

  e. Technological dualism–in same country, one sector may be technologically advanced while the production techniques of another sector may be old and labor intensive.

  f. Appropriate technology–can be labor intensive, intermediate or capital intensive.

  g. Boomerang effect–Japan becoming less willing to sell its technology to Korea because of fear that Korea will become a tougher competitor tomorrow. Fear of the boomerang effect has caused some American firms to restrict the sales of their technology to the Japanese.
Government controls–Worldwide trend of developing country governments to limit after-sale control of technology by the provider.

5. Education

  a. Education yardsticks–literacy rate, amount spent on education, enrollments, and kinds of schools. Such data may underestimate the size of the vocationally trained group in developing nations because many learn their trade in informal apprenticeships.

  b. Educational mix–study of medicine, law and humanities emphasized in developing nations.

  c. Brain drain–the rising unemployment among the highly educated in developing countries had led to a brain drain, the emigration of highly educated professionals to another country. An UNCTAD study estimates that 500,000 professionals have left Third World countries since World War II. [See Table 9.1, p. 323, for the number of scientists and engineers admitted on permanent visas between 1988 and 1998. Figure 9.4, p. 324, shows the regions from which they came.

d. Reverse brain drain–in some developing countries from which scientists have emigrated to industrialized nations, organizations and governments have "reverse brain drain" programs to lure their citizens back to their homelands.

e. Adult literacy–many governments giving priority to primary education to achieve universal literacy.

f. Women's education–Nearly every government has a goal of providing free and compulsory education for both genders. Figure 9.5, p. 325, shows the improvement from 1960 enrollment to the estimated enrollment estimated for the year 2025. These statistics are significant to businesspeople. Educated women have fewer, healthier, and better-educated children. They also achieve higher labor force participation and higher earnings. This leads to an increased role for women in family decision making.

6. Language

   a. Spoken language–key to culture.

      (1) Languages delineate cultures–four languages, four cultures. It does not follow from this generalization that cultures are the same wherever the same language is spoken. Chile and Mexico are not culturally similar.

      (2) Foreign language–where many spoken languages exist in a nation, often a foreign language is the lingua franca or "link" language.

      (3) English, the link language of business–use of English as the business lingua franca is spreading in Europe.
          The European Commission reported in 1996 that over half of EU adults could speak English and one-third speak it as a second language. The Commission also stated that 83 percent of EU secondary students are learning English compared to 32 percent learning French and 16 percent learning German. A number of international firms have adopted English as their house language.

      (4) Must speak the local language–even though many businesspeople speak English, when they buy, they insist on speaking their own language. The seller who speaks it has a competitive edge.
          Figure 9.7, p. 329, shows a map of major languages of the world.

   b. Translation

      (1) Use two translations. Translation by a bilingual native which is then translated back by a bilingual native in the other language. Result is compared with the original.

      (2) Technical words–international businesspeople should know that some governments have programs to keep their languages pure and free from foreign words. Although the French government and other defenders of the French language are fighting to maintain a French presence on the Internet, they are losing. An estimated 85 percent of the world's Internet sites are in English and 80 percent of the information is stored in English. Experts say that people will have two languages: one for conversation with friends and one for communicating with the formal world.

      (3) No unpleasantness–reluctance in many areas to say anything disagreeable.

   c. Unspoken language

     (1) Gestures–meanings for same gesture differ among countries. Foreigner should leave gestures at home.

     (2) Closed doors

     (3) Office size–never gauge people's importance by the size and location of their offices.

     (4) Conversational distance–Anthropologists say that conversational distances are smaller in Middle East and Latin America than in the U.S.

   d. The language of gift giving

     (1) Acceptable gifts–chocolates, red roses, Scotch whiskey

     (2) Bribes–pervasive worldwide. See the Bribe Payers Index, p. 334.

     (3) Questionable payments–expediting payments or bribes?
A non-governmental agency, Transparency International, founded in 1993, surveys businesspeople and political analysts and then publishes a Corruption Perception Index. Fourteenth-ranked U.S.' score has dropped from 8.41 for the period 1980-1992 to 7.8 in 2000. See Figure 9.8, p. 335 for 2000 scores and rankings.

7. Societal Organization
Every society has a structure or organization which is the patterned arrangement or relationships defining and regulating the manner by which its members interface with each other. They are based on kinship or are formed on the basis of free association of individuals.

   a. Kinship

     (1) Extended family includes blood relatives and relatives by marriage.

     (2) Member's responsibility to extended family

     (3) Pedro Diaz Marin–use of maternal and paternal surnames

   b. Associations
May be formed by age, sex or common interest.

     (1) Age–in many countries, children exert less influence in product choice than in the United States. Older people continue to live in extended families and have a strong voice in family affairs.

     (2) Gender–generally, the less developed the country, the less equal are the genders with respect to job opportunities and education. This is changing, however.

     (3) Common interest–management must identify common interest groups.

   c. Class Mobility
Ease of moving from one social class to another lies on a continuum from rigid caste system in India to relatively flexible social structure in the United States. Developing countries tend to be less flexible. Increased industrialization generally weakens barriers to mobility.

V.   Entrepreneurial Spirit

The desire to be an entrepreneur may be more widely shared than we commonly assume. A 23-country survey showed that over one-quarter to three-quarters of the population in these countries would like to own their own business. Results are shown in Figure 9.9. page 337. Interestingly, nearly 80% of the sample in Poland wanted to own their own business, while in Russia the percentage was much lower.

VI.   Understanding National Cultures

To help IBM managers understand the many national cultures in which the firm operates, Geert Hofstede, a Danish psychologist, interviewed thousands of employees in 67 countries. He found differences in their answers to 32 statements could be based on four value dimensions: (1) individualism vs. collectivism, (2) large vs. small power distance, (3) strong vs. weak uncertainty avoidance, and (4) masculinity vs. femininity. Table 9.3, p. 338 presents scores for Hofstede's value dimensions.

Plots of Dimensions and Management Implications

Figure 9.10, page 339, plots the scores for selected Anglo and Latin American nations on the power distance and uncertainty avoidance dimensions. The lines of communication in organizations in these countries are vertical and employees know who reports to whom. The Anglo nations in the fourth quadrant scored low on both dimensions. Organizations in these countries are characterized by less formal control and fewer layers of management.

The scores for individualism and power distance are plotted in Figure 9.11, page 339. The Latin countries (first quadrant) scored relatively high on power distance and low on individualism. Employees tend to expect their organizations to look after them and defend their interests. They expect close supervision and managers who act paternally. People in Anglo countries (third quadrant), who scored low on power distance and high on individualism, prefer to do things for themselves and do not expect organizations to look after them. Hofstede's four dimensions have given managers a basis for understanding how cultural differences affect organizations and management methods.

Answers to Questions

1. A national culture has two components-(1) surface culture (fads, styles, food, etc.) and (2) deep culture (attitudes, beliefs, and values). Less than 15% of a region's culture is visible so international businesspeople, knowing there are two components, will make an effort to look below the surface and not accept at face value what they first see.

2. The Japanese operator of Disneyland made popular the idea that family outings could be fun. This used to be seen by fathers as a duty. Disney executives believed they could change the French attitude of not wanting to take their children from school during the school year as Americans do or to take more short breaks during the year instead of taking one vacation during August. The executives also did not build large restaurants because they were told that Europeans didn't eat breakfast. When the park opened, everyone wanted breakfast, and Disneyland had no place to feed them.

3. Symbols and colors are especially important to members of a culture. Marketers must verify that colors they intend to use have no special, unfavorable meaning before using them for products, packaging, or advertisements. they must check symbols for unfavorable connotations. There also may be local preferences for form that could affect the design of the product or package. Even the need for different kinds of music for commercials must be considered.

4. Managers can use the demonstration effect to motivate employees to work harder or reduce absenteeism by offering awards of products as well as money. A vacation in an expensive resort

for an employee who would not normally go there might be a great motivator for the employee and spouse. When announcing such a contest at a meeting of employees, the employer can use a film of the resort to create interest through the demonstration effect. Advertisers commonly use it in ads to show consumers how they could have greater prestige or pleasure by utilizing their goods or services.

5. New products do not have the appeal that they have in the United States in other markets where people are more reluctant to change. Where this is true, marketers must be careful to show that any new product is an evolutionary, not revolutionary change; in other words, they need to relate it to what the consumers have been using. The same is true for production mangers or office managers when they install new processes.

    Not only are people reluctant to change because they have to learn something new, but often they don't want to change because it involves discarding that is still useful. It is extremely difficult to persuade workers to use new production machinery, for example, if the older, slower, machinery is still working as it always has. Houses where Americans lived were always part of the daily scavenger hunts of Brazilians who made a living cleaning and repairing American discards that for them had plenty of life left.

6. Religion is responsible for many of the beliefs and attitudes affecting human behavior. Knowing the basic tenets of the more popular religions will help to explain why attitudes vary so widely from country to country.

7. Buddhists teach that if their followers have no desires, they will not suffer. However, if they don't desire anything, marketers have no sales arguments to use with them. Also, without desires, well-known motivators such as production bonuses and offers of overtime to earn more money won't make much of an impact on workers who practice Buddhism.

8. Technological superiority enables a firm to compete or even attain leadership in world markets. It can be sold or used to obtain better conditions for a foreign investment when the host government wants the technology that only a particular firm has (case of IBM in Mexico). It also enables a firm with just a minority position in a joint venture to control it and keep it as a captive customer for inputs that the home plant produces.

9. The extended family can be a desirable source of employees or it can be undesirable if a supervisor loads up his department with distant cousins. Often they feel they owe their loyalty to him rather than to the firm. It is desirable if there is a need for the kind of workers that presently are working out well at the firm, although in some areas, managers need to be careful about too many from one location. If the workers are from certain racial minorities, this can cause problems in some countries. Managers have to be on the alert to see that employees in the purchasing department are not favoring members of their extended families for the wrong reasons. Also, loyalty to the extended family may be the cause for high absenteeism during harvest time.

10. Adams has worked for years using participative management in the United States, which scores low on both power distance and uncertainty avoidance. In contrast, Latin American countries score relatively high on both dimensions. This means that the production superintendent comes from an organization characterized by less formal control, fewer layers of management, and more informal communication among members. The workers, however, expect close supervision and managers who act paternally. The lines of communication are vertical. Adams will likely find it difficult to get workers to talk seriously directly with him: they are used to going through their foreman. Getting feedback or suggestions on how to improve processes and procedures will be more difficult also, as Adams is the boss and he should know more than the workers and thus shouldn't ask them how to do things (their opinion of participative management).

Our experience indicates that a small group of employees can be educated to speak up during discussions, but it takes time. Adams is going to have to make some changes in his management style or at least postpone aspects of it for a while.

Answers to Internet Problems

1. The answers to these questions come from an extensive source on body language and gestures, webofculture.com/worldsmart/gestures.htm.

    a. In Bulgaria, to signal NO, Bulgarians nod their heads up and down. To say YES, they shake their heads back and forth.

    b. A Spaniard stretches his arms out, with palm down, and makes a scratching motion toward his body with the fingers.

    c. Make a motion with both hands as if you were signing your name on a piece of paper.

    d. It may signify that the meeting is finished.

    e. The Brazilian has enjoyed the meal very much. A less enthusiastic gesture is to grab the right earlobe with the right hand.

    f. Related sites include The Nonverbal Dictionary (members.aol.com/nonverbal2/diction1.htm) and the Brazilian Body Language page (www.maria-brazil.org/gestures.htm).

2. The source is www.usdoj.gov/criminal/fraud/fcpa.

    a. The FCPA makes it unlawful to bribe foreign government officials to obtain or retain business. However, the 1998 amendment provides an explicit exception to the bribery prohibition when the payments are "reasonable and bona fie expenditures" for "promotion, demonstration, or explanation of products or services or the execution or performance of a contract with a foreign government or agency thereof."

    b. The statute lists the following examples of :routine government action" (1) obtaining permits, licenses or other government documents, (2) processing governmental papers, such as visas, and work orders, (3) police protection, (4) mail pickup and delivery, (5) providing phone service, power and water supply, (6) loading and unloading cargo, (7) protecting perishable products, and (8) scheduling inspections associated with contract performance or transit of goods across the country.

    c. You may want to note to students that the FCPA was amended in 1988 and again in 1998. The major change in 1998 was a reduction in some penalties for violation of the statute.

TM 9.1
Figure 9.1 **Major Religions of the World**

Christian
- Roman
- Eastern
- Protestant
- Sects, Various
- → Extension Of
  Christian Influence

Hindu
- Also Christian, Sikh,
  Buddhist, Etc.

Judaic
- And Widely Scattered
  Communities

Local
- Animist, Etc.

Japanese
- Buddhist And Shintoist

Chinese
- Buddhist-Taoist-Confucian

Muslim
- Sunni
- Shia

Buddhist
- Lamaist
- Southern
- Uninhabited

Estimated Religious Population of the World

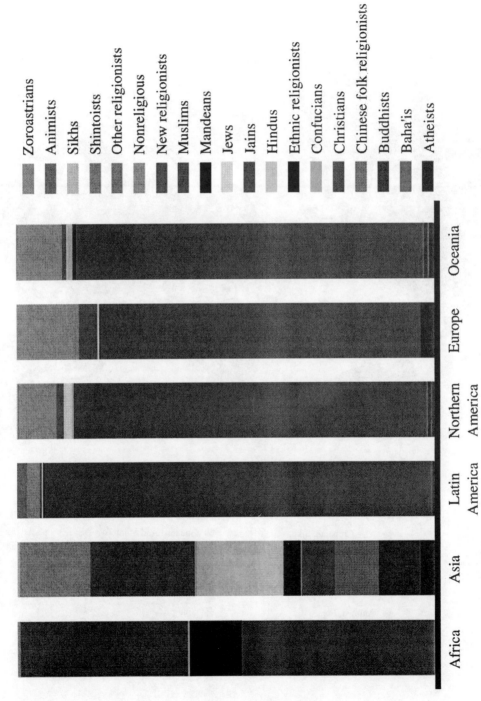

Zoroastrians
Animists
Sikhs
Shintoists
Other religionists
Nonreligious
New religionists
Muslims
Mandeans
Jews
Jains
Hindus
Ethnic religionists
Confucians
Christians
Chinese folk religionists
Buddhists
Baha'is
Atheists

Africa   Asia   Latin America   Northern America   Europe   Oceania

Area

Figure 9.3

Percentage of Adults Age 20 to 24 in Post-High School Education

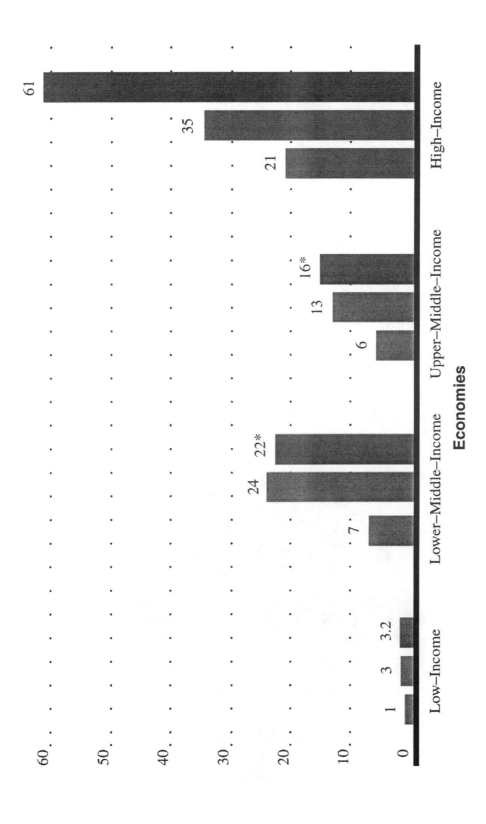

McGraw-Hill/Irwin

Table 9.1　　　　　**INS Permanent Visas Issued, by S&E Occupation (Thousands)**

INS Permanent Visas Issued, by S&E Occupation (Thousands)

Year	Total, All Immigrant S&E	Engineers	Natural Scientists	Mathematical Scientists and Computer Specialists	Social Scientists
1988	11.0	8.1	1.2	1.2	0.5
1989	11.8	8.7	1.2	1.5	0.4
1990	12.6	9.3	1.2	1 .6	0.5
1991	14.1	10.5	1.3	1.7	0.6
1992	22.9	15.6	2.8	3.4	1.1
1993	23.6	14.5	3.9	4.2	1.0
1994	17.2	10.7	3.1	2.8	0.7
1995	14.1	9.0	2.4	2 .1	0.6
1996	19.4	11.6	3.7	3.3	0.8
1997	17.1	10.3	3.5	2.6	0.7
1998	13.5	7.9	2.5	2 .5	0.6

Source: Appendix Table 3-24, *Science & Engineering Indicators—2000*, www.nsf.gov/sbe/srs/seind00/frames.htm.

Figure 9.4　　　　　**Place of Birth of Foreign-Born Science and Engineering Degree Holders, 1997**

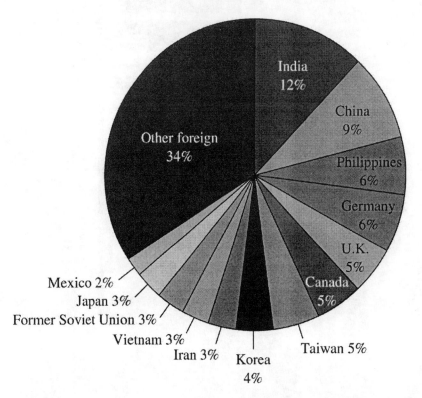

Figure 9.5

Gross Enrollment Ratios for Primary Education by Sex (percent)

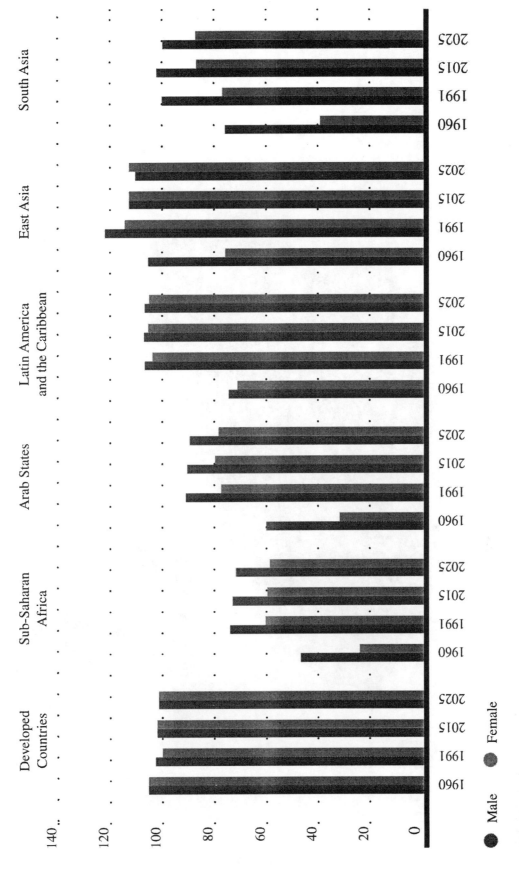

McGraw-Hill/Irwin

TM 9.6

Figure 9.6 How Language Divides Belgium

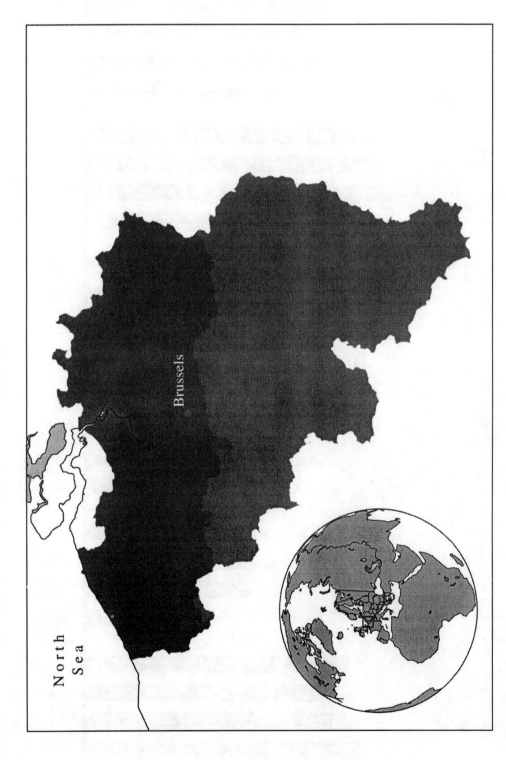

North Sea

Brussels

● Flemish-Speaking ● French-Speaking

McGraw-Hill/Irwin

TM 9.7

Figure 9.7   Major Languages of the World

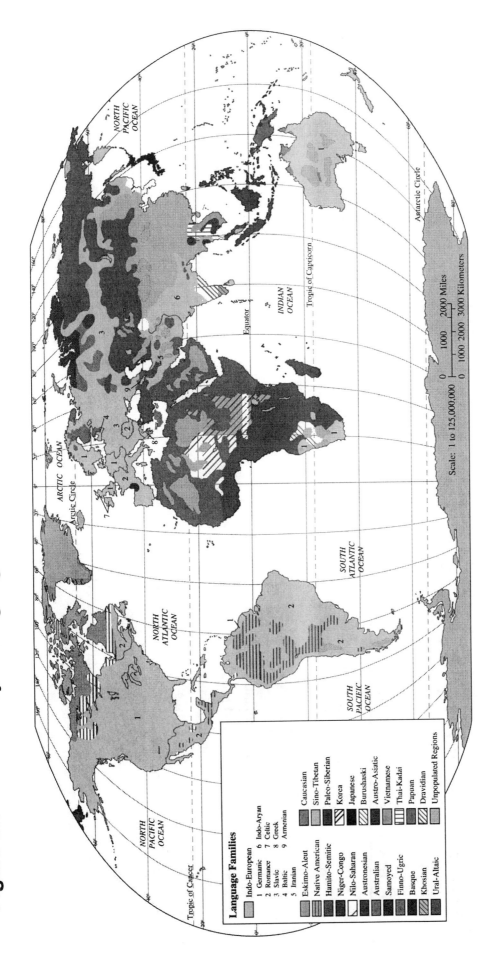

Language Families

Indo-European	6 Indo-Aryan
1 Germanic	7 Celtic
2 Romance	8 Greek
3 Slavic	9 Armenian
4 Baltic	
5 Iranian	

Caucasian
Sino-Tibetan
Paleo-Siberian
Korea
Japanese
Burushaski
Austro-Asiatic
Vietnamese
Thai-Kadai
Papuan
Dravidian
Unpopulated Regions

Eskimo-Aleut
Native American
Hamito-Semitic
Niger-Congo
Nilo-Saharan
Austronesian
Australian
Samoyed
Finno-Ugric
Basque
Khoisan
Ural-Altaic

Scale: 1 to 125,000,000

McGraw-Hill/Irwin

1999 Bribe Payers Index

Rank	Country	Score	Rank	Country	Score
1	Sweden	8.3	11	Singapore	5.7
2	Australia	8.1	12	Spain	5.3
2	Canada	8.1	13	France	5.2
4	Austria	7.8	14	Japan	5.1
5	Switzerland	7.7	15	Malaysia	3.9
6	Netherlands	7.4	16	Italy	3.7
7	United Kingdom	7.2	17	Taiwan	3.5
8	Belgium	6.8	18	South Korea	3.4
9	Germany	6.2	19	China	3.1
9	United States	6.2			

Source: From Transparency International (TI), *B & M 2000–2001 Update*, p. 27. Copyright Transparency International. Reprinted with permission.

McGraw-Hill/Irwin

TM 9.9
Figure 9.8   2000 Corruption Perception Index Scores and Ranking

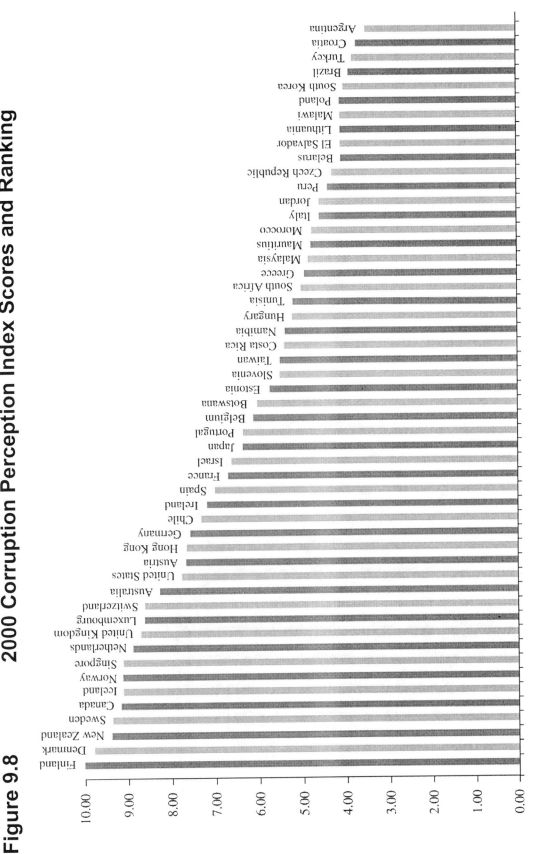

Source: "TI Press Release," http://www.gwdg/de/~uwvw/2000Data.html (November 14, 2000)

© The McGraw-Hill Companies, Inc., 2002 All Rights Reserved.

McGraw-Hill/Irwin

TM 9.10
Figure 9.9

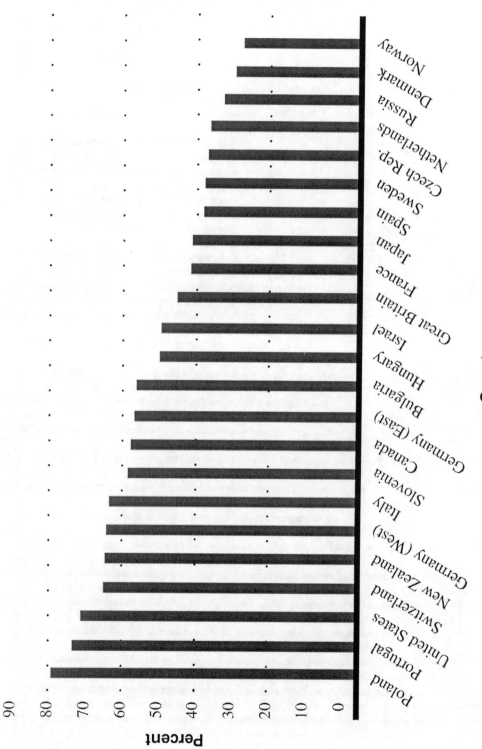

Percent Preferring to be Self-Employed

Source: David Blanchflower and Andrew Oswald, "Countries with the Spirit of Enterprise," *The Financial Times*, February 17, 2000, p. 27.

McGraw-Hill/Irwin

TM 9.11

Figure 9.10   **Plot of selected nations on power distance and uncertainty avoidance**

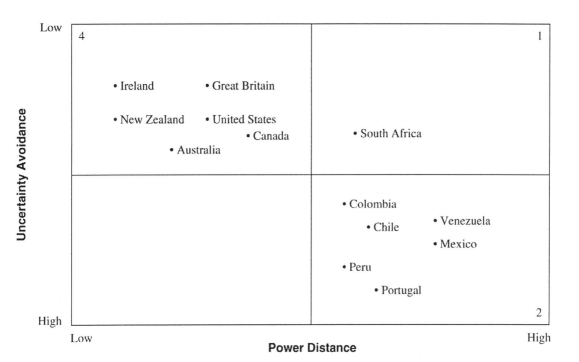

Plot of selected nations on individualism and power distance

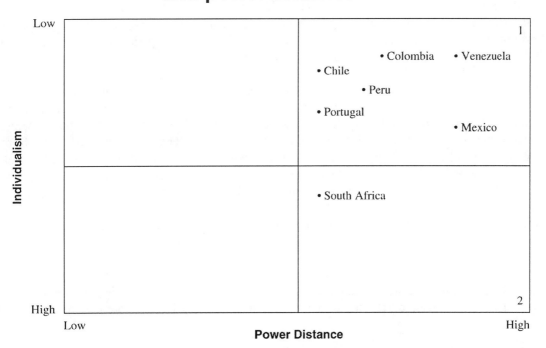

CHAPTER 10
POLITICAL FORCES

Learning Objectives

1. The students should be made aware that business does not operate in a vacuum, free to do what it wishes and to deal with customers without government interference.

2. Government is everywhere, regulating or owing business. The students should learn that the ideology of the home and host government are important to understand.

3. Nationalism as a powerful force with political repercussions should be explained.

4. It should be made clear that governments not only regulate or own businesses. Government should also protect business from terrorism or invasion.

5. The growing political force of international organizations and labor unions should be pointed out.

6. Students should know that large companies have some political clout of their own.

Overview

International business has become more and more sensitive to political forces as it plans operations. Legal forces which are dealt with in Chapter 11 are related to political forces, so Chapters 10 and 11 are companions. Laws and their enforcement reflect ideology and political points of view.

A hospitable political atmosphere permits business to flourish even though the country is poor in natural resources. The opposite is also true, and some countries blessed with natural resources are poor because of government instability or hostility.

In a communist country all major factors of production are government owned and labor unions are government controlled. Of course, there are not many avowedly communist countries left, and one of those, the People's Republic of China (PRC) is an odd combination with a strict communist government in Beijing coexisting with a fast-growing private business sector–complete with stock exchanges–in the coastal provinces. The formerly communist-run countries of Eastern Europe and the ex-Soviet Union are trying in their own ways at their own speeds to become market economies and democracies.

Capitalism in its pure form does not exist. Even in so-called capitalist countries, government regulation of business is extensive and many companies are government owned. Socialism advocates government ownership or control of major banks and businesses, but a number of countries which refer to themselves as socialist leave much finance and business in private hands. The story entitled "I'm from the Government, and I'm here to help you" is a good–if sad–demonstration of how difficult and frustrating a government can make it for a citizen to make a gift to the government. And that was in Germany which was governed by the Christian Democrats, no the more Socialist Democrats.

The words *conservative* or *right wing* and *liberal* or *left wing* have ideological meanings in most countries but one should not oversimplify. For example, in Europe *liberal* has a different political coloration than in the United States.

Left and right political advocacy organizations are important to business. They spend hundreds of millions of dollars and other currencies to lobby in Washington and U.S. State capitals as well as in

Brussels and European country capitals, and in other countries. Just as important, they litigate precedent setting lawsuits that affect judicial decisions for years to come.

Nationalism is an emotional force with which foreign business must deal. It probably exists in all countries but can be particularly strong in the LDCs.

Terrorism disrupts business as managers or their families are kidnapped and held for ransom or as offices or factories are bombed or burned. The perpetrators may be motivated by ideological or religious hate. They are sometimes financed, trained and protected by governments.

One function of government is to protect its businesses from violence and destruction, domestic or foreign. Not all countries have succeeded in doing that, and terrorism of various kinds adversely affects business in several countries. Likewise, government stability and policy continuity toward business are important for business to succeed. However, management cannot take stability and continuity for granted.

International business executives must recognize that certain national, religious or tribal hostilities may affect their policies. The Arab-Israeli hostilities with the resulting boycotts and laws are a case in point.

Labor organizations have had political powers within nations for years. Now they have begun to influence business internationally.

Of increasing importance to international business is forecasting risks in countries where they may wish to do business. The Procedures are called country risk assessment (CRA).

Suggestions and Comments

1. In the media currently and in a great deal of published material, there are countless references to the ideological forces we discuss. You can use those easily available sources to enliven the course and demonstrate current applicability of the book's discussion.

2. There are studies of the efficiency of government-owned industries as compared to privately owned business. Some assignments in those studies should prove interesting.

3. Terrorism and traditional hostilities are other subjects very much in current public attention. You can use newspaper, radio and TV material to illustrate the points of terrorist and traditional hostilities' effects on business.

Student Involvement Exercises

1. The story about I'm from the government, is an excellent example of bureaucracy at work. Have your students find other examples and report them to the class.

2. We have attempted to avoid a controversial presentation of the ideological forces material. Nevertheless, it is quite controversial, and you might get lively discussions of the pros and cons of "right" vs. "left," "conservative" vs. "liberal," etc.

3. Your students may have, or be encouraged to have, some interesting views on terrorism, e.g., on whether it is a legitimate political tool or on what measures governments should utilize to suppress it.

4. You might call for research into policies, rules and regulations of international organizations which affect ICs.

5. Your students might be interested also in research into the new internationalization of labor unions.

Guest Lecturers

1. Professors of political science at your school could expand on the ideological forces subjects.

2. Economics professors could be helpful. For example, professors of history of economic thought, state and local governments or international economics might discuss the backgrounds and relative economic performance of government-owned and privately owned businesses.

3. Someone in your local police department may be willing to speak about terrorism and counter-measures against terrorism.

4. A labor union official may be found who is knowledgeable about international labor activities.

Lecture Outline

I.   The story about I'm from the government shows how government can frustrate and complicate the simplest activities.

   A. Mr. Much tried to donate his fishing boat to a national coastal park in Germany.

   B. Permits of one sort or another were required from seven government agencies.

   C. Although the boat was finally placed in the park, people would not understand why because the explanatory notices had been removed because there was no planning permission for them

   D. Mr. Much had gone fishing in frustration.

II. Chapter 10 on political forces and Chapter 11 on legal forces can be a study unit.

   A. Chapter 10 deals with political forces including ideologies, government ownership or control of business, government attitudes toward business and government protection of business.

   B. Chapter 11 discusses some of the laws, their interpretations and enforcement, which reflect the ideologies and attitudes of governments as well as government stability and continuity.

   C. Figure 10.1 is a world map of political freedom. See page 314.

III. Ideological Forces

   A. Communism–Under communist government all major factors of production are owned by the government. Labor unions are government controlled.

      1. Communism as conceived by Karl Marx was a theory of social change directed to the ideal of a classless society.

      2. As developed by Lenin and others, communism advocates:

         a. seizure of power by a conspiratorial political party.

         b. maintenance of power by stern suppression of internal opposition, and

         c. commitment to the ultimate goal of a worldwide communist state.

      3. When a communist government takes over a previously non-communist country, it *confiscates* all major factors of production.

         a. International law recognizes a government's rights to *expropriate* foreign-owned property if the government pays the foreign owners promptly, adequately and effectively.

         b. If government does not pay, the government seizure of the foreign-owned property is called confiscation and that is not recognized as legal.

   B. Capitalism

The capitalist, free enterprise ideal is that all factors of production be privately owned. Government should be restricted to only those functions which the private sector cannot perform such as national defense and international relations. No such county exists.

1. Government regulation of business. The reality in so-called capitalist countries ins that government controls business through countless laws and regulations covering subjects such as
   a. taxes
   b. employment conditions
   c. wages
   d. retirement
   e. safety
   f. pollution
   g. zoning
   h. and many more
2. Compliance with the myriad government regulations requires skilled lawyers, accountants and engineers, much red tape is very costly.

C. Socialism

This doctrine calls for government ownership of the basic means of production, distribution and exchange. Profit is not an aim.

1. In practice, some self-styled socialist governments act more capitalist than socialist. This has been true in
   a. Germany
   b. the Scandinavian countries, and
   c. Singapore, among other places.
2. Most LDCs refer to themselves as socialist. Typical in LDCs are shortages of capital and trained people so that production and distribution facilities are usually government owned. However, they are sometimes privately owned as when:
   a. Foreign private capital invests in a LDC or
   b. Local private capital–perhaps with help from the IFC–creates or buys production or distribution facilities.

D. Right wing or left wing

Political parties are sometimes said to have right wing or left wing members. The meaning is that these wings deviate from the center of the party.

1. The right wing advocates less government ownership and intervention and more private and individual ownership and freedom.
2. The left wing pushes for government involvement

E. See The Worldview on page 353 for the origin of left and right terminology.

F. Conservative or liberal

In general political usage in the United States, the term *liberal* is similar to the left wing although usually not as extreme. That meaning of *liberal* does not, however, travel to Europe. Read the experience of one of the authors in the test.

G. Another different use of the words conservative and liberal occurs when the media is discussing the former communist countries of eastern Europe and the U. S. S. R. , and the communist government of the PRC. There, conservative is used to refer to forces favoring a return to or maintenance of a strong central government. Recall, that is the opposite of what they mean by conservative in the West which is the weaker central–and other–government, and more private ownership and management.

IV. Government Ownership of Business

In the communist countries, all significant business is government owned and that is the doctrine–although frequently not followed–in socialist countries. Perhaps surprisingly, large segments of business are owned by governments of countries which do not consider themselves communist or socialist.

A. Why governments nationalize business

1. Government suspects the company is concealing profits.

2. Government believes it can run the company more profitably.

3. Ideological; when left wing governments take over, they sometimes nationalize businesses which has occurred in:

   a. Britain

   b. Canada, and

   c. France, among other countries.

4. To put dying industries on life support systems (paid for by government) which may be disconnected after elections. This saves jobs and gets votes for political officeholders.

5. Because government pumped money into a weak industry, and control usually follows the money, or

6. Happenstance, as with the nationalization of German-owned companies outside. Germany during and after WW II.

B. Competition between government and privately owned companies. Complaints by the private companies include

1. Government companies can cut prices aggressively because they do not have to make profits.

2. Government companies get subsidies and other free or low-cost financing from the government

3. They get preference on government contracts.

4. They get expert assistance.

5. Figure 10.2 illustrates some of the differences in the objectives of private-owned as compared to government firms.

V. Privatization

During the 1980s and 1990s many countries sold state-owned assets to private buyers. The countries were in Asia, Europe, Latin America and North America; Britain has been a leader in the movement while the United States has lagged. Privatization does not always involve ownership transfer from government to private hands. Governments may contract out the management of some activities, or may lease state-owned facilities to private entities. Most studies indicate privately run businesses are more efficiently run than government companies. Such studies have been conducted in the United States, Britain, Australia and Italy.

A. Figure 10.3 shows percentage of privatization in transition countries which are countries of the former Soviet Union (USSR) or Eastern European countries that were dominated by the USSR.

B. See Figure 10.4 for the percentages of privatization by region.

C. A different twist on airport privatization is being implemented by the U. K. airport management company, BAA, and the Dutch operator of Amsterdam's Schiphol. They are successfully improving retail sales results of airport shops in a number of cities including Brisbane, Indianapolis, Melbourne, Naples, New York, Pittsburgh, and Vienna.

D. The government of Mozambique brought in a private British company to run its customs service.

E. The communist government of the PRC is permitting private, even foreign, ownership of businesses.

F. Privatization of previously government-owned companies in formerly communist countries of central and eastern Europe has proceeded at three speeds, depending on differing government approaches.

G. In most instances, buyers of newly privatized companies are profiting.

VI. Nationalism

Nationalism has been called the "secular religion of our time." It is an emotion found in varying degree of strength in almost every country, and is frequently quite strong in LDCs. Some of the results of nationalism on multinational companies are:

A. Requirements for minimum local ownership or local product assembly or manufacture.

B. Reservation of certain industries for local companies.

C. Preference of local suppliers for government contracts.

D. Limitations on number and type of foreign employees.

E. Protectionism.

F. Seeking a "French solution," i.e., a local rather than a foreign takeover of a local firm or

G. Expropriation in the most extreme cases.

VII. Government Protection of Business

An historic function of government of whatever ideology has been the protection of economic activities–farming, mining, manufacturing or whatever–within the country. The activities must be protected from foreign invasion and domestic terrorism.

A. The Iraqi invasion of Kuwait in 1990 had important political reasons, probably most important, control of most of the world's petroleum reserves. Even if Iraq did not invade Saudi Arabia, if it had been unchallenged in Kuwait, it could have intimidated the Saudis with its superior armed might. Saudi Arabia has the world's largest proven oil reserves so that Iraq could dictate oil and other policy matters, a prospect that frightened many.

B. A UN military operation led by the U. S. drove the Iraqis out of Kuwait, and in gratitude for U. S. leadership, Kuwait and the other Gulf Cooperation Council countries bought billions of dollars worth of American arms. Then another political force intervened. The UN Security Council of which the PRC is a permanent member imposed economic sanctions against Iraq for its failure to abide by its agreements which ended the UN military operation. In 1997, the PRC threatened to withdraw its support of those sanctions unless Kuwait bought PRC howitzers instead of superior American-made ones. Kuwait bought the Chinese howitzers.

C. Terrorism became a major world problem in the 1970s and continued into the 1990s. Several countries' politicians and companies' executives were victimized.

1. Many executives were kidnapped and held for ransom. It is said industry in Argentina has paid the equivalent of several hundred million dollars ransom to retrieve kidnapped executives.

2. In Italy terrorism has struck politicians and executives. The Italian company, Fiat, said acts of terrorism cut its output more than 12 percent and sharply increased costs.

3. Government and companies are taking countermeasures against terrorism. The Italian government gave its police more powers. Fiat fired several hundred insubordinate workers and the firings were upheld by an Italian labor court and supported by the labor union.

4. As the counter-terrorist measures took hold, there were many defections from the terrorist organizations, and some of the defectors gave police information which led to the arrest, trial and convictions of large numbers or organizations members. Terrorism lost its charisma among the young and fewer young Italians took that route. the remaining organizations are less idealistic and have more Mafia and other criminal group ties.

5. Government-sponsored terrorism is an act of war. Nevertheless, there is strong evidence that certain governments have sponsored and assisted terrorists. Countries named include Iran, Syria and Libya.

D. Terrorism is worldwide, but there are countermeasures.

1. The geographic spread of terrorism can be understood by the locations of some of the most active terrorist groups. They include the Irish Republican Army (although by 1995 there were negotiations and hope that the IRA might crease operations); the Hamas and other Islamic fundamentalist groups which are strong in the Middle East, but which are accused in the New York World Trade Center bombing; the Basque separatist movement (ETA) most active in Spain; the Japanese Red Army; and the German Red Army Faction. Of course, in 1995 a terrorist bomb destroyed a government building in Oklahoma City, and perpetrators were apparently U. S. citizens.

2. Kidnapping of executives for ransom is a terrorist tactic. Countermeasures include:

   a. commando management by which high-ranking executives fly into dangerous countries with a minimum of notice and publicity and fly out as quickly as their jobs are done;

   b. ransom insurance;

   c. antiterrorist schools;

   d. kidnap' negotiating specialists; and

   e. caution by informed executives

E. In 1997, Peru executed what was called "among the great counter-terrorist operations in history."

F. Terrorism is changing. Now there is:

   (a) ethnoterrorism with 'racial cleansing" as has been practiced in the former Yugoslavia and in Burundi and Rwanda; (b) necular terrorism; and (c) Islamic fundamentalist terrorism.

G. See Figure 10.5 and 6 for precautions to be taken by travelling executives.

H. In the U. S., training is available in anti-terrorist detection and defensive, evasive vehicle driving. An American company has gone international with armoring vehicles for protection of business and government officials.

VIII. Government Stability

Economic activities can prosper where government is stable with economic policies which are clear and which change only slowly. Government instability or sudden policy changes make successful conduct of business difficult or impossible. Some examples:

A. Lebanon was until 1974 the business and tourist headquarters of the Middle East.

1. It was highly prosperous and achieved prosperity with virtually no natural resources or rich farmland. Its prosperity was the work of an industrious, intelligent people given political stability.

2. Then civil war broke out, the political stability was shattered and with it went nearly all the prosperity, the business and tourist activities.

3. By 1997, relative peace had returned to Lebanon and people, hope and money were returning.

B. Bolivia enjoyed a rare treat of political stability from 1972 until 1979. During that period, new investment flowed into Bolivia and its untapped natural riches began to be developed. Unfortunately, political unrest began again in 1979, and the continuation of Bolivia's development remains in question although in 1985 a new president was democratically elected who took drastic steps to cuts inflation and battle the cocaine industry, which had become Bolivia's biggest business. Good progress was made and the president elected in 1989 pledged to continue the same policies.

C. One success story in Bolivia is in the Santa Cruz region in the east. Thanks to political stability, it has been able to greatly increase production and export of soybeans, cotton and oil. The exportation is being much expedited at lower costs due to the development of a new deep-water port at Puerto Aguire from where products can be shipped through an international waterway to the Atlantic in Uruguay.

D. Another success results from uses of the funds paid by foreign investors for privatization (although the Bolivians do not call it that) of government-owned assets. The funds went into trust funds to earn and pay pensions to poor Bolivians into the future.

E. Bolivia, once not notorious for the frequency of its military coups, conducted in 1997 its fifth consecutive peaceful, democratic election since 1982.

F. Permanence or Continuity of Government Policy toward Business

Sudden, radical changes of policy have been defined as a form of government instability. They make profitable business operations difficult or impossible.

IX. Government Assistance Gaining Export Business
The Small Business in the Global Economy feature illustrates how a small business was able to obtain export orders by joining trade missions sponsored by the U. S. Department of Commerce

X. Traditional Hostilities

There are long-running hostilities arising from political, ideological, racial or religious differences. One need name only a few such hostilities to illustrate their impact on business and trade.

A. Arab-Israel. This has generated trade boycotts and American legislation on the subject.

B. The peoples of Cambodia and Vietnam have been hostile to each other for centuries. Cambodia was occupied for years in the 1970s and 80s by Vietnamese troops.

C. The Sinhalese and Tamils have been locked in deadly combat in Sri Lanka for years. The 1991 assassination of Rajiv Ghandi was blamed on Tamils who hated him for sending Indian troops to Sri Lanka to try to put down the Tamil uprising.

D. The Bosnians, Croats and Serbs are killing each other in the former Yugoslavia while the Armenians and Azerbijanis fight in their parts of the former USSR.

E. The ancient and lethal hostilities between the Hutus and Tutsis in Burundi and Rwanda have been mentioned.

XI. International Organizations

Many UN agencies have become highly politicized. The World Bank Group, IMF and WTO exercise powers with political ramifications. OPEC has used its muscle for specific political purposes. The EU is gathering political power from its members, and the OECD "Guidelines for Multinational Enterprises" has had political results.

XII. Labor

Historically unions have operated, for practical purposes, almost exclusively within individual countries. This is changing.

A. Domestic Operations. Unions are usually ideologically oriented and usually toward the left. In every noncommunist, developed country, unions are powerful political forces, sometimes dominating political parties, sometimes working for or against political candidates or legislation.

B. International Operations Unions have begun to cooperate across national borders to affect international business.

XIII. International Companies (ICs)

Although a company's sales are not directly comparable to a nation's GNP, large sales do give a company power just as a large GNP is one mark of a powerful country. As you can see from Table 1-3 in the text, some companies' sales figures exceed the GNP of most nations. Some IC devices to exercise their powers are:

A. Create competition among prospective host governments for new or additional investments, technology or R&D.

B. Get help from the IC home country governments in negotiations with host countries, or

C. Permit local citizens to participate in ownership of the affiliate in the host country.

XIV. Country Risk Assessment (CRA)

It has become extremely important for a company or bank considering selling to, investing in or lending to a foreign entity–government or private–to first identify and measure the risks. The risks are compared to those which could be expected from expending the efforts and funds at home or in a different foreign country. The risks may be:

A. Political
    1. War
    2. Revolution
    3. Election of hostile government

B. Economic
    1. Balance of payments deficits
    2. Credit availability
    3. Inflation
    4. Exchange controls
    5. Recession
    6. Labor productivity
    7. Infrastructure efficiency

C. Social
    1. Labor unrest
    2. Poverty
    3. Population growth
    4. Terrorism
    5. Available, fair court system

As can be seen, several of the above items are interrelated. One may cause or be affected by others. The nature of the business is important as is the length of time the company's personnel and assets will be in the host country. CRA may be done by experts working for the company. Companies also may subscribe to outside CRA services or have special studies prepared.

D. The LDC debt crises which erupted in the 1980s have some lessons for CRA analysts.
   1. Many LDCs are vulnerable to external shocks.
   2. Debtor countries' economic policies are important.
   3. Sustained economic growth is necessary for high-debt countries to service the debt without too heavy a burden on the people.
   4. Social and political costs of over indebtedness combined with austerity are high.
   5. Global ripple effects of seemingly independent events must be considered.
E. Figure 10.7 shows country risk ratings by The Economist Intelligence Unit.

Answer to Questions

1. a. It is a belief in some political system or tendency such as capitalism, communism, socialism, conservative, liberal, right or left.
   International company managers know they cannot own factors of production in communist countries, but they may be able to do substantial business with those countries. They know they may or may not be able to own factors of production in socialist countries because among so-called socialist countries or governments, there is great latitude in application of socialist doctrine. In so-called capitalist countries, company managers know they must study carefully the laws and regulations regulating business.
   b. Generally speaking, private companies are more welcome under "conservative" governments than under "liberal' ones, as those words are used in the United States. Extremism of the left or right wing varieties tends to make company management uneasy. It prefers stable governments with clear policies not subject to sudden or radical change.

2. a. The capitalist, free enterprise ideal would be a government which performed only those functions the private sector could not. They would include defense and international relations. Every other activity would be conducted by individuals or private business.

   b. Reality in so-called capitalist countries is that government is very much involved with private business even to the extent that some business is government, not privately, owned. Companies not owned by government are subject to countless laws and regulations by all levels of government, for example in the United States by national state and local governments. Laws, etc., deal with all manner of subjects, e.g., taxes, antitrust, work conditions, wages, transportation rates and routes, securities sales and more.

3. Terrorism discourages investment and all productive activities. People are injured or killed and property is destroyed.

4. Business is regulated by governments of all countries where it is not owned by government. Governments impose all manner of regulations on businesses which must comply. Compliance is frequently expensive and sudden changes of government policies can be too costly for the companies to bear. Gradual change can usually be coped with more easily and is less burdensome.

5. Traditional hostilities such as that between Israel and the Arab countries can force a company to choose whether to deal with one or the other group.

6. International companies are not without political clout. When considering investments in a country which will bring to the country capital, technology management and markets, the ICs can bargain for favorable government policies. The IC may threaten to invest elsewhere. In some instances the IC's home government may intercede on the company's behalf with the host government.

163

7. The dynamic nature of the countries involved in CRA make the practice more of an art than exact science. All the information required for MNE to be able to analyze a country to a degree of complete certainty could never be obtained.

8. a. Most Vulnerable
   General Reasons–Long-term nature, high capital investment, high profile, strategic nature of industry, high work force involvement.
   Activities–Mines, oil fields, oil refineries, heavy equipment manufacturers, automobile manufacturers.
   Least Vulnerable
   General Reasons–Short-term nature, low capital investment, low profile, nonstrategic industry, low work force involvement.
   Activities–Banks, cosmetic manufacturers, personal hygiene products manufacturers, hotels
   b. High Profile
   Employ nationals, operate under a "local name.

9. There are five lessons: (a) Many LDCs are vulnerable to external shocks, (b) Debtor countries' economic policies are important, (c) sustained economic growth is necessary for high-debt countries to service the debt without too heavy a burden on the people, (d) Social and political costs of over indebtedness combined with austerity are high, (e) Global ripple effects of seemingly independent events must be considered.

10. The full answers to this question are complex and beyond the scope of this book. An oversimplified list would include poverty in Islamic countries; hostility toward other religions, particularly Christianity; and Judaism, hostility toward Western countries, particularly the U. S. and West Europe; and hostility of the Shia and Sunni Moslems toward each other.

Answers to Internet Problems

1. (a) Norwegian Labor Party
   Conservative Party
   (b) 65
   23
   (c) Labor Party: Equal Right to Education and an increase in welfare programs.
   Conservative Party: Increased Health benefits and Privatization of Government owned business.

The Internet Directory in this text contains many Web sites for specific countries. These Web sites contain material on political parties. Specifically, the Web site at http://www.agora.stm.it/politic/europe.htm contains information on many political parties in Europe

2. There are several Web pages that will give the answer. For political, economic and financial risk, visit the Web site at http://snoopy.asial.com.sg/realstk/start.html

Discussion of Minicase 10-1: Newly Privatized Company: What Do We Do Now?

The denationalization of the company gives management new opportunities to become more effective in a dynamic business environment. New policy formulation in the area of human resource management and marketing could contribute to a successful future.

A plan for profit sharing by the employees could act as a motivator when implemented. The concept of *quality circles*, which involves employee participation in decision making, should be considered. Training and development in the areas of maintenance and safety may need to be upgraded. Additionally, interdepartmental competitions based on energy consumption of safety records could contribute to cutting expenses. From a marketing viewpoint, the company would begin with a complete market research of its industry. This study may lead to more advertising or increases in the research and development budget.

1994 Map of Freedom

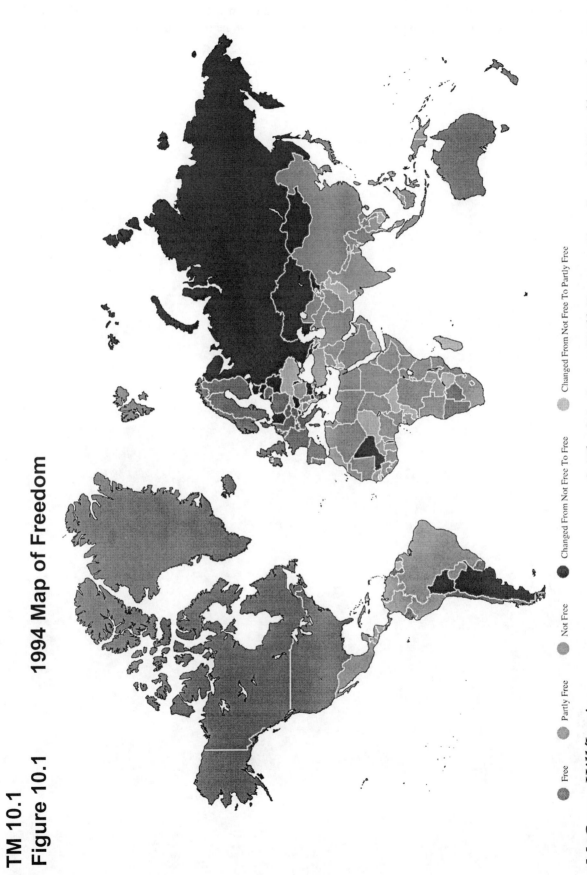

Free   Partly Free   Not Free   Changed From Not Free To Free   Changed From Not Free To Partly Free

TM 10.2
Figure 10.2   Planners and Business Investors—Why Can't They Collaborate?

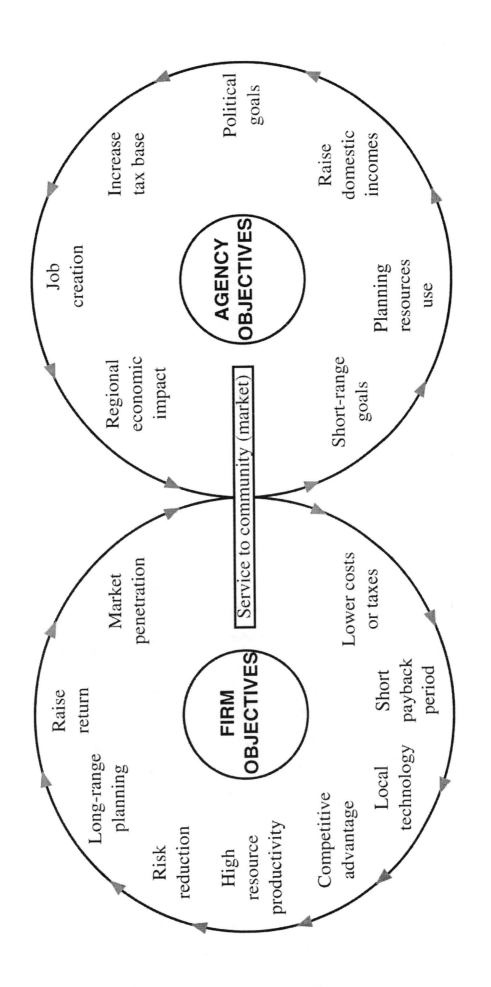

AGENCY OBJECTIVES

Increase tax base

Political goals

Job creation

Raise domestic incomes

Regional economic impact

Planning resources use

Short-range goals

Service to community (market)

FIRM OBJECTIVES

Market penetration

Lower costs or taxes

Raise return

Short payback period

Long-range planning

Risk reduction

High resource productivity

Competitive advantage

Local technology

McGraw-Hill/Irwin

TM 10.3
Figure 10.3

Transition Progress

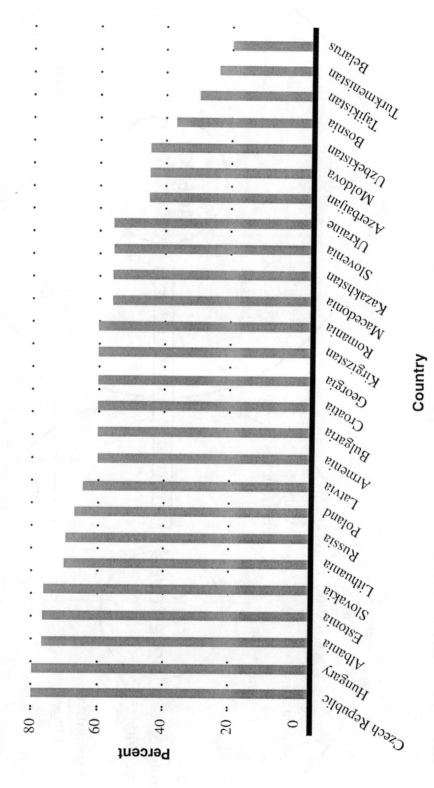

Country

Source: European Bank for Reconstruction and Development

McGraw-Hill/Irwin

TM 10.4
Figure 10.4

Privatizations by Region

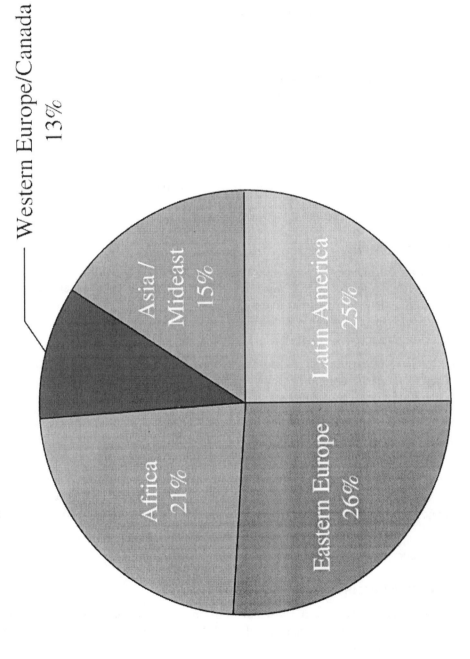

Western Europe/Canada
13%

Asia /
Mideast
15%

Africa
21%

Latin America
25%

Eastern Europe
26%

Source: "Privatization World Summary," Prepared for the Transnational Corporations and Management Division of the United Nations. Used here by permission of the author, Michael S. Minor.

McGraw-Hill/Irwin

CHAPTER 11
LEGAL FORCES

Learning Objectives

1. Emphasize the added dimensions of legal forces on a business operating internationally. It must cope with the laws of its home country, the laws of every other country in which or with which it is involved, and a growing new sort of legal force: international organization rules and procedures.

2. Show the various purposes for which taxes are used and introduce different national tax rates.

3. Point out some of the many subjects dealt with by law, e.g. antitrust, industrial espionage, employment, contracts, patents, trademarks, tariffs, exportation, product liability and price and wage laws, to name only a few.

Overview

The purpose of this chapter is to alert the students to the size and complexity of legal problems facing international business. They should be aware that there are potential legal problems about which they should consult experts.

Suggestion and Comments

1. To help illustrate differences between taxes, explain that only an income tax depends on the taxpayer making a net profit. Capital gains tax is levied on the difference between adjusted cost and the sales price. Due to inflation there may be no real net profit. Sales taxes are a percentage of the goods' sales price and value added taxes (VATs) are levied at each step of a production and distribution, in each case, regardless of whether any profit is realized.

2. You can illustrate antitrust law applications by referring to reports of ongoing cases and investigations in current publications such as *The Wall Street Journal, Financial Times,* or the financial pages of a good newspaper.

3. The same is true about product liability. There are frequent accounts in the newspapers about companies being sued because their products are alleged to be dangerous and to have caused death, injury or damage.

4. Your school probably has a business law course which covers contracts. You could borrow the textbook used in that course and brush up on contract enforcement within the United States. Then expand that to include a contract between an American seller and a foreign buyer.

5. Similarly, brush up on the rudiments of American patent and trademark protection. Then expand those concepts to include protection in other countries.

Student Involvement Exercises

1. To illustrate the use of taxes for purposes in addition to income, have your students learn the percentage of the tax portion of the price of a bottle of whiskey, a package of cigarettes, and a gallon of gas relative to other goods.

2. Assign research in current publications for examples of businesses or labor unions demanding tariff protection for their products or jobs.

3. Stimulate discussion, or perhaps an in-class debate, about the pros and cons of domestication. What are the advantages and disadvantages for the host country and for the foreign company?

4. Some writers oppose and others defend U.S. policies in antitrust, taxation, foreign corrupt practices and Arab boycott. Have the students find arguments pro and con and stimulate class discussion or debate about them.

Guest Lecturers

1. Accountants or lawyers specializing in tax matters could add to or clarify tax discussion, and probably some of them are knowledgeable about international tax matters.

2. Find lawyers to speak on antitrust and restrictive trade practices as they differ in the U.S. and elsewhere.

3. Import-export executives or customs officers could enlarge on tariffs, quotas and other trade obstacles.

4. Present or former officials of price and wage stabilization agencies could speak about price and wage controls, as could someone from the economics department of your school.

5. Lawyers may speak on contract enforcement and arbitration problems when two or more countries are involved.

6. Patent agents or lawyers could speak about protection or properties such as patents and trademarks.

7. If your school offers a course on the international legal aspects of business, ask its professor to speak to your students.

Lecture Outline

I.   Chapter Openers: International Law and Local Issues

    A. The opening photograph in this chapter is the Peace Palace in The Hague in the Netherlands, which is the home of the International Court of Justice, commonly called the World Court. The text discusses activities of the World Court.

    B. "When a Local Issue Can Have International Ramifications" is a piece about the attempt by Massachusetts lawmakers to set policy affecting those who do business with the state government in Massachusetts. Massachusetts attempted to prohibit businesses who do business in Myanmar (Burma) from doing business with the Massachusetts state government. The United States Supreme Court held that the Massachusetts law was unconstitutional. Based on the Constitution's Supremacy Clause, the Supreme Court found that the Massachusetts law conflicted with federal law and stuck down the Massachusetts law. Under the Constitution, the president and congress have power to set foreign policy. State laws that violate those Constitutional mandates will be struck down. Source: U.S. Supreme Court: Crosby v. National Foreign Trade Council, No. 99-474, 530 U.S. 363 (2000).

II.   "The Legal Forces Which Affect International Business" is far too broad and deep a subject to cover adequately in one course, much less in one chapter of a book. Nevertheless, business managers would have a dangerous blind area if they did not realize that many legal forces would affect them and prepare to get expert assistance to deal with them.

III. Taxation

    A. Government purposes in levying taxes include:

        1. Revenue

2. Income redistribution
    a. Provide national defense, police, fire, education and other services.
    b. Encourage research and development in selected areas.
3. Discourage consumption of products such as alcohol or tobacco.
4. Assistance for domestic producers and their employees by making import competition more expensive or scarcer.
5. Compliance with a tax convention (treaty) with another country.

B. With so many purposes for taxes and so much money involved powerful groups push and fight for tax legislation and regulations, which favor them.

C. From country to country there are different kinds of taxes and different approaches to their enforcement.

1. Tax levels vary from zero to over 100 percent.
    a. Some countries' tax rates can exceed 100 percent. The taxpayer must then use other sources of income or property to pay.
    b. In some tax haven countries, the tax rate can be zero on the certain kinds and sources of income.

2. Tax types differ
    a. Capital gains taxes exist in a few countries, notably the U.S. In the U.S., a taxpayer who buys a capital asset and later sells it for more than the adjusted cost pays a capital gains tax on the difference. The fact that the sale price may be higher due to inflation (so there was no real profit) does not reduce or eliminate capital gains taxes.
    b. Income taxes exist in most developed countries. It is the major income source for the U.S. government. There must be an excess of income over allowed expenses or credits before income tax is due. See Figure 11.1 and accompanying discussion.
    c. The value-added tax (VAT) is common in Europe. It is a tax levied at each stage of the production and distribution of a product. See Table 11.1 and accompanying discussion in text for more on VAT.
    d. A number of Americans want the U.S. to lower its income tax and impose VAT. One reason for that is that WTO rules permit an exporter to collect from its government a rebate of the VAT taxes paid on an exported product thus lowering its cost and making it more competitive in the world markets. WTO rules do not permit any income tax rebate.

3. Tax laws and regulations vary in their complexity. Many consider the United States to have the most complex tax system. The internal revenue code runs over 5,000 pages in length and official interpretations add more than 10,000 pages to that. In addition, there are thousands of pages of judicial rulings.

4. Attitudes vary as to compliance with and enforcement of tax laws.
    a. The United States and Germany are among the most strict.
    b. Italy is lax. The attitude of the Italian tax advisors can be understood when you see the variety and number of taxes levied on Italian businesses.

5. Taxation of income according to its source and the nationality of its recipient differ.
    a. The United States taxes the income of its citizens from every source regardless of where they live and work. This is referred to as the national tax approach.
    b. Most other countries do not tax the income of their citizens if they live and work abroad. This is referred to as the territorial tax approach.

6. There are many other tax law differences too numerous to mention, but some are:
    a. Tax incentives to make certain investments.
    b. Exemptions, costs and depreciation allowances.
    c. Tax credits, and
    d. Double taxation of corporate profits and then of dividends received by shareholders.
7. Particularly among the developed countries, there are many tax conventions (treaties). They provide for exchange of information between the tax authorities, reduction of tax on certain types of income, and they define terms, such as
    a. income,
    b. source,
    c. residence, and
    d. what constitutes taxable activity.
8. See Figure 11.2 for a list of countries with which the U.S. has tax conventions.

IV. Antitrust-Restrictive Trade Practices

The antitrust laws of the United States are venerable, the first having been enacted in 1890. The similar type laws in the Europe Union are called competition policy.

A. Aside from terminology there are differences between U.S. and European approaches.
    1. The United States has been more vigorous in enforcement.
    2. The United States has tried to enforce its laws extraterritorially (outside the United States) against nonresident foreigners. The EU has started extraterritorial application in actions such as review of the 1997 merger of Boeing and McDonnell Douglas.
    3. Certain conduct such as price fixing or cartels are illegal *per se* in the United States. That is, price fixing or cartels are illegal even though no damage can be shown. No such concept applies in Europe, and if a cartel allows its customers a fair share of the benefits– it can be legal in Europe.
B. Among industrial countries, the antitrust laws of Japan are the least effective. Its enforcement agency is called a toothless tiger.

V. Tariffs and other Trade Barriers.

Trade barriers were discussed at length in Chapter 3. Suffice it to point out here that they are legal forces with which international business must cope. The small business feature, "When is a Duck Not Like a Bedspread?" illustrates unhappy features of bureaucracies at work. In this case, it is the U.S. Customs and the Justice Department. Customs ruled that TV ducks, cloth animals that perch on couch arms with pockets which could hold TV remotes or magazines, belonged in the same tariff schedule as bedspreads. Bedspreads are subject to U.S. textile quotas so that the small business desiring to import and market the ducks would have to purchase a textile quota visa that would have doubled their price and made them unprofitable. The story is about the firm's battle to reverse the ruling.

VI. Product Liability

This is manufacturer's legal liability for faulty or dangerous products.

A. Liability can be civil and the company must pay money damages.
B. Liability can be criminal in which case fines or imprisonment may be imposed.
C. Both types of liability have been imposed in the United States, France, and Britain.
D. The EU is moving to standardize and toughen manufacturers' liability laws.

E. There are features unique to U.S. product liability law which make it much more potentially costly to defendants than in other countries. They are:

    1. Contingency lawyers' fees.

    2. Extensive discovery procedures.

    3. Punitive damages.

    4. Jury trials.

F. The punitive damages aspect of U.S. product liability laws have caused foreign firms to keep their medications and health products out of the U.S. Within the country, research of all sorts has declined precipitously because drug companies know a jury may blame the company for alleged damages caused by a new drug and award huge punitive damages to the plaintiffs. The silicone breast implant lawsuits are given as examples.

VII. Currency Exchange Controls

Most countries, and all developing countries, have laws dealing with the purchase, possession, and sale of foreign currencies.

A. A country must impose currency exchange controls when it cannot earn enough hard currency through sales of its products and services to foreigners.

    1. Soft currency is currency which will not be accepted by nonresidents of the issuing country or will be accepted only at a lower value than that established by the issuing government.

    2. Hard currency is acceptable worldwide at or near the same value.

    3. Soft currency is called nonconvertible because it is not readily convertible into other currencies. Hard currency is convertible.

B. Persons entering or leaving countries with exchange controls frequently must declare the types and amounts of currencies they are carrying. The objectives are:

    1. To prevent smuggling in of the local currency and

    2. To encourage bringing in hard foreign currencies.

VIII. Miscellaneous Laws

When doing business and/or traveling internationally it is necessary to be conscious of and sensitive to laws of the host country which frequently are very different from those of the home country.

A. The severity of the punishment may be the main difference. All countries have laws against production, sale, possession or use of narcotics. Western countries enforce their laws as best they can, and when a person is convicted the sentence is a fine and maybe a prison term. Two Australians were executed by Malaysia for possession, and an Englishman was hanged for trying to smuggle narcotics out of Malaysia.

B. The laws may be unique to the host country. Some examples are given in the text, and the students may be encouraged to research for others.

IX. International Legal Forces

A. What is International Law?

    1. Each sovereign nation is responsible for creating and enforcing laws within its jurisdiction. Once laws cross international borders, the matter of enforcement is complicated by the necessity of agreement between nations. The same concepts that apply to domestic laws do not always apply to international law.

        a. Public international law includes legal relations between governments, including laws concerning diplomatic relations between nations and all matters involving rights and obligations of sovereign nations.

b. Private international law includes laws governing transactions of individuals and companies crossing international borders. For example, private international law would cover matters involved in a contract between businesses in two different countries.

2. Sources of international law. International law comes from several sources. The most important source of international law is found in the bilateral and multilateral treaties between nations. Treaties are agreements between countries and may also be called conventions, covenants, compacts, and protocols. Another source of international law is customary international law. International rules derived from customs and usage over the centuries form what is called customary international law

B. International Dispute Settlement

1. Litigation in the United States. The United States has a long tradition of using lawsuits to solve dispute between parties. Businesses in the U.S. have grown accustom to resolving disputes though litigation. The United States has well developed court systems that facilitate litigation. Litigation can be extremely complicated and expensive. In addition to the trial itself, most lawsuits also have lengthy pre-trial activities including a process called discovery. Discovery is the means of finding facts relevant to the litigation known to the other side including obtaining documents in possession of the other side. Some discovery methods can seem quite intrusive since courts grant parties great latitude in obtaining information in the possession of the opposing side. Indeed, one reason many people from outside the U.S. dislike litigation in the U.S. is the process of discovery.

2. Arbitration. Many people outside of the United States dislike the U.S. system of discovery. For this reason, it is common for U.S. business people entering into contracts with business people abroad to agree that any disputes will be resolved by arbitration and not by litigation. Arbitration is a dispute resolution mechanism that is an alternative to litigation. Arbitration is usually quicker, less expensive, and more private than litigation. Arbitration is also usually binding on all parties.

C. Contract Enforcement

1. Frequently, at least one part to an international contract is a government. This is often true when dealing with developing countries and always true with communist countries.

a. A government, when sued for breach of contract, may plead sovereign immunity. That is the government's immunity to being sued without its permission.

b. A company contracting with a government's immunity to being sued without the government's permission.

2. Even if both contracting parties are nongovernmental, problems can arise. International contracts may be designed to avoid some of the problems by containing agreements such as:

a. Jurisdiction, where lawsuits may be brought.

b. Applicable law, e.g., the law of New York or France.

c. Arbitration.

d. Which language (where there are two) shall govern ambiguities or contradictions of translations.

3. Arbitration can be superior to courts of law in settling disputes. It can be faster because the courts of most countries have backlogs of pending cases. Arbitration procedures are less formal and can be confidential. Enforcement of an arbitration award, in most countries, is easier than enforcement of the decision of a foreign court. The reason is that

most UN member countries have ratified the UN Convention on the Recognition and Enforcement of Foreign Arbitral Awards.

4. When the contract involves investment in a foreign country, disputes may be referred to a tribunal at the World Bank. That tribunal is called the International Center for Settlement of Investment Disputes.

5. A body of law governs contracts for the international sale of goods. It is the U.N. Convention on the International Sale of Goods, and it has been ratified by the United States and a number of other countries.

6. In 1991, a regulation was promulgated under the Treaty of Rome, which governs the law of the contract when parties from two or more EU countries are involved.

7. Worldwide business law is being promoted by other organizations. The International Chamber of Commerce's Incoterms and its Uniform Rules and Practice on Documentary Credits enjoy almost universal acceptance. Rules on Bills of Lading sponsored by the International Law Association have been adopted by a number of countries.

D. Patents

1. Patent protection is standardized to some degree under the International Convention for the Protection of Industrial Property (the Paris Union and the Inter-American Convention.)

2. Patent application and protection harmonization has been achieved in Europe by the European Patent Organization (EPO). A patent filed and granted in any member country in that country's language is effective in all member countries.

E. Trademarks are the subject of the Madrid Agreement, the General American Convention for Trademark and Commercial Protection and of several bilateral friendship, commerce and navigation treaties. In 1988, the EU instituted a community-wide trademark system. A single European Trade Mark Office will be responsible for recognition and protection of proprietary marks in all EU countries.

F. Trade names are covered by the Paris Union. Goods bearing forged trade names are subject to seizure at importation.

G. Copyrights are protected under the Berne Convention and the Universal Copyright Convention.

H. Trade secrets are protected by laws in most countries.

I. Industrial espionage and intellectual property piracy are common.

1. Industrial espionage is the theft, by whatever means, of a company's trade secrets.

2. Intellectual property piracy is the use (without the owner's permission) of patents, trademarks, trade names or copyrights.

J. Intellectual property rip offs cost U.S. (and other) firms billions of dollars. In a survey, 325 American companies reported 32 cases of theft of intellectual information per month entailing losses of some $5.1 billion. Ranked by nationality and frequency of complaints, the top perpetrators were Chinese, Canadian, French, Indian, and Japanese.
Trademarks, recorded music, machinery spare parts, and pharmaceuticals are counterfeited and sold at prices far below those charged in legal markets. Turkey is said to be the world's top producer followed by China, Thailand, Italy, and Colombia. India is the source of much of the counterfeited pharmaceuticals.

1. At American request, the PRC closed private factories that were producing CD-ROMs, music CDs, and video CDs. In 1998, the resulting gap was filled quickly by entrepreneurs in Hong Kong and the neighboring Portuguese colony of Macao. In 1997 there were no CD factories in Macao, but by 1999 about 80 had sprouted up.

In brightly lit stores, pirated software and CDs are offered to customers quite openly. They can be had for less than $3 a disc.

The old arguments about the poor quality of pirated cassette tapes no longer hold with digital products. Indeed, the counterfeited software tends to be more up to date than that found in the few Hong Kong stores still selling legal software. Often the pirates even fix the bugs in the legal version.

2. In fact. Hong Kong police caught and arrested 16 of them in dawn raids on four illegal software factories in June 1998. The Hong Kong government said it had made a world record pirate software seizure worth more than HK$90 million. U.S. Trade Representative Charlene Barshefsky said she was pleased by the action and commented that "the size of the raid is staggering."

X. International Standardizing Forces

A. Tax convention between countries follow patterns.

B. Articles 81 and 82 of the Treaty of Rome are standardizing restrictive trade practices laws in the EU.

C. Contract arbitration is the subject of a U.N. convention.

D. Chapter 4 covered a number of international organizations, many of which have harmonizing or standardizing effects in their areas of operations.

E. Two standardizing organizations are the International Organization for Standardization and the International Electrotechnical Commissions. Government and company buyers worldwide are demanding products which meet the specifications set by these two organizations.

XI. U.S. Laws Which Affect International Business of American Firms.

A. Taxation. We have remarked that the U.S. tax system is one of the world's most complex. Other aspects of U.S. taxation we should be aware of include:

1. Taxing Americans Who Work Abroad. The United States taxes its citizens who live and work abroad on their incomes from every source. Other nations do not tax their citizens on their foreign source income if they live and work abroad. The U.S. law is a national tax jurisdiction approach, which means that if you are a citizen or permanent resident of the U.S., you are taxable there even though you live and work abroad. Other countries follow a territorial tax jurisdiction approach in accordance with which if you neither live nor work in the territory of the country, you receive no benefits from its services and are therefore not taxable by the country. The U.S. Internal Revenue Code (IRC) permits Americans living and working abroad to exempt an amount of earned income from U.S. income tax. Congress changes the amount allowed frequently, and you might assign students to research the current IRC provision. Earned income is salary, wages, commissions, allowances, or bonuses. No part of "unearned" income is exempt. Unearned income includes interest, dividends, and royalties.

2. The U.S. IRC can discriminate against U.S. international companies compared to foreign based ICs in terms of interest deductibility when investing in the United States.

B. There are numerous federal laws attempting in some manner to prevent unwarranted discrimination in employment. Major federal employment laws include Title VII of the federal Civil Rights Act of 1964, Age Discrimination in Employment Act of 1967, and the Americans With Disabilities Act of 1990. Congress specifically intended these federal employment laws to apply extraterritorially. Title VII, the ADEA, and the ADA generally cover U.S. citizens working for U.S. companies abroad. For example, if a woman who is U.S. citizen is denied a promotion because of her gender while working in Germany for an American company, she may bring an action in the United States under Title VII against her employer for unlawful discrimination in employment. Congress enacted one exception to the extraterritorial application of the federal employment laws, though, and that is an exception for local foreign laws. It is not a violation of United States law for an employer to engage in conduct that ordinarily would constitute illegal behavior if such behavior is required by local law in which the conduct took place. For example, certain countries prohibit women from engaging in certain activities such as driving. If a U.S. company is complying with the laws in a nation with such laws, the U.S. company would be protected from suits in the U.S. for discrimination if the discrimination is necessary to comply with local laws. Exceptions, however, are extremely unusual.

   C. Foreign Corrupt Practices Act (FCPA). Revelations during the 1970s of "questionable" or "dubious" payments by U.S. companies to foreign officials caused Congress to pass the FCPA effective in 1978.

      1. The OECD adopted an anti-bribery convention in 1999.

      2. Finally, other people and organizations are beginning to join the U.S. in combating corruption. Transparency International (TI) was founded in 1993. It publishes the "Corruption Perception Index." Its Web site is given in the text. Institutions that are discussing battling bribery include the Council of Europe, the Inter-parliamentary Union, the Organization of American States, the EU and the OECD.

   D. Anti-boycott Law. The Arab countries boycott companies which do business with Israel. Companies wishing to do business with Arab countries must swear they do no business with Israel or that goods sold do not come from Israel.

      1. In 1977, the U.S. government passes a law forbidding American companies to make such statements. The law is being enforced.

      2. Few other countries have such a law or policy.

      3. According to studies and statements, the anti-boycott law is causing American companies to lose business with Arab customers, which include some of the oil-rich countries.

      4. There were complaints that the anti-boycott law was being enforced unenthusiastically. Possibly in response to the complaints, the Department of Commerce stepped up enforcement, more companies were charged with violations and stiffer fines were levied.

      5. During the 1990's there were vigorous efforts to bring peace between Israel and its Arab neighbors. There were some successes, and some hopes that the Arab League would relax or end the boycott.

   E. Some U.S. agencies and offices assist American exporters and international businesses.

      1. The U.S. Department of Commerce actively encourages U.S. companies to export and provides helpful information and customer contacts.

      2. U.S. embassies and consular offices can be helpful with information and introductions for U.S. companies that wish to export to or invest in foreign countries.

XII.   Common Law–Civil Law

   A. Historically, common law was created by courts as they decided specific cases which decisions were recorded for study and precedent. The European civil law was based on decrees by kings or bills passed by legislatures. As time passed, those distinctions blurred.

   B. Current differences stem largely from differing attitudes in Europe and the United States toward government and different forms of government. In Europe, governments tend to be more feared or respected than in the United States. In addition, the same political party usually controls both the executive and legislative branches of European governments, whereas quite commonly different parties control one or both houses of U.S. federal and state legislatures, or the legislature is held by one party while the executive is of a different party.

The results are fewer compromises in European legislation and fewer court challenges than are prevalent in the United States.

C. Differences Between the U.S. and England. The text discusses five differences in the legal systems between the United States and England:

1. England has a split legal profession with barristers and solicitors.
2. England has no jury for civil court actions.
3. England allows no contingent fee arrangements.
4. Award of costs to the winner in civil litigation.
5. Pre-trial discovery is more restricted in England.

Answers to Questions

1. To encourage or discourage consumption of specific products; to encourage or discourage location of new businesses; to redistribute income or to grant reciprocity to resident foreigners called for by a tax convention.

2. It is argued that VAT is relatively simple in comparison to the complex U.S. tax laws. Another argument involves WTO regulations. WTO permits the rebate of VAT at the time a product is exported from the country but does not permit rebate of income taxes.

3. National tax system levies tax based on the nationality or citizenship of the taxpayer regardless of where the income was earned.

4. The U.S. antitrust laws and attitudes are different from those operating in other countries. In general they are the most restrictive and strictly enforced. When the U.S. attempts to enforce these laws overseas, countries object claiming their international operations are not subject to U.S. jurisdiction as they have their own laws governing their trading practices.

5. Frequently, Americans abroad who run afoul of a local law, have not received much help from the U.S. embassy or consulate.

6. Some of the advantages of arbitration as compared to court proceedings are speed and informality. The parties can choose their arbitrators and get into arbitration immediately. In addition, arbitrators are not bound by court procedures. They can admit and consider any evidence they feel is relevant and important.

7. No. There are quotas, packing and labeling requirements, health requirements, classifications and many others.

8. Yes. When a faulty product injures or kills someone.

9. a. No. A bribe made to expedite non-discretionary official actions is legal under that Act. It may not be under other laws.
   b. No.
   c. The Arab League talked about relaxing the boycott, however, there has been little evidence of relaxation.

10. a. A new law is made in Europe after consensus is achieved among most of the people, business, and government agencies which will be affected. In the United States, law is written, implemented and interpreted by three independent branches of government. In contrast to U.S. practices, European legislation is rarely amended and regulations are rarely revised. European courts are not as often asked to give their interpretations, and if they are, decisions are rarely appealed. U.S. laws and regulations are constantly being amended or revised by the legislatures and the agencies.

b. Differences in European and U.S. law practices can be attributed to historical reasons. Governments in Europe have traditionally been more feared and respected than in the United States. Because U.S. laws are not based on consensus, people feel free to challenge the legal system.

Answers to Internet Problems

1. (a) It is the responsibility of the Court of Justice to ensure that the law is observed in the interpretation and application of the treaties establishing the European Communities and of the provisions laid down by the competent Community institutions.

   (b) The Court of Justice comprises 15 judges and 9 advocates general. The judges and advocates general are appointed by majority vote by the Member States for a renewable term of six years. One of the judges is selected to be president of the Court for a renewable term of three years.
   Information on the European Court of Justice can be found at the Web site
   http://europa.eu.int/cj/index.htm

3. US Trademark Law, Patent Cooperation Treaty
   You can find information on the European patent office at http://www.european-patent-office.org/index.htm and on the United States Patent Office at http://www.uspto.gov.

Discussion of Minicase 11-1: Italian Law

This sort of impasse is not unusual in international contracting, but it probably is to your local lawyers who have no international experience. You should find and consult experienced international lawyers or have your law firm bring in at least one such lawyer of counsel for advice in drafting this contract and future international contracts.

One solution such a lawyer might suggest is arbitration of any disagreements by the International Chamber of Commerce in Paris. Another solution could be arbitration by a tribunal of one arbitrator chosen by your company, one chosen by the Italian customer and the third chosen by a Swiss or other third country judge. In either event, the decision is a nationality-neutral with the decision being made by a third party who is neither American nor Italian.

TM 11.1
Figure 11.1

In OECD countries there is often quite a difference between the highest "all-in" rate of taxes on wage income and the highest standard rate of personal income tax imposed by central government. In Denmark the standard rate is over 20% whereas the "all-in" rate is over 60%. The standard rate in the United States is much higher than in Denmark, but the 'all-in' rate is much lower, at about 46%.

"All-in" rates include all "taxes" imposed on wage income which are above the standard rate, such as social security contributions and local taxes.

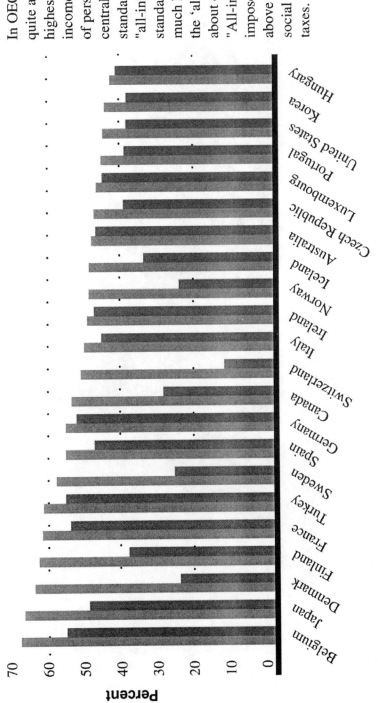

● "All-in" rate   ● Standard rate

McGraw-Hill/Irwin

TM 11.2
Figure 11.2

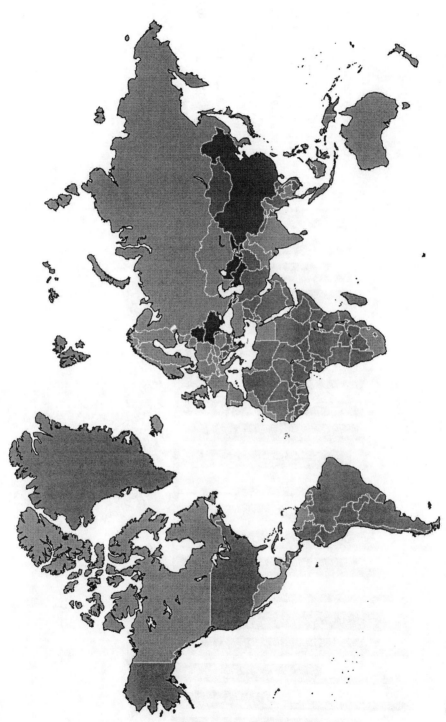

- Countries in which the United States has tax treaties with.

- The U.S.—U.S.S.R. income tax treaty applies to the countries of Armenia, Azerbaijan, Belarus, Georgia, Kyrgyzstan, Moldova, Tajikistan, Turkmenist, Ukraine, and Uzbekistan.

- The United States has tax treaty with People's Republic of China, but does not include Hong Kong.

McGraw-Hill/Irwin

TM 11.3
Figure 11.3

Corporate income tax, top rates, %

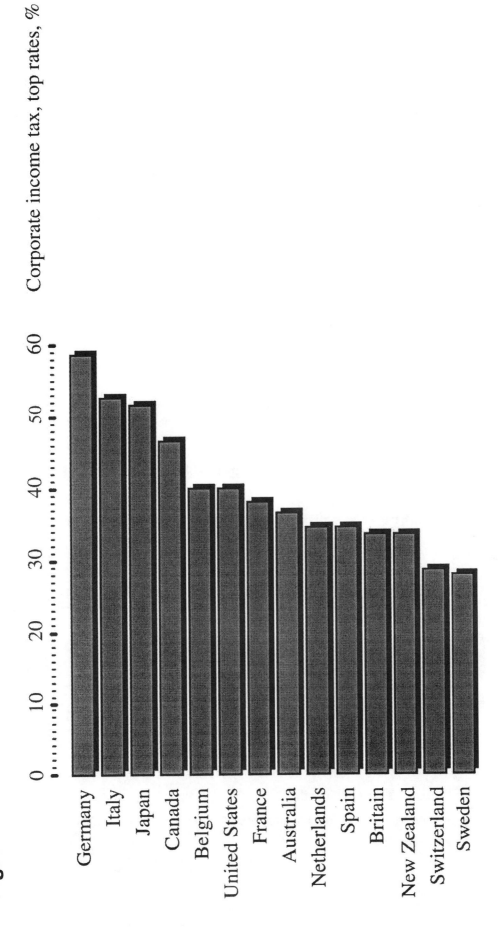

McGraw-Hill/Irwin

CHAPTER 12
LABOR FORCES

Learning Objectives

1. Point out that pools of available labor may be found among the natives of the country where a company operates or among refugees or guest workers who have entered the country.

2. Discuss the immigration system in the United States and how the process by which a non-citizen is admitted to the United States.

3. Indicate how the composition of a nation's labor force can affect productivity and discuss other influences on productivity.

4. Explain why a foreign employer must consider host country attitudes toward social status, gender, race, traditional society and minorities.

5. Introduce differences in labor union strengths and philosophies and the growth of the labor-in-management movement.

6. Show the differences in unemployment rates in most of continental Europe as compared to North America and discuss some of the reasons for those differences.

Overview

Although classical economists assumed the immobility of labor, modern experience has demonstrated labor to be quite mobile. It has moved as 'guest workers' in Europe; people seeking better jobs moving from Mexico to the United States, or as refugees fleeing such varied homelands as Cuba, Vietnam, and several African countries. Moving workers create problems and benefits for both the receiving and losing countries. Immigration has become a major concern for many U.S. based companies as they attempt to fill positions.

Labor productivity results from the skills of the labor force supplemented by the capital equipment supplied to the labor force by management. A country's tax policies and inflation rate affect the propensity of its people to save. The greater the savings, the more money is available for R&D and investment in more and better capital equipment to enhance labor's productivity.

Management of a foreign company must be aware of host country prejudices, practices, superstitions, mores and laws regarding several sensitive subjects. They include social status, women's rights, race, traditional societies, and minorities.

In some countries labor unions are stronger and more vocal than in others. Labor unions have become active across national borders. The EU now requires large international companies to establish works councils to improve workers' rights to information and consultation.

Suggestions and Comments

1. Emphasize the extent and areas of labor mobility.

2. Explain the reasons for such mobility.

3. Compare labor productivity in the United States with that in other countries and discuss the reasons.

4. Point out the importance of observing host country attitudes about race, gender, social caste, etc.

5. Discuss the differing implementations of the EU's works councils requirements.

Student Involvement Exercises

1. Have the students read the "Job Sharing" articles at the beginning of the chapter and then research how the problem of unemployment is being dealt with in different parts of the world.

2. Ask the students to update the labor mobility information in the book and research how well the new refugees are faring.

3. Assign studies of labor productivity. Have students compare productivity in two or more countries and discuss the reasons for the differences.

4. A study that will interest a number of your students is the women's rights movements in various countries and areas of the world. Encourage discussions of why they differ so widely.

5. Encourage study, discussion, and debate of the pros and cons of the new EU work councils requirements.

Guest Lecturers

1. Your school may have a course in labor economics and the person who teaches it could enlarge on problems and uses of labor.

2. Someone from your school's sociology department might enlarge on the material about management problems with host country attitudes toward social or caste status, gender, race traditional society, and minorities.

3. Personnel or labor relations managers from firms in your area might be interesting speakers on labor relations.

4. On the same subject you might also get labor union officials who might offer perspectives.

5. Ask an immigration attorney to speak on immigration policy.

Lecture Outline

I. The "Job Sharing" articles show a German approach to cutting labor costs while avoiding lay offs. The second article demonstrates that approach may not be the best method of minimizing unemployment. The "Small Business and Jobs" feature on page 424 discusses some steps being taken in the EU to assist small businesses in creating jobs.

II. Labor Mobility

Although international business management usually finds most of its labor among the natives of the host country, a growing phenomenon in recent years has been a mobile, immigrant labor force, people who move from another country.

    A. Some of the areas which have been heavily affected by labor migration are:

        1. Europe where "guest workers" went from south to north.

        2. Arab OPEC countries attracted workers from Egypt, Algeria, Morocco, Pakistan, and India.

        3. Iran and Pakistan have several million Afghanistani refugees.

        4. Southeast Asia and Philippines where many Vietnamese have fled.

5. North America which is absorbing millions of refugees from Cuba, Central America, Haiti, Mexico, Vietnam, and other Southeast Asian countries.

6. South Africa into which over 200,000 people trek every year for work.

B. United States immigration policy is a good reference point for examining labor mobility. Immigration refers to the process of leaving one's home country to reside in another country. For people who are not citizens of the United States, the United States can be a difficult country to enter. Even for people from Canada and Mexico, the United States can be a difficult country to enter.

1. The Immigration and Naturalization Service (INS) in the U.S. Department of Justice is the federal agency responsible for all immigration matters, including naturalization, which is the process of becoming a U.S. citizen.

2. Background. The text gives a brief history of immigration to United States.

3. Nonimmigrant Visas. Nonimmigrant visas are issued to those coming to the United States for a temporary visit. These visas are broken into specific categories (such as workers, students and tourists) and are identified by letters. Those discussed in the text are:

B - The B visa is issued for a short-term stay, usually six months or less for either business (B-1) or pleasure (B-2).

E - The E visa is for trade or investment.

F - The F visa is for students.

H - The H visa is for workers. Included in the H is the H-1B for specialty occupations such as professionals and highly skilled workers. Many high-tech workers are admitted for temporary stays under the H-1B category.

I - The I visa is for members of the media.

J - The J visa is for exchange scholars.

L - The L visa is for intracompany transferees.

4. Immigrant Visas. Immigrant visas are for those individuals desiring to remain permanently in the United States and are called permanent residents or green card. There are two main categories for issuance of immigrant visas: family reunification and employment based immigration.

5. Refugees/Asylum Seekers. Throughout history, there have been flights of people from persecution. These individuals are called refugees or asylum seekers. If refugees are able to get to a safe country, they are in a position to seek asylum. In order to be admitted to the United States as a refugee or asylum seeker, one must establish a well founded fear of persecution based on one's race, religion, nationality, membership in a particular social group, or political opinion. People who are economically depressed cannot seek asylum for economic reasons.

6. Immigrant workers in the United States provide both high and low skilled positions. Of the 12.7 million new jobs created in the United States between 1990 and 1998, 5.1 million (38%) were filled by immigrants.

C. Population pressures are being created by booming population growth in a number of developing countries. Women bear the brunt and most of the burdens of the baby booms as their constant work of bearing and raising children hinders their education and other productive work.

D. The United Nations High Commission for Refugees (UNHCR) attempts to assist refugees.

III. Guest Workers and Labor Shortages

Countries with high birthrates or which receive many refugees may have too many people for the available jobs. Other countries, notably in northern Europe, found they had too few workers during the post-WW II boom years up to 1974. They imported guest workers, but now problems developed for those countries and their guest workers.

A. Economic Problems. Due to contagious inflation, the post-WW II boom ended in the early and mid-1970s. The OPEC price increase then deepened the recessions, and many native citizens of northern European countries found themselves unemployed. They then wanted back the jobs the guest workers had been imported to fill.

    1. Some countries deported seasonal workers and refused to issue new visas for them to return.

    2. Other countries offered "go home" bonuses to encourage their guest workers to leave.

B. Employment. Figure 12.1 is a chart from the OECD showing total employment in the OECD member countries.

C. Labor Shortages. The beginning of the 21st century saw low unemployment in many industrialized nations, including the United States. Figure 12.2 shows that the unemployment rate in the United States is less than five percent, which is the lowest unemployment rate in recent history. In order to meet necessary staffing requirements, many companies are resorting to unique avenues to reach potential employees. Marriott sent recruiters into laundromats, bus terminals, and senior centers in southern California in an attempt to find employees for its hotels. The Walt Disney Company asked annual Disneyland pass holders if they knew anyone who would want to work.

IV. Composition of the Labor Force and Comparative Productivity

A. Refugees. These people are fleeing oppression and everyone who can get out does so. Thus, the receiving country's labor force receives men, women and children of all ages and conditions of health. Some will have the skills and strength to enter the work force immediately. Most cannot. National productivity probably suffers.

B. Guest Workers. These people come prepared to do specific jobs and are not granted visas unless they are ready to work. Frequently, they are not permitted to bring their families. National productivity probably improves.

C. Immigrants Can Boost Productivity. From the 1960's through 1997, immigrants, refugees, or others, permitted the U.S. economy to grow faster than its long-term trend without igniting inflationary flames. Immigrants are said to have saved New York City, which has absorbed some 113,000 a year during the 1990's before which the city was experiencing a potentially catastrophic population drain.

D. Other Effects and Productivity

    1. Inexperienced workers such as adult women reentering the work force and young people entering the work force instead of a university or the armed forces.

    2. Research and development, tax policies and savings rates, all of which affect the capital and capital equipment available to improve workers' productivity. See Figure 12.4 for comparison of countries productivity.

V. Social status, sexism, racism, traditional society, or minorities: Considerations in Employment policies. International employers must be cautious when they hire employees in a host country. Most countries have local traditions, practices, discriminations, attitudes or laws about people about which the foreign management should be aware.

A. Social Status. There are societies, notably India, where one's social position is established by the caste into which the person is born. There is bitterness and strife between castes, and an employer must be careful about hiring them to work together.

Although not as well known as the Indian below class untouchables, there is an under class in Japan called burakumin whose members are despised by other Japanese. A non-burakumin, Sue Sumii, sympathized with the burakumin and wrote articles and stories about them, spending most of her adult life exposing what she considered the idiocy of Japan's class system.

B. Sexism. Although women's rights have made good advances in the United States, in other countries women's rights range from small to none.

    1. In those places, local business and government may not accept a woman in the labor force, not to mention in management or the professions. There are examples in the text of how women fare, or are treated, in several countries, including Japan, Pakistan, Saudi Arabia, India, the People's Republic of China, the former Soviet Union, and Afghanistan.

    2. Even in the United States today, women have made great advancements yet continue to face discrimination, especially in advancing into the higher levels of business management. As indicated in Figure 12.5, even though women make up 46.5 percent of the U.S. labor, they constitute a relatively small percentage of senior positions in the Fortune 500 companies.

    3. Women's Education. Studies show a persistent correlation between the length of women's schooling and birthrates, child survival, family health, and a nation's overall prosperity. Very low levels of education are almost always present in societies in which girls and young women are forced into prostitution or otherwise brutalized at a young age by techniques such as female genital mutilation. The World Health Organization, a UN agency, says that people in these societies believe that they are doing the right thing for their daughters by subjecting them to genital mutilation and do not see the link between genital mutilation of a young girl and the pain, infections, ill health, and possible death she may suffer.

    4. Unemployment for women. As indicated in Figure 12.6, with respect to the countries in the OECD, in almost every country the unemployment rate for women is higher than the unemployment rate for men. Figure 12.7 shows that in the OECD countries, men still earn substantially more than women do.

    5. Opportunities for Women in International Business. As in many areas, opportunities abroad are increasing for women. The text discusses a study done on international opportunities for women as well as examples of companies giving women opportunities.

C. Racism. Race relations create problems worldwide. Foreign management must be sensitive to host country attitudes and laws in racial matters.

D. Traditional Society. Some developing countries have barely begun to modernize and many of their people are still relatively primitive. Here the foreign employer may find itself in the paternal position of a traditional tribal chief rather than an employer in the usual sense. Family and tribal loyalties are important and nepotism is the rule.

E. Minorities. Traditional societies combined with racial attitudes sometimes create situations where minorities of foreigners dominate the banking and business of a country. Examples are Indians and Pakistanis in East Africa and Chinese in Southeast Asia.

    1. Advantages for foreign employers of such minorities include that they are probably industrious and skilled as well as multilingual.

    2. Disadvantages are that they are probably unpopular with the majority population of the country and could isolate foreign management.

VI. Employer-Employee Relationships

A prudent investor and to-be employer in a host country should examine labor availability, attitudes and practices. Labor peace is important.

A. Look Behind Labor Strike Statistics
   1. Was the period abnormal?
   2. Were the strikes peaceful or violent?
   3. Were the strikes industry-wide or only against selected employers?
   4. Were the strikes wildcat or was there usually advance warning?
   5. Do the unions and workers abide by labor agreements and what can the employer do if they do not?

B. There are good information sources.
   1. *Foreign Labor Trends* from the Bureau of International Labor Affairs of the U.S. Department of Labor.
   2. *Handbook of Labor Statistics* from the Bureau of Labor Statistics of the U.S. Department of Labor.
   3. *Yearbook of Labor Statistics* from the International Labor Office of the U.N.

C. Labor Unions: European Different than American and Japanese.
   1. European unions are usually identified with political parties and socialist ideology. European workers frequently gained freedom from feudalism and various rights and power through collective action.
   2. American unions tend to be more pragmatic. U.S. workers had already gained many civil rights, including the vote, before the union movement became important. During the 1996 election campaigns in the U.S. the big American labor unions AFCL/CIO and Teamsters became much more active and promised to continue and intensify their activity.
   3. Japanese unions are enterprise-based rather than industry wide, and as a result, tend to identify strongly with the interests of the company. There is an account of an example of where that backfired.
   4. Figure 12.8 shows that workers in OECD countries used the strike weapon much less frequently during the 1990's than they did in the 1980's. Labor union membership trends have been downward in most OECD countries, including the United States.

D. International Labor Activity.
   For years, unions were active and effective within individual countries but very little abroad. That is changing and unions are cooperating internationally, exchanging information and pressuring ICs in several countries. As the EU proceeds to unite its 15 member countries, and its businesses will serve the entire market, labor organizations are also working cooperatively. The European Trade Union Confederation is an umbrella group with headquarters in Brussels, which is the seat of the EU Commission.

E. Worker Participation in Management.
   In Germany a movement was begun in the 1950's called codetermination which required by law that large companies give representatives of their work force places on their boards of directors. It was expected that this practice in Europe's largest economy would be the pattern and would spread throughout Europe and perhaps beyond. That did not occur.
   1. Other American companies and some in other countries have tried to improve communications and relations between management and labor. Terms such as industrial democracy and worker participation are sometimes used.
   2. In 1996 in the EU, there came into effect a directive requiring most international companies operating in the EU to set up work councils. The aim is to improve labor's right to information and consultation.

F. Workers of the World
1. How much they cost is the subject of Figure 12.10.
2. Unemployment rates differ greatly within the EU and between the EU and North America. Within the EU, Britain and the Netherlands have the lowest unemployment rates due, it is said, to relatively easy rules about hiring and firing workers and lower unemployment benefits. Similar rules are said to be the reason for lower unemployment and much greater job creation rates in the U.S. as compared with continental Europe. Other obstacles to hiring in Germany include restrictive laws about shop-opening hours and private employment agencies.

Answers to Questions

1. a. The employer's bargaining strength is stronger. Good employees can be hired at lower pay.
    b. An excess of qualified employees frequently means business recession and possible social and political unrest

2. No. One reason for labor mobility is a shortage of certain categories of workers, frequently in agriculture, construction, hotel or restaurant fields, in a country and availability of people in other countries who are willing to do those sorts of jobs. The people who migrate to take those jobs often do so legally and are called guest workers. Other reasons for labor mobility are economic or political. People emigrate from countries where there are insufficient jobs. People also flee persecution.

3. The guest workers possess skills desired by the host country and become legal immigrants. They frequently do not bring families and thus require a minimum of social services such as food, housing, education, etc. The refugees come in all ages and conditions, without reference to skills possessed or needed. They are frequently illegally in the country and they need many social services.

4. People coming to the United States for temporary stays are generally coming for job related reasons or for pleasure. The text outlines the major visas for temporary stays. Those coming to the United States for permanent stays generally are coming for job related reasons or for family reunification.

5. Often, productivity suffers. In times of low employment, unskilled workers fill necessary jobs.

6. More efficient tools and machines result in more extensive and effective research and development. The amount of money for R&D depends on company priorities and governmental tax policies.

7. Such minorities are typically unpopular with the local majority which can damage the companies' government relations or product acceptance. Too great reliance on such minorities can insulate foreign management from local realities.

8. European unions tend to be more ideological and political. U.S. unions tend to be more pragmatic and more focused on specific collective bargaining agreements. U.S. unions have tended to be much more politically active in recent years, though. Japanese unions are enterprise-based, rather that industry-wide, and, as a result, tend to identify strong with the interests of the company.

9. Employment laws and regulations are more permissive in the U.K. and U.S. than they are in France and Germany. When business is bad, employers can more easily fire unneeded employees, and are therefore more ready to hire new employees when business improves. Unemployment benefits are sufficiently high on the European continent that lower paying jobs

offer little incentive for people to take them and give up the benefits.

In addition, particularly in Germany, there are restrictive laws about hours businesses can operate on weekends and evenings.

10. Not good due to nationalistic union attitudes and ideological differences. If it comes, the EU is a good bet as the first location.

11. Works councils are organizations of workers, with some management participation. They keep workers informed about company developments and give them opportunities to have input in company plans. They are now required for most international companies that operate in the EU.

Answers to Internet Problems

1. Japan's ministry of labor was established in 1947 with the aim of promoting workers welfare. The Internet Directory in this text has information on many governments around the world. Japan's Ministry of Labor is located at http://www.mhlw.go.jp/english/index.html

2. Labor statistics show that there are more unemployed men than women (Dec 97) in Australia. Information on Australia's labor statistics can be found at http://www.abs.gov.au/

Discussion of Minicase 12-1: Staffing Your Operations Abroad

The issues of this case deal with racial, political and guest worker problems, when operating in a foreign country with an internationally segregated work force. Losing favor with the Luau government is a problem which could potentially threaten the whole Asian market. This anti-company trend is the result of the government and nationals feeling the IC is favoring the Chinese and possibly discriminating against the locals.

The Chinese staff would be aware of the resentment between the nationalities and probably are noticing the negative trend in attitude. However, for their own job security they would be hesitant to admit this. In addition, they would be accustomed to uncooperative relations with the Micronesians and therefore would not view this as a significant or unusual development.

To win back a favorable attitude the company should implement some training and career programs. The locals should be strongly encouraged to apply for jobs with the company and employed where possible. If locals can take a few of the positions, it is more likely that the Micronesians will not feel they would be surrounded by Chinese if they were employed by the company. A good public relations move would be to offer U.S. university scholarships to Micronesians. For those already qualified, training in the United States may enable them to assume a position of major responsibility in the Luau operations. These types of programs if well publicized, would be very visible to the community and favorable to the government.

MINICASE 12-2

The purpose of this minicase and Minicase 12.3 is the have the students think about immigration categories. The best visa for Ms. Lund would be a H-1B, a temporary noniminigrant visa for specialty occupations such as professionals and highly skilled workers. As an architect, she should be able to qualify.

MINICASE 12-3

The best visa for Mr. Naguib would be an E visa, which is a visa for those coming to the United States to direct an operation in which the non-citizen has invested money.

World of Work: Employment as Percent of Working-Age Population

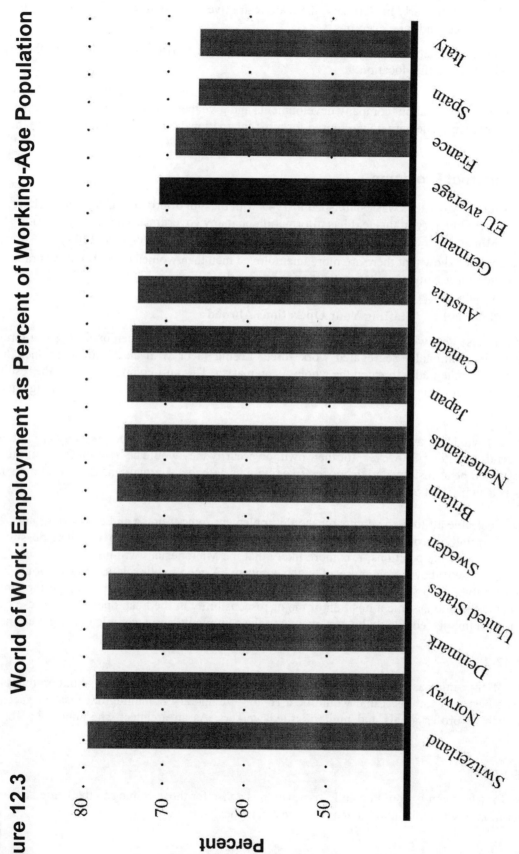

TM 12.2
Figure 12.4   Productivity: Output Per Hour in Manufacturing

Productivity America led other rich countries in the rise in manufacturing productivity in 1999. According to preliminary data from the Bureau of Labor Statistics, American labor productivity increased by 6.2% over a year earlier. The countries with the next-biggest rises were Britain and France. Belgium came last in our table with an increase of 0.7%. In Canada, Italy, and Japan, productivity grew in 1999 after declines in 1998. Britain, France, and Sweden showed better gains in 1999 than in 1998, but productivity growth in Belgium and Germany decelerated. This seems to support the common complaint of European economists that their countries have failed to reap productivity gains from the Internet. Hours worked in manufacturing declined between 1979 and 1999 in all countries for which data were available except Canada, where hours rose at an average annual rate of 0.3%.

Percentage increase on a year earlier, 1999

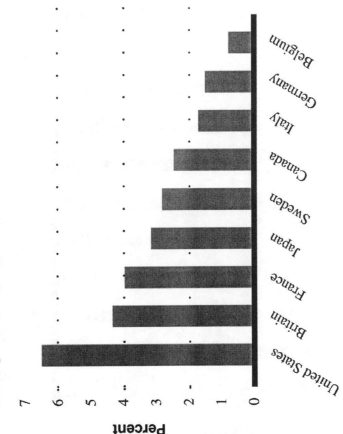

Source: US Department of Labor; and *The Economist*, November 18, 2000, p. 122.

McGraw-Hill/Irwin

Female Wage Gap: Difference Between Female and Male Full-Time Earnings Percent

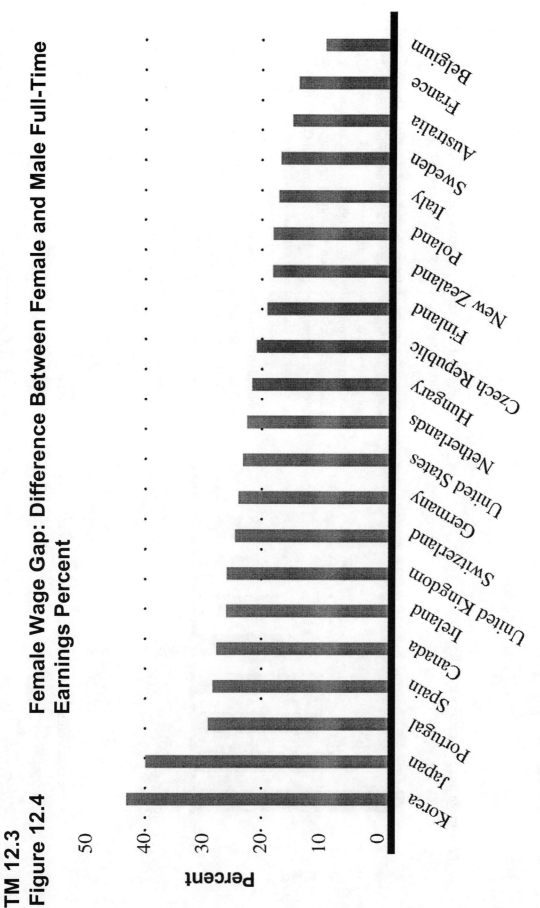

Source: OECD in Figures, 1999, p. 83.

McGraw-Hill/Irwin

Strikes

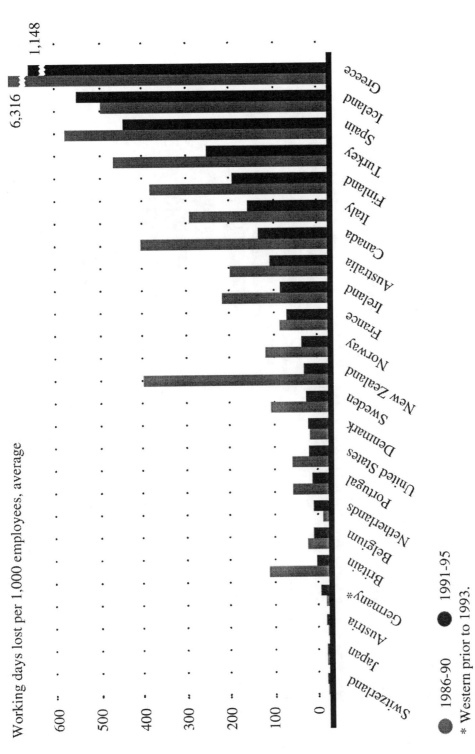

Working days lost per 1,000 employees, average

● 1986-90   ● 1991-95

* Western prior to 1993.

Source: UK Office for National Statistics; *The Economist*, April 26, 1997, p. 108.

McGraw-Hill/Irwin

TM 12.5
Figure 12.10   **Labor Costs**

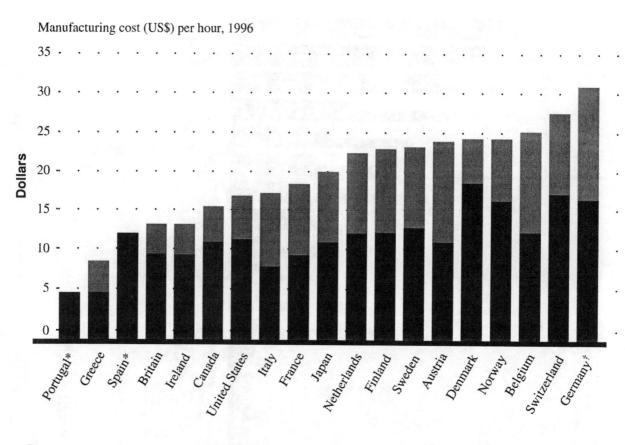

Manufacturing cost (US$) per hour, 1996

Wages not linked to time worked (e.g. Holiday pay, Social Security contributions, etc.)

Wages for time worked

*Breakdown not available   †Western

Source: *The Economist*, May 24, 1997, p. 104.

CHAPTER 13
COMPETITIVE FORCES

Learning Objectives

1. Make students aware of the presence of increasing worldwide competition among firms in the United States, Japan, the EU and the Asian nations.

2. Show students that the responsibility for increasing the worldwide competitiveness of the United States lies with management, labor, government and consumers.

3. Show students how the U.S. is regaining competitiveness and the growing importance of competition from Asian NICs and NIEs.

4. Discuss competitor assessment.

5. Describe the impact of counterfeit products and industrial espionage.

Overview

World competition has intensified and there are four nations and groups of nations whose firms are in worldwide competition with each other-Asian countries (NICs, NIEs and China), United States, EU, and Japan. Nations do not compete with each other, their firms do, but most economic and social conditions as well as political actions affect the ability of all of a nation's firms to compete. Using the term, *national competitiveness*, is a convenience.

In the case of the United States, as the dollar's value rose, American companies experienced difficulty in competing in world markets, but its high value was only one of the reasons. Various non-price factors were also responsible. The government, industry, labor and consumers all can contribute to the return of American competitiveness. Japan is facing the same competitive problems that the United States and Europe have been facing. Counterfeiting and industrial espionage are also competitive problems. Although competitive assessment is not new, its use is increasing and companies are establishing competitor intelligence systems.

Suggestion and Comments

1. Students at this level are usually unaware of the extent to which some firms go in their competitor analysis. You might assign someone to give a short report on this subject. See Student Involvement Exercises.

Student Involvement Exercises

1. You may want to ask students to do an update on Europe 92. Ask them to identify what has changed, such as laws, industry structure, and so forth, and what changes they expect to see in the next 3 to 5 years, including possible admission of new members to the EU.

2. Assign someone to report on competitor analysis. You should get a lively discussion on the ethics involved in obtaining information about competitors.

3. You can begin the study of this chapter by discussing question 2. The discussion will be interesting if you have a good political mix of students.

4. You could ask some students to do a report comparing keiretsu, chaebol, and grupos. Note the definitions in our glossary. It didn't occur to us to talk about their similarities until after we had finished the chapter.

Guest Lecturers

1. Try to get someone from a consulate of an EU member to discuss the impact of the euro and of possible admission of new members on the EU and on businesses in the EU.

2. Ask your district office of the U.S. Department of Commerce to send someone to talk about Commerce' efforts to alert U.S. businesspeople about developments in the EU, Japan, and the Asian NICs, NIEs and China.

3. Get someone from the headquarters of a multinational in your area to tell the class how his or her firm prepared for Europe 1992 and/or NAFTA.

4. International marketing managers or someone on their staff can provide the class with some interesting experiences about the analysis of competition.

Lecture Outline

I.   Opening Section
      The Opening Section shows that according to an ex-military man, the principles of war may be applied to business. Many firms have installed intelligence systems and some have hired ex-intelligence officers to rune them.
      World competition has intensified and four nations and groups of nations whose firms are in worldwide competition with each other have emerged–U.S., Japan, EU, and the Asian nations (NICs, NIEs and China).

II.   Competition at the Macro Level (National Competitiveness)
      Although nations do not compete against each other, most economic and social conditions as well as political actions affect the ability of a nation's firms to compete in world markets and so we speak of national competitiveness.

      A. United States
          1. Declining Competitiveness in the 1970s and 1980s
              a. The lag in national competitiveness began in the 1970s American firms first experienced competition from European and Japanese firms which began buying U.S. companies when the cheap dollar made them inexpensive in their currencies. As the dollar's value rose, U.S. firms had difficulty competing in U.S. and foreign markets and American protectionist sentiment grew. This prompted more foreign firms to invest in the United States. When the dollar's value fell again, foreign firms exporting to the United States had problems competing price wise with domestic products so they set up U.S. production facilities.
              b. The overvalued dollar was one of the principal reasons for the decrease in American competitiveness, but non-price factors such as quality, delivery time, after-sales service, reliability of supply and trade barriers to U.S. exports were also important.
          2. Improving Competitiveness of the U.S.
              a. From the mid-1980s through the mid-1990s, efforts were undertaken in the U.S. to improve the financial situation (e.g., budget deficit, savings and loan industry), streamline regulations, open global markets, and improve industrial productivity by restructuring operations, enhancing quality, reducing costs, investing in information and computer technologies, and reducing time to market.

b. A 1994 Council on Competitiveness (COC) study revealed that the U.S. had significantly improved its position in areas where it had been lagging and had maintained its strength in areas where it had been strong in the 1991 report.

c. A decade-long (1985-1995) assessment by the COC, *Competitiveness Index 1996*, found that the U.S. had increased its global market share of goods by over 23 percent, had generated a large and growing surplus in services trade, had led the major industrial nations in growth of industrial output during the last 5 years of analysis, had a lower unemployment rate than all major industrialized nations except Japan, and had strengthened its competitive position overall.

d. Growth in U.S. manufacturing productivity during 1985–95 was lower than the growth of other nations, but by the end of the 1990s, the U.S. was the clear leader, achieving productivity growth nearly 50 percent higher than its nearest competitor, the U.K. (Figure 13.2).

3. Ranking U.S. competitiveness.

   a. The *World Competitiveness Scorecard* consistently ranked the U.S. first throughout the 1994-2000 period, followed by Singapore. Ratings of other nations have varied over the years (Table 13.1)

   b. The *Global Competitiveness Report* also ranked the U.S. first in 2000, replacing Singapore, which had been ranked highest from 1996-1999 (Table 13.2).

   c. Comparing the *World Competitiveness Scorecard* and the *Global Competitiveness Report*, the U.S., Singapore, and the Netherlands are ranked consistently in the top 5 in each report. All of the top 20 countries in each report are in the top 25 in both reports, despite differences in their rank order.

4. Dawn of a "New Economy?"
   Recent U.S. economic and export growth has been generated mostly by a relatively small number of industries, particularly related to information and communications technology (ICT). ICT accounts for up to 75 percent of the rise in U.S. productivity growth during the second half of the 1990s. Some analysts suggest the ICT sector has provided the basis for a "new economy," characterized by a permanent increase in productivity growth, lower levels of unemployment while still maintaining low inflation, and more stable growth in output. Emergence of the claimed "new economy" has been promoted by several interrelated forces, including technological advances, liberalization of financial markets, globalization, greater flexibility in labor markets, improved management of the macroeconomy, and an environment supportive of entrepreneurship. Evidence regarding the existence of a "new economy" remains mixed, however.

5. Continued challenges to U.S. competitiveness. Despite improvements in competitiveness during the 1990s, the U.S. faces challenges to maintaining international competitiveness. This section identifies key challenges to the sustained competitiveness of U.S. industry and increased U.S. exports, including:

   a. Innovative capability and investment in research and development. Technological innovation has a central role in productivity improvement, long-term economic growth, and improvement of a nation's standard of living.

      (1) The Economic Creativity Index 2000 ranks the U.S. as the leading country overall and for each of the creativity, technology, and startup dimensions (Table 13.3). A 1999 study by the COC found that the U.S. and Switzerland had achieved sustained leadership in innovative capabilities across the prior three decades, although their lead has declined over time. Since 1985, the U.S. has had a decline in the growth rate of R&D funding and employment, flat or declining

spending on education as a percentage of GDP, a decline in its relative international openness, and the underlying environment for technological innovation in the U.S. has become relatively less supportive.

(2) Although overall R&D expenditures in the U.S. are higher than other major nations, growth in R&D spending since 1991 is the lowest since the early 1970s (Figure 13.3) and total expenditures on basic research have declined substantially as a percentage of GDP. The U.S. government's share declined from nearly 60 percent of total U.S. R&D expenditures in 1970 to around 30 percent in 1997. Increased R&D investment by businesses has only partially made up the difference.

(3) To address this situation, the U.S. government must reverse recent declines in support for R&D. The government should encourage initiatives that will promote private R&D spending, especially on long-term projects. Promotion of basic research within universities, independently or in cooperation with the private sector, is also essential.

b. A shortage of knowledge workers.

Increased global competition has placed an increasing premium on skilled workers, yet the proportion of R&D workers in the total U.S. workforce has been declining since the late 1980s. The U.S. outspends all other industrialized nations in education and leads the world in the percentage of students graduating from universities. Despite this, test scores from secondary level students have failed to improve since 1985 and compare poorly with the scores of other nations (Table 13.4). To address these challenges, the U.S. must initiate significant changes and investments in improved primary and secondary education, and undertaking concerted efforts to rebuild university education in technical disciplines.

c. More conducive regulatory environment.

Government policy and institutions such as universities can create an environment that can promote, or inhibit, firms' innovativeness. Government activities per se are not bad for national competitiveness. However, in addition to the previously mentioned encouragement of R&D and reform of education, more can be done by the U.S. government. This includes tax reform, opening of foreign markets, protection of intellectual property rights, reducing dependence on foreign capital, and industrial targeting.

(1) Tax reform. The bipartisan Competitiveness Policy Council recommended reducing double taxation of dividends and double taxation of corporate retained earnings, two significant tax code impediments to long-term capital formation in the high-growth and start-up sectors.

(2) Market-opening efforts. A key initiative by the U.S. government involves leadership activities in opening markets, including the threat of retaliation if other governments fail to remove trade barriers to U.S. exports. These efforts must be sustained and perhaps expanded to allow effective competition by U.S. firms and help address record high U.S. trade deficits.

(3) Protecting intellectual property rights. The U.S. government has used the threat of retaliation to promote the protection of intellectual property rights and eliminate another barrier to U.S. exports in international markets, particularly in Asia—competition from illegal copies of U.S. products.

(4) Dependence on foreign capital. An area in which U.S. competitiveness may be vulnerable is reliance on foreign capital. During the late 1990s and in 2000 the

U.S. experienced unprecedented inflows of capital from abroad. The U.S. economy could be vulnerable to changes such as renewed inflationary pressures, a rapid depreciation of the currency, slowed growth, or declines in projected corporate profits and stock prices. These changes could quickly reverse the flow of capital, possibly reducing the availability of funds for investment and choking economic growth.

    (5) Industrial targeting. The government can do more to support U.S. companies that face competition from targeted industries. Industrial targeting, the practice of government assisting selected industries to grow by a variety of means, has been common in Europe, Japan, and many developing nations.

B. European Union

Formation of the European Union created a large market that attracted new competitors from within and outside Europe (Figure 13.4). By 2003, the EU is expected to begin adding additional members, particularly Central and Eastern European countries, ultimately incorporating 27 or more nations into a "greater Europe" trading area. Such developments can create important new opportunities for business, as well as creating new competitive challenges. The Lomé Convention is a source of competition from the developing nations, although the EU and developing nations must reform the agreement to be compatible with WTO guidelines.

1. European competitiveness

    a. There are some indications that the EU's competitiveness as a whole has declined relative to the U.S., even though several member nations have recently improved their international competitive position.

        (1) During the 1990s (Table 13.5), growth in the EU's export volume has lagged the level of most of the world. The 1999 increase (3.5 percent) was only 37 percent of the EU's level for 1997, and 70 percent of its average for 1990-1996. The EU's imports have also been growing at a slower rate than most of the world. The 1999 increase of 4.0 percent was the same as its average for 1990-1996, but less than half its performance of 1997 and 1998.

        (2) The EU has had lower growth in real GDP and higher unemployment than the U.S. for each year, 1992-1999 and the EU's relative fiscal surplus has been worse than the U.S. for each of the years 1993-1999. These trends are projected to continue through at least 2002.

        (3) OECD indicators for trade coverage ratios (exports/imports) for "high-tech," "medium-tech," and "low-tech" industries reveal that European firms appear to specialize in low-tech products for export, followed by medium-tech and then high-tech products. Export/import ratios for U.S. and Japanese firms are in the reverse order.

        (4) European expenditures on R&D as a percentage of GDP are consistently lower than those of Japan and the U.S. (Figure 13.5). Business-funded R&D in major European countries is also lower in the late 1990s than a decade before. EU expenditures per capita in 1999 on information and communication technology (ICT) were less than 60 percent the U.S. level, and the EU has an increasing deficit with the U.S. in ICT trade.

2. Barriers to European competitiveness

    a. Labor costs and productivity. Wages, salaries, and fringe benefits are higher in 11 European countries than they are in the U.S. when stated in U.S. dollars. The hourly rates of 9 European countries are higher than those of Japan. The high cost of labor in the EU is compounded by productivity that lags the U.S. and other competitors. McKinsey & Co. released a study claiming that thousands of jobs may have to be cut if industries such as the automotive, telecommunications, and banking industries are to be as efficient in France and Germany as they are in Japan and the U.S.. The report stated that if the U.S. were to bring the minimum wage to the French level from where it is now (55 percent of that level), 30 million U.S.s would be thrown out of work.

    b.   Education. Many EU nations have achieved high standards of performance in their primary and secondary school systems, often superior to the U.S. (Table 13.4). However, university education in Europe tends to be more theoretical, more rigid, and less adaptable to the changing needs of industry than in the U.S.

    c.   Conflicting positions of member nations. Constraining efforts to improve overall competitiveness of the EU is continued disagreement among member nations regarding key issues. The EU has significant differences in relative economic prosperity among member nations, complicating efforts to achieve consensus on monetary and taxation policies, economic development and industrial subsidies, expansion of the EU through adding new member nations, and other initiatives.

    d.   Cultural biases. One reason for Europe's technological lag is an aversion to using tools that are overly "U.S." These biases can hinder the EU's efforts to improve competitiveness in an increasingly knowledge-driven world.

    e.   International E-Commerce in Europe. The EU's enterprise commissioner says that Europe has 3 to 4 years to overtake the U.S. and become completely competitive in internet technology. While 30 percent of U.S. and Canadian populations are connected to the internet, in most EU nations less than 15 percent are. Development of EU E-businesses is hindered by the lack of an entrepreneurial culture and an under-developed risk capital market.

3.   Signs of improvement in European competitiveness.

    a.   The *Global Competitiveness Report* (Table 13.2) showed that 6 of the top 10 (15 of the top 25) nations in 2000 are from the EU or EFTA, versus only 3 of the top 10 in 1996. Similarly, the *World Competitiveness Scoreboard 2000* (Table 13.1) lists 8 European nations among the top 10 (versus 6 of 10 in 1996). At a business level, only the U.S. has more firms than the EU on *Fortune's* Global 500 list for 2000.

    b.   The *Corruption Perceptions Index 2000* (Table 13.6) shows that European nations account for 7 of the leading 10 nations on this list, and 13 of the top 20. This can influence the competitiveness of working with (or against) European firms, in the EU and elsewhere in the world.

    c.   In terms of competitiveness in innovation, the *Economic Creativity Index 2000* (Table 13.3) lists 7 European nations among the world's top 10 (13 of the top 25). The COC found that several EU nations, particularly Denmark, Finland, and Ireland, have made major gains in their innovative capacity, allowing them to gain position relative to the U.S., Japan, and leading EU innovation leaders.

    d.   One step that many EU firms, especially larger international companies, are taking to improve their production efficiency is closing older plants and concentrating their production at their most efficient facilities.

    e.   Although the EU experienced subdued economic performance and continued high levels of unemployment during 1991-1996, economic growth has improved since that time. Strong gains have been made in employment during the late 1990s and 2000, particularly in part-time and fixed-term employment in the services sector.

4. Competition from Japan.

   a. Fearing that when trade barriers were abolished among EU countries after 1992, they would be replaced by new obstructions for nonmembers, Japanese auto firms, including Nissan, Toyota, and Honda, established production plants within the EU. Japanese imports have nearly eliminated the EU motorcycle industry. The EU runs a large trade deficit in electronics. Japanese cameras and watches are market leaders, and every small color TV tube used in Europe is made by Japanese electronic companies with local production facilities.

   b. At the beginning of 1996, there were 727 Japanese manufacturing affiliates in Europe employing over 200,000 people. The United Kingdom has been the favorite location of Japanese investors.

   c. Japanese service companies have also invested in the EU and are competing with local firms in retailing, advertising, hotels, distribution, tourism, and insurance. Many have come because Japanese manufacturers frequently prefer to bring their service providers with them instead of having to use local suppliers.

   d. EU manufacturers are concerned that Japanese manufacturers are buying local distributing companies. Buying distributors in Europe permits them to maintain high prices and makes it difficult for small competitors to get distribution.

5. Competition from the U.S.

   European firms face competition from U.S. exports as they do from Japan, but unlike Japan, U.S. companies have had Europe-based manufacturing facilities for a long time. U.S. companies have generally been well accepted in Europe. Yet EU governments are working to help national companies compete with U.S. firms (e.g., Airbus, the Fourth Framework Programme for Research and Development, and Eureka).

6. Competition from Asian Nations.

   Companies from Asian nations that used to receive investment from Europeans taking advantage of lower labor costs are now investing in Europe. While firms from all the Asian tigers have production facilities in Europe, South Korea's industrial conglomerates—the chaebol—have been leading an Asian investment drive into Europe. However, the Asian economic turmoil that began in 1997 resulted in the near collapse of the Korean economy. Many planned chaebol investments have been delayed or cancelled, helping to slow the onslaught into Europe of Korean and other Asian competitors.

C. Japan

1. Japan experienced impressive economic growth between 1960 and 1985. In the late 1980s the Japanese economy over-expanded and capital was misallocated. A sustained downturn resulted from the subsequent collapse of the "bubble economy," in which prices of Japanese stocks, real estate, and other property plummeted.

2. Average annual growth in real GDP was less than 1 percent from 1992-1999. High levels of corporate debt and stagnant domestic demand resulted in record numbers of bankruptcies. Unemployment increased by 135 percent between 1990 and 1999, from 2.0 percent of the workforce to 4.7 percent. The government's fiscal budget declined from a 1.5 percent surplus in 1992 to a 7.0 percent deficit in 1999. Japan's public debt is the highest among the OECD nations. The end of the 1990s saw deflation.

3. In the past, Japanese firms could export the country out of its economic problems relatively easily. Large devaluations of Southeast Asian and South Korean currencies cut into Japanese exports, causing Japan's trade surplus with those countries to fall sharply in 1997 and 1998. Exports declined by 1.5 percent in 1998 due to the region's financial crisis (Table 13.8) and only rebounded by 2.0 percent in 1999. Despite this, Japan had

1999 trade surpluses with the EU and the U.S. of $38.4 billion and $69.6 billion, respectively (Figure 13.1), increasing pressure from abroad to open Japanese markets to competition.

4. Declining ranking on competitiveness. In the Global Competitiveness Report (Table 13.2), Japan's ranking declined from 13 to 21 between 1996 and 2000. The World Competitiveness Scorecard (Table 13.1) suggested an even greater decline in Japan's relative competitiveness, from 3 to 17 between 1994 and 2000. Several factors that help explain Japan's declining competitiveness during the 1990s include:

   a. Declining productivity. The rate of improvement in productivity has declined from 4.3 percent annually between 1985 and 1995 to 3.1 percent in 1999 (Figure 13.2). Part of the explanation for declining productivity is traditional reluctance of Japanese employers to discharge loyal employees. This has resulted in overstaffing and reduced hiring of young workers, thus creating a mismatch of skills due to inability to recruit younger workers with new knowledge bases.

   b. Declining investment in R&D. The COC ranks Japan as a leading nation in terms of international innovativeness. Many Japanese companies have invested heavily in R&D during the 1990s, despite the overall economic problems in Japan, and they have established strong international positions as a result of their innovativeness. Overall Japanese investment in R&D has declined substantially since the early 1990s, however.

   c. Barriers to innovation.

      (1) Japan ranked 20th in the Economic Creativity Index 2000 (Table 13.3)

      (2) Japan was lowest ranked among the top 25 nations in terms of the start-up index, reflecting barriers to entrepreneurial initiative within that country. Despite some progress in recent years, it remains difficult for entrepreneurs and small businesses to gain access to capital. This problem is particularly great for businesses in emerging knowledge-based sectors, which involve higher risk and fewer assets to serve as collateral.

      (3) The costs of establishing a new manufacturing facility in Japan is also significantly higher than in other developed countries (Table 13.7). This problem has been compounded by high costs for telecommunications and internet connections in Japan. Japanese internet penetration continues to lag that of the U.S.

      (4) Japan's trade in information and communication technologies (ICT) has grown more slowly than the world as a whole. Between 1996 and 1999, Japan's share of the world's ICT exports declined from 15.1 percent to 12.5 percent, and its share of ICT imports declined from 7.0 percent to 5.9 percent.

   d. Regulations and Restructuring.

      (1) Despite continued pressures to promote restructuring and deregulation, limited progress was achieved by the Japanese in the 1980s and early 1990s. The keiretsu continued to exercise strong influence, the financial sector was insulated from international competitiveness, and inefficient, often corrupt practices characterized many public works projects. In a cultural setting that did not allow for corporate or bank failure, problems were merely papered over, not resolved, which prolonged the post-"bubble economy" crisis and permitted a chronic lack of confidence to settle in.

(2) Pressured by a broad recognition that the sustained economic malaise would not disappear on its own, the Japanese government has recently begun to promote a number of institutional changes. Efforts were undertaken to restructure, including banking, financial services, and retailing sectors.

e. Japan's Keiretsu.

    (1) One of Japan's best-known institutions is the keiretsu, a group of financially connected firms that tend to do business with themselves rather than with others. Both U.S. businesspeople and trade officials have contended for many years that the keiretsu system contributes greatly to the huge Japanese-U.S. trade imbalance..

    (2) After the collapse of the "bubble economy," regulations were relaxed to permit greater access to international financial markets, and both banks and companies became less dependent on the keiretsu. Sustained domestic economic stagnation, internationalization of capital markets, and pressure for reform of corporate governance have begun to loosen traditional relationships among affiliated members of keiretsu. In addition, many Japanese banks are merging and selling their cross-share holdings.

f. Improving Japanese competitiveness

    (1) During the 1990s, to improve their competitiveness when the yen rose past 100 to the dollar, Japanese firms invested billions of dollars in Asian production facilities to take advantage of cheaper labor, land, and manufactured components. Their strategy was to dominate local sales with local production and keep out U.S. exports, while expanding their exports to the rest of the world. Low-cost imports from their Asian subsidiaries, both finished products and components used in Japanese-made products, enabled Japanese firms to compete at home against U.S. imports. Emergence of the Asian economic crisis in 1997 hampered short-term economic returns from this strategy, however it also provided an opportunity for further investments at reduced rates, including purchasing shares from financially-strapped local partners. These actions are expected to lower overall costs and improve international competitiveness during the 2000s.

    (2) It appeared that the Japanese economy began to enter a recovery phase in mid-1999. Performance remained tenuous in 2001, with continued overcapacity in many industrial sectors and sustained high personal savings rates due to individuals' uncertainty about their financial prospects. Restructuring continues to put a damper on the economy, but has helped to promote improved transparency and external monitoring of corporate governance, facilitating changes in traditional management practices

    (3) Government deregulation, technological advances, diversifying consumer tastes, and increasing internationalization of Japanese society have opened up Japan to increased foreign direct investment from other nations. A record high of $12.7 billion of investment was received from abroad in 1999. Although less than 5 percent of the level of investment flowing into the U.S. ($282.5 billion in 1999), these inflows were nearly 4 times Japan's 1998 total of $3.3 billion.

g. Competition from the U.S. and Europe

    (1) The Japanese economy has been in a repetitive cycle for the last 25 years in which the government allows the yen to fall against the dollar to boost exports, while also restricting domestic growth to dampen imports. Japan's trade surplus takes off. Then the U.S. reacts by demanding that the Japanese government

(1) allow the yen to rise against the dollar, (2) reduce restrictions on U.S. imports, (3) permit U.S. firms more freedom in doing business in Japan, and (4) stimulate its economy to increase demand. The Japanese response is to make some concessions on U.S. imports, reduce some of the restrictions on U.S. firms doing business in the country, and drive up the value of the yen. However, often the yen rises too much and recession results. The country was coming out of its fifth such cycle in 2001

2) Bargain hunting is in; high prices are out. The recession and high costs have motivated Japanese consumers and businesses to search for cheaper products and are creating new distribution channels for U.S. imports made cheaper by increased U.S. competitiveness and the strong yen.

3) Continued easing of regulations and decline in land prices have encouraged further activity by foreign firms in Japan's distribution, service, and retail sectors. An increasing number of foreign firms are also entering Japan's service sector, many areas of which have previously been protected from competition due to regulations. Foreign firms, which are 90 percent more productive than Japanese non-manufacturing firms and 70 percent more productive than Japanese firms as a whole, are stimulating rapid change in business practices.

h. Competition from Asian nations

1) Much of the competition in Japan from Asian countries is the result of Japanese firms moving their production to those countries in the mid-1990s to avoid high labor costs at home and increase or recover their international competitiveness. Key industries, such as electronics manufacturers, are being accused of hollowing out, that is, closing their local production facilities and becoming marketing organizations for other, generally foreign, producers. Those companies that are continuing to do their own manufacturing are shifting to other countries where production costs are lower. South Korea, which long depended on Japan for investment and technology, is now successfully competing against it in the export of high-tech goods such as electronics, petrochemicals, machinery, and steel

2) This new Japanese strategy is creating regional groups capable of competing worldwide and also ties Asian nations to the Japanese economy. Some Asian countries welcome their ties with Japan, while others remain concerned about being excessively dependent on the Japanese

D. Developing Nations and the NIEs of Asia

One factor that stands out in this analysis of competitive forces is that products made by Asian firms are competing strongly with the output of older, more experienced producers from Europe, the U.S., and Japan. Japanese companies driven by the strong yen to build plants in East Asia are increasingly exporting their output (called *reverse exports*) back to Japan. U.S. investment in East Asia has increased, rising to nearly $6 billion between 1987 and 1999.

1. An economic crisis hits the region.

a. The Asian NICs, NIEs, and China developed rapidly over the past two decades, and a major factor driving these nations' growth has been international trade (Table 13.8).

b. Rapid growth in the 1980s and early 1990s was accompanied by excess capacity, high levels of debt, and rapid inflation in real estate and other asset values. Ironically, the financial system that had allowed these nations to achieve rapid growth through access to easy money, often based on political connections and other factors, was

206

ultimately one of the main reasons for later problems. In 1997, a financial crisis in Thailand spread quickly to other Asian nations, resulting in a decline of local currencies of up to 80 percent versus the U.S. dollar. Many of these nations experienced similar declines in stock prices, as about $400 billion in value was erased from Asian stock markets in 1997. Most of the region experienced deep economic recession as part of one of the largest economic collapses the world has ever experienced

    c.   The International Monetary Fund came to the assistance of many of the affected nations, committing over $110 billion in short-term loans just to Thailand, Indonesia, and South Korea. To obtain these loans, the borrowing nations had to agree to a number of actions, including economic deregulation, banking reform, and tight macroeconomic policies. There was also pressure for substantial structural reforms, including reduced government spending, scaling back of government efforts at industrial targeting, reform of banking systems, removal of barriers to foreign investment, and a breakup or sell-off of indebted companies.

2.   Recovery is faster than expected.

    a.   There are signs that most Asian economies are emerging from the wreckage. For the first time for many of them, management of Asian companies are concentrating on earning profits instead of trying to break production records at any price. Formerly powerful conglomerates in Korea, Indonesia, and other nations have been forced to sell off portions of their businesses to pay debts. Banks that served as conduits for directing a country's savings to the conglomerates' favored entities must now function as normal commercial banks.

    b.   Since 1999, substantial economic recovery has occurred in most Asian countries. Many nations have resorted to exporting as a means of dealing with their financial problems (Table 13.8). These strategies have been facilitated by a booming U.S. economy. The collapse of Asian currencies caused these countries' goods to be much less expensive than prior to the crisis, allowing Asian nations to ship vast quantities of merchandise, particularly computers and electronics goods. In the first half of 2000, electronics goods alone accounted for 60 percent of Thailand's exports, 53 percent of Hong Kong's, 34 percent of Taiwan's, 33 percent of China's, 25 percent of Malaysia's, 19 percent of Korea's, and 14 percent of Singapore's exports

3.   E-commerce has a promising future. While Asian NIEs, NICs, and China currently lag the U.S., Europe, and Japan in internet access and e-commerce, the gap is expected to narrow. The number of internet users in the Asia-Pacific region is projected to increase from 73 million in 2000 to 233 million in 2005. In terms of e-commerce, Hong Kong, Korea, and Singapore have the greatest potential in the near-term, especially for business-to-consumer applications. However, government actions may pose a barrier in some nations, due to restrictive attitudes toward the internet and e-commerce. For example, in 2000, the Chinese central government introduced regulations on foreign ownership of internet portals, which could constrain that country's web development.

4.   Questions remain regarding the future.

    a.   Since mid-1997, short-term foreign debt levels have become more manageable, though still equaling 20 percent of the region's total output, and foreign exchange reserves have grown in most of the Asian nations. While government efforts to provide stimulus packages have helped to hasten the rate of economic recovery, several nations are running budget deficits of about 5 to 6 percent of GDP. In several nations, the pace of structural reform has been slower than anticipated and there are still many weak banks and companies with problem loans. In many nations, output remains below pre-crisis levels.

    b.   It remains to be seen if the Asian NICs and NIEs can soon regain the sustained high growth rates that existed before the crisis. To do so will require their governments to implement structural reforms. Slowing growth in the U.S., especially in high-technology sectors supplied by Asian companies, and continued economic difficulties in Japan may also limit the effectiveness of traditional national economic development strategies based on export-driven growth.

5. China, a case unto itself.

    a.   China is the world's most populous nation, with over 1.3 billion people. Over the past 20 years, China has had strong sustained growth, even by comparison to the Asian NICs and NIEs. It has achieved average growth in merchandise exports of 15 percent per year during the past 2 decades and has a large trade surplus. With $87.8 billion in imports in 1999, the U.S. is China's largest trading partner. Exports from China to the U.S. grew at an average rate of 21 percent during the 1990s, and the growing trade deficit has caused concern among U.S. politicians and business people. China's performance in international trade and as a destination for large flows of foreign direct investment helped that country to largely escape the 1997 Asian economic crisis that hit most of its neighbors.

    b.   China has been trying to join the World Trade Organization for over 13 years. The country views WTO membership as a necessary element in its quest to establish a sustainable market economy. However, entry into the WTO will require China to eliminate many trade barriers and other practices that currently protect its business sector from foreign competitors. The transition will require many changes in government and business practices, and concerns remain regarding China's vulnerability to the type of currency problems that struck other Asian nations.

E. Counterfeiting and Piracy: A Challenge to Business Worldwide

1. A special kind of competition confronting unwary consumers and international companies in both developed and developing nations is counterfeiting. The International Chamber of Commerce estimates that 8 percent of world trade consists of counterfeit products. According to the Global Anti-Counterfeiting Group, counterfeiting and piracy cost U.S. manufacturers $200 billion per year.

2. Besides the production of exact copies of branded items, other kinds of counterfeiting include making (1) close copies with different names, (2) reproductions that are not exact copies, and (3) imitations that are cheap copies and fool no one. Piracy, a kind of counterfeiting, is the copying of trade-related intellectual property protected by patents, copyrights, and trademarks.

3. Increasingly, the sale of counterfeit goods is occurring on the Web. There are about 25,000 websites selling consumer luxury products, and from 20 to 30 percent of them sell counterfeit goods or misuse a manufacturer's trademark.

4. Counterfeiting is extremely common in Asian nations such as South Korea, China, Hong Kong, Malaysia, Thailand, and Indonesia. Taiwan has been one of the major sources of counterfeit products. Under heavy pressure from the U.S., the Taiwanese government passed strong copyright laws and banned the export of pirated products. Despite a decline in the proportion of seizures of products from Taiwan since 1999, that country remains a major source of illegal products. Organized crime, particularly Chinese crime syndicates known as Triads, has become increasingly involved in product counterfeiting. The Federal Bureau of Investigation considers counterfeiting and other forms of theft of intellectual property to be "the crime of the 21st Century."

5. Despite pressure from business groups and the passage of new laws in many nations which have been major sources of counterfeit goods, the problem of counterfeiting appears to be growing. There was a 40 percent increase in seized counterfeit goods in 1998 over the 1997 levels, a 31 percent increase from 1998 to 1999, and a further increase of nearly 100 percent is suggested by data from the first half of 2000. In terms of product categories seized in 1998 and 1997, pirated software, motion pictures, and music topped the list. During the first half of 2000, China was the source of nearly three times the value of counterfeit items as the next largest nation, Taiwan (Table 13.9). Malaysia was the third largest source, followed by Hong Kong and Panama.

6. China, the biggest offender. Around the world, China has earned the status as the world's biggest source of counterfeit goods. Foreign companies have hired detectives, conducted raids, filed court cases, lobbied Beijing, and pressed for sanctions by their own governments against China, only to see the problem continue to escalate. It is estimated that counterfeit products account for a quarter of Chinese manufacturing, and ending the production of such products could wreak havoc in some sectors of the Chinese economy.

   Counterfeit products can be dangerous. In addition to counterfeiting luxury goods, pesticides, fertilizers, drugs, and aircraft parts are routinely copies. The FAA reported that fake parts were involved in at least 166 U.S.-based aircraft accidents from 1973 to 1993.

   Combating imitations. Industry associations are working to stop product counterfeiting.

7. Industrial espionage

   a. For years, firms have acquired information about competitors by hiring their employees, talking to their customers, etc. Firms such as Mitsubishi and Hitachi have committed illegal acts to obtain information on competitor's products.

   b. General Motors accused its former head of global purchasing of arranging an enormous act of industrial sabotage when he left to join Volkswagen, taking data on GM's future products and information on suppliers and parts costs. There are claims that the French government participates in industrial espionage. American intelligence experts caution American businesspeople not to fly on Air France because of bugged seats and French government spies posing as businesspeople. Government employees routinely enter hotel rooms of visiting businesspeople to look through their briefcases.

III. Analysis of the Competitive Forces
In a survey of over 100 major American firms conducted in 1997 by a consulting group specializing in competitor intelligence systems, only 60 percent of all respondents had organized competitor intelligence systems. However, 82 percent of the companies with revenues of $10 billion or more had them.

A. Is Competitor Assessment New?
Competitor assessment has been going on for a long time. The difference is that management recognize that increased competition has created a need for more in-depth and broader knowledge of competitors' activities. Some even hire former CIA agents to handle data gathering and analysis.

B. Sources of Information.

1. There are five sources of information about the strengths, weaknesses, and threats of a firm's competitors.

   a. within the firm

   b. published material, including computer databases

   c. suppliers/customers

       d.   competitors' employees

       e.   direct observance or analyzing physical evidence of competitors' activities

  2.   Benchmarking is a way for firms to measure themselves against world leaders.

  3.   Managers can use one or more of the four basic types of benchmarking

       a.   internal-comparing one operation in a firm with another

       b.   competitive-comparing a firm's operation with that of a competitor

       c.   functional-comparing similar functions of firms in one's industry

       d.   generic-comparing operations in totally unrelated industries

Answer to Questions

1. Although firms, not nations, compete against each other, most economic and social conditions as well as political actions affect the ability of all of a nation's firms to compete in world markets. An example is a nation's exchange rates. If its currency is expensive relative to other currencies, all the country's companies find it harder to compete against foreign firms.

2. *U.S. government*–can pressure other governments to lower their barriers to U.S. exports and protect U.S. patents. It can eliminate double taxation of corporate profits. Promote increased R&D spending. Improved education systems at the primary, secondary, and varsity by levels. The government can support U.S. firms that face competition from foreign targeted industries, promote protection of intellectual property rights, and manage dependence on foreign capital.

   Management–Managements must make product quality and increased productivity their top priorities and must be willing to invest long term instead of expecting an immediate return. They must be persistent and more aggressive against foreign competition. Workers should be involved in decision making.

   Labor–must also take the long-term view and must work with management instead of taking the traditional adversarial position. Work rules can be loosened.

3. According to the McKinsey report, in inflation adjusted terms, minimum wages have doubled in both France and Germany over the past 25 years. They blame this increase in inflation-adjusted minimum wages for keeping low-skilled people out of the workplace, essentially by raising their costs above their level of productivity and potential for adding economic value to companies. The report suggested that if the U.S. raised the minimum wage to the level of the French (from a current level of about 55% of the French minimum wage), 30 million Americans would lose their jobs.

4. Another group of nations has emerged to become a fourth important region, with a combined GDP over $2 trillion. This group includes the four East Asian NIEs, the two NICs, Malaysia, Thailand and China. There are extremely strong trade flows among the Asian NIEs and between the NIEs and the members of ASEAN. Firms from Asian NIEs export more to other NIEs and ASEAN members than they do to Japan. They are also important investors in ASEAN members. Moreover, there is no longer a division of labor just between Japan and other Asian countries. Significant cost differences exist between the Asian NIEs and the Asian NICs and between the Asian NIEs and the ASEAN nations. South Korean firms have moved production to lower cost nations such as Indonesia, for example.

5. They claim that the keiretsu construct informal barriers to the sales of foreign goods in Japan. Toyota can assemble an automobile from parts supplied only by its keiretsu, for example. This makes it very difficult for potential suppliers outside the keiretsu to obtain any of Toyota's business. Remember that Toyota owns small amounts of stock in each of the main keiretsu members.

After the collapse of the "bubble economy," regulations in Japan were relaxed to allow greater access by companies to international financial markets. This allowed both banks and companies to become less dependent on the keiretsu, which could reduce the power of the keiretsu over the individual members. In addition, sustained domestic stagnation since the early 1990s, internationalization of capital markets, and pressure for reform of corporate governance in Japan have begun to further loosen traditional relationships among affiliated members of keiretsu. Many of the Japanese banks have been merging as well as selling their cross-shareholdings, making a gradual breakup of the keiretsu system seem like an increasingly likely outcome.

6. Industrial targeting is a government practice of assisting selected industries to grow by various means: subsidies, low-cost loans, keeping the domestic market just for the local targeted firms. The United States government has targeted the flat-panel display industry whose products are used in notebook computers, video games, and control panels in jet aircraft.

7. Counterfeiting, putting well-known manufacturers' names on copies of their merchandise, is estimated to cost the legitimate owners $200 billion annually. Piracy is a kind of counterfeiting involving copying of trade related intellectual property protected by patents, copyrights, and trademarks. Products commonly pirated include software, videos, compact discs, and books. It is estimated that $12 billion are lost annually in sales of pirated software.

8. To boost exports, the Japanese government allows the yen to fall against the dollar to both increase imports and restricts domestic growth to dampen demand for imports. Japan's trade surplus increases rapidly. The U.S. reacts demanding that the Japanese government (1) allows the yen to become more expensive, (2) reduces import restrictions on U.S. goods, permits American firms more freedom in doing business in Japan, and (4) stimulates the economy to increase demand. The Japanese make some concessions on American imports, reduces some of the restrictions on U.S. firms doing business in Japan, and drive up the value of the yen to make Japanese exports more expensive.
   But, generally, the yen overshoots and recession follows. The government again tries to export its way out of the recession without making any other changes, and the cycle repeats itself.

9. Competitor intelligence systems gather information from all areas within the firm, published material, competitors' employees and direct observation. Depending on the methods used, intelligence gathering from these sources may be ethical or not. If a company advertises job openings it does not have to attract competitors' employees to interviews, this is considered to be unethical. It would be unethical to enter a competitor's premises to take pictures, participate in plant visits without informing the company visited of the participants' industrial affiliation or steal a competitor's waste.

Answers to Research Problems

1. The site address for the Business Software Alliance's table on losses and illegal copying rates for software for 1999 is http://new.bsa.org/usa/globallib/piracy/piracystats99.phtml. This website has the report, "1999 Global Software Piracy Report," published May 2000.

   For the 25 countries with the highest rates of software piracy in 1999, the report lists the following:

Country	Piracy Rate	Retail Software Revenue Lost to Piracy (US$ millions)
Vietnam	98%	13.1
China	91	645.5
CIS-less Russia	90	43.5
Russia	89	165.5
Lebanon	88	2.1
Oman	88	9.8
Indonesia	85	42.1
Bolivia	85	5.1
Paraguay	83	8.2
El Salvador	83	16.7
Pakistan	83	18.9
Bahrain	82	6.0
Thailand	81	82.2
Kuwait	81	13.2
Romania	81	12.1
Nicaragua	80	6.8
Qatar	80	4.5
Guatemala	80	15.6
Bulgaria	80	11.2
Egypt	75	33.2
Jordan	75	3.3
Honduras	75	6.3
Turkey	74	98.3
Other Latin America	72	37.4
Dominican Republic	72	15.3

The 2 countries with the highest rates of piracy are in Asia. Most of the countries with the highest rates of piracy are in Asia, Eastern Europe/CIS, the Middle East, and Latin America.

The regions with the highest dollar losses in 1999 were North America and Western Europe, where their large economies and the largest PC and software markets resulted in large dollar losses despite relatively low piracy rates. Nevertheless, on a dollar basis for the value of software revenues lost to piracy among the 25 countries with the highest rates of piracy, China is by far the leading country ($645.5 million), followed by Russia ($165.5 million), Turkey ($98.3 million), and Thailand ($82.2 million).

Discussion of Mini-Case 13-1: Wal-Mart Takes on the World

1. Many skeptics have claimed that Wal-Mart's business practices were distinctly American and could not successfully be transferred internationally. Yet, during the 1990s and early 2000s, the company has internationalized at a rapid pace. By January 2001, the company had 1,068 retail units outside the U.S., employing over 255,000 associates and accounting for approximately 14% of the company's sales.

2. When Wal-Mart began to internationalize, it did not start with the large European retail market, where there were strong, established competitors. Instead, Wal-Mart focused on emerging markets with large populations – in Latin America, this included Mexico, Argentina, and Brazil. In Asia, they aimed at China.

3. Wal-Mart used learning from partners to facilitate international expansion. When first entering foreign markets, in 1991 in Mexico City, Wal-Mart relied on a 50-50 joint venture with a leading local retailer. When they entered Brazil 4 years later, they had the majority position in a 60-40 joint venture with a leading local retailer. When the company later expanded into Argentina, it entered on a wholly owned basis. Then, in 1997, Wal-Mart expanded further in Mexico by acquiring a controlling interest in the leading Mexican retail conglomerate, Cifra.

4. Wal-Mart was one of the first international retailers to enter China. It initially planned to enter China with a partner, Charoen Pokphand, a Thai conglomerate with extensive investments in China and a strong track record with joint ventures. However, the venture ended after 18 months due to disagreements over control. Wal-Mart then formed a venture with 2 politically connected partners, with the first store in a rapidly growing city near Hong Kong (the proximity to Hong Kong was expected to help the company manage its operations while learning about China). The company learned many things about the differing needs of Chinese consumers, the problems of working with less-modernized Chinese suppliers, and the importance of building relationships with government agencies and local communities. By 1991, Wal-Mart had 11 stores in China and was poised to take advantage of the phasing out of Chinese restrictions on foreign participation in its retail market after an expected entry of China into the World Trade Organization.

5. After initially focusing on large developing nations, Wal-Mart began to focus on the Canadian and European markets, where they would confront strong, entrenched competitors. Due to difficulty in building market share from scratch in such a marketplace, Wal-Mart entered via acquisitions. In Canada, it acquired 122 Canadian Woolco stores in 1994 and now has a 35 percent share of the Canadian discount- and department-store retail market. In Europe, Wal-Mart entered both Germany and the U.K. through acquisitions, which allowed the company to quickly build market share within the highly advanced and competitive European retail market. From this base, the company expects to grow through a combination of new stores and further acquisitions.

6. Even in Europe, Wal-Mart encountered difficulties, including overextension of its limited European infrastructure, problems with suppliers unfamiliar with its operating practices, and resistance from competitors, regulators, and labor to some of its policies.

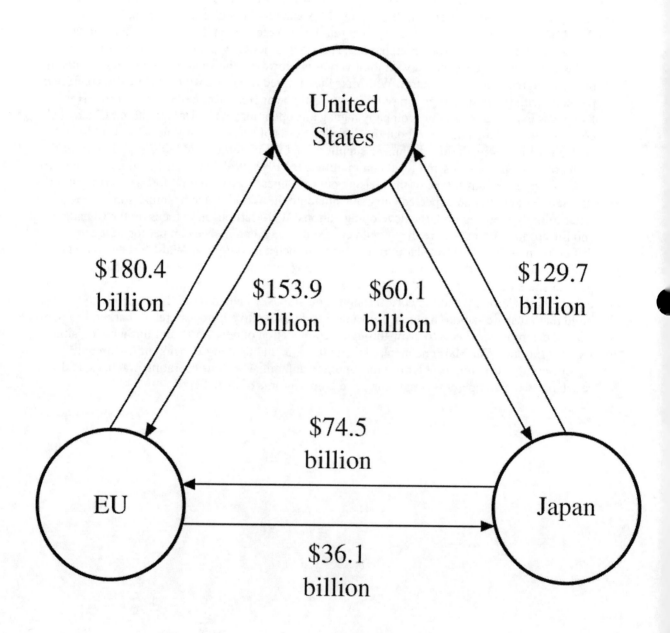

TM 13.2
Figure 13.2

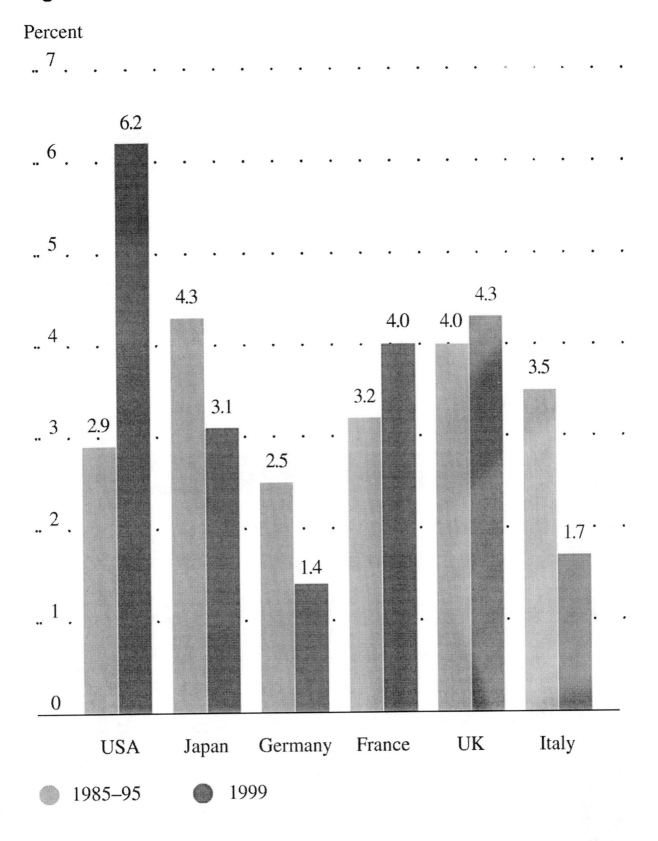

Percent

USA   Japan   Germany   France   UK   Italy

● 1985–95   ● 1999

TM 13.3
Figure 13.3

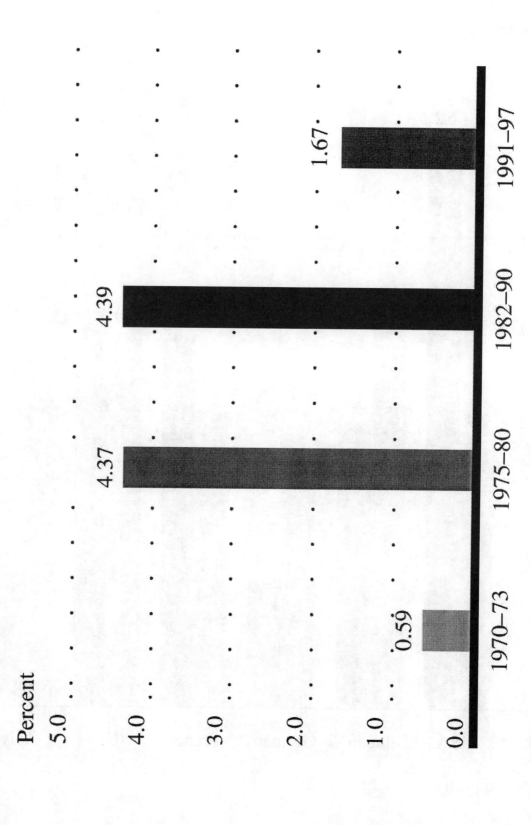

Percent

5.0

4.0   4.37   4.39

3.0

2.0   1.67

1.0
         0.59

0.0
    1970–73   1975–80   1982–90   1991–97

McGraw–Hill/Irwin

TM 13.4

Figure 13.4

Iceland
$8/0.3

Atlantic
Ocean

Finland
$124/5.2

Sweden
$227/8.9

Norway
$146/4.4

United
Kingdom
$1,357/59.1

Denmark
$175/5.3

Ireland
$82/3.7

Netherlands
$382/15.7

Germany
$2,134/82.0

Belgium-Luxembourg $275/10.6

France
$1,427/58.8

Austria
$212/8.1

Switzerland
$264/7.1

Italy
$1,172/57.6

Black
Sea

Portugal
$107/10.0

Spain
$553/39.4

Mediterranean Sea

Greece
$121/10.5

● EU members   ● EFTA members

TM 13.5
Figure 13.5

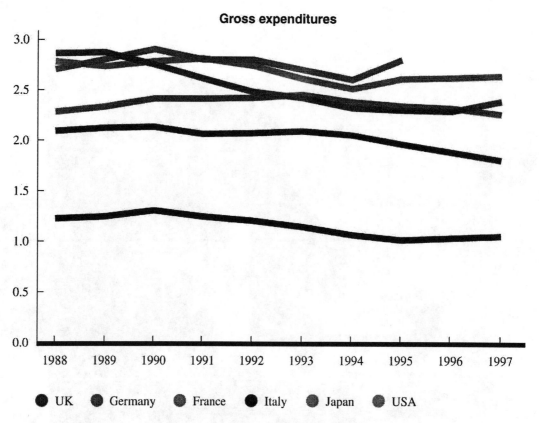

Gross expenditures

● UK ● Germany ● France ● Italy ● Japan ● USA

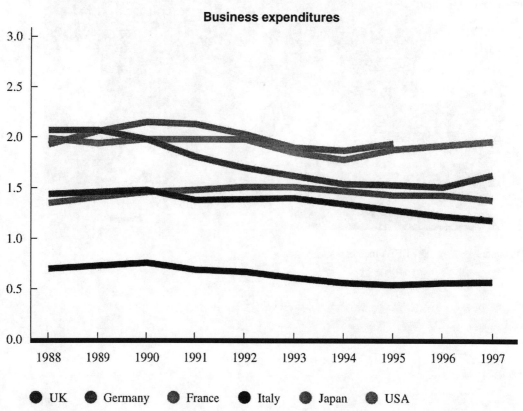

Business expenditures

● UK ● Germany ● France ● Italy ● Japan ● USA

The World Competitiveness Scoreboard: Ranking as of April 19, 2000

Country	Score	Ranking						
		2000	1999	1998	1997	1996	1995	1994
United States	100.00	1	1	1	1	1	1	1
Singapore	75.22	2	2	2	2	2	2	2
Finland	74.01	3	3	5	4	15	18	19
Netherlands	72.13	4	5	4	6	7	8	8
Switzerland	68.49	5	6	7	7	9	5	5
Luxembourg	68.09	6	4	9	12	8	—	—
Ireland	64.83	7	11	11	15	22	22	21
Germany	64.49	8	9	14	14	10	6	6
Sweden	63.86	9	14	17	16	14	12	9
Iceland	63.52	10	17	19	21	25	25	—
Canada	63.42	11	10	10	10	12	13	20
Denmark	63.38	12	8	8	8	5	7	7
Australia	63.12	13	12	15	18	21	16	16
Hong Kong	60.47	14	7	3	3	3	3	4
United Kingdom	59.36	15	15	12	11	19	15	14
Norway	57.79	16	13	6	5	6	10	126
Japan	57.36	17	16	18	9	4	4	3
Austria	57.19	18	19	22	20	16	—	—
France	54.33	19	21	21	19	20	—	—
Belgium	53.34	20	22	23	22	17	—	—
New Zealand	52.77	21	20	13	13	11	9	10
Taiwan	51.10	22	18	16	23	18	—	—
Israel	50.30	23	24	25	26	24	—	—
Spain	47.28	24	23	27	25	29	—	—
Malaysia	42.12	25	27	20	17	23	23	18
Chile	41.44	26	25	26	24	13	—	—
Hungary	40.90	27	26	28	36	39	—	—
Korea	38.36	28	38	35	30	27	—	—
Portugal	37.97	29	28	29	32	36	—	—
Italy	34.71	30	30	30	34	28	—	—
China	34.32	31	29	24	27	26	—	—

Sources: IMD, "The World Competitiveness Scoreboard," http://www.imd.ch/wcy/factors/overalldata.html (August 23, 1998); and http://www.imd.ch/wcy/ranking/ranking.cfm (April 25, 2000).

Global Competitiveness Report
of 25 Top-Ranked Nations

Country	Growth Competitiveness Rank				
	2000	1999	1998	1997	1996
United States	1	2	3	3	4
Singapore	2	1	1	1	1
Luxembourg	3	7	10	11	5
Netherlands	4	9	7	12	17
Ireland	5	10	11	16	26
Finland	6	11	15	19	16
Canada	7	5	5	4	8
Hong Kong	8	3	2	2	2
United Kingdom	9	8	4	7	15
Switzerland	10	6	8	6	6
Taiwan	11	4	6	8	9
Australia	12	12	14	17	12
Sweden	13	19	23	22	21
Denmark	14	17	16	20	11
Germany	15	25	24	25	22
Norway	16	15	9	10	7
Belgium	17	24	27	31	25
Austria	18	20	20	27	19
Israel	19	28	29	24	24
New Zealand	20	13	13	5	3
Japan	21	14	12	14	13
France	22	23	22	23	23
Portugal	23	27	26	30	34
Iceland	24	18	30	38	27
Malaysia	25	16	17	9	10

Source: World Economic Forum, The Global Competitiveness Report, 2000 and 1999 editions, www.worldeconomicforum.com (November 29, 2000). Reprinted with permission of World Economic Forum.

Economic Creativity Index 2000 for the 25 Top-Ranked Nations

Country	Economic Creativity Index Rank	Economic Creativity	Technology Index	Start-up Index
United States	1	2.02	2.02	2.02
Finland	2	1.73	2.02	1.43
Singapore	3	1.63	1.95	1.31
Luxembourg	4	1.44	1.37	1.51
Sweden	5	1.36	1.52	1.21
Israel	6	1.35	1.55	1.15
Ireland	7	1.31	1.74	0.87
Netherlands	8	1.26	1.20	1.32
United Kingdom	9	1.22	1.08	1.36
Iceland	1 0	1.16	0.80	1.51
Switzerland	11	1.11	1.62	0.60
Hong Kong	12	1.10	0.58	1.63
Denmark	13	1.07	1.25	0.88
Germany	14	1.04	1.66	0.41
Canada	15	0.99	1.21	0.77
Australia	16	0.97	0.91	1.04
Taiwan	17	0.97	0.90	1.04
Belgium	18	0.95	1.00	0.90
Norway	1 9	0.80	0.61	0.98
Japan	20	0.69	1.59	−0.21
Hungary	21	0.66	1.06	0.27
New Zealand	22	0.64	0.73	0.56
Malaysia	23	0.59	1.08	0.11
France	24	0.59	1.36	−0.18
Poland	25	0.56	1.14	−0.01

Source: World Economic Forum, The Global Competitiveness Report 2000, www.worldeconomicforum.com (November 29, 2000). Reprinted with permission of World Economic Forum.

Who Is Head of the Global Class?

A study of 15,000 students and 1,500 schools from 21 countries, sponsored by the International Association for the Evaluation of Educational Achievement, found that factors in students' homes have more of a bearing on success than do class size, amount of homework, and other instructional factors. Listed below are the average scores at the eighth grade or its equivalent for a selection of the countries studied.

Country	Overall Average	Science Tasks	Mathematics Tasks
Singapore	71	72	70
England*	67	71	64
Australia*	6 5	63	6 6
Switzerland	65	65	66
Sweden	64	63	65
Scotland	62	64	61
Norway	6 2	58	6 5
Czech Republic	61	60	62
Canada	60	59	62
New Zealand	60	58	62
Netherlands*	60	58	62
United States*	55	55	54
Spain	5 4	56	5 2
Iran, Islamic Republic of	52	50	54
Portugal	47	47	48
Cyprus	46	49	44
International average	59	58	59

*Countries not satisfying guidelines for sample participation rates.

Source: *Performance Assessment in IEA's Third International Mathematics and Science Study (TIMSS)*, International Association for the Evaluation of Educational Achievement, September 1997, http://timss.bc.edu/TIMSS1/TIMSSPDF//Pareport.pdf.

TM 13.10
Table 13.5

Growth in Volume of World Merchandise Trade by Selected Regions (annual change in percentage)

	Exports						Imports					
	Average, 1990–96	1995	1996	1997	1998	1999	Average, 1990–96	1995	1996	1997	1998	1999
World	**5.5**	**8.5**	**4.0**	**10.5**	**4.5**	**4.5**	**6.0**	**8.5**	**4.5**	**—**	**—**	**—**
North America*	7.0	9.5	5.5	11.0	3.5	4.5	7.0	8.0	5.5	13.0	10.5	10.5
Mexico	—	—	—	19.5	11.0	13.5	—	—	—	28.0	15.5	15.0
Latin America	8.5	12.0	11.0	11.5	7.5	7.0	11.0	3.0	10.5	22.5	8.5	-2.0
Western Europe	5.0	7.5	4.0	9.5	5.5	3.5	4.0	6.5	3.0	9.0	8.5	3.5
European Union (15)	5.0	8.0	4.0	9.5	6.0	3.5	4.0	6.0	2.5	8.5	8.5	4.0
Transition economies	3.5	14.5	3.5	10.5	5.0	-3.0	2.5	11.5	12.0	13.5	5.0	-10.0
Asia	7.0	9.5	2.5	13.0	3.5	6.0	9.5	14.0	4.5	5.5	-8.5	9.0
Japan	1.0	3.5	20.5	12.0	-1.5	2.0	6.0	12.5	2.5	1.5	-5.5	9.5
East Asian traders†	10.0	14.5	3.5	16.5	13.0	11.5	10.5	15.5	4.0	3.0	-22.5	17.5

*Canada and the United States.

†Hong Kong, the Republic of Korea, Malaysia, Singapore, Taiwan, and Thailand for 1990–1996 data. Indonesia, Republic of Korea, Malaysia, Philippines, and Thailand for 1997–1999 data.

— = data not available.

Sources: World Trade Organization, "International Trade," April 4, 1997, http://www.wto.org/intltrad/intlorg.htm (July 9, 1997); and "Developing Countries' Merchandise Exports in 1999 Expanded by 8.5%—about Twice as Fast as the Global Average," http://www.wto.org/english/news_e/pres00_e/pr175_e.htm (April 6, 2000).

McGraw-Hill/Irwin

The Year 2000 Corruption Perceptions Index: Top 20 and Bottom 10 Countries

Rank	Country	2000 Corruption Perceptions Index Score
1	Finland	10.0
2	Denmark	9.8
3	New Zealand	9.4
3	Sweden	9.4
5	Canada	9.2
6	Iceland	9.1
6	Norway	9.1
6	Singapore	9.1
9	Netherlands	8.9
10	United Kingdom	8.7
11	Luxembourg	8.6
11	Switzerland	8.6
13	Australia	8.3
14	United States	7.8
15	Austria	7.7
15	Hong Kong	7.7
17	Germany	7.6
18	Chile	7.4
19	Ireland	7.2
20	Spain	7.0
81	Mozambique	2.2
82	Kenya	2.1
82	Russia	2.1
84	Cameroon	2.0
85	Angola	1.7
85	Indonesia	1.7
87	Azerbaijan	1.5
87	Ukraine	1.5
89	Yugoslavia	1.3
90	Nigeria	1.2

Rankings are based on multiple surveys from 1998 through 2000. The rankings are based on the degree to which corruption is perceived to exist among public officials and politicians. The index is a composite, drawing on 16 surveys from eight independent institutions. Surveys incorporate the perceptions of businesspeople, the general public, and country analysts.

Source: Transparency International, www.transparency.de/documents/cpi/2000/cpi2000.html (September 14, 2000).

© Copyright Transparency International 2000.

International Comparisons of Initial Investment Costs in the Manufacturing Sector

		Japan	United States	United Kingdom	Germany	France
Manufacturing plant	Price of space in industrial park	100	13	12	17	2
Office	Lease guarantee	100	8	81	7	10
Setting up a company	Registration costs	100	7	139	76	2
Hiring costs	Factory manager	100	67	82	78	79
	Administrative Manager	100	11	19	44	44
	Engineers	100	20	34	81	81
	Headquarters staff, factory workers	100	18	3	5	8
Housing, school	Rent guarantee	100	12	20	25	29
	Admission fee. tuition	100	85	62	46	59
Visa	Visa fee	100	158	283	67	333
Ratio		100	14	24	20	9

Note: Japan = 100. Costs are based on a wholly owned subsidiary with 500 million yen of capital, a 5,000-square-meter factory with 3,000 square meters of factory space in an industrial park in a provincial city, 500 square meters of office space in a major city, one expatriate representative director with three dependents (spouse and two school-aged children) and 150 square meters of rental housing in a major city, and local hires of one factory manager, one administration manager, 20 engineers, clerical workers for the headquarters, and factory workers.

Source: JETRO Inward Foreign Direct Investment Survey (Tokyo: Japan External Trade Organization), www.jetro.go.jp/ip/e/access/inward_foreign_direct_investment.html (November 12, 2000).

Average Annual Increases in Merchandise Exports for Selected Countries, 1980–1995

	Average Annual Growth Rate, 1980–1990 (%)	Average Annual Growth Rate, 1990–1999 (%)	Growth Rate in 1997 (%)	Growth Rate in 1998 (%)	Growth Rate in 1999 (%)	Value in 1999 ($ billions)
World	4.7%	6.5%	10.5%	5.0%	5.0%	$5,473
Japan	5.0	2.5	12.0	−1.5	2.0	419
China	11.4	—	—	—	—	195
Hong Kong	15.3	9.0	6.0	−4.5	3.5	174
South Korea	—	15.0	25.0	17.0	12.0	145
Taiwan	5.9	5.5	8.0	1.0	5.0	122
Singapore	16.2	11.0	7.0	−0.5	5.5	115
Malaysia	17.8	13.5	9.5	4.0	20.0	85
Thailand	21.6	10.0	7.5	8.0	12.0	58
United States	3.6	6.5	12.0	2.5	4.5	695
Mexico	12.2	14	15	6	16	137
Germany	4.6	5.5	12.0	7.0	4.0	542

Sources: *World Development Indicators, 1997* (Washington, DC: World Bank, 1997), pp. 154–56, 158–60; and *International Trade Statistics 2000* (Geneva: World Trade Organization, 2000), pp. 17, 44, 51, 60–61, 83.

McGraw-Hill/Irwin

CHAPTER 14
STRATEGIC PLANNING, ORGANIZATIONAL DESIGN, & CONTROL OF THE GLOBAL FIRM

Learning Objectives

1. To understand international strategy and competencies and their role in achieving international competitive advantage.

2. To study the steps in the global strategic planning process.

3. To see examples of corporate mission statements, objectives quantified goals and strategies.

4. To examine new directions in strategic planning.

5. To study various organizational forms and understand the concept of the virtual corporation.

6. To emphasize the importance of controls for an IC and the elements of determining where decisions should be made.

7. To explain how an IC can maintain control of a joint venture or other organization in which it has less than 50% ownership.

8. To list the types of information an IC needs from its units around the world.

9. To understand de-jobbing.

Overview

The first three sections of this book have primarily focused on the broad environmental context in which international businesses compete. This discussion has included the theoretical framework for international trade and investment, the international monetary and other organizations that influence international business, and the financial, economic, physical, social, political, legal, and other institutions found in various nations. In this chapter, we begin to shift our attention away from the external environment, and we focus instead on the business itself, including the actions managers can take to help their companies compete more effectively as international businesses.

To succeed in today's global marketplace, a company must be able to quickly identify and exploit opportunities wherever they may occur, domestically or internationally. To do this effectively, managers must fully understand why, how, and where they intend to do business, now and over time. This requires managers to have a clear understanding of their company's mission, a vision for how they intend to achieve that mission, and an understanding of how they plan to compete with other companies. In order to meet these challenges, managers must understand their company's strengths and weaknesses and be able to accurately compare them to those of their worldwide competitors. Strategic planning provides valuable tools for helping managers address these global challenges.

International strategy is concerned with the way firms make fundamental choices about developing and deploying scarce resources internationally. International strategy involves decisions that deal with all of the various functions and activities of a company, not merely a single area such as marketing or production. To be effective, a company's international strategy needs to be consistent among the various functions, products, and regional units of the company (internal consistency) as well as with the demands of the international competitive environment (external consistency).

The goal of international strategy is to achieve and maintain a unique and valuable competitive position, both in a nation as well as globally, a position that has been termed "competitive advantage." This suggests that the international company either must perform different activities than its competitors, or else perform the same activities but in different ways. To create a competitive advantage which is sustainable over time, the international company should try to develop skills, or competencies, that (1) create value for customers, and for which customers are willing to pay, (2) are rare, since competencies shared among many competitors cannot be a basis for competitive advantage, (3) are difficult to imitate or substitute for, and (4) the firm must be organized to allow it to exploit fully the competitive potential of these valuable, rare, and difficult to imitate competencies. In attempting to develop competitive advantage, a company's managers are forced to make choices regarding what to do, and what *not* to do, now and over time. Different companies make different choices, and these choices have implications for each company's ability to meet the needs of customers and to create a defensible competitive position internationally. Without adequate planning, managers are more likely to make decisions that do not make good sense competitively, and the company's international competitiveness may be harmed.

Many global and multinational companies have instituted formal worldwide strategic planning to identify opportunities and threats, formulate strategies to handle them and stipulate the means to finance them. Global strategic planning provides a formal structure in which managers analyze the firm's external environments, analyze the firm's internal environments, define the company's business and mission, set objectives, quantify goals, and formulate strategies and tactics to achieve them. Operating managers do the planning and the planning staff assist them.

Organizational design generally follows strategic planning and both are commonly done during the planning process. Firms may (1) have an international division, (2) be organized by product, function or region (3) have a mixture of them (hybrid form). Some firms have tried a matrix form to attain a balance between product and regional expertise, but its disadvantages have led some firms to use a matrix overlay over the traditional product, regional or functional form instead of a matrix. Management's are now examining two organizational forms, the virtual corporation and the horizontal corporation.

Because the operations of an IC are far flung in countries around the world and because events in one country may affect the entire enterprise, two things become essential. They are *information* and *control.*

When decisions must be made which affect more than one unit of the IC, balance must be struck between the interests of the parent company, the subsidiary companies and the enterprise as a whole. If a decision is made to favor the parent or one subsidiary at the expense of the other, measurements must be devised in order that management of the slighted subsidiary does not suffer because of losses beyond their control.

Control, decisions and measurements are easier when the subsidiary is 100 percent owned than when it is less than 100 percent owned or when an independent joint venture company is involved. In the latter situation, measures to try to control include keeping the technology necessary, keeping the key positions (such as general manager, treasurer or production manager), providing the capital or marketing the product.

Good information is essential about many subjects. Important areas are financial, technology, markets, political and economic. Accurate management evaluation depends on good information.

Suggestions and Comments

1. We find that the students like the material in this chapter because it gives them the "big picture." Those who have had management courses on organization are seeing this material for a second time.

2. Probably the easiest way to present the material on planning is to put Figure 14.1, page 485, on the screen.

3. Point out the importance for an IC to control activities of its units and efforts around the world.

4. Give examples of reasons up-to-date, accurate information is necessary for successful IC operations.

Student Involvement Exercises

1. Have students analyze why certain types of decisions should be made by the IC parent company while others should be made by subsidiary and other IC units.

2. Have students report on sources of different types of information which should be reported by IC units to the parent.

Guest Lecturers

1. Your school's management organization people could speak on control and information.

2. Executives from ICs located near you could add to those subjects.

3. Almost any manager can speak about how planning is done. Perhaps you can get someone from the planning function itself.

Lecture Outline

I. Opening Section

The opening section discusses the question, "Is Strategic Planning Dead?" Some management experts say it is while others say it isn't. However, upon examination, those who say strategic planning is dead, are talking about the old, top-down variety performed by the firm's top senior executives in seclusion with little input by people outside the small planning group.

New strategic planning is done by teams of line and staff managers from different business and functional areas and include both junior staff members that have show the ability to think creatively and experienced veterans. Planners interact with suppliers and customers during the planning process to have first-hand experience with the firm's markets.

II. What is International Strategy, and Why Is It Important?

A. International strategy is concerned with the way firms make fundamental choices about developing and deploying scarce resources internationally. To be effective, strategy needs to be consistent among the company's various functions, products, and regional units (internal consistency) and with the demands of the international competitive environment (external consistency).

B. The goal of international strategy is to achieve competitive advantage, both in a nation and globally. To create a competitive advantage which is sustainable over time, a company must develop competencies that (1) create value for which customers are willing to pay, (2) are rare, (3) are difficult to imitate or substitute for, and (4) the firm must be organized to allow it to exploit fully the competitive potential of these competencies.

C. The challenge for international companies is that resources are always scarce, there are many alternatives for using these scarce resources (for example, which nations to enter), and these alternatives are not equally attractive. Managers must make choices regarding what to do, and what _not_ to do, now and over time. Without adequate planning, managers are more likely to make decisions that do not make good sense competitively.

III. Global Strategic Planning
  A. Why Plan Globally?
  Formal global strategic planning provides a means for managers to identify opportunities and threats, formulate strategies to handle them and stipulate how to finance their implementation. Plans provide for consistency of action among the managers.
  B. Standardization and Planning
  There is a growing tendency to standardize marketing strategies and total products. Their standardization can also be the result of strategic planning.
  C. Global Strategic Planning Process
  The process provides a formal structure for (1) analyzing firm's external environments, (2) analyzing firm's internal environments, (3) defining company's business and mission (4) setting corporate objectives, (5) quantifying goals, (6) formulating strategies and (7) making tactical plans. See Figure 14.1, page 485.
    1. Analysis of domestic, international and foreign environments. Managers must know not only what the present force values are, but also where they appear to be going.
    2. Analysis of corporate controllable variables–this also will include a situational analysis and a forecast. The various functional areas will provide input to the planning staff, if there is one, who will prepare a report for the strategy planning committee. The committee wants to know where the company is heading, what are its strengths and weaknesses and so forth.
    3. Defining corporate business, vision, and mission statements. These broad statements communicate to the firm's stakeholders what the company is and where it expects to go. Some firms have all three statements; others combine two or more. Examples include Ford, DuPont, and Amazon.com.
    4. Set corporate objectives
      a. Objectives direct the firm's course of action.
      b. Goodyear mentions 5 objectives to strengthen its focus as a growth company capable of consistent earnings improvement.
    5. Quantify the objectives
      a. When objectives can be quantified, they should be.
      b. However firms frequently do have non-quantifiable or directional goals.
    6. Formulate the corporate strategies
      a. Action plans that seem plausible, taking into consideration the directions of external forces and the firm's strengths, weaknesses, opportunities, and threats.
      b. Strategies may be general at the corporate level.
      c. Scenarios–"what-if" scenarios help managers become aware of critical elements in the uncontrollable environment forces. See the Worldview, "Rehearsing the Future," page 489, for a description of the manner in which Shell employs scenarios.
      d. Contingency plans–managements prepare contingency plans for worst-and best-case scenarios.
    7. Prepare tactical plans–these spell out how the objectives will be reached.
  D. Management tools
  According to a survey of 9,000 managers they stated that the most commonly used tool (90%) is the missions statement, followed by the customer satisfaction survey (90%). Least used tools are value chain analyses (27%), Porter's 5 forces (24%), mass customization

(20%) and dynamic simulation (20%). However, frequency of use of management tools does not necessarily indicate the relative value of these tools.

E. Strategic Plan Features and Implementation Facilitators

1. Sales forecasts and budgets–these are two prominent features of the strategic plan. They are both a planning and a control technique.

2. Plan implementation facilitators
   Two of the most important are policies and procedures.

   a. Policies are broad guidelines issued by upper management to assist lower level managers to handle recurring problems.

   b. Procedures describe how certain activities will be carried out, thus ensuring uniform action throughout the firm

F. Kinds of Strategic Plans

1. Time horizon–short, medium and long term

2. Level in the organization–If firm has three organizational levels, there will be three levels of plans. (See Figure 14.2, p. 491). Each will be more specific and for a shorter time frame than it is at the level above.

G. Methods of Planning

1. Top-down planning–corporate headquarters develops and provides guidelines.

   a. Disadvantages–restricts initiative at lower levels and shows some insensitivity to local conditions.

   b. Advantages–headquarters should be able to formulate plans that ensure optimal use of firm's resources.

2. Bottom-up planning–lowest levels inform top management of what they expect to do.

   a. Advantage–those responsible for attaining the goals are formulating them

   c. Disadvantage–no guarantee that the sum total of the goals will coincide with those of headquarters.

3. Iterative planning–combine aspects of bottom-up and top-down planning. (Figure 14.2, p. 491).

H. New Directions in Planning
Changes have been made in three areas: (1) who does it, (2) how it is done, and (3) contents of plan.

1. Who does it–senior operating managers, not planning staffs

2. How is it done–a decided move to less structured format and a shorter document. Top managements generally accept the fact that a good strategic planning process must allow ideas to surface from anywhere and at any time. See the 3M example on page 494 for a discussion of "planning by narrative."

3. Contents of plan–more concerned with issues, strategies and implementation–Shell example.

I. Summary of the Planning Process–Frederick Gluck.

1. Top management must assume a more explicit decision-making role.

2. Planning must change from forecasting to an exercise in creativity.

3. Planning processes and tools must be obsessed with being first to recognize change.

4. Planner must be a crusader for action.

5. Strategic planning must be restored to the core of line management responsibilities.

IV. Organizational Design

Organizing normally follows planning. In designing the organizational structure, management is faced with two concerns: finding the most effective way to take advantage of specialization of labor and coordinating firm's activities to enable it to meet its overall objectives.

A. Evolution of the Global Company

1. Companies often enter foreign markets by exporting , then forming sales companies and finally setting up production facilities.

2. As its foreign involvement changes, the firm's organization often changes. Each domestic product division may be responsible. When firm begins to invest overseas, it might form an international division which usually is organized on a regional basis. Figure 14.3, page 496.

3. As overseas operations increase in importance, some firms eliminate international divisions and establish worldwide organizations based on product, region or function. In some cases, customer classes are also a top-level dimension.

4. Global corporate form–product

The product division is responsible for global line and staff operations. Each division will have regional experts, so, although this organizational form avoids duplication of product experts common in a company with an international division, it creates a duplication of area experts. Some firms have a group of regional experts in an international division which advises the product divisions but has no line authority over them. See Figure 14.4, page 497 for diagram of this type of organization.

5. Global corporate form–geographical regions.

These firms put the responsibility for all activities under area managers who report directly to the CEO. This form used for both multinational and global companies. It appears to be popular with companies that manufacture products with low, or at least, stable technological content that require strong marketing ability. Product coordination across regions presents problems and management often places specialized product managers on the headquarters staff to provide input to corporate decisions regarding products. See Figure 14.5, page 497.

6. Global corporate form–function

Few companies organized by function at top level. Commonality among users of this form is a narrow and highly integrated product mix. See Figure 14.6, page 498. Examples are provided for Exxon-Mobile and GM.

7. Hybrid forms

In a hybrid organization, a mixture of organizational forms is used at the top level. Figure 14.7, page 498 is a simple hybrid form. See example of Ford.

8. Matrix organizations

Has evolved from management's attempt to mesh product, regional and functional expertise while maintaining clear lines of authority. Figure 14.8, page 499 illustrates a simple matrix.

a. Problems with the matrix–managers from each dimension of the matrix must agree on a solution. This often leads to sub-optimal compromises, delayed responses and power politics. The problem goes higher in the organization when the managers cannot agree.

b. Matrix overlay–because of these problems, some firms have maintained their organization based on product, region or function, but have built into the structure accountability for other organizational dimensions. a firm organized by product, for example, might have regional specialists in a staff function with the requirement that they have input to product decisions.

    c.   Strategic Business Units–business entities with a clearly defined market specific competitors, the ability to carry out its business mission, and a size appropriate for control be a single manager. Most SBUs are based on product lines.

B. Change in Organizational Forms

The rapidly changing business environment is pressuring managements to look for organizational forms that will enable their firms to act more quickly, reduce costs, and improve product quality.

Also new is the acceptance by many managements of the need for frequent reorganizations called *reengineering* by many. CEOs are striving to make their organizations lean, fast-to-respond, and innovative. See Shell and Coke restructuring stories in text. See the small and medium-sized example of ACT Manufacturing on pages 502-503 for a company that has prospered from outsourcing to other firms, but that has also had to restructure as it has grown.

C. Current Organizational Trends

Two organizational forms are now receiving the attention of many CEOs: the virtual corporation and the horizontal corporation.

    1.   Virtual corporation

Also called a network organization. It enables companies to come together quickly to take advantage of a specific marketing opportunity. These alliances enable each member to concentrate on what it does best, its core competency. A virtual corporation can have capabilities superior to those of any member. When the opportunity ends, the virtual corporation disbands. Similar to consortia which have existed for decades.

    2.   Horizontal corporations

A form of organization characterized by lateral decision processes, horizontal networks, and a strong corporate wide business philosophy. Has been adopted by some large technology-oriented global firms such as AT&T, GE, and DuPont to give them flexibility to respond quickly to advances in technology and be product innovators. The idea is to substitute cooperation and coordination for strict control and supervision.

D. Corporate Survival into the 21st Century

Managers will make greater use of the dynamic network structure that breaks down major functions of the firm into small companies coordinated by a small-sized headquarters organization. Business functions such as marketing and accounting may be provided by separate organizations connected by computers to a large central office. The firms of tomorrow must learn how to be large and entrepreneurial. Small is not better, focused is better. See Worldview, "How to become more globally competitive" on page 504.

V.   Control

Every successful company uses controls to put its plans into effect and to evaluate and reward or correct executive performance. An element of controls is whether decisions are made by the parent company, the subsidiaries or by a combination.

A. Product and Equipment

    1.   Subsidiaries may favor product and equipment designed specially for the market and conditions of the host country.

    2.   The parent company may prefer product and equipment be standardized in order to multiply source options and simplify procurement and maintenance.

B. Confidence in Subsidiary Management and Headquarter' Reliance on It. With greater confidence, more decisions will be delegated or left to subsidiaries.

1. Moving subsidiary managers into parent operations or into other subsidiaries widens the executives' knowledge of the system and knowledge of each other.

2. Moving parent managers into subsidiaries widens their knowledge of subsidiary problems to which the parent might not be sensitive otherwise.

C. Stages of an International Company's Growth

1. As the company grows, more and more of its parent's executives will have served abroad and will have knowledge of the system and confidence. More decisions will tend to be made at parent headquarters.

2. As growth continues and operations become more complex, there come to be too many decisions for parent management. Then a tendency to decentralization begins. Parent management establishes guidelines for subsidiary executives and reserves decision to itself in only the most important matters.

3. During the 1980s and early 1990s, it became something of a management fad to empower subsidiary managers and decentralize. As do most fads, this practice faded by the mid 1990s, and IC began to recentralize power at the parent company in the home country.

D. Decisions Which May Benefit the IC to the Detriment of a Subsidiary

1. Move production facilities or invest in new ones.

2. Where the parent and/or one or more subsidiaries could fill an order, who gets it?

3. Multi-country production.

4. Which subsidiary books the profit? That material in the text with the accompanying numbers illustrate the tax considerations.

E. Frustration of Subsidiary Management
An objective of all businesses is to obtain and keep able, loyal executives. If subsidiary managers are not allowed to make important decisions, regarding their operations, they may resign or become hostile. Some companies reporting such developments in the mid 1990s were IBM, CS First Boston, and European International.

F. Subsidiaries Less Than 100 Percent Owned by the Parent and Joint Ventures
Control is not as easy as it is with a 100 percent owned subsidiary. The other shareholders or the joint venture partner may make it difficult or impossible for the parent or other partner to make the sort of decisions mentioned above. With a subsidiary less than 100 percent owned, there are some ways to exercise some control.

1. Keep the technology secret.

2. Appoint the important officers such as the managing director and treasurer, the production manager or the purchasing officer.

3. Furnish key components for the project.

4. Control marketing channels.

G. Control is impossible without prompt, accurate information reporting by subsidiaries. Reports should cover:

1. Financial information.

2. Technology, new products, inventions, or methods.

3. Market opportunities.

4. Political land economic developments.

H. In the U.S. you can find variations on each of the above approaches. In fact, some of the practices Americans are said to have learned from abroad, originated in the U.S. For example, lean production and total quality management were invented in the Bell Labs in the 1920s and became central to America's World War II production. As discussed in Chapter 20, the occupying Americans taught them to the Japanese, who then retaught them to their teachers in the 1970s and 80s.

VI. De-jobbing

Big firms where many of the good jobs used to be are unbundling activities and farming them out to smaller organizations. New computer and communications technologies are de-jobbing the workplace, changing from traditional fixed job approach to one in which teams perform tasks.

A. The transformation is from a structure built out of jobs into fields of work, or projects, needing to be done.

B. As the project develops, the person's responsibilities change as does the composition of the team, and the person may move to a new project.

C. Hierarchy implodes, and people no longer take their cues from a supervisor. Signals come from the changing demands of the project.

D. Traits of companies with de-jobbed workers are four.

1. Employees are encouraged to make the kinds of operating decisions that used to be reserved for managers.

2. Employees are given the information they need to make those decisions.

3. Employees are given training to understand business and financial issues that used to concern only an owner or executive.

4. Employees are given a stake in the fruits of their labor–a share of profits.

VII. Managing in a world out of control, the Internet may be the closest thing to a working anarchy the world has ever seen. It has been built up without any central control because the U.S. Defense Department wanted to ensure it could survive a nuclear attack. The consequences for management in a world out of control as presented by one author seem deceptively simple.

A. do simple things first

B. learn to do them flawlessly

C. add new layers of activity over the results of the simple task

D. don't change the simple things

E. make the new layer work as flawlessly as the simple, and

F. repeat ad infinitum

G. Increasingly, the most successful companies will advance by involving and adapting in this organic, bottom-up way.

VIII. Successful leaders will have to

A. relinquish or at least relax control

B. honor error because a break through may at first be indistinguishable from a mistake.

C. constantly seek disequilibrium

Answer to Questions

1. Probably, your company will want to step up its activity in the home market of your German competitor to distract its attention somewhat from the American market. You will be sending signals to the German competitor that an attack in your home market will be answered by increased activity in its home market. Because it appears that the dollar will continue to be strong against the mark, it appears that trying to compete in the German market by exporting to it may not be feasible. Your competitor already has a plant in the United States. Your company needs to think seriously about setting up production facilities in Germany.

2. You had better construct a scenario about what OPEC might do with respect to supplying crude to Israel. Will Arabian members try to persuade OPEC members to reduce their supplies to Israel (political pressure to force Israel to negotiate with the PLO)? Is there a possibility of war or at least increased terrorist activities? How strong is Iran's influence on OPEC?

3. This is a situation for iterative planning. Give them some broad goals and time frames from headquarters and then ask them to present their plans within these constraints. Possibly, the process will have to be repeated once again before the subsidiaries and headquarters are in agreement.

4. Set up an organization based on product or region and install a matrix overlay. Establish a group of regional experts at headquarters if your new organization is based on product. Make clear to the product managers that the regional experts will have input to the product decisions.

5. You could break up Pozoli and put its product divisions in the Mancon divisions Pozoli is already a multinational that has been in business for years. Its brand names are well known all over the world. Probably better to locate the entire company in the international division unless this division's job is only to handle exports for the two product groups. If so, either you need to change the international division's thrust or establish Pozoli as a separate division on the same level as the international division and the two product divisions.

6. The firm makes an acquisition whose business is significantly different from the present businesses and so new expertise is needed. Perhaps the company is entering new markets and needs regional expertise it doesn't have now. An important customer changing a JIT or synchronous production could force the firm to change also as Ford, GM, Campbell and many others have required their major suppliers to do. This alone could require the firm to make numerous changes in the organization.

7. If the subsidiary's market is large and different enough, it may make economic sense to design and produce equipment and products for that one market. Management of the subsidiary would probably make those decisions.
    Otherwise, it may be more economic to standardize on a worldwide basis. Such standardization could save on procurement, training, and maintenance costs. It could give the organization a choice of sources; if one subsidiary had difficulties, the product could be furnished by another.

8. Headquarters would make these decisions.
    a. Decisions to channel business through a low tax country subsidiary rather than a high tax country sub, or decisions based on capacity utilization or production costs to let one subsidiary bid for a contract while forbidding others to complete.
    b. Such decisions would most likely be made at IC headquarters.

9. The company can exercise control if it is providing necessary ingredients such as money, technology, management skill, production management or sales distribution.

10. Computer and communications technology will polarize the work force with a relatively small elite group controlling automated production and de-jobbing everyone else.

Answers to Internet Problems

1. The URL is the one appearing in footnote 4. Instructors can direct their students to the DuPont company Web site at www.dupont.com. The answers to the questions can be found in various places, including in the annual report or in the investor relations sections.

    a. For example, in the investor relations section at www.dupont.com/corp/ir/profile.html, it is stated that, "The company aims to deliver at least a 15 percent total shareholder return and 10 to 12 percent earnings growth annually over time."

b. As shown in the answer to part (a) above, the company has more than one quantified goal. In particular, the company states it has a goal of (1) at least a 15 percent total shareholder return, and (2) 10 to 12 percent earnings growth annually. The company also states that its goal is "at least doubling the rate of revenue growth."

c. The company refers to "value creation strategies" that include: (1) global leadership, (2) innovation, (3) alliances and acquisitions, (4) productivity, and (5) customer focus. The annual report and other sources provide additional detail on strategy, particularly by business area.

2. Endnote 42 gives the Internet address in the U.K. of the Andersen Consulting article, www.ac.com/outlook/o_clos_1.html.

   a. They say "functional departments and geographic divisions fragment and compartmentalize the various activities that go into serving the customer. Ultimately, this fragmentation means that information about the customer rarely finds its way far enough into the organization to provide useful feedback. As a result, customized service is difficult, and organizations tend to take a one-size-fits-all approach to the market-a powerful impediment to building closer relationships with specific segments of customers."

   b. Companies are taking a more process-centered approach to customer relationship management. There's a growing trend toward managing all activities that identify, attract, and retain customers in an integrated manner-managing them as a process that cuts across functional departments by addressing these activities as a set of customer relationship management process.

   c. The "best customers" are the most profitable for the organization. the companies must shift resources away from those who are not their best customers and, in many instances, get rid of the high maintenance, low-margin customers.

Discussion of Minicase 14–1: Electrix, Incorporated–Must it Reorganize?

At this time, what is needed is a matrix overlay. The president can reorganize the company with product divisions and have an international division on the staff as shown in Figure 14.4, page 497. The president can require that the International Division be notified about all proposed product changes and given an opportunity to discuss them with the appropriate product division. The International Division and the product division must be in agreement in matters affecting sales outside the United States. The marketing manager in the Japanese subsidiary should send his reports to the head of marketing in the company, but a copy of his report should also go to the International Division.

It looks as though the Japanese subsidiary must have its own design team in Japan as it cannot wait for designs to come from the United States. This seems a better solution than one using horizontal linkage.

Discussion of Minicase 14–2: Competition Within the IC

One decision you almost surely will not make is to leave to Paraguayan Railways (PR) to split up its order among W's factories . W already has the PR order, and Pr's option to allocate production among W's factors was not a factor in getting the order. In addition, having the W factories submit competitive bids would cause competition and possible hostility among them rather than the cooperation and mutual assistance W encourages. finally, financially W can certainly get no more for the locomotives than the amount established in the order it has in hand, and opening up competitive bids among its factories would likely result in a lower total payment by PR divided b PR as determined among W's factories.

Country risk analysis (CRA) is in order here to calculate how much political risk would accrue to a factory due to continuing unemployment and left-wing attacks if a factory does not get orders. The other side of that is to calculate how much benefit would accrue if a factory does get orders. Benefits could be tax concessions by government, wage or hour concessions by labor, or political goodwill in the community or country.

Intra IC goodwill can be garnered by the American factory sharing the latest technology with the subsidiary factories. The American factory will deserve compensation for such sharing in the form of royalty payments and/or significant parts of the PR order.

Transportation costs from the factories to PR must be considered. Paraguayan import costs, e.g., tariffs, and restrictions on product from the countries involved are factors in the decision.

The Global Strategic Planning Process

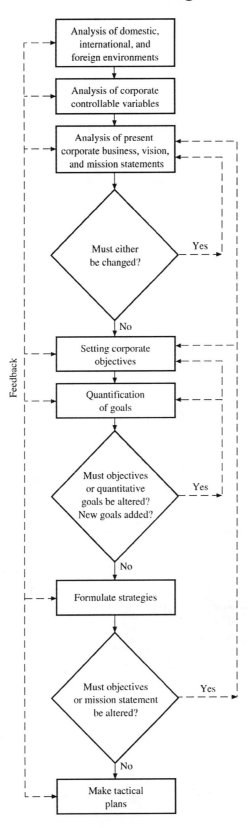

TM 14.2

Figure 14.2　　　　**3M Strategic Planning Cycle**

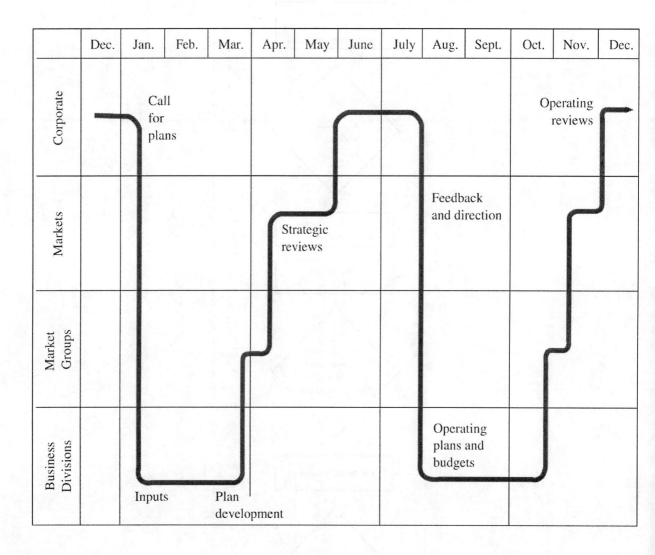

TM 14.3

Figure 14.3   **International Division**

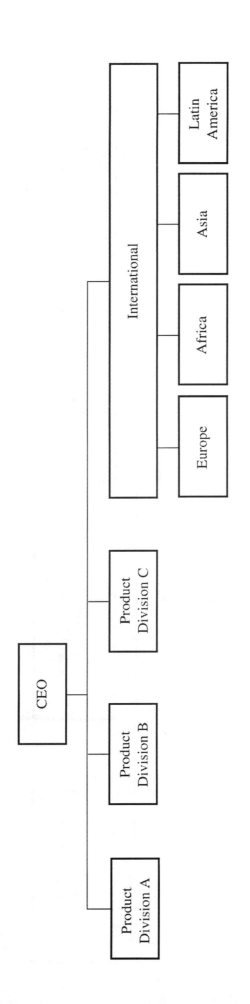

McGraw-Hill/Irwin

TM 14.4
Figure 14.4 **Global Corporate Form--Product**

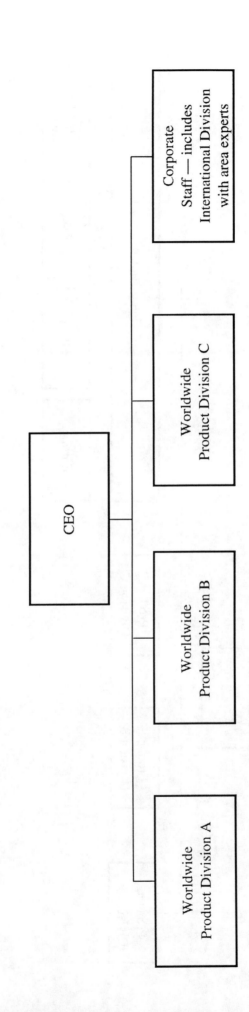

McGraw-Hill/Irwin

TM 14.5
Figure 14.5

Global Corporate Form—Geographical Regions

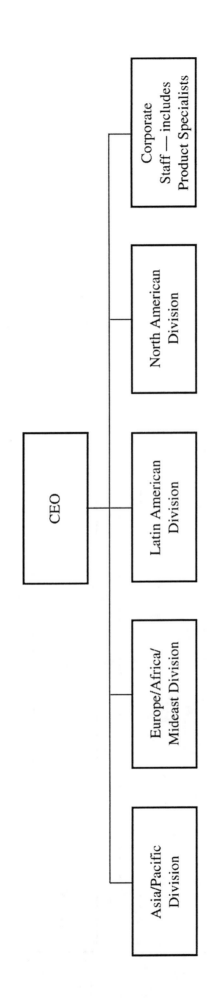

CEO

Asia/Pacific Division

Europe/Africa/ Mideast Division

Latin American Division

North American Division

Corporate Staff — includes Product Specialists

McGraw-Hill/Irwin

TM 14.6
Figure 14.6   **Global Corporate Form--Function**

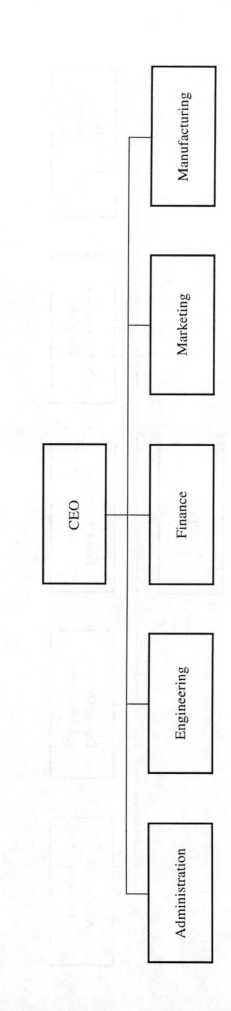

Hybrid Organizational Form

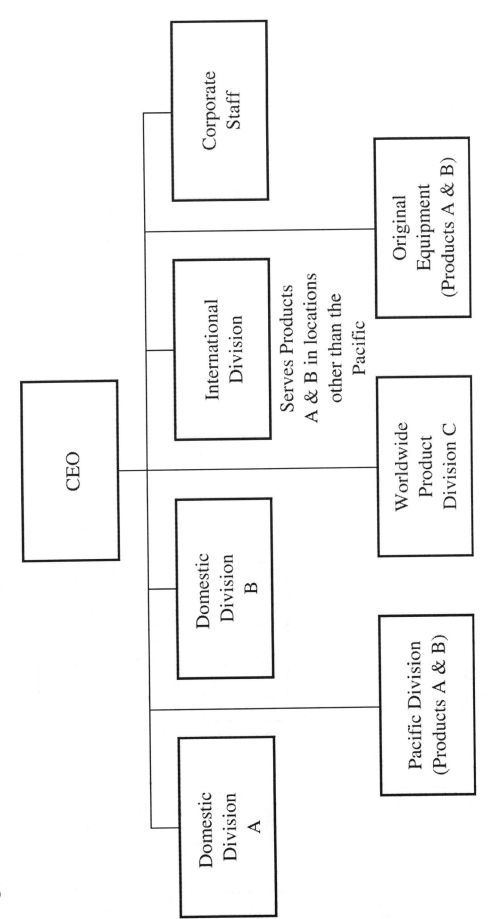

```
                        ┌──────────┐
                        │   CEO    │
                        └────┬─────┘
   ┌──────────┬─────────┬────┴────┬──────────────┬──────────────┐
┌────────┐ ┌────────┐ ┌──────────────┐ ┌──────────────┐ ┌──────────┐
│Domestic│ │Domestic│ │International │ │              │ │Corporate │
│Division│ │Division│ │  Division    │ │              │ │  Staff   │
│   A    │ │   B    │ │              │ │              │ │          │
└───┬────┘ └────────┘ └──────────────┘ └──────┬───────┘ └──────────┘
    │                  Serves Products        │
    │                  A & B in locations      │
    │                  other than the          │
    │                  Pacific                  │
┌──────────┐      ┌──────────┐      ┌──────────────┐
│ Pacific  │      │Worldwide │      │ Original     │
│ Division │      │ Product  │      │ Equipment    │
│(Products │      │Division C│      │(Products A&B)│
│ A & B)   │      │          │      │              │
└──────────┘      └──────────┘      └──────────────┘
```

McGraw-Hill/Irwin

TM 14.8

Figure 14.8 **Regional Product Matrix**

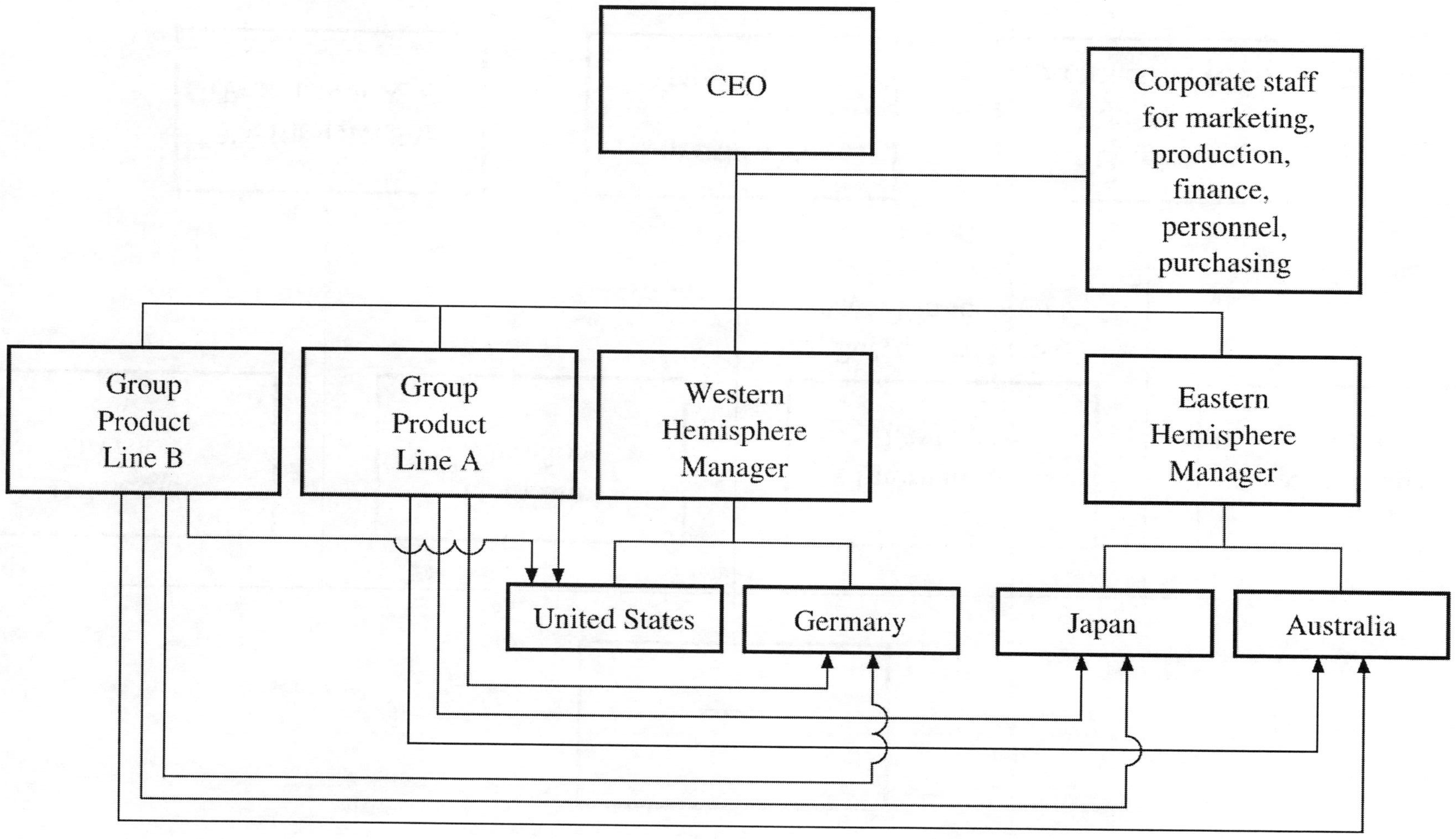

CHAPTER 15
MARKET ASSESSMENT AND ANALYSIS

Learning Objectives

1. Inform students about environmental analyses and a modified version, market screening, used for market assessment and analysis.

2. Explain some of the problems market researchers encounter in foreign markets.

3. Provide students with an opportunity to put to use the information from Section III, Foreign Environments.

4. Explain the utility of market indicators and market factors.

5. Introduce the utility of the internet as a source of market research data.

6. Provide sources of information for the screening process.

Overview

This chapter introduces a screening process to assist in the analysis and assessment of foreign markets based on the environmental forces of Section III. This process consists of an examination of the forces in succession and the elimination of countries or markets at each step. The sequence uses has been chosen so that there will be a smaller number of prospects to consider at each of the succeedingly more difficult stages. Unlike previous editions, we suggest both country screening and a newly-introduced topic, segment screening.

Often the commitment of the financial and human resources is so great that managements will also require primary research to be done in the market. Researchers will frequently find that obtaining these data is more difficult than it is in the home country because of cultural problems and technical difficulties. Examples of the cultural problems are low level of literacy, language, barriers and distrust of strangers. Among the technical difficulties are the lack of maps, telephone directories and adequate mail services.

Suggestions and Comments

1. This chapter should not prove difficult because in one sense it brings together the forces the students have been studying in Section III, Foreign Environment.

2. One part, the sections on statistics and marketing research, may be a little rough, if the students have not had statistics or marketing research. However, because this material is descriptive, the worst that can happen is that they will fail to appreciate the importance of the difficulties we describe. We have students from Arts and Sciences who take this course in their International Business minor without the above prerequisites and they are able to manage it.

Student Involvement Exercises

1. Teams of three or four students can use the screening process on three or four countries and a product that you choose. If the class has been doing the continuous exercise, they can report on the countries they have been researching.

2. Ask students to select a country and a product they wish to export to it. Have them report on the sources of information available to enable them to decide if the market is worth entering.

Guest Lecturers

1. Someone with experience in doing marketing research overseas from a nearby multinational, export management company or an export merchant can tell the class how his or her company analyzes markets.

2. The foreign trade representative from the Department of Commerce district office often will have experience in helping firms obtain market data. Usually Commerce people are willing to address a class.

Lecture Outline

I.   Opening Section
     This shows the students how a veteran marketer was able to obtain the data he needed when they were not available as in the United States. He was not stopped by lack of data but used ingenuity to get what he needed.

II. Market Screening
     Market screening is a method of market analysis and assessment that allows management to identify a small number of viable markets by eliminating those that are unattractive. The countries are subjected to a series of screenings based on the environmental forces of Section III. (Figure 15.1, page 521). Screenings have been ordered so that the less difficult and less expensive to do come first.

     A. Initial Screening

         1. Basic need potential–First screening based on the need potential. If firm produces air conditioners, it will look for countries with warm climates.

         2. Foreign Trade and Investment – By examining where similar products are going now or where producers are setting up plants to produce them, analysts can identify some prospects. Note that this information is usually provided in less detail than we would ideally prefer. The UN's *International Trade Statistics Yearbook*, Volume II, will show which countries export and which import a firm's products and the dollar amounts involved. Table 15.1, page 535, reproduces a page from the *Yearbook* showing international trade in chocolates.

     B. Second Screening – the Financial and Economic Forces. After the initial screening, there will be a smaller list of prospects for the second screening. The analyst will look at such factors as trends in inflation rates, exchange rates, and interest rates. Credit availability, paying habits of customers and ROI on similar investments are other factors to consider. Two measures of market demand based on economic data are (1) market indicators, and (2) market factors.

         1. Market indicators

             a. Economic data which serve as yardsticks for measuring the relative market strengths of various geographic areas.

             b. An example of a multi-country index developed for the needs of a specific industry is the index of e-commerce potential for Latin America (Table 15.2, page 525). This index contains general economic factors as well as more industry-specific indicators. The summary e-commerce potential index is composed of three indices: market size, market growth rate, and e-commerce readiness.

         2. Market factors

             a. Market factors are data which tend to correlate highly with market demand for a given product. These factors allow us to use estimation by analogy when we cannot estimate demand directly.

     b.   Example 1: If one-fifth of existing home computers are replaced annually in the U.S., in a similar country we can expect similar demand for replacements.

     c.   Example 2: If each household in a similar country has an average of 1.3 television sets, then 1.3 x the number of households in the country under study should indicate the size of market potential.

  3. Trend analysis
     If historic growth rates known, the analyst can construct a time series or use the arithmetic mean of past growth rates.

  4. Cluster analysis and other multivariate techniques
     Divide objects into groups so that the variables within each group are similar. Multidimensional scaling, factor analysis and conjoint analysis are other techniques for examining differences and similarities among markets.

  5. Periodic updating
     All analyses should be updated periodically because conditions change.

C. Third Screening–Political and Legal Forces
   Analyst will look for such elements as:

  1. Entry barriers to market

  2. Profit remittance barriers

  3. Political and policy stability. Instability makes planning difficult or impossible.

D. Fourth Screening–Sociocultural Forces

  1. Can hire consultants

  2. Can study publications and visit Web sites mentioned in text

  3. Can attend area seminars on "How to Do Business in _____."

E. Fifth Screening–Competitive Forces–Factors to be considered:

  1. Number, size, financial strength of competitors

  2. Their market shares

  3. Their apparent marketing strategies

  4. Apparent effectiveness of their promotional programs

  5. Quality levels of their product lines

  6. Source of their products–imported or locally produced

  7. Pricing policies

  8. Levels of after-sales service

  9. Their distribution channels

  10. Their coverage of the market (could market segmentation produce niches that are currently poorly served?)

F. Final Selection of New Markets
   These countries should be visited by an executive of the firm:

  1. Field Trip

     a.   Should be unhurried

     b.   May be able to join a government-sponsored trade missions or visit a trade fair

  2. Government-Sponsored Trade Mission and Trade Fairs

  3. Sometimes Local Research is Required

4. Research in the Local Market
    a. Researchers will try to obtain secondary data but if unavailable, they must collect primary data.
    b. Here they face cultural problems and technical difficulties
        (1) Cultural problems–transportations, low level of literacy, distrust of strangers, fear of tax collectors.
        (2) Technical difficulties–no up-to-date maps, streets not numbered, no telephone directories, poor mail system.
5. Research as Practiced
    a. Highly developed in industrialized nations
    b. In developing areas, the tendency is to do less research and to use simpler techniques.
    c. The most common techniques are trend analysis and querying of knowledgeable people such as salespeople, channel members, customers. If demand is high (seller's market) then less market research is done.

III. Segment Screening
    A. We naturally think in terms of countries, but markets often extend across borders. What's important are needs and wants, not political boundaries. Similar age, income, and lifestyles usually determine market segments.
    B. Criteria for determining the viability of market segments -
        a. Definable – can identify and measure the segment.
        b. Large – segments must be large enough to be worth serving.
        c. Accessible – we must be able to reach the segment for promotion and product distribution.
        d. Actionable – must be able to use the 4 Ps to compete for the segment.
        e. Capturable – segment cannot be completely captured by the competition.
    C. Two Screening Methods, Reconsidered
        a. We view the world in terms of political borders but should think in terms of market segments that may extend across borders.
        b. Given existence of subcultures within nations, market segments can be smaller than a country as well as extending across multiple countries.

Answers to Questions

1. The Appendix after this chapter lists many sources for all screening steps.

2. The suggested order is based on the idea of performing the least difficult screening first. Successive screenings which become more difficult will deal with fewer countries.

3. The export manager can consult *U.S. Foreign Trade Highlights* at the International Trade Administration site (www.ita.doc.gov/).

4. A country's imports don't completely measure market potential for many reasons: lack of foreign exchange, high prices and political pressures among others. Furthermore, import data only show what the country has been importing: sales from local production usually will be higher. In other cases, a ban on imports may have been lifted.

5. (1) Entry barriers, (2) profit remittance barriers, (3) unstable governments, and unstable policies.

6. An executive from the firm must corroborate the facts uncovered by the desk study. Moreover, someone from the firm must see firsthand what the conditions are because no amount of secondary

data will substitute for the experience of seeing prospective customers, competitors and government officials.

7. Company representative will learn firsthand about the market, meet important customers face to face, and make contacts with customers interested in representing the firm in the local market. The cost should be less than if the firm's representatives were to make the trip alone. The impact of a visit of various companies is greater than is the visit of just one. Moreover, embassy officials will give the trip of a mission advance publicity and will arrange for facilities and interviews.

8. *Cultural* problems (foreign language, interviewing wrong people, receiving wrong answers from respondents fearing the interviewer to be a tax assessor), and *technical* difficulties (lack of maps and telephones, out-of-date, telephone directories, questionnaires difficult to mail, mail often not delivered).

9. The market size index is a measurement of the potential market for goods and services. The index is a ratio of several consumption and production items for each country compared to the regional total for the same items.

Answers to Internet Problems

1. The students will find the home page of Big Emerging Markets is www.ita.doc.gov/bems/
   a. The Department of Commerce states that over the next two decades, these are the markets that "offer the greatest commercial opportunities. "Already, exports to the BEMs exceed combined exports to Europe and Japan and their combined GDP of more than $2 trillion is as much as that of Germany and the United Kingdom. Current sales to these countries comprises one-fourth of total American exports
   b. China including Hong Kong and Taiwan, India, South Korea, Mexico, Brazil, Argentina, South Africa, Poland, Turkey, and ASEAN (Indonesia, Brunei, Malaysia, Singapore, Thailand, the Philippines, and Vietnam.
   c. According to Commerce, industrial and farm machinery, electric power transmission, transportation equipment, and a wide range of high-tech products-all sectors where American producers have an advantage over the competition.

2. This is to show students the contents of the FT900. This report is published monthly and includes monthly and cumulative totals. There is also a year-end report. First, go to www.census.gov/foreign-trade/Press-Release/2001pr/01/. Then click on "Exhibit 18. Exports and Imports of Motor Vehicles & Parts by Selected Countries," which is the report they need.
   a. cars-less
      trucks-less
      parts-less

   b. Canada
      Mexico

   c. Canada
      Japan

   d. Canada
      Mexico

Answers to Minicase 15.1 The SugarDaddy Chocolate Company

1. Yes, $7.2 billion in world exports for 1998.
2. Six largest importing nations:
   a. France/Monaco - $926 million
   b. Germany - $903 million
   c. U.S.A. - $593 million
   d. United Kingdom - $542 million
   e. Japan - $287 million
   f. Canada - $275 million
3. Actually, every one of the six imported more in 1998 than in 1994.
4. Export competition (1998 exports):
   a. Germany- $1.1 billion
   b. Belgium - $960 million
   c. France/Monaco - $782 million
   d. United Kingdom - $ 579 million
   e. Netherlands - $511 million

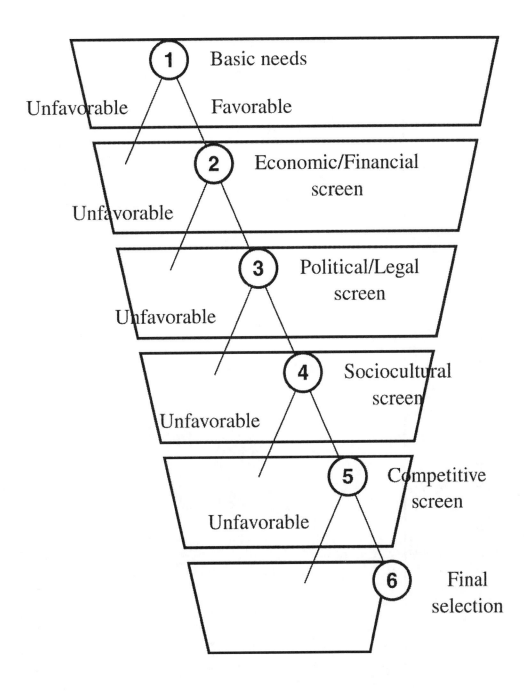

E-Commerce Potential: Rankings for Latin America

Countries	Market Size	Market Growth Rate	E-Commerce Readiness	Overall E-Commerce Potential
South America				
Argentina	4	10	1	2
Bolivia	16	9	9	6
Brazil	1	12	6	3
Chile	5	1	2	1
Colombia	8	17	7	2
Ecuador	13	16	14	15
Paraguay	12	15	11	14
Peru	11	7	1	1
Uruguay	7	13	4	1
Venezuela	3	19	4	6
Caribbean				
Dominican Republic	14	3	8	6
Haiti	20	14	15	18
Jamaica	6	8	13	9
Central America				
Costa Rica	9	6	9	6
El Salvador	15	4	6	2
Guatemala	16	11	17	16
Honduras	18	18	20	19
Mexico	2	14	3	3
Nicaragua	19	20	18	19
Panama	10	2	10	5

Source: Michael S. Minor and Alexandra Brandt, "A Possible Index of E-Commerce Potential for Latin America," Working Paper, January 29, 2001. Reprinted with permission of Michigan State University-CIBER.

CHAPTER 16
MARKETING INTERNATIONALLY

Learning Objectives

1. To show students why multinational marketing managers may wish to standardize the marketing mix worldwide.

2. To show the importance of the total product concept when deciding if the marketing mix can be standardized worldwide.

3. To demonstrate the effect of the uncontrollable forces on the marketing mix.

4. To examine the intricacies of transfer pricing.

5. To present the Foreign Environmental Constraints to Marketing Mix Standardization Matrix.

Overview

Although the marketing functions are the same for marketing domestically and internationally, the markets served vary greatly because of the differences among the environmental forces. There are advantages in the worldwide standardization of the marketing mix but frequently environmental differences necessitate a modification of the domestic mix or the development of a new one. The extent of the change will depend on the type of product, the forces, and the degree of market penetration desired by management. Product, price, distribution and promotional strategies are discussed in this context.

Suggestions and Comments

1. You will note that in this and the chapters to follow, we have reversed our treatment of the functions and the effect of the uncontrollable forces on them. In Section III we discussed each group of forces and illustrated how a given set of forces (ex: legal) affected all of the functional areas of the firm. In this chapter and those that follow, we reverse the procedure and examine the functional areas one by one and illustrate how a number of the forces influence them.

2. Chapter 16 is rather long. (How do you write a short chapter on marketing internationally?) If you cover all of the material, you can easily spend three class periods on it. We have been able to do it in less time by opening with a question, "Why do marketing managers want to standardize the marketing mix worldwide?" and then use Table 16.3 as a basis for all class discussion in which the class can pull from this chapter and all of the chapters in Section III.

3. You probably will want to spend a few minutes on formulating six product strategies from three product and message alternatives.

4. Robert F. Hartley's *Marketing Mistakes and Successes* (8th edition, 2001) provides some interesting examples of marketing errors.

Student Involvement Exercises

1. If you have any foreign students as we generally have, you can ask them to compare the way the same product is promoted in their country and in the United States. This helps to reinforce the six product strategies discussion. Other students can research foreign magazines in the library to compare ads for the same product in different countries.

2. Question 1 at the end of the chapter might start a discussion on total vs. physical product.

Guest Lecturers

1. A member of the advertising staff of a multinational can provide some insight as to how the firm plans and controls its overseas advertising campaigns.

2. A member of the headquarters marketing staff can discuss the company policy with respect to international standardization of the marketing mix. He or she will have some good "war stories" about campaigns that made it and those that failed because of environmental differences. We have found that the speaker was well keyed-in when we loaned him or her a copy of the text so that the discussion would be built around our framework. Not everyone will take the time to do it, of course, but those who do really relate to the students.

Lecture Outline

I.   Opening Section

The opening section describes the evolution of P&G's international marketing strategy. In the 1940s, the company exported its core products from the U.S. to build demand. Once attained, it either established local sales companies or factories. None of its products were launched with global distribution in mind. P&G also had a policy of using the same policies and procedures overseas that had been successful in the United States.

In the early 1990s, the CEO changed the firm's marketing strategy. Instead of waiting to introduce a product globally until after P&G had accumulated U.S. experience, it tried to introduce them on a worldwide scale early in their development to avoid giving competitors time to react in all of its markets. When necessary, local management adapted them to satisfy what they believed were local demands.

The new CEO adopted another strategy. The company now uses autonomous core teams composed of representatives from markets worldwide for core product lines such as hair care, diapers, and laundry. The intent is to produce true global products and marketing strategies from the outset rather than make them and then adapt them to local conditions.

P&G management calls the company a truly global corporation. Since 1980, it has quadrupled the number of consumers it can serve with its brands—about 5 billion. P&G now has operations in over 70 countries and sells its products in more than 140 countries, making it one of the biggest and most successful consumer goods companies in the world.

II.   Added Complexities of International Marketing

The basic marketing functions are the same everywhere but marketing internationally differs from marketing domestically because of the great variations in the uncontrollable environmental forces. Moreover, even the controllable forces vary greatly.

III.   The Marketing Mix (*What* and *How* to Sell)

The international marketing manager must decide if (1) the firm can standardize worldwide, (2) it must make some changes, or (3) it must formulate a completely different marketing mix.

A. Standardization, Adaptation or Completely Different?

1. Management would prefer standardization for the following reasons: (1) lower costs, (2) easier control and coordination from headquarters, (3) reduction in the time and effort needed to prepare marketing plans.

2. In spite of these advantages, sometimes it is necessary to modify the present mix or develop a new one. The extent of the changes depends on the type of product (consumer or industrial), environmental forces, and the degree of market penetration.

B. Product Strategies

1. When formulating product strategies, managers must consider the total product (Figure 16.1) because a new product may be created without changing the physical product. This will reduce manufacturing costs and permit international standardization of the production process which is a goal of most managers.

    a. Total and physical product – much of the confusion about whether a firm can have global products is due to the facts that discussants fail to clarify whether they are referring to the total product, the physical product, or the brand name. Cadbury-Schweppes' tonic water and chocolate and Nestlé instant coffee are examples used in the text.

    b. Type of product (see Figure 16.2, page 545)

        (1) Industrial goods can often be sold worldwide with either easy-to-make changes, or none at all.

            a. Some industrial products need to be modified, however, for use in developing countries because of tendencies to overload equipment and slight maintenance

        (2) Consumer products often require more modification than do industrial products. However, they can be sold unchanged to certain market segments such as the foreign-educated and well-travelled (the "jet set"), and expatriates.

            a. Note that certain other products (French perfume, American hamburgers) must be sold virtually unchanged since their "foreignness" is a critical part of their consumer appeal.

            b. Generally, the lower the economic and social strata, the greater the dissimilarities with respect to cultural and social values.

        (3) Services are generally easier to market globally than consumer products. Consulting firms such as Accenture (formerly Andersen Consulting) find that they can offer similar services worldwide. The credit card industry is also largely global. On the other hand, employment agencies may not be able to operate in some countries because they are illegal.

            a. You might ask students whether hotels and higher education are standardized global industries as well.

    c. Foreign environmental forces

        (1) Sociocultural forces–Dissimilar cultural patterns generally necessitate changes in foods and consumer goods. At times, a brand name, label, or the standard colors of the package are unsuitable for cultural reasons. However, marketers must investigate the truthfulness of the stories about these problems because, some of them have no basis. An example is the extensively circulated Nova story. See the photo of the Pemex Nova gas pump.

        (2) Legal forces–Firms must adhere to a nation's laws which may be a formidable constraint in the design of product strategies. Also, brand piracy can be a problem.

        (3) Economic forces–Another obstacle to worldwide product standardization. Products from industrialized nations may be too expensive for developing countries or they may not withstand more difficult operating conditions. Smaller markets may not permit as extensive a product mix as in the home country.

        (4) Physical forces–Climate and difficult terrain may require product adaptations or even different products.

C. Promotional Strategies
1. Promotion both influences and is influenced by the other marketing variables. It is possible to formulate 9 distinct strategies by combining the three alternatives of (1) marketing the same physical product everywhere, (2) adapting the physical product for foreign markets, and (3) designing a different physical product with (a) the same, (b) adapted, or (c) different promotional messages.
   a. Although 9 strategies are possible, 6 are most commonly used.

   b. (1) same product – same message, (2) same product – different message, (3) adapted product – same message, (4) adapted product – adapted message, (5) different product – same message, (6) different product – different message for the same use.

2. Advertising
Advertising is the promotional mix element with the greatest worldwide similarities. Advertising everywhere is based on American techniques.
   a. Global or regional brands – Manufacturers are increasingly using global or regional brands because:
      (1) Cost is most often cited. Producing one commercial for use across a region can result in a saving of up to 50% of the production costs.
      (2) There is a better chance of obtaining one regional source to do high-quality work than of finding multiple sources in several countries.
      (3) Some marketing managers feel their companies must have single image through a region.
      (4) Companies are establishing regionalized organizations where many functions, such as marketing, are centralized.
      (5) Global and regional satellite, cable television and the Internet are becoming widely available.
   b. Global or national brands – National brands still retain appeal. Management has to be careful about eliminating them simply to achieve scale economies.
   c. Private brands – these also compete (often successfully) with global or national brands. Examples include the Wal-Mart brand, and SPAR, the world's largest food retailer.
   d. Availability of media – Many media are available.
      (1) TV – Satellite and cable (Star TV, MTV, etc.) offer choices and an audience that is increasing rapidly.
      (2) International print media – again, the choices seem to continue to increase.
      (3) Cinema and videocassette advertising – these reach audiences in novel ways. Videotape ads are popular in the Middle East where other media choices may be limited.
   e. Internet advertising – The Internet offers several attractive elements as a promotional medium:
      (1) An affluent, reachable audience.
      (2) Interactive contacts with potential customers.
      (3) Consumers may help shape the messages they receive, that is, messages can be customized.
      (4) It may reach some groups such as teenagers for which good media alternatives aren't available.

(5) But (see the section on personal selling later in the chapter) it may be difficult to build trust over the Internet.

    f. Type of product – Buyers of industrial goods and luxury consumer goods usually act on same motives the world over.

    g. Foreign environmental forces – Basic cultural decision is whether to position product as local or foreign. For international market segments, advertisers can formulate global advertising campaigns. Legal forces affect product claims. Strong tendency for governments to control advertising.

    h. Globalization versus localization – one school of thought looks for similarities across countries in order to capitalize on them by providing promotional themes with worldwide appeal. Another school of thought believes it preferable to develop separate appeals to take advantage of differences among customers in different cultures and countries.

    i. Neither purely global nor purely local – for most firms, neither purely global nor purely local is best way to handle international advertising. One ad agency head said that 15% had a global approach, another 15% had a local approach, and the rest are "glocal." They develop a strategy for large regions, but not for the world.

    j. Gillette's panregional approach – Gillette has organized its advertising in regional and cultural clusters: pan-Latin America, pan-Middle East, pan-Africa and pan-Atlantic. Is based on the belief that the firm can identify the same needs and buying motives in regions or countries linked by culture, consumers' habits, and level of market development.

    k. Programmed-management approach – a middle-ground advertising strategy between globally standardized and entirely local programs. This approach gives the home office a chance to standardize those parts of the campaign that may be standardized but still permits flexibility in responding to different marketing conditions.

3. Personal Selling
The importance of personal selling in the promotional mix depends on relative costs, funds available, media availability, and type of product sold.

    a. Personal Selling and the Internet. The Internet won't eliminate the need for personal selling. Personal selling depends on trust. The Internet makes communication easier, but trust-building harder. Computer-mediated communication transmits much less nonverbal information, including emotions, expressions of cooperation and trustworthiness. Also, feedback during message delivery is lost.

    b. International standardization

       (1) Sales force organization, sales presentations and training methods similar to those in home country.

       (2) Because of high costs of sales calls, many firms in Europe are using telemarketing and direct mail to qualify prospects. Since 1992, Dell Computers had been employing both methods to sell computers in Japan and Europe.

    c. Recruitment of sales force difficult in some markets because of social stigma attached to selling.

4. Sales Promotion

    a. Sociocultural and economic constraints.

       (1) Premium must be meaningful to consumer

       (2) Contests and raffles often successful

b. Two unsuccessful sales promotions-Hoover in the U.K. gave 2 free tickets to continental Europe or the U.S. to anyone buying Hoover products for $150. Cheapest pair of tickets cost $750 so 200,000 customers rushed to buy inexpensive vacuum cleaners for $180. Hoover sent a team from U.S. headquarters to fire managing director and set up a task force to issue tickets. The company is taking a $72.6 million charge against its profits.

Pepsi-Cola began a promotion in the Philippines which would award cash prizes for winning numbers under bottle caps. When the winning number was announced, the firm found that the winning number had been printed on 900,000 caps. The firm has paid out $10 million, but people still threaten to sue.

5. Public Relations

   a. Many international firms fail to inform the public of their activities.

   b. Overseas subsidiaries of American firms support public-service activities locally; in Japan, Coke spends $5 million on programs for children and the handicapped, IBM Japan puts 1% of its profits into good works. Warner-Lambert, pharmaceuticals, began a program, Tropicare, to train local health care providers in preventive medicine. This has been successful in Africa and Latin America.

   c. McDonald's sued two people who were distributing leaflets in London accusing the company of destroying rain forests, exploiting children in its advertising, starving the third world, and cruelty to animals. After 3 years in court and spending $16 million, McDonald's won $98,000 in libel damages in 1997. The defendants said they had no intention of paying McDonald's anything.

D. Pricing Strategies

   1. Pricing, a Controllable Variable

      a. Effective price setting is more than a mechanical markup, price is a controllable variable.

      b. Price setting is complex because of its interaction with other elements of marketing mix. See Table 16.3 at end of chapter.

   2. International Standardization

   Managements must be concerned with (1) foreign national pricing and (2) international pricing for exports.

      a. Foreign national pricing–Government price controls, cost differentials of different markets, diverse competition, product in different stage of product life cycle.

      b. International pricing (transfer pricing)–special kind of exporting (intracorporate sales). Management may order an affiliate to sell another affiliate at less or more than market price for tax reasons. See Figure 16.3, page 566 to see how firms hide profits with transfer pricing

E. Distribution Strategies

   1. Markets must concern themselves with getting the goods to foreign marketers and distributing the goods within each market.

   2. Interdependence of Distributive Decisions–Care must be taken when making distribution decisions to analyze their interdependence with other marketing mix variables.

   3. International standardization–Two constraints to international standardization–variations in the availability of channel members and inconsistent influence of environmental forces.

      a. Availability of channel members.

b. Foreign environmental forces–legal, economic and sociocultural—make standardization of distribution channels difficult. French and Japanese laws have slowed the growth of large retailers although the Japanese law has been scrapped.

4. Disintermediation. This long, difficult word refers to unraveling of traditional distribution structures. Primary reasons for the change are the combination of the Internet for ordering combined with fast delivery services – FedEx, UPS. Increasingly can offer rapid delivery without specialized or dedicated distribution channels.

F. Channel Selection
1. Direct or Indirect Marketing
   Will management use middlemen or sell directly?
2. Factors influencing channel selection
   a. Market characteristics
   b. Product characteristics
   c. Company characteristics
   d. Middlemen's characteristics

G. Foreign Environmental Forces and Marketing Mix Matrix
   Table 16.3, page 569, summarizes many of the constraints to the internationalization of the marketing mix.

Answers to Questions

1. The question is not whether global brands can be standardized. For many products, consumers are standardized globally. It depends on how culturally sensitive the product is. It also depends on whether we are considering the total or physical product. Wherever there is a single campaign, the advertiser of necessity uses common denominator advertising–a campaign to attract the largest market segment. Of course, he uses the term disparagingly.

2. Global advertising for luxury goods and industrial products has been used well before the Levitt article as you know. As mentioned in the text, there is an increased use of global *brands* by international firms. Many firms have gone to regional promotion which was made possible by European cable and satellite TV. EC 92 has been a motivating force. Gillette is a good example of a firm that has pan-European promotion, but there are other American firms such as Coca-Cola, IBM, Kelloggs, P&G and Quaker. Ford's signing a single contract for ad placement in 84 magazines around the world is noteworthy.

3. Managers are interested in internationally standardizing their marketing mixes because often important cost savings can be obtained. Logistics and acquisition of inputs are simplified. Standardized pricing enables important worldwide customers to be charged the same price no matter from where they are sourced.

4. Manufacturers are increasing their use of global and regional brands for a number of reasons:
   a. Less expensive to produce one TV commercial to use throughout a region than to produce commercials in a number of countries.
   b. Better chance to obtain one regional source to do high quality work than trying to find sources in various countries.
   c. Many believe their companies must have a single image throughout a region.
   d. Firms are establishing regionalized organizations where many functions such as marketing are centralized.
   e. Global and regional satellite TV are becoming available to permit global and regional promotion.

5.   Gillette looked ahead to the EU well before its inception. Pan-European media availability enabled Gillette to take a regional approach to promotion. Gillette's products lend themselves to the regional approach because they are consumed in the same way in the region, they are low priced, and are bought for the same reasons.

6.   As you go down the economic and social strata in each country, you tend to find greater dissimilarties among countries with respect to social and cultural values.

7.   Just as in the United States, European and Japanese women are being forced to find jobs to contribute to the support of the family and they don't have time to shop and prepare meals from "scratch." Frozen food sales and one-stop shopping in hypermarkets have risen in Europe. Japanese women are patronizing convenience stores such as 7-11 and ordering convenience food by TV with home delivery.

8.   Many products marketed in industrialized countries are too expensive for developing countries so they must be simplified or different, less expensive ones must be produced–Gillette's plastic tube of shaving cream and Hoover's simpler washing machine. Poor infrastructure may require product change–hand operated instead of electrically operated machines. Product mixes may have to be simpler–no Cadillacs.

9.   This discussion comes from page 560. Firm A can expect to be most successful. Since the Internet doesn't help with building trust at the early stages of a relationship because there is no non-verbal interaction, which helps transmit information about emotions, cooperation, and trustworthiness. But this won't be a problem for Firm A, which expects the Internet only to continue relationships already established by face-to-face interaction. Firm B, on the other hand, expects to make sales on the Internet without building on prior relationships. This method is more likely to fail.

10.   When the United States affiliate buys the item for $100 and sells it for $200. Tax paid by the British subsidiary is 0, but that paid by the American company is $34. Using the transfer pricing shown in Figure 16.3, no tax was paid.

Answers to Internet Problems

1.   Students will find this information at www.adage.com/dataplace/archives/dp405.html. Remember that you or your students may be able to find more recent data than the 1998 data to which we are referring.
     a.   Unilever doesn't lead in any of the other countries.
     b.   Proctor & Gamble leads in Mexico, Peru, Puerto Rico and Venezuela.

     The remaining questions refer to the table "Top 100 Global Marketers 1999." The address is www.adage.com/dataplace/archives/dp409.html. Again, your students may find an updated table.

     c   They are (1) Proctor & Gamble, (2) Unilever, (3) Volkswagen, (4) Nestlé, (5) Ford.
     d.   Three are consumer products firms, but two are automakers.
     e.   For 1998, P&G spent about 10% ($280.9 million) more on advertising outside the U.S. than did Unilever, and $1.038 billion (2 and a half times) more inside the U.S.

2.   The students will find the "Preparing..." section under "Companies" at P&G. The Preparing section is specifically mentioned. The address is www.pg.com/info/financial_center/annual_report/ourshareholders/preparing.html. It is also in endnote 43.

     a.   Head & Shoulders, Tide, Always, Whisper, Vicks, Ariel, and Pampers are named in the report as being global brands.

b. "Brands falling into the trap of merely shifting value with me-too line extension will quickly fall behind the market leaders that create value with fundamentally better, new products."

c. The company filed for 17,000 patents.

d. Report says global concerns will bring innovations to market at a much faster pace than today–and not just in one or two countries at a time, but worldwide.

Discussion of Minicase 16–1: U.S. Pharmaceutical of Korea

1. The company should use the carrot and stick approach. Sloane can offer a discount for prompt payment which will compete with the return that the wholesaler can get by investing the money short term. To force them to be consistent in settling their accounts, he might offer an additional year-end bonus payable in merchandise to those with an acceptable payment record for the year. The stick is the constant pressure on the wholesaler to pay coupled with a threat to discontinue supplying merchandise if the account is not settled within the proper time. According to the article, 90 days are considered to be reasonable.

2. It could be that the serious distributors resent USPK's selling directly to big retailers and important end-users while leaving them the smaller, low volume retailers. Sloane might discuss the situation with some of the larger wholesalers. He perhaps can offer them exclusive territories in return for their handling only USPK's products. His sales representatives can work with the wholesalers' representatives rather than competing with them. Sloane has to make his franchise wanted. He will get cooperation when the conditions are such that the wholesalers want his product line.

3. Sloane may be able to convince the larger competitors to form an industry association which will formulate guidelines for channel members. The companies may even agree on the kinds of clients to whom they will sell. For example, they might get wholesaler loyalty by agreeing **not** to sell directly to retailers or end-users.

4. The industry association might be the answer to handling demands for gifts. The larger, more important manufacturer should be able to agree on a no-gift policy. American subsidiaries can also explain that they are prohibited by the Foreign Corrupt Practices Act. If they have been offering gifts, they can say that the home offices are tightening up because they fear investigation if they do not.

Discussion of Minicase 16–2: An Ethical Situation

1. Demands that women sign a document confirming that they are aware of the risks involved and that they will take the proper precautions against pregnancy when using the product. With such signed proof, women should not be able to claim they were unaware of any after effects.

2. Explanations and warnings are provided with the product in easy to understand language.

3. The press has been informed of the dangers involved when using the product. Reporters were invited to seminars to be briefed.

4. For the first time, Hoffman-LaRoche is warning general practitioners against prescribing a dermatology product. It is restricting supplies, as far as legally possible, to skin specialists.

5. For the first time, control is kept on each package so that precise monitoring is possible through registration of the prescribing physician and pharmacist.

6. By means of letters, brochures, telephone, lectures, films and trade journal announcements, physicians in each country where the product is marketed are being kept well informed.

7. For the first time, Hoffman-LaRoche has appointed a special manager in Basel headquarters to be responsible for seeing that all Roche companies observe its guidelines on the product. Normally, Hoffman-LaRoche allows its national subsidiaries to be independent of Swiss headquarters.

TM 16.1
Figure 16.1

Components of the Total Product

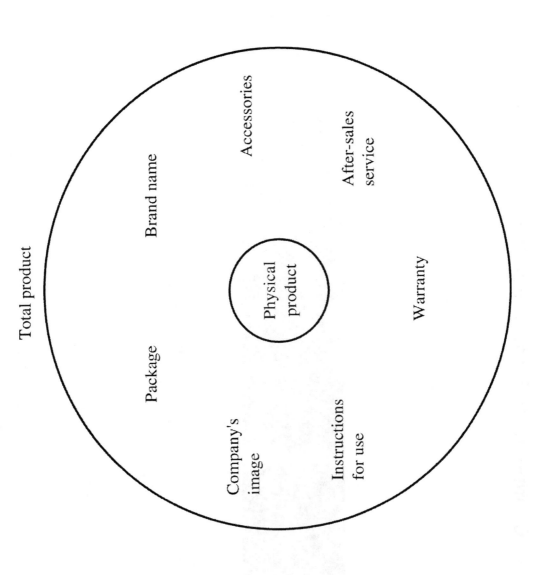

McGraw-Hill/Irwin

TM 16.2
Figure 16.2 **Continuum of Sensitivity to the Foreign Environment**

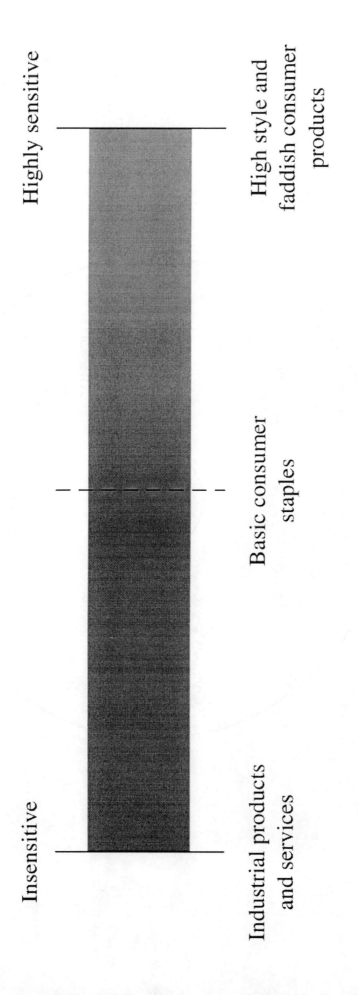

Insensitive ——————————————————— Highly sensitive

Industrial products and services

Basic consumer staples

High style and faddish consumer products

McGraw-Hill/Irwin

TM 16.3
Figure 16.3   **Hiding Profits with Transfer Pricing**

GREAT BRITAIN

JAMAICA

UNITED STATES

An item costs $100 to produce. It is sold to a Jamaican subsidiary for $100.

Tax rate: 52%
Tax paid: $0

The Jamaican subsidiary resells the item for $200 to a U.S. subsidiary.

Tax rate: 5%
Tax paid: $5

The American subsidiary sells the item at cost for $200. No profit earned. No tax paid.

Tax rate: 34%
Tax paid: $0

© *The McGraw-Hill Companies, Inc., 2002 All Rights Reserved.*

McGraw-Hill/Irwin

CHAPTER 17
EXPORT AND IMPORT PRACTICES AND PROCEDURES

Learning Objectives

1. To show the class that exporting is important not only for small export firms, but is also significant for the large multinational and global firms.

2. To convince the class that the three problem areas cited as reasons for not exporting by management's: (1) location of foreign markets, (2) payment and financing procedures, and (3) export procedures can be surmounted rather easily.

3. To provide students with information concerning the Department of Commerce services.

4. To teach the students about the kinds of export documents required, the kinds of payment terms that are offered and some sources of export financing.

5. To describe important innovations in materials handling in sea and air transport.

6. To introduce students to the basics of importing.

Overview

Exporting is an important facet of international business for both large and small firms. No company can afford to have local production facilities in every one of its overseas markets. Some markets must be supplied by exporting from either the home plant or from a foreign subsidiary. In spite of the fact that exporting can be profitable, only a small percentage of the U.S. GDP is exported. The major problem areas for those who do not export are (1) location of foreign markets, (2) payment and financing procedures, and (3) export procedures.

Market screening described in Chapter 15 will enable the firm to locate foreign markets. The terms of payment employed in the export market are (1) cash in advance, (2) open account, (3) consignment, (4) letters of credit, and (5) documentary drafts. A number of private and public sources of financing are available. OPIC, FSC and Foreign Trade Zones are some of the other government incentives to export.

Export procedures are considered a problem because of the documents involved. In addition to the usual domestic documents, goods for export require export licenses and export bills of lading. Marine insurance is necessary because ocean going steamship companies assume no responsibility for their cargo. The documents for collection generally include (1) commercial invoices, (2) consular invoices, (3) certificates of origin, and (4) inspection certificates.

To eliminate errors and reduce the costs of preparing export documents, U.S. Customs has designed the Automated Export System (AES) which uses the Electronic Data Exchange (EDI). Customs has another system which permits importers to file import documents, pay Custom's fees and import duties electronically all in one transaction. This speeds the flow of cargo.

Innovations in materials handling such as containerization, huge freight planes, RO-RO and LASH ships, have opened up new markets to exporters.

Importing is in one sense the reverse of exporting, but many of the concerns of importers and exporters are similar. The text describes various ways to find sources of imports.

Suggestions and Comments

1. This chapter covers the highlights taken from our course, Export-Import Procedures. We try to arouse the students' interest in exporting by illustrating that this is a function of large global and multinationals as well as the smaller export companies. Table 17.0, page 581, which shows who the 20 largest exporters are, is a great help.

2. If you bring in a speaker from the list of guest lecturers, we believe that will help also, especially the international trade specialist from the Department of Commerce district office.

3. We believe that all business students should be acquainted with the basics of exporting and should know where to begin to gather information. Unfortunately, Department of Commerce district offices no longer provide assistance to beginners unless they represent a going firm that wants to export. The text explains where to begin.

Student Involvement Exercises

1. Ask the students to interview people involved in exporting such as members of a bank's international department, foreign freight forwarders, export departments of a local multinational, the foreign trade specialists in the Department of Commerce or the manager of a Foreign Trade Zone. Report to the class what these people do.

2. Some of the class can report on an article pertaining to exporting that they find in Business America published by U.S. Department of Commerce.

3. Ask the students to choose a product and a country to which they wish to export it. Assume an FOB factory selling price and prepare a quotation using one of the terms of sale in the text. Specify export payment terms. What other documents will be required?

4. Have 7 students role play a letter of credit transaction. There will be (1) buyer, (2) seller, (3) issuing bank, (4) correspondent bank, (5) foreign freight forwarder, (6) customhouse broker in the buyer's country and (7) the shipper (air or water). The seller starts by making offer to buyer who either accepts terms of sale or asks for different terms. The seller then goes to the issuing bank and so forth. If you live in a port city, you may ask students to get the forms such as a bill of lading, etc. to use in class.

Guest Lecturers

1. If you have a foreign freight forwarder in your area, invite him or her to explain the firm's services to exporters. A good forwarder can help a newcomer to get started and is one person who is knowledgeable about the entire exporting process.

2. Someone from an Export Management Company or an export merchant can provide the class with good information.

3. The international trade specialists from the district office of the Department of Commerce can describe the valuable assistance that Commerce offers to those desiring to export. The area served by each district office is divided among the district office's specialists so that no matter where you are located, there is someone responsible for your area and that person should be available for your class. You can also ask the specialist to send you samples of some of the Commerce material mentioned in the text.

4. The person in charge of exporting in a local company is a good source of information. Don't think that your city has to be a large international business center to have firms that export. Check all the companies in your area. You may be surprised.

5. If your institution has a Small Business Development Center, ask one of the persons that counsel newcomers to exporting to talk to your class. Great in-house expertise because generally they have been trained by Commerce people from the district office.

Lecture Outline

I. Opening Section

The opening section gives examples of DuPont, a large international firm, that exports $4 billion annually and Crosskeys Systems Corporation, a Canadian firm that began in 1992 with no exports. In just 5 years, the firm's export revenues reached C$17.3 million and then went to C$32.2 million. The company now services over 165 customers in 45 countries, illustrating that firms of all sizes export.

DuPont is typical of the large firms that export even though they also have overseas production facilities. Of the 20 largest exporters listed in Table 17.1, only the aircraft manufacturers have no foreign plants.

II. Who Exports?

The U.S. Bureau of Census reported that manufacturers accounted for the largest proportion of exports in 1997 (69%). The survey showed that the top 50 manufacturers accounted for 45% of the known export value while 202,185 small and medium-size firms were responsible for 31% of the known export value.

III. Why Export?

A. No firm can produce every product in every market.

B. The host government may require it.

C. Export to remain competitive in home market.

D. Test the market first with exports.

E. Accidental exporting-firm is requested to export.

F. To offset cyclical sales of the domestic market.

G. To achieve additional sales, which allows firm to use excess capacity to lower unit fixed costs.

H. Extend product's life cycle.

I. Distract foreign competitors in firm's home market by exporting to their home markets.

J. Partake in the success that other firms have in exporting.

K. Improve equipment utilization rates.

IV. Why Don't They Export?

A. Preoccupation with the vast American market

B. Reluctance to become involved in a new and unknown operation

C. What are their specific problem areas?

1. Locating foreign markets

2. Payments and financing procedures

3. Export procedures

V. Locating Foreign Markets

The screening process in Chapter 15 is a procedure that can be used by experienced market analysts, but newcomers to exporting may wish to use any one of a number of export assistance programs.

A. Sources of Export Counseling
   1. Trade Information Center – individuals and firms new to exporting may call the Trade Information Center (TIC) at 1-800-TRADE, which is a one-stop source of information on federal assistance programs offered by all federal agencies. Before calling the TIC, an individual is advised to visit its Web site. On its index page, there are links to government export programs, trade promotion events, and trade lead information. The purpose of the TIC Web site is to inform newcomers to exporting what resources are available before they contact the Trade Information Center directly for assistance. Firms that are already exporting may bypass the Trade Information Center and go directly to the nearest district office of the Commerce Department's International Trade Administration (ITA).
   2. Small Business Administration (SBA)
      The SBA has an Office of International Trade that offers assistance at its SBA district offices.
      a. SCORE programs – experienced executives offer free counseling to small firms.
      b. SBDC/SBI programs – Small Business Development Centers
   3. Department of Agriculture also has a single contact point for agriculture exporters seeking information.
B. Department of Commerce Export Assistance Program
   1. Foreign Market Research
      a. After learning about the company and its products, the international trade specialist might advise the potential exporter to consult the National Trade Data Bank (NTDB), a service that selects the most recent trade promotions and other useful information and puts it on a CD-ROM that is updated monthly. Among other things, the NTDB contains the Foreign Traders List–a list of foreign importers with descriptions of each and the products they wish to import. From this list, the exporter can prepare a mailing list of those interested in its products and make a bulk mailing. An individual can subscribe to the NTDB as part of the trade and economic information available at the Commerce Web site for $175 annually or receive CD-ROM discs monthly for $575 annual subscription fee. The discs are usually in university SBDCs offering export assistance and in the Government Documents section of university libraries. The trade specialist may suggest using the Trade Opportunities Program (TOP), which provides current sales leads from overseas firms wanting to buy or offering to represent their products or services. These leads are also published in The Journal of Commerce. The exporter can also advertise in the Commercial News, a catalog-magazine published 10 times a year to promote American products in overseas markets.
      b. Smaller number of markets – After a smaller number of potential markets have been identified, they can be researched using the Country Commercial Guide stored on the NTDB or can be seen at the State Department's home page at www.state.gov/www.services.html under "Business." Another useful business publication is Business America, a Commerce biweekly with a section containing announcements about U.S. promotions abroad in which the firm can participate, foreign concerns looking for licensors, distributorships, and joint partners, and opportunities to make direct sales.

    c.   Direct or indirect exporting-if the firm chooses to obtain its own overseas representation, it can try broad-based mailing or use the Commerce Agent/Distributor Search service for a fee of $250 per market. It can obtain information on their commercial activities and competence by obtaining an International Company Profile from Commerce. D&B, FCIB, and the exporter's bank will also supply credit information.

2. Show and sell-Commerce organizes trade events to help locate foreign representatives and make sales. There are 4 kinds:

    a.   U.S. Pavilions-Commerce selects about 100 global trade fairs annually to recruit American firms for a U.S. Pavilion. Exhibitors receive extensive support from Commerce.

    b.   Trade Missions-5 to 12 business executives from an industry sector. Participants are given advanced publicity, logistical support and pre-arranged appointments with government officials and potential buyers.

    c.   Product Literature Center-Commerce Trade Development specialists represent U.S. companies at international trade shows. they distribute literature and talk to visitors. They then inform the firms who the interested visitors were for follow-up.

    d.   Reverse Trade Missions-the U.S. Trade Development Agency funds visits to the U.S. by representatives of foreign governments to meet with American industry and government officials. They are interested in buying American equipment for specific projects.

C. Other Sources of Assistance

1. World Trade Centers Association–over 300 World Trade Centers provide access to an online trading system. Exporters need only a computer and a modem to place offers to sell in an electronic database. Access can be gained with a local telephone in 800 cities in 100 countries.

2. District Export Councils–Department of Commerce has 51 district export councils composed of volunteer business and trade experts who assist in workshops and arrange for consultations for newcomers.

3. State governments–All states have export development departments offering assistance to exporters by providing sales leads, locating overseas representatives, and counseling.

D. Export Marketing Plan

1. The plan, like the domestic plan, must state what must be done when, who should do it, and how much money will be spent. See the Appendix for a plan outline.

2. The export marketing mix has been discussed in Chapter 16, but there are two aspects worthy of discussion here, export pricing and sales agreements with foreign representatives.

    a.   Pricing policies

       (1) The terms of sales usually offered are FAS, Port of Exit; CIF, Foreign Port; CFR, Foreign Port; and DAF.

       (2) Preferred pricing method is to use factory door cost to which is added to the direct cost of making sale plus a percentage of the general administrative overheads, and profit.

    b.   Sales agreement
       Similar to domestic agreement, but attention must be given to designation of the

responsibilities for patent and trademark registration and designation of country whose laws will govern a contractual dispute.

V. Payment and Financing Procedures

A. Export Payment Terms
These may be (1) cash in advance, (2) open account, (3) consignment, (4) letters of credit, and (5) documentary drafts.

1. Cash in Advance
Few customers will pay cash in advance.

2. Open Account
Seller assumes all risk so these terms must be offered only to reliable customers in economically stable countries.

3. Consignment
Seller assumes all risk.

4. Letters of Credit
Document issued by buyer's bank which promises to pay the seller a specified amount when the bank has received certain documents specified in the letter by a specified time.

a. Confirmed and irrevocable
Letter will usually be confirmed and irrevocable. When letter is confirmed by a bank in the seller's country, that bank is obligated to pay if exporter conforms to letter's terms.

b. A pro forma invoice (looks like an invoice but is really a quotation) frequently requested by buyer before order is placed. Bank will use it when opening letter of credit.

c. Letter of credit transaction (Figure 17.2, page 592).

5. Documentary Drafts

a. An export draft is an unconditional order drawn by seller on buyer instructing buyer to pay amount of draft upon presentation (sight draft) or at an agreed future date (time draft). (Figure 17.3, page 593.)

b. No guarantee that buyer will accept and pay a documentary draft whereas a confirmed letter of credit will be paid if documents are in order.

B. Export Financing
The competition forces exporters to offer credit. They must be familiar with private and public sources of export financing.

1. Private Sources

a. Private banks

b. Factoring–discounting export accounts payable without recourse.

c. Forfeiting–purchase of obligations arising from sale of goods and services which fall due at some date generally between 90-180 days. These are sold without recourse.

2. Export-Import Bank provides direct loans, intermediary loans, and guarantees.

3. Other Government Incentives
These are other government incentives to trade which are not strictly a part of export financing.

a. Overseas Private Investment Corporation (OPIC)–a government corporation which offers investors insurance against expropriation, currency inconvertibility and damages from wars or revolutions.

b. Foreign Sales Corporations (FSCs) have replaced Domestic International Sales Corporations (DISCs) as a means of granting tax benefits on export transactions occurring after December 31, 1984. The new entity was created in answer to complaints by U.S. trading partners that the DISC law provided export subsidies that were considered illegal under GATT. The EU is contesting the FSC in WTO.

c. Foreign Trade Zones (FTZ)–the American version of a free trade zone. Goods may be brought into an FTZ and stored, inspected, repackaged or combined with American components. No import duties need be paid while goods are in the FTZ.

VI. Export Procedures
Exporters are confronted with five or six times as many documents a are domestic shippers. However, foreign freight forwarders will handle much of this work.

A. Foreign Freight Forwarders
1. Act as agents for exporters.
2. Prepare documents, book space with carriers and will supply marine insurance if asked.

B. Export Documents
1. Shipping documents include domestic bill of lading, export packing list, export licenses, export bill of lading, export packing list, export licenses, export bill of lading, insurance certificates, and Shipper's Export Declaration.

a. Export Licenses
All goods except those going to U.S. possessions or Canada require either a general export license or a validated export license.

b. General export license requires no special authorization.

c. Validated export license requires special authorization for a specific shipment and is needed for strategic materials and all shipments to communist countries.

d. Export bill of lading-service three purposes:1) contract for carriage between shipper and carrier, (2) receipt from the carrier for the goods shipped, (3) certificate of ownership. Bills of lading for foreign shipments are called air waybills (air shipments) and ocean bills of lading (steamships) A straight bill of lading is non-negotiable whereas an order bill may be endorsed like a check.

e. Insurance certificate–evidence that insurance coverage has been obtained to protect shipment from loss or damage while in transit. There are three kinds of marine insurance: (1) basis perils, (2) broad named perils, and (3) all risks.

2. Automated Export System (AES) –Customs has introduced a single information collection and processing center for electronic filing of the export documentation required by the government.

C. Collection Documents
Documents that seller must provide the buyer in order to receive payment: (1) commercial invoices, (2) consular invoices, (3) certificates of origin, and (4) inspection certificates.

VII. Export Shipments
The tremendous advance in materials handling techniques over the past two decades such as containerization, RO-RO and LASH, provide cost savings and enables exporters to reach new markets.

A. Containers

Containers are large boxes 8' x 8' in cross section by 10, 20 or 40 feet in length which seller fills in its own warehouse. They are sealed and not opened until goods arrive at final destination. Materials handling time is reduced and the risks of damage and theft are minimized.

B. RO-RO (Roll On-Roll Off) ships permit anything on wheels to be driven on and off. Loaded trailers can be driven off in ports which do not have lifting equipment to unload containers.

C. LASH (Lighter Aboard Ship) vessels carry 60-foot long barges which are unloaded in deep water and towed to shallow river ports where they are filled with cargo. the barges are then brought back to the anchored LASH ship and loaded aboard.

D. Air Freight

Air freight has had a profound effect on international business because shipments which required 30 days for delivery by ocean freight are now delivered in 24 hours. Huge freight planes can carry 200,000 pounds of cargo. Although air freight rates are higher than ocean rates, the total cost of shipping by air is frequently less expensive. Table 17.2, page 602 compares the total cost of the two modes. Even when total costs for air freight are higher, it may still be advantageous to ship by air when production and opportunity costs are considered. Also the firm may be air-dependent, the products may be air-dependent and air freight may enable the exporter to compete with overseas manufactures.

VIII. Importing

Many of the concerns of exporters and importers are similar. The prospective importer identifies import sources in a number of ways:

A. If similar products are already in the market, inspect them at a retailer who sells them to see where they are made. Imported products are required by law to have country of origin clearly marked. Then call the country's embassy and ask for names of manufacturers. Also call foreign chambers of commerce that are in major American cities. Once you have names and addresses, write for quotations.

B. If product not being imported, try the sources in point 1 and try international department of banks as well.

C. Try the electronic bulletin board of the World Trade Centers. You can put your name in their data banks that are seen around the world. The Internet has many sites where exporters from other countries are offering their products to importers.

D. When you visit foreign countries, look for articles to import.

E. Customhouse Brokers

Help importers import. They are to importers what foreign freight forwarders are to exporters. They can provide such services as arranging transportation for the goods after they leave Customs and advising clients as to import quotas. They can arrange to place goods in a bonded warehouse when necessary.

F. The Automated Commercial System (ACS)

Customs has another system, ACS, that it uses to track, control, and process all U. S. imports of commercial goods. Importers who use the ACS to file documents can also pay Customs fees and import duties electronically in one transaction.

G. Import Duties

Every importer should know how Customs calculates import duties and the importance of product classification.

1. The Harmonized System–is an important classification system used by all developed nations. A firm that feels it is paying excessive import duties can take the matter to court if it cannot reach an agreement with customs officials.
2. HTSUSA–See Figure 17.5, p. 605, for a page from this American version of the Harmonized System. Page 606 in the text explains the meaning of the initials in the column headed. "Special." Notice column 2 in Figure 17.5 contains duties that are significantly higher than those of Column 1 which are rates for nations friendly to the U. S.

Answers to Questions

1.   a. FAS, Port of Exit–Seller pays all transportation and delivery expense to the ship's side. The buyer is responsible for any damage or loss to the goods from that point on.

        b. CIF, Foreign Port–The seller pays all insurance, transportation and miscellaneous charges to the named foreign port. The buyer is responsible for loss or damage to the goods after they have been delivered aboard ship if it required an on-board bill of lading. There is a received-for-shipment ocean bill of lading for which responsibility for loss and damage passes to the buyer when the goods are delivered to the custody of the carrier, but we know of no instance where this is used. The standards requirement of buyers is a clean on-board bill of lading.

        c. CFR, Foreign Port–The same conditions as for a CIF shipment except for no insurance

2.   a. (1) Cash in Advance, (2) Open Account, (3) Consignment, (4) Letter of Credit, (5) Documentary Draft

        b   Cash in Advance and Letter of Credit.

3   Figure 17.2, page 592 illustrated the merchandise and document flows and path of letter of credit.

4.   The bank manager can do nothing but pay if the exporter has delivered all the documents required by the letter of credit.

5.   The *Foreign Trade Zone* is the name given to the American version of a free trade zone. Imports can be brought in, stored, examined, repackaged or reprocessed without payment of import duties. For custom purposes, goods in an FTZ are deemed *not* to have landed in the U. S.

6.   The export bill of lading serves three purposes: (1) contract for carriage between the shipper and the carrier and (2) it is evidence of title to the merchandise, and (3) receipt from carrier for goods shipped.

7.   No, the importer should not do this in an FTZ because the shirts are not considered to have entered the U. S. if they go to a foreign trade zone. If the adornments were sewn on there, the shirts would have to pay the higher duties that these shirts pay when they are imported in the normal way. To avoid the duty, the adornments have to be *attached* after the shirts pass Customs.

8.   Import sources are listed in "Importing" section.

9.   A customhouse broker assists the importer pass its goods through Customs. The customhouse broker acts as the importer's agent. It can also arrange for transportation after the goods leave Customs and for storage in an FTZ or bonded warehouse if necessary.

10. Germany
$5,000 + 0.058 = $5,000 + $290 = $5,290.00
Canada
$5,500 + $0 = $5,500 + 0 = $5,500.00
Azerbaijan
$4,000 + 0.4 = $4,000 + $1,600 = $5,600.00

Answers to Internet Problems.

1. Your students will find two useful addresses under "Export and Import Information," www.customs.gov/impoexpo/abaesint.htm and www.census.gov/foreign-trade/aes/aesfact.html.

   a. The AES is the central point through which export shipment data by multiple agencies is filed electronically with U.S. Customs. The exporter or its forwarder transmits the exporter's export information and the carrier or the forwarder transmits the transportation data via AES. The AES generates either a confirmation message or an error message. There are several advantages to the AES. The system requires the user to correct errors as they occur, thus eliminating the I in 2 chances of errors that occurred before the AES. The costly delays of paper handling are also decreased and duplicate reporting is eliminated.

   b. The AES, with its editing system and the exporter's subsequent corrections, ensures the exporter's compliance with current U.S. export reporting requirements. The AES system allows the exporter to correct errors at any point in time. The AES has demonstrated the ability to collect complete and accurate data because of the immediate feedback to the user when data are omitted or are incorrect.

   c. Yes, SEDs are no longer needed because the AES provides an alternative to filing a paper Shipper's Export Declaration.

   d. There is no export clearance requirement in AES. Participating exporters and carriers operate under the premise that all shipments can be exported unless they receive a Hold message. This allows cargo to proceed without delay.

   e. AES collects the required SED information and manifest data, verifies shipments against previously-approved licenses and transmits the transaction to the appropriate Partnership Agency.

2. The Internet address for INCOTERMS 1990 is cited in Endnote 9 and appears in the Internet directory under "Export & Import Information" and also "Legal Information." Students have to click a descriptive page for the definition of each term (DAF descriptive page, for example)

   a. DAF stands for "Delivered at Frontier" (named place). It means "that the seller fulfills his obligation when the goods are made available, cleared for export, at the named point and place at the frontier, but before the customs border of the adjoining country."

   b. "When the goods have been made available at the names place in the country of importation. The seller has to bear the costs and risks involved in bringing the good thereto (excluding duties, taxes, and other official charges payable upon importation) as well as the costs and risks of carrying out customs formalities."

   c. "The seller fulfills his obligation to deliver when he has made the goods available to the buyer on the quay (wharf) at the named port of destination, cleared for importation. The seller has to bear all risks and costs including duties, taxes, and other charges of delivering the goods thereto."

d. FAS (port of exit) requires the seller to pay the delivery expenses up to the ship's side at the port of exit, whereas when DEQ is used, the seller has the obligation to deliver at the wharf at the port of <u>destination.</u>

e. Group C – shipment terms. Main carriage pad to destination

  Group D – Arrival terms. Seller bears all costs and risks to bring goods to country of destination

  Group E – Departure term-Seller makes goods available to buyer at the seller's own premises.

  Group F-Shipment terms. Main carriage is unpaid. Seller is called on to deliver goods to a carrier named by the buyer.

Discussion of Minicase 16–1: State Manufacturing Export Sales Price

If Mason chooses to use the factory door approach, he will deduct the sales expense and the advertising and promotional expense from the $21,500. He will *not* deduct R&D expense, of course. The factory door price for export will be:

```
 $21,500
-  4,300   (20% sales expense)
  17,200
-  2,150   (10% advertising and promotional expense)
 $15,050
```

He probably will, in the future, add something to cover the cost of his own time. He must add to the factory door cost the expense items provided by the freight forwarder. The CIF Foreign Port price would be:

1.	"Factory door price"	....	$15,050.00
2.	Containerization	....	200.00
3.	Inland freight/handling	....	798.00
4.	Forwarding and documentation	....	90.00
5.	Ocean freight	....	2,633.00
6.	Commercial Risk Insurance	....	105,.00
7.	Marine Insurance	....	124.58
	($18,876 x 1.1) = $20,763.60 x $0.60/$100		
		CIF Foreign Port	$19,000.58

Discussion of Minicase 16–2: Morgan Guaranty Trust Company Letter of Credit

1. Bank of South America.

2. It is irrevocable

3. It has been confirmed.

4. By Morgan Guaranty Trust.

5. John Doe in Puerto Cabello, Venezuela.

6. Smith Tool.

7. Sight draft.

8. a. Commercial invoice in triplicate.
   b. Consular invoice in triplicate visa by Venezuelan consul.
   c. Negotiable insurance, policy covering marine and war risk.
   d. Full set of straight ocean bills of lading.

9. CIF Puerto Cabello, Venezuela

10. March 31 19–

11. To Morgan Guaranty Trust Co., New York City.

12. Seller–Smith Tool.

13. Seller–Smith Tool.

14. No.

15. An "on board" bill of lading is not required.

TM 17.1
Figure 17.1   Letter of Credit

THE MERCHANTS NATIONAL BANK OF MOBILE
MOBILE, ALABAMA

FOREIGN DEPARTMENT

Confirmed Irrevocable Straight Credit

Smith & Company
P.O. Box 000
Towne, Alabama 36000

Credit No. 0000
Mobile, Alabama, April 1, 20—

DEAR SIRS:

WE ARE INSTRUCTED BY Banco Americano, Bogota, Colombia

TO ADVISE YOU THAT THEY HAVE OPENED THEIR IRREVOCABLE CREDIT IN YOUR FAVOR FOR ACCOUNT OF

Compañia Santadereana de Automotores Ltda. "Sanautos", Bucaramanga, Colombia

UNDER THEIR CREDIT NUMBER 111-222 **FOR A SUM OR SUMS NOT EXCEEDING A TOTAL OF** $40,000.00

(FORTY THOUSAND NO/100 U.S. DOLLARS)

AVAILABLE BY YOUR DRAFTS ON US AT Sight   **FOR INVOICE**

VALUE OF 100%

TO BE ACCOMPANIED BY
1.   Commercial Invoice: five copies signed by the beneficiaries with sworn statement
        regarding price and origin of merchandise.
2.   Air Waybill: three non-negotiable copies, cosigned to the order of: Sanautos, Carrera
        15 Calle 29, Bucaramanga, for notification of same.
3.   Consular Invoice: three copies.
4.   Certificate of Origin: three copies
5.   Copy of the airmail letter addressed to: Sanautos, Apartado Aereo No. 936,
xxxxxxxxxxxxxxxxxxx Bucaramanga, Colombia, remitting original of shipping documents
        requested.
6.   Packing List: three copies.
7.   Copy of the airmail letter addressed to: Colombia de Seguros Bolivar, Calle 36, No.
        17-03, Bucaramanga, Colombia, covering details of shipment of merchandise, for
        insurance purposes.
Evidencing shipment of: "Repuestos para vehiculos automotores, registro de importacion No.
67038 del. 21 de Noviembre de 19—." Port of Shipment: any American port. Destination:
Bucaramanga, Partial shipments are permitted.
    ALL DRAFTS SO DRAWN MUST BE MARKED DRAWN UNDER THE MERCHANTS NATIONAL BANK OF MOBILE CREDIT

NO. 0000, Banco Americano No. L/C 111-222

    THE ABOVE MENTIONED CORRESPONDENT ENGAGES WITH YOU THAT ALL DRAFTS DRAWN UNDER AND IN COMPLIANCE WITH THE TERMS OF THIS CREDIT WILL BE DULY HONORED ON DELIVERY OF DOCUMENTS AS SPECIFIED IF PRESENTED AT THIS OFFICE ON OR BEFORE June 27, 19—   **:WE CONFIRM THE CREDIT AND THEREBY UNDERTAKE THAT ALL DRAFTS DRAWN AND PRESENTED AS ABOVE SPECIFIED WILL BE DULY HONORED BY US.**

    UNLESS OTHERWISE EXPRESSLY STATED, THIS CREDIT IS SUBJECT TO THE UNIFORM CUSTOMS AND PRACTICE FOR COMMERCIAL DOCUMENTARY CREDITS FIXED BY SEVENTH CONGRESS OF THE INTERNATIONAL CHAMBER OF COMMERCE AND CERTAIN GUIDING PROVISIONS ALL AS ADOPTED BY CERTAIN BANKS AND OTHER CONCERNS IN THE U. S. A.

YOURS VERY TRULY,

ASSISTANT MANAGER	**VICE PRESIDENT, ASSISTANT CASHIER**
John Doe, Vice President	Allen Jones, Vice President

cc Banco Americano, Bogota, Colombia

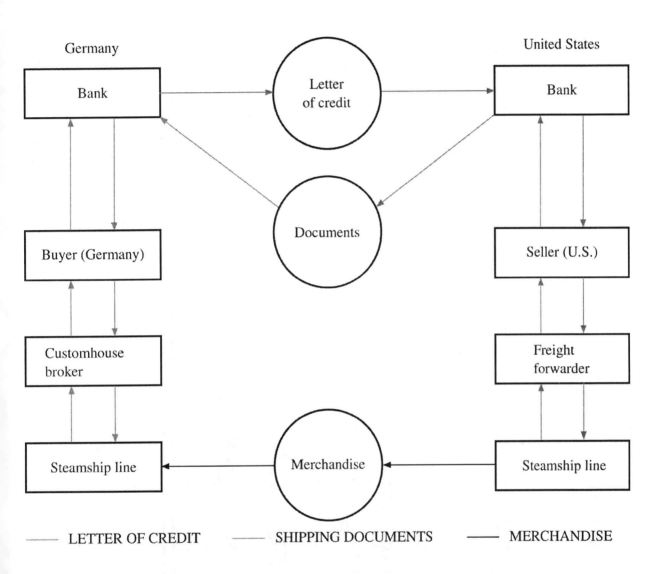

TM 17.3
Figure 17.3   Sight Draft

MOBILE, ALA., July 6,   20

$ 2,500.00

Sight D/P   PAY TO THE ORDER OF

Clayton Motor Company

Two Thousand Five Hundred   DOLLARS

VALUE RECEIVED AND CHARGE SAME TO ACCOUNT OF

CLAYTON MOTOR COMPANY

To   First National Bank of Mobile
      P. O. Box 1467   BY
      Mobile, Alabama   36621   John P. Clayton, President

FIRST NATIONAL BANK
st
MOBILE
ALABAMA

McGraw-Hill/Irwin

TM 17.4
Figure 17.4   Page from the HTSUSA

HARMONIZED TARIFF SCHEDULE of the UNITED STATES (1995)
Annotated for Statistical Reporting Purposes

Heading/ Subheading	Stat. Suf- fix	Article Description	Units of Quantity	Rates of Duty — 1 General	Rates of Duty — 1 Special	2
8461		Machine tools for planing, shaping, slotting, broaching, gear cutting, gear grinding or gear finishing, sawing, cutting-off and other machine tools working by removing metal, sintered metal carbides or cerments, not elsewhere specified or included:				
8461.10		Planing machines:				
8461.10.40		Numerically controlled	....	4.4%	Free (A,CA,E,IL,J, MX)	30%
	20	Used or rebuilt	No.			
	60	Other	No.			
8461.10.80		Other	....	4.4%	Free (A,CA,E,IL,J, MX)	30%
	20	Used or rebuilt	No.			
	40	Other, valued under $3,025 each ...	No.			
	80	Other	No.			
8461.20		Shaping or slotting machines:				
8461.20.40	00	Numerically controlled	No. ...	4.4%	Free (A,CA,E,IL,J, MX)	30%
8461.20.80		Other	....	4.4%	Free (A,CA,E,IL,J, MX)	30%
	30	Used or rebuilt	No.			
	70	Other, valued under $3,025 each ..	No.			
	90	Other	No.			
8461.30		Broaching machines:				
8461.30.40		Numerically controlled	....	4.4%	Free (A,CA,E,IL,J, MX)	30%
	20	Used or rebuilt	No.			
	60	Other	No.			
8461.30.80		Other	....	4.4%	Free (A,CA,E,IL,J, MX)	30%
	20	Used or rebuilt	No.			
	40	Other, valued under $3,025 each ..	No.			
	80	Other	No.			
8461.40		Gear cutting, gear grinding or gear finishing machines:				
8461.40.10		Gear cutting machines	....	5.8%	Free (A,CA,E,IL,J, MX)	40%
	10	Used or rebuilt	No.			
		Other:				
	20	For bevel gears	No.			
		Other:				
	30	Gear hobbers	No.			
	40	Gear shapers	No.			
	60	Other	No.			
8461.40.50		Gear grinding or finishing machines	....	4.4%	Free (A,CA,E,IL,J, MX)	30%
	20	Used or rebuilt	No.			
	40	Other, valued under $3,025 each ..	No.			
		Other:				
	50	For bevel gears	No.			
	70	Other	No.			
8461.50		Sawing or cutting-off machines:				
8461.50.40		Numerically controlled	....	4.4%	Free (A,CA,E,IL,J, MX)	30%
	10	Used or rebuilt	No.			
	50	Other	No.			
8461.50.80		Other	....	4.4%	Free (A,CA,E,IL,J, MX)	30%
	10	Used or rebuilt	No.			
	20	Other, valued under $3,025 each ..	No.			
	90	Other	No.			
8461.90		Other:				
8461.90.40		Numerically controlled	....	4.4%	Free (A,CA,E,IL,J, MX)	30%
	10	Used or rebuilt	No.			
	40	Other	No.			
8461.90.80		Other	....	4.4%	Free (A,CA,E,IL,J, MX)	30%
	10	Used or rebuilt	No.			
	20	Other, valued under $3,025 each ..	No.			
	80	Other	No.			

TM 17.5
Morgan Guaranty Trust Company Confirmation Letter

MORGAN GUARANTY TRUST COMPANY
OF NEW YORK
INTERNATIONAL BANKING DIVISION
23 WALL STREET, NEW YORK, N.Y. 10015

March 5, 20___

Smith Tool Co. Inc.
29 Bleecker Street
New York, N.Y. 10012

> On all communications please refer to
>
> **NUMBER IC — 152647**

Dear Sirs:

   We are instructed to advise you of the establishment by
. Bank of South America, Puerto Cabello, Venezuela . . . .
of their IRREVOCABLE Credit No. 19845 . . . .
in your favor, for the account of John Doe, Puerto Cabello, Venezuela . . . .
for U. S. $3,000.00 (THREE THOUSAND U. S. DOLLARS) . . . .
available upon presentation to us of your drafts at sight on us, accompanied by:
Commercial Invoice in triplicate, describing the merchandise as indicated below

Consular Invoice in triplicate, all signed and stamped by the Consul of Venezuela

Negotiable Insurance Policy and/or Underwriter's Certificate, endorsed in blank, covering
marine and war risks

Full set of straight ocean steamer Bills of Lading, showing consignment to the Bank of
South America, Puerto Cabello, stamped by Venezuelan Consul and marked "Freight Prepaid",

evidencing shipment of UNA MAQUINA DE SELLAR LATAS, C.I.F. Puerto Cabello, from United
States Port to Puerto Cabello, Venezuela

Except as otherwise expressly stated herein, this credit is subject to the Uniform Customs and Practice
for Documentary Credits (1974 revision), International Chamber of Commerce Publication No. 290.

The above bank engages with you that all drafts drawn under and in compliance with
the terms of this advice will be duly honored if presented to our Commercial Credits
Department, 15 Broad Street, New York, N. Y. 10015, on or before March 31, 20* on which
date this credit expires.

   We confirm the foregoing and undertake that all drafts drawn and presented in
accordance with its terms will be duly honored.

Yours very truly,

Authorized Signature

   Immediately upon receipt, please examine this instrument and if its terms are not clear to
you or if you need any assistance in respect to your availment of it, we would welcome your
communicating with us. Documents should be presented promptly and not later than 3 P.M.

CHAPTER 18
HUMAN RESOURCE MANAGEMENT

Learning Objectives

1. Be familiar with regional or cultural differences in labor conditions.

2. Methods to create jobs and avoid unemployment differ from region to region and culture to culture.

3. There are three sources of executives for ICs, the home country, and a host country, or a third country.

4. Language training is extremely important for IC executives in part to help them avoid the language trap.

5. Women are more and more being utilized as IC executives.

6. As two career households become more common, the trailing spouse problem arises when one of them is offered a juicy job abroad.

7. IC executive compensation packages are complicated.

Overview

Effective managers for ICs are in high demand but short supply. Difficulties are illustrated in China and Latin America where cultural considerations cause failures. One expert on China says sending someone with Chinese language capability but without "Chinese Values" can be worse than sending a westerner whom no one expects to have those values. The problem in Latin American is to operate in the dual mode of U.S. efficiency and the more personal Latin approach.

Some of Japan's largest companies are leading a move away from the country's job-for-life culture The psychological blow is particularly hard on middle-aged men when they lose their jobs and are not placed in other work.

The huge wage gaps between eastern and western Europe are well exemplified on the German-Polish border. One result is a large number of undocumented Poles working in Germany.

Child (ages 4-15 years) labor is common in many LDCs in living and working conditions that are repugnant to many Westerners. LDC officials say the children would be worse off without the jobs.

The U.S. and to a lesser extent, Japan, have done better at job creation than has Europe. Reasons include differing unemployment benefits.

Sources of IC managers may be the home country, a host country, or a third country.

Knowledge of two or more languages is increasingly important. Avoid the language trap.

Women are moving in and up IC executive ranks. More and more are getting foreign posting.

Common-sense rules must apply to selection and promotion of IC executives. They should be reviewed.

Suggestions and Comments

1. National and international periodicals frequently have articles about working conditions in different counties.

2. You will also find material there about IC executive selection and compensation.

3. There and in scholarly publications there is information about international business and language training.

Student Involvement Exercises

1. Students may refer to the periodicals referred to above and other sources to prepare reports about working conditions in different countries.

2. Have the students study government and labor policies which results in different unemployment rates in different regions.

3. From *The European* and many other sources, students should find it most interesting to research job-search tips and leads.

Guest Lecturers

1. Human Resource Management professors in your school, particularly if they have international experience or knowledge.

2. Personnel officers from companies in your area may be able to contribute.

3. Professors from the Economics Department may speak on labor economics.

Lecture Outline

I.   The comment by Asghar presents a common attitude in LCDs about working children.

II.   The article about the right stuff illustrates some difficulties ICs encounter in staffing management positions in China and Latin America.

III. Japan's Jobs-for-life culture fading

    A. Led by Toyota, Japanese companies are hiring on a contract basis.

        1. The workers may be of any age or nationality.

        2. They are hired and promoted based on merit without regard to seniority.

    B. For various reasons, Japanese companies are moving production abroad to non-yen countries.

        1. This is contributing to the end of jobs-for-life and increasing unemployment.

        2. Among the worst affected by these trends are middle-aged men without jobs for the first time. There is psychological damage as they hide in their homes because of embarrassment. Marriages suffer.

IV.   The East-West Europe wage gap is exemplified on the German-Polish border.

    A. In Poland, wages can be as low as 150-200 deutsche marks (DM) a month compared to DM 1,500 to DM 2,500 in Germany.

    B. Such disparity, of course, draws many Poles to work, legally or not, in Germany.

    C. As the EU expands, probably including Poland, and labor can move more freely, such wage gaps will narrow.

V.   Child labor, ages 4 to 15 years, is common in many LDCs and in some developed countries.

    A. The children's working and living conditions are miserable.

B. Western opinion often expressed by the Brussels-based International Federation of Free Trade Unions or the ILO, calls for improvement of the children's conditions.

C. Officials of the LDCs resent such calls. They argue:

    1. Cheap labor is one of the only strengths they have in a competitive world.

    2. The children would be even worse off without the jobs.

D. Another example of the type of campaign resented by the LDC was a 1996 call by the United Nations Children's Fund, which urged international companies to adopt child labor codes. One response was by the World Federation of Sporting Goods Industries, which drew up a code of practice aimed at eradicating child labor in its member companies and their suppliers.

VI. ICs from industrial countries frequently must adapt practices when they operate in non-industrial LDCs, even though the people learn industrial skills rapidly. More difficult is their adaptation to factory life, such as:

A. Reporting to work at the same time and place each day.

B. Production schedules.

C. Factory teamwork.

D. Industrial hierarchy.

E. Safety equipment and rules.

VII. According to the Mercer Consulting Group, the world's largest employee benefits consultancy, 90 percent of American-based international companies plan to boost expatriate assignment by the year 2000. Such positions require more and different skills than do purely domestic executive jobs. Among the skills are

A. Be bi-or multi-cultural

B. Know the employer's business policies and practices.

C. Understand business practices and customs in the host country.

D. Know the host country language.

VIII. Three sources of staffing for IC executives are: the home country, a host country, or a third country.

A. The home country national.

    1. Will know the home country language and culture, but

    2. Will be unlikely to know host or other countries' languages or cultures.

B. The host country national

    1. Will know the host country language and culture, but

    2. Will be unlikely to know the home or other countries' languages or cultures.

C. Generalizations such as made above about home and host country nationals are subject to many exceptions, and no generalizations of those sorts should be even attempted about third country nationals. They may:

    1. have gone aboard for one company and switched to another,

    2. have been U. N. or other international agency employees,

    3. have been hired out of European, North American or other business schools.

IX. Subsidiaries in host countries sometimes welcome home or third country nationals for sensitive negotiations with the host country government, for example when requesting high-level, large amount payment guarantees by the government. The home or third country foreigner to the host country presents advantages:

A. Lack of patriotism or host country loyalty is not involved.

B. After the negotiations, the home or third country person can depart leaving the subsidiary to get on with its government, blaming any hard feelings on the foreigner.

X.   An expatriate management assignment can be your passport to the company's top executive positions. Or it can be the end of your career with that company. Precautions to observe to improve your chances of success include:

A. Try to get someone fairly high in the company's hierarchy to be your mentor who will keep you informed of developments at headquarters and prevent people there from forgetting your.

B. Insist that the company tell you exactly what it expects you to accomplish.

C. You may be forgotten in spite of your mentor's efforts, and to protect yourself in such a case you should have done that best possible job for your company, learned the host country culture, language, and markets and met and mingled with as many other company executives as possible. You may be attractive to another company with the skills and knowledge you have accumulated. That is a major source of third country executives.

XI. The expatriate's family: Nine out of ten failures of an expatriate's assignment are family related. Unhappy spouses, referred to as trailing spouses, are the biggest reason for employees asking to go home early which can be very expensive for the employer in addition to the loss of the employee. Companies are taking steps to prevent unhappiness, steps such as culture and language training, assistance with housing, education, shopping, recreation, and others.

XII. The expatriate as one of a two-career couple is becoming more common. In these cases the employer may assist the trailing spouse to get a job in the host country or may even hire the person itself.

XIII. The language trap can catch you if you speak only one language, usually English.

A. English has become the lingua franca of the world.

B. English-only speakers do not understand communications in other languages but can be understood by the many people with English as a second language.

XIV. Women are moving into IC executive suites–as executives, not secretaries.

A. The Washington-based organization, Women in International Trade, can assist IC female executives.

B. The number of women being posted abroad by ICs is growing.

C. Although about half U. S. business school students are women, the rapid increase in their numbers in business has slowed.

D. Growing numbers of women are abandoning corporate life due to feelings of not belonging there. While some are taking temporary breaks until their children reach school age, more and more are starting their own businesses. Ironically, the tough climb up the first rungs of the corporate ladder often prepares women to succeed as entrepreneurs better than men. One women commented, "The need for risk taking that was instilled early on made me better suited to start my own business."

XV. Resumes are marketing tools; they are prepared and read with that in mind. Nevertheless, they are usually reasonably accurate, Robert Half International, a worldwide executive search firm has collected and published bloopers from actual resumes, that have been submitted to it by job seekers. A list of the types of statements not to put in resumes, is in the text..

XVI. Selection and promotion of managers do's and don'ts include:

A. Other qualities being equal, promote from within the company.

B. If other qualities are not equal, and the outsider is better qualified, give that person the nod.

C. Important as language ability definitely is, don't choose or promote a person without other qualifications.

D. Assess the total person
    1. Functional skills
    2. Language proficiency
    3. International business and culture savvy
    4. The combination of such qualities is found frequently in natives of small countries such as Belgium, Denmark, Luxembourg, the Netherlands, or Switzerland.

XVII. Compensation of IC executives who are expatriates in three parts.
    A. Salaries are usually standard for each level of the management hierarchy throughout the IC.
    B. Allowances are payment to compensate expatriates for extra costs of living abroad, such as:
        1. Housing
        2. Cost-of-living. See Figure 17-2
        3. Tax differentials
        4. Education of children
        5. Moving and orientation
    C. Bonuses are paid in recognition that expatriates and their families undergo hardships and inconveniences and make sacrifices living abroad. They include:
        1. Overseas premiums
        2. Contract termination payments
        3. Home leave reimbursements

XVIII. Compensation packages are complicated
    A. What percentage to pay in host country currency, or home or other country currency.
    B. Currency exchange rates are constantly changing.
    C. Inflation rates change and differ from country to country.

XIX. International status is given the top people whom the IC wants to retain. Among the perks given a manager with international status are:
    A. Company cars, perhaps with chauffeurs
    B. Private pension plan
    C. Retirement payment
    D. Life insurance
    E. Health insurance
    F. Company house or apartment
    G. Foreign subsidiary directorship
    H. Seminar and vacation travel
    I. Club membership
    J. Hidden slush funds

XX. Near the end of this chapter are Figures and Tables which can be interesting and helpful.
    A. Figure 18.4 compares living expenses in 26 cities around the world.
    B. Figure 18.5 gives CEO pay numbers in 24 countries.
    C. Figure 18.6 shows a source of help for expatriates.
    D. Table 18.1 compares the costs of over indulgence in 18 cities.
    E. Figure 18.7 is a view of business environment in 25 cities.
    F. Figure 18.8 illustrates office space costs in 10 locations.

Answer to Questions

1. LDC representatives say cheap labor is one of their few advantages in a competitive, interrelated world. They also say the children would be even worse off without the jobs, bad as they are.

2. It gave an extended mid-day break so the employees could go home to tend their crops and animals and care for children. Without the break, the employees were becoming hostile and potentially dangerous. The employees worked weekend hours to make up for the time lost during the breaks.

3. Problems involving the trailing spouse of expatriate executives are increasing in numbers because of the growing prevalence of two-career couples. There are several ways companies are coping with them. They are helping trailing spouses find suitable employment in the host countries, working with them on their resumes, setting up appointments and interviews, paying executive search firms, and other ways. They are arranging training in the host country culture and language. If all else fails, the companies sometimes will hire the spouse in there own organization.

4. Home country nationals know the language and culture of the home country. However, in an IC they need to deal with other languages and cultures with which they may be less familiar.

5. People who speak only English do not understand what is being said or written in another language. However, as English becomes a lingua finaca, most other people understand what the English speakers are saying and writing.

6. Third country nationals have experience as expatriates and are likely to know host country language and culture.

7. Expenses are usually higher, and expatriate life is frequently more difficult or inconvenient.

8. There are many more factors to consider. A few are different expenses and taxes, different inflation rates, currency exchange rates, currency controls, and living conditions.

9. Some host countries may be hostile to female executives or uncomfortable dealing with them.

10. Costs of living, safety, medial facilities, education, housing, recreation, and shopping.

Answers to Internet Problems

1. Visit the Web site http://homefair.com/home. The site provides comparisons of living costs between selected cities in the world. According to this Web site, a person making $30,000 a year in Long Beach, California would need to make $55,641 in Oslo, Norway to maintain the same standard of living.

2.   a. ABWI is one of many organizations working for women in international business. Specifically, the Web sit at http://www.abwiword.com has information on the organization, Women in International Trade.
          b. Women in Technology International has a Web page listing several activities. The Internet Directory in this text has information on countries and regions containing specific information on the status of women. One such Web site is http://www.witi.org.

Discussion of Minicase 17-1: Female Executives in International Business

In both these situations the arguments against giving the job to a woman have been heard often. The first paragraph of the case is the foundation of the arguments. They say the male executives of banks, customers, governments or joint ventures outside the United States will not accept or cooperate with female executives of any nationality. They say the situation is bad everywhere outside the United States and worst in Africa, Asia and Latin America.

Aside from the unfairness of denying hiring and promotion opportunities to qualified women, there is the point that the only way to break down the barriers is to let women executives try in the international arena. Perhaps they will be able to deal successfully with male executives abroad as representatives of American companies.

In 1981, the cause of female executives of U.S. firms in international business got a boost. A U.S. Court of Appeals held an American company could not deny a woman an executive position because she might not be acceptable to foreign customers. The court said, "Nor does stereotyped customer preference justify a sexually discriminatory practice.:

However, the court also said the woman must be as well qualified as a male competitor or the firm is not required to give her the job. In this case there was a better qualified male employee who got the position, director of international operations, and the court did not order the firm to fire him and hire her.

The position in that case is headquartered in the United States. Your decisions involve positions in Mexico and Japan. The language of the court would seem to apply regardless of where in the world the job is located, but there are factual differences faced by you.

One difference is that the woman applying for the Mexico job is better qualified for the job than anyone else in the company. Unless you find a better qualified male outside your company, the court decision probably applies to your situation. Moreover, in Mexico there are some examples of women in business and the professions, and your new female executive vice president might be well accepted.

As to the Japanese job, the applicant seems qualified but may not be best qualified. You should accumulate evidence on that subject.

An additional problem might confront the woman who wants the job in Japan. She is one half Japanese, and Asians, including Japanese, can be hostile to mixed blood persons. Here is a racial problem added to the sexual question. Presumably, the court's reasoning would apply equally to racial attitudes of foreign customers as to their sexual prejudices, but the court was not faced with a racial question.

One factor in favor of both women is that in your company, international experience is a must before an executive can hope to get into top management. Therefore, if you pass over these women, you are not only denying them the specific jobs, you are also damaging their entire careers.

TM 18.1
Figure 18.2

OPPORTUNITIES FOR
ECONOMISTS, PLANNERS AND ENGINEERS

We are a Tokyo-based consulting firm with full-time and project-based positions available in developing countries for economists, planners and engineers. We work in various sectors (e.g. transport. environment. education, tourism, energy) and offer excellent remuneration.

If interested, please send a detailed CV to:

PADECO Co., Ltd., Izumikan Sanbancho Bldg.
3-8 Sanbancho, Chiyoda-ku, Tokyo 102-0075
Fax: 81-3-3238-9422 Email: admin@padeco.co.jp
Homepage: http://www.padeco.co.jp

CENTRE OF PLANNING AND ECONOMIC RESEARCH
ATHENS, GREECE

Research Officers in Economics

The Centre of Planning and Economic Research is seeking to appoint up to 13 Research Officers in the following areas of economics:

Macroeconomics, Public Economics, Industrial Economics, Monetary Economics, Applied Econometrics, Economics with emphasis to Social Policy, Applied Microeconomics, Labour Economics.

Applicants should hold a Ph.D. degree and be Greek or EU nationals.

The closing date for applications is the 10th of July, 2000.

For further details please contact: tel. 0030 1 3643771; fax 0030 1 3630122; e-mail: kepe@kepe.gr

---

Founded in 1823, Birkbeck is based in Bloomsbury and has the highest proportion of research active staff of any college or university in the greater London area.

Birkbeck UNIVERSITY OF LONDON

Lecturer/Senior Lecturer/ Reader in Management

The department of Management is seeking to make an appointment in any area of management or business. You will teach challenging, experienced students at undergraduate, postgraduate and PhD level and contribute to the research reputation of the department and the School of Management and Organizational Psychology as a whole.

Applicants should have a PhD, or equivalent, in a relevant social science area and have developed, or for appointment at lecturer level show evidence of developing, an international research programme and publications.

Salary ranges: £19,372 to £24,713 pa or £25,655 to £32,199 pa or £33,697 to £37,804 pa inc, depending on qualifications and experience.

**For details and application forms please send a large (A4) sae to the Personnel Department, Ref: CMB143/G, Birkbeck, Malet Street, Bloomsbury, London WC1E 7HX.
Closing date: 27 June 2000
Birkbeck web site: http://www.bbk.ac.uk**

JOB HUNTING INTERNATIONALLY?

Executive $75K-500K+. Career searching into, within or out of Asia / Europe / M.East / U.S.? Contact for **Free** Info & Critique

www.careerpath.co.uk

	Fax:	Email:
USA/Canada	+1 202 4781698	cpamerica@careerpath.co.uk
Europe	+44 20 75048280	cpeurope@careerpath.co.uk
Asia / M. East / Aus	+66 2 2674688	cpasia@bkk.loxinfo.co.th

Commercial Research analyst

A leading international commodity trade house with a global presence in the sugar market as principal traders, brokers and refiners is seeking a highly numerate graduate with demonstrable analytical and presentation skills. Working in the research department, initially the role requires you to develop detailed knowledge of the European Community legislative environment though it is vitally important to identify commercial opportunities and develop direct links with our clients. The successful candidate will have a good degree in Economics or closely related discipline, excellent communication and computer skills and a keen interest in agriculture policy. We will provide full in-house training, travel opportunities and a competitive salary and benefits package.

Send a cv to Box 4106, 25 St James St, London SW1A 1HG, England

---

Executive Director, AZERBAIJAN

Open Society Institute seeks an Executive Director for its national foundation in Baku, Azerbaijan. The executive director, in conjunction with and under direction of OSI Azerbaijan's board of directors, develops strategy, plans and implementation for operating and grantmaking programs. The director supervises staff; interacts with foundation board of directors; oversees the foundation's annual budget.

REQUIRES: Fluent English and Azeri, Turkish and/or Russian; 4+ years ngo management; 2+ years field exp. in Central and Eastern Europe or preferably, in the former Soviet Union; exp. working with a board; strong financial management, organizational, interpersonal and writing skills; BA with Masters or other advanced degree preferred. Extensive travel.

Send cover letter/CV to: **Open Society Institute**
Human Resources - Code AZERB, 400 W. 59th Street, NY, NY 10019, or fax to: (212) 548-4607.

PEMBROKE COLLEGE AND THE JUDGE INSTITUTE OF MANAGEMENT STUDIES
CAMBRIDGE

The Bristol Myers Squibb Research Fellowship In Pharmaco-Economics

Bristol Myers Squibb are supporting a Research Fellowship in Pharmaco-Economics to be held jointly at Pembroke College and The Judge Institute of Management Studies. The appointment will run from 1 October 2000 or as soon as possible thereafter.

The Judge Institute of Management Studies is the University of Cambridge's business school. It aims to be an internationally-recognised centre for research and education of the highest quality to provide a forum for the debate of key management issues by leaders from around the world.

Pembroke College is one of the constituent colleges of the University of Cambridge, and has strong accademic connections with the corporate world.

Applications are sought from candidates with a strong research record in the field of health/pharmaco-economics. The appointment is for an initial 3-year term, with the possibility of renewal thereafter. Salary is negotiable depending on experience.

Completed applications should reach the College by 24 July 2000. Further particulars and application forms are available from the Senior Tutor's Secretary, Pembroke College, Cambridge CB2 1RF (pat.whitby@pem.cam.ac.uk).

Pembroke College is an equal opportunities employer.

Source: *The Economist*, June 10, 2000, p. 103.

TM 18.2
Figure 18.5   Chief Executives' Pay

As a multiple of manufacturing employees' pay, 1999

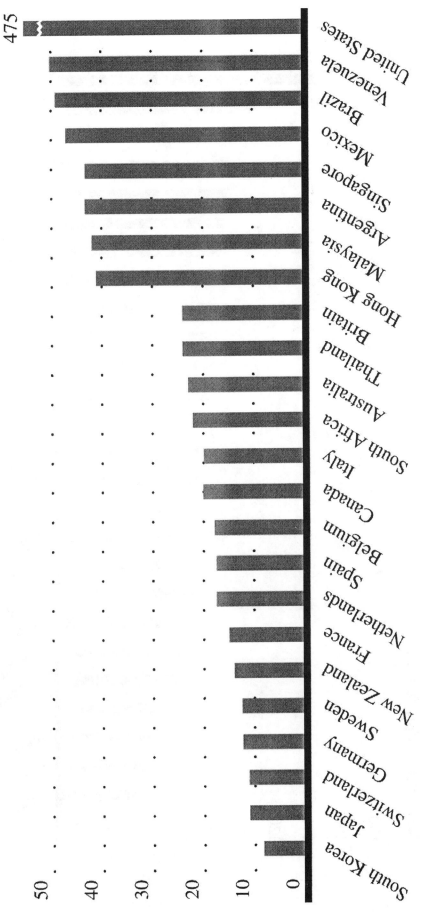

Source: *The Economist,* September 30, 2000, p. 110.

McGraw-Hill/Irwin

Figure 18.4   Cost of Living

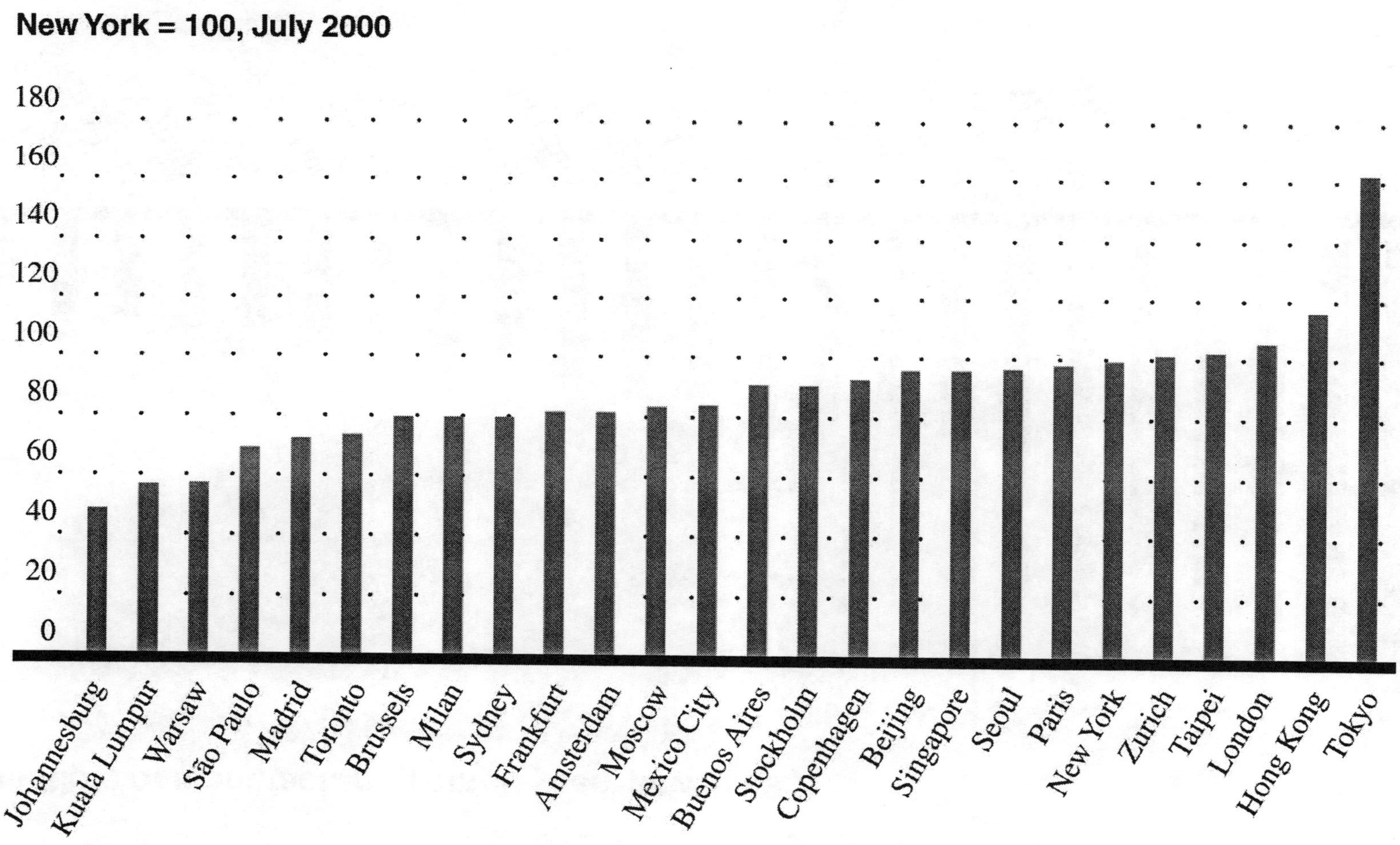

New York = 100, July 2000

Source: *The Economist*, July 22, 2000, p. 98

McGraw-Hill/Irwin

TM 18.4

Figure 18.7   Comparative Business Environment in 25 Cities

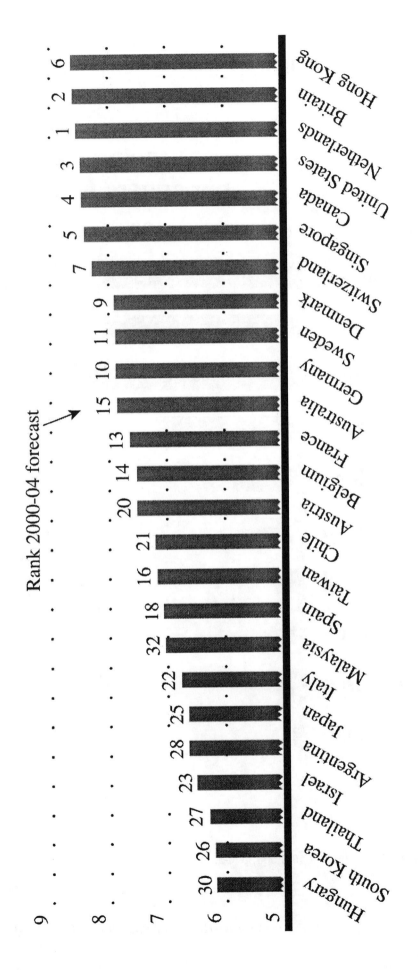

Rank 2000-04 forecast

Source: *The Economist*, May 20, 2000, p. 126

McGraw-Hill/Irwin

Paying the Price for Office Space

Source: *Los Angeles Times*, August 10, 2000, p. C3.

CHAPTER 19
FINANCIAL MANAGEMENT

Learning Objectives

1. Remind the student that currencies fluctuate in value in terms of each other and that some are hard and convertible while others are not.

2. Explain the business risks caused by those fluctuations and the measures companies may take to protect themselves.

3. Explain the growing use of countertrade.

4. Point out that ICs' treasuries can be converted to profit centers.

5. Introduce the subject of derivatives and their uses to protect an IC against value fluctuations.

Overview

International business has contacts, investments, assets and liabilities in more than one currency. Inasmuch as currency values fluctuate in terms of each other, the companies may gain or lose depending on what currencies they hold. The companies face several types of risks: two of them are transaction and translation.

Some of the steps management can take to protect against those risks include hedging, accelerating or delaying payments, exposure netting price adjustments, balance sheet neutralizing and swaps.

Two other types of risks (or opportunities) encountered by ICs arise from capital raising and investing. Financial management must determine or estimate (1) what currency to raise, (2) strength or weakness of that currency, (3) whether to use equity or debt, (4) source of the capital, (5) if the source is a capital market, which one, (6) how much money for how long and (7) other sources such as a joint venture or a government investment incentive program.

A growing number of sales are made, without money because the buyer has too little hard, convertible currency. Generally more information is available from non-communist LDCs than from communist countries. In addition, such LDCs can usually get more aid from international agencies such as the IMF or the World Bank.

Some companies have established international finance centers where all internal and external invoices are handled. Such centers can help weak currency subsidiaries shop the money markets and reduce hedging and similar protection expenses through the use of derivatives.

Suggestions and Comments

1. Illustrate a transaction loss with an example of an obligation of an American importer to pay a French exporter five million French francs (Ff) in 180 days. Assume the exchange rate on the date of sale to be Ff 8 = Us$ 1. Show the financial result if the rate changes during the 180 days to Ff 9 = US$1 or to F$f$ 7 = US$ 1.

2. Explain that importers and exporters usually do not want to bear currency exchange risks but that others are in the business of doing so. Banks or currency market makers or traders take such risks.

3. Show how the importers and exporters can use hedging and other devices to avoid currency exchange risks.

4. Illustrate how currency rate changes can affect a firm's profit and loss statement. When assets and liabilities or payables and receivables within an IC group of companies are denominated in different currencies, they must all be translated to a single currency, usually that of the home country where the IC parent company is located. This is referred to as the translations risk.

Student Involvement Exercises

1. When a DC based IC has a subsidiary in a country which imposes currency exchange controls, the subsidiary may not be able to dividend its profits to the parent. Have your students make a list of uses to which that trapped money may be put.

2. The story at the beginning of chapter 6 about how McDonald's locked in a favorable currency exchange rate to pay for the ingredients it needed to import shows the importance of such operations. Have your students research for other examples.

3. Encourage research of the various capital markets of the world, the differences, advantages and disadvantages of each.

4. Countertrade is becoming more and more important to international business. Have your students find as many examples as possible of its application.

Guest Lecturers

1. International department officers of banks could speak on hedges, swaps and banks as capital sources for ICs.

2. Accountants may be found to speak on translation risks.

3. Someone from the financial department of companies which deal with transactions and investment risks should be interesting.

4. The same sort of person might speak on decisions involved in capital sourcing.

Lecture Outline

I.   Fluctuating Currency Exchange Rates
      As currencies change value in terms of each other, firms doing international business are subject to several resulting risks,

      A. Transaction Risk
         In any transaction which involves payment or receipt in the future of a foreign currency, there is a transaction risk that the foreign currency's value is vis-à-vis the home currency will change. The party which bears the risk can protect itself in several ways.

         1. Currency exchange forward, option or futures market hedges.

            a. The forward hedge involves a contract between the party who bears the currency transaction risk and a second party, almost always a bank, in the terms of which the bank agrees to deliver to the party at risk upon an agreed future date, in that party's home currency, an amount close to the amount of the transaction. Thus the bank assumes the currency exchange risk for which it charges a fee.

b. The option market hedge is a big activity of the Philadelphia stock exchange although that is not the only place to deal in options. To conduct an option hedge on the stock exchange, the party at risk must deal with a broker with a seat on the exchange. If the party at risk is to receive a foreign currency in the future, it would buy a put option giving it the right to put, i. e. deliver, the foreign currency to the party who wrote the option who in turn agrees to deliver to the party at risk upon an agreed future date, in that party's home currency, an amount close to the amount of the transaction. Thus, the option writer assumes the currency exchange risk for which it charges a fee. The party at risk who bought the option will exercise it only if the currency values have changed so that it would otherwise lose money. In our example that would be the case if the foreign currency had lost value in terms of the home currency and would therefore buy less of the home currency than it would have at the time of the transaction. Otherwise, if the currencies' relative value had not changed or if the foreign currency had strengthened in terms of the home currency and would now buy more of it, the party at risk would not exercise the option but would let it lapse. It had bought protection which turned out not to be needed.

c. The futures market hedge is the activity of the international monetary market of the Chicago Mercantile Exchange (CME) although that is not the only place to deal in futures. To conduct a futures hedge on the CME, the part at risk must deal with a broker with a CME seat. If the party at risk is to receive a foreign currency in the future it would buy a futures contract to deliver close to that amount of that currency at a fixed date. This is in the nature of a short contract, which goes up in value if the foreign currency goes down in the value vis-à-vis, the home currency. Thus, any loss the party at risk would incur because the foreign currency lost value would be offset by the increased value of the short contract. The futures market does not offer the flexibility the party at risk would enjoy in the forward or option hedge because contracts on the CME are in fixed amounts for each currency dealt in there, and settlements of contracts are at fixed dates each year. See Table 19-1 for the ticker codes of the currencies traded on the international monetary market. That market is part of the Chicago Mercantile Exchange, an advertisement for which is shown in Figure 19-1.

d. In our example, the party at risk using either a forward or futures hedge is short the foreign currency. A short may be covered or uncovered. In a covered short, the party either has the foreign currency in its possession or has the contractual right to receive it on or before the date agreed to deliver that currency. In an uncovered short, the party has neither the currency nor a contractual right to it.

2. Credit hedge
   a. This involves borrowing the foreign currency the party at risk will get in the future.
   b. Converting it immediately to the home currency, and
   c. Repaying the loan when the foreign currency is received.

3. Acceleration or delay of payment
   a. When a debtor is obliged to make a future payment in a foreign currency, it will study the comparative strength of the foreign currency vis-à-vis the home currency.
   b. If the home currency is stronger, the debtor will delay buying the foreign currency until the last moment in hopes less home currency will be required to buy the same amount of foreign currency.
   c. If the home currency is weaker, the debtor might buy the foreign currency at once.

    d.   Acceleration or delay of payment between unrelated companies can work hardship on the creditor which receives late payment.

    e.   Within an IC, the enterprise unit which suffers–or its management–can be otherwise rewarded or compensated by the IC.

4. Exposure netting

    a.   In currency groups such as the EMS, assets or liabilities in two or more of the currencies could be expected to offset each other. A caveat is in order here. During 1993 and 1994, the EMS encountered some rough going, and the currencies were permitted to fluctuate in value in ranges of 15% above and 15% below the set exchange rates and yet remain in the EMS. That 30% range in more like a floating currency regime than the fixed system the EMS was designed to be.

    b.   In 1999, the EMS was succeeded by the European economic and monetary union (EMU), and by 2001, twelve of the 15 EU countries had joined. One EMU program is to replace their 12 individual, national currencies with one, the euro. Thus exposure netting is no longer possible with those 12 currencies against each other. However, there remain the currencies of the three EU countries that have not joined EMU and, of course, the currencies of all the other countries of the world.

    c.   An asset (or a liability) in a strong currency could be offset (netted) by an asset (or a liability) in w weak currency.

5. Price adjustment

    a.   If a seller accepts future payment in a weak currency, it can boost the price in an attempt to cover the risk.

    b.   Between unrelated companies, such price increases can be difficult or impossible due to competition.

    c.   Between IC units, such price adjustments can be beneficial for the enterprise and the unit paying the higher price– or its management– can be otherwise rewarded or compensated.

6. See Figure 19.2 for illustrations of the protection methods outlined above.

7. A new development has brought some currency-risk hedging within the reach of medium and small size businesses. In 1990, the Federal Reserve permitted American banks to hold foreign currency deposits in the U.S.

B. Translation Risk

1. While transaction currency exchange risks arise from underlying transactions involving foreign currency payments in periods up to one year, translation risks involve longer term exposures arising from investment in different countries.

    a.   The investor hopes for rent, dividend, interest on royalty payments for years in the future. Those payments will usually be in currencies other than that of the investor's home country, and, of course, those currencies will fluctuate in value, becoming stronger or weaker thus, buying more or less home-country currency

    b.   The fixed investments in other countries, e.g., stocks, bonds, land, or buildings, have values expressed in the currencies of those countries. All those assets and accompanying liabilities, payables and receivables must be expressed in the currency of the home country in order to be comprehensible to bankers and other creditors, stockholders and government regulators of the home country. Thus, all those numbers must be *translated* from the "foreign" currencies to the home country currency.

2. To minimize translation-caused profit/loss swings, management can:

a. Neutralize the balance sheet by trying to equalize assets and liabilities in each currency in which the firm does business.
   b. Use parallel loans or swaps. See Figures 19.3 and 4.
   c. Use bank swaps which frequently involve one hard currency and one soft currency.
   d. Hedge.

II. Capital Raising and Investing
Fluctuating currency values are important considerations for companies raising capital or investing abroad, but their concerns are usually for longer time periods than in transaction situations.

   A. Management Decisions
      1. In which currency to raise capital.
      2. Long-term estimate of that currency's strength.
      3. Should the capital be equity or debt?
      4. Capital source, e.g.
         a. Ordinary commercial bank loan.
         b. Bank swap.
         c. Swap with another company.
         d. From another unit of the IC.
         e. One of the world's capital markets.
      5. If a capital market source is chose, which capital market?
      6. How much money for how long?
      7. Other sources such as joint venture partner or a government incentive to the firm's investment.
      8. Interest rate swaps
      9. Currency swaps

   B. Up-to-Date, Accurate Information
      In order to optimize its decisions, management needs the best available information. For that it should maintain good relationships with officers of international banks and other IC financial management.

   C. Sources of Information or Swap/Hedge Partners.
      More and more, the IC financial managers and, of course, people form their international finance centers, are attending conferences and seminars which are attended also by their counterparts from banks, government, and international agencies, and other ICs. The word "networking" may be overused, but the practice can be useful. Whether you need to countertrade (see below), hedge, invest, swap or other financial operation, the people you met or learned of at the various meetings can usually assist you.

III. Derivatives
For some, particularly in the media, "derivatives" became a dirty work in 1994. A number of companies and agencies lost money because their officers misused derivatives and many commentators blamed "derivatives." That is much like blaming automobiles for damage they cause when operated by incompetent (for whatever reason) drivers.

   A. Derivatives are financial instruments, the values of which are tied to price movements of underlying commodities or other instruments.
   B. Hedges we have discussed, such as futures and options, are derivatives as are swaps. You will recall that we discussed them as means of avoiding or protecting against risks.

C. It is true that derivative use can be complex, and if badly done, costly.

D. It is suggested that many managers should seek expert advise to:

1. Identify where risks lie.

2. Design an appropriate strategy for managing them, and

3. Select the right tools to execute the strategy.

E. Table 19.2 shows the 10 top derivatives exchanges around the world.

IV. Sales Without Money

Countertrade has been said to come in six varieties. They are (1) counterpurchase, (2) compensation, (3) barter, (4) switch, (5) offset and (6) clearing account arrangements. Countertrade is now extremely important in world trade and its use in growing. Industrial cooperation is another device used in trading and dealing with countries which are short of hard, convertible currencies. Five type of industrial cooperation have been identified. They are (1) joint venture, (2) coproduction and specialization, (3) subcontracting, (4) licensing and (5) turnkey plants.

At least one of the countries involved in countertrade or industrial cooperation is usually, but not always, and LDC. As we have learned, instability, high illiteracy, authoritarian governments, poverty, and corruption frequently characterize LDCs. As such circumstances bear on countertrade and industrial cooperation, the following generalizations can be made.

A. Accurate and timely information may be scarce, but

B. the LDCs often get help in compiling accurate statistics from the World Bank, regional developments banks, the IMF or some UN agency, and

C. one or more of those organization or aid agencies of developed countries may provide large amounts of needed hard currency financing.

D. When LDCs pay in products made in their factories, there are two common problems, quality and timely delivery. Two methods of dealing with those problems are.

1. Inspection by reliable, third-party organization.

2. Guarantee of quality and timely delivery by a bank in the LDC country.

E. Figure 19.6 shows membership by industry of the American Countertrade Association.

V. International Finance Centers/In-House Banks

Some ICs have established autonomous international finance centers where complex decisions can be made about financial problems and opportunities of a multinational. Such financial centers/in-house banks have been established as profit centers rather than mere service departments by a number of international firms. Some of the activities in which the centers can save or make money for their firms are:

A. Hedge currency risks by matching open positions of the several multinational units and hedge outside only positions not thus covered.

B. Maximize intra-enterprise capital utilization and raise capital outside only if no multinational unit can provide it economically.

C. When raising capital outside, shop the markets and methods to obtain it most economically.

D. Maximize hard, strong currency holdings and minimize those of weak currencies.

E. Assist IC units in weak currency countries.

F. Handle invoicing for both intra-enterprise and outside trading.

G. We have emphasized the great potential value of the correct uses of derivatives by an IC. But, there are also great risks with the incorrect uses of derivatives, and the IC needs highly competent, skilled people to manage and oversee derivatives operations. Such people are rare, and what better utilization could there be of an international finance center than concentration of derivatives operations for all parts of the IC?

Answers to Questions

1. Because if the value of the foreign currency goes down compared to your currency during the six months, the foreign currency paid you by the importer will not buy as much of you currency.

2. Yes. It can buy a forward hedge in the foreign exchange market, borrow in the money market, net its exposures or raise its price. It can also hedge on the futures or options market.

3. On the date of sale (payment by the importer to be made in six months), the exporter borrows an amount which, plus six months' interest, equals the amount of the sale. The borrowing is in the importer country's currency. The exporter immediately converts that currency to the currency of its country and lends it or uses it as operating capital for six months. When the importer pays, that money is used by the exporter to repay its borrowing.

4. The smaller company dealing with other separate companies benefits from payment acceleration or delay at the cost of the other company which will resist such actions. The IC can look to the benefit of the entire enterprise and reward management for contributing. The enterprise benefits by using payment acceleration or delay to maximize currency holdings in high interest countries where credit is tight; to hold more strong and less weak currencies and to minimize holdings of currencies of countries where exchange controls exist or are expected.

5. You would net an asset in one currency against a liability in the other.

6. See the answer to question 4.

7. Important business decisions such as dividends, pricing new investment, asset location, etc. must be based on the consolidation into one currency of all assets, liabilities, payables and receivables. It is unrealistic for management to base key decisions on the assumption that exchange rates have not and will not change.

8. Yes. When two ICs (A and B) each have a company in the same two countries, a loan by A to the affiliate of B in one country is offset by a loan by B to the affiliate of A in the second country.

9. Because the buyer does or will have goods or products or commodities which the buyer can deliver to the seller which can, in turn, sell them to pay for what it sold to the buyer. These processes are referred to as countertrade or co-production, among other terms.

10. There are two ways to deal with those problems. Independent inspection agencies can monitor to the production process in the LDC factories and inspect the products for quality. Second, more and more LDC banks will guarantee product quality and timely delivery of products from plants in their country.

Answers to Internet Problems

1. Due to technological advances currency trading occurs 24 hrs a day and currency rates are constantly changing. There are many sites that include financial information CNNfn's web site (http://www.cnnfn.com) , for example, lists the value of currency trading and the time of the last trade.

2. International managers can predict changes by monitoring economic and political changes in the world. The Internet Directory in this text has information on economic information in many countries. One such site is http://www.devocapital.com. Internet users can find detailed information on most world countries by following links on the page.

Discussion of Minicase 19–1: Dealing with the Transaction Risk Caused by Fluctuations of Relative Currency Values

1. You could use a *foreign exchange market hedge* which works as follows. On the day of sale –180 days before payment is due–you sell short for your company Ff 5 million for 180 days. You could accomplish this through your bank or your commodity broker with a contract on the International Monetary Market, although most large, commercial hedge operations are done with the bank.
    In either event, you have entered a contract to deliver to the bank or other party Ff 5 million in 180 days. In return, the bank or other party has agreed to deliver you $ million in 180 days. You have used the day of sale exchange rate of FF 5 –US$1, and you have assured your company it will receive the desired $1 million, regardless of what happens to the Ff – US$ rate.
    In 180 days the French importer pays our company Ff 5 million to cover its obligation under the import contract. The company pays that Ff 5 million to the bank or other party, which at the same time pays US$ 1 million to your company. The actual amount you receive may not be exactly $1 million but will depend on the premium or discount in the forward market on the day of the short sale.

2. A credit market hedge is similar in principle but different in mechanics. On the day of the sale–180 days before payment is due–you borrow Ff 5 million from a French bank or other lender for your company. You immediately convert the Ff 5 million to US$ 1 million and use the $1 million however most useful or profitable for your company for 180 days, On the 180th day the French importer pays Ff 5 million and use the $1 million however most useful or profitable for your company for 180 days. On the 180th day the French importer pays Ff 5 million to your company which uses that payment to repay its French borrowing. The amount borrowed would usually be a little less than Ff 5 million; it would be an amount which, plus interest, would equal Ff 5 million in 180 days. Thus, the importer's payment would completely and exactly repay the French borrowing.

Minicase 19-2

Countertrade

An American company and a Soviet foreign trade organization (FTO) have reached agreement on all the technical aspects of the product that the company wants to sell and the Soviet Union wants to buy All export license problems have been cleared, but one obstacle remains. The Soviet Union is not willing to pay in a hard convertible currency.

The product includes late technology, but it has some relatively simple components. The company has not sold previously to the East or to any customer for which U.S. dollar availability was a difficulty.

The company turns to you, an international business consultant with extensive experience in dealing with communist and Third World customers. What inquiries will you advise your client to make? what steps would you advise the client to take in efforts to consummate the sale and get the U.S. dollars it needs?

Discussion of Minicase 19-2: Countertrade

You should point out to your client that although they are unfamiliar in dealing without U.S. dollars, this may not be a problem as options are available. Industrial cooperation with the Soviets has a degree of risk, but if the lack of hard currency would stop the deal from materializing, it should certainly be considered.

The American company must do a cost/benefit analysis to determine which of the following actions would be best:

a.   Forget the deal and incur the losses on expenditure already put into negotiations,

b.   co-production and specialization,

c.   licensing.

The financial consequences of the first option are relatively easily measures. Co-production and specialization is a form of industrial cooperation where the Soviets would produce the relatively simple components of the product while the Americans continue to produce the rest. There would be an exchange of components and independent assembling and marketing.

Minicase 19–3

LDC DELIVERY DIFFICULTIES

In your countertrade experience, you have encountered two serious problems. Sometimes the quality of the goods supplied by the LDC/C partner is not up to specifications. On other occasions, the LDC/C partner was late in making deliveries or delivered only part of the goods promised.

What are two methods you might try to avoid those problems in future contracts?

Discussion of Minicase 19–3: LDC Delivery Difficulties

The two possible methods to protect your interests are, first with agreement of the LDC plant management, hire an independent, third-party inspection firm. This firm will monitor the production assuring quality components and raw materials and on-time results. The finished product is inspected for quality and conformity with specifications.

A second method is to get a bank in the LDC to guarantee quality and timely delivery of the product.

Minicase 19–4

CFO DECISIONS WHEN THE COMPANY HAS A TEMPORARY SURPLUS OF FUNDS

You are the chief financial officer (CFO) of an IC. The parent company has a temporary surplus of funds. You do not foresee an operating need for the money. $5 million, for about six months.

What are some possible uses for that money by the parent? What uses are possible within the IC system? What considerations will govern your decision as to how best utilize the money?

Discussion of Minicase 19–4: CFO Decisions: Temporary Surplus of Funds

First, we will make the assumption that the dollars quoted in the case are US$. The easiest option to initially consider would be the best deal available on a short-term (six months) fixed deposit on the U. S. money market. The return calculated could be used as the benchmark on which alternatives can be compared.

Within the multinational system there may be a division or subsidiary requiring a short-term loan. Whether the money would be lent to this subsidiary would depend on the need for the loan, the payback period and interest rate chargeable. The firm may consider converting the US$s into another currency for other financial reasons. Investment in a high interest rate country may result in a more profitable short-term deposit than the U. S. benchmark. Investigation in this area may prove to be worthwhile as some countries periodically offer high interest short-term bonds for special economic development projects.

Determination of the present strong and weak currencies must be done initially as this information would influence all options, unless the company wants to play with stock or commodities. The option of buying one or more contracts in the currency forward markets is available. You should look at trends and decide on which currencies and whether to be covered, or if uncovered, to go long or short.

The final decision must be balanced judgment considering all the conditions, needs, and expectations of financial outcomes.

Minicase 19–5

USING A TEMPORARY FUND SURPLUS TO MAKE SOME PROFIT IN CURRENCY FORWARD MARKETS

Assume your decision in Minicase 18–4 was to use the $5 million buy one or more open contracts in the currency forward markets. The first contract was long in British pounds at 1.5137 for 30 days with your $5 million.

How may pounds and pence is your company long?

In 30 days, when you cover the contract, the price is 1.5347. Did you make or lose money for your company? How much? (For purposes of these minicases, ignore commissions.)

Discussion of Minicase 19–5: Profit in Currency

The currencies used in this case were chosen to highlight the exception as to how currencies are quoted in relation to each other. All currencies with the exception of the British are primarily quoted in terms of how much is needed to buy a U. S. dollar, e.g. US$ 1 – Ff 8.4075 and £1 = US$ 1.5138.

In this case, you buy long, the £ appreciates and therefore the gain (calculated below) is how much you make for your currency:

Contract payout:

$$\frac{1.5347}{1.5138} \times \$5 = US\$ 5,069,031.60$$

Gain or (loss):

$5,069,031.60 - $5,000,000 = US$ 69,031.60

Gain of $69,031.60

MINICASE 19–6

SHORT THE FRENCH FRANC

Use the same facts as in Minicase 18–5. Your decision is to invest the $5 million in a contract shorting the French franc at 8.0475 for 30 days. How many francs and cents are you short? In this instance, you cover at the end of the 30-day contract a 7.8992. Did you make or lose money for you company? How much?

Discussion of Minicase 19–6: Short the French Franc

The quoted currencies describe two rates of how many French francs can be traded for one U. S. dollar. In this case, you sold short, the franc appreciated against the dollar and therefore a loss was incurred (as calculated below):

Contract payout:

$$\frac{8.0475}{7.8992} \times \$5 = \$5,093,870.30$$

Gain or (loss)

$5,000,000 - $5,093,870.30 = ($93,870.30)

Loss of $93,870.30

Foreign currency trading is not as foreign as you think.

The potential of CME foreign currency futures, and options on futures, is easy to understand. They're volatile. They offer low margins. And they're exceptionally liquid, with average daily volume close to 100,000 contracts.

Most important, CME currency contracts trend well, year after year. And they respond to familiar, fundamental economic factors—the kind you follow every day in the news.

What's more, with CME foreign currency options, you can take advantage of opportunities in the market with limited risk.

Of course, trading foreign currency futures and options at the CME does involve risk. But if you can afford to assume it, they offer everything a speculator could want.

More bang for the buck. The mark. And the yen.

To learn more, call your futures broker. And call the CME toll–free at 1–800–331–3332. Dept. "W", for our free brochure.

CHICAGO MERCANTILE EXCHANGE
FUTURES AND OPTIONS WORLDWIDE

International Monetary Market Index and Option Market

30 South Wacker Drive Chicago, Illinois 60606 312/930-1000
67 Wall Street New York 10005 212/363-7000
27 Throgmorton Street London EC2N 2AN 01/920-0722

More bang for your buck!

To learn more, call our toll–free number or send this coupon to: Chicago Mercantile Exchange, Marketing Services, 30 South Wacker Drive, Chicago, Illinois 60606.

Name

Address

City   State   Zip

Telephone

10/15/86WSJ

TM 19.2
Figure 19.2

Hedging Currency Risks

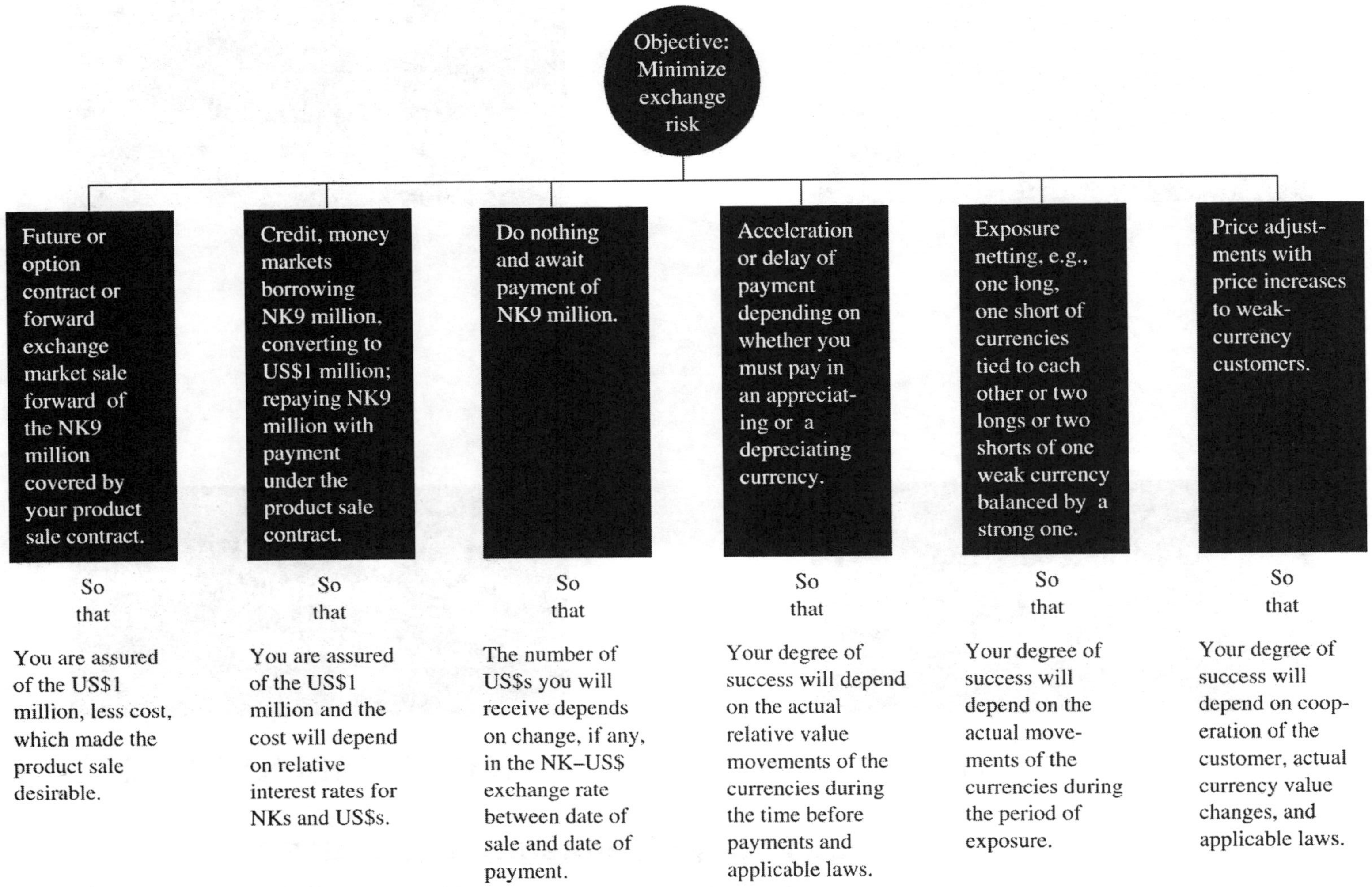

Objective: Minimize exchange risk

Future or option contract or forward exchange market sale forward of the NK9 million covered by your product sale contract.	Credit, money markets borrowing NK9 million, converting to US$1 million; repaying NK9 million with payment under the product sale contract.	Do nothing and await payment of NK9 million.	Acceleration or delay of payment depending on whether you must pay in an appreciating or a depreciating currency.	Exposure netting, e.g., one long, one short of currencies tied to each other or two longs or two shorts of one weak currency balanced by a strong one.	Price adjustments with price increases to weak-currency customers.
So that	So that	So that	So that	So that	So that
You are assured of the US$1 million, less cost, which made the product sale desirable.	You are assured of the US$1 million and the cost will depend on relative interest rates for NKs and US$s.	The number of US$s you will receive depends on change, if any, in the NK–US$ exchange rate between date of sale and date of payment.	Your degree of success will depend on the actual relative value movements of the currencies during the time before payments and applicable laws.	Your degree of success will depend on the actual movements of the currencies during the period of exposure.	Your degree of success will depend on cooperation of the customer, actual currency value changes, and applicable laws.

McGraw-Hill/Irwin

**Parallel Loans by Two Parent Companies
(Each to the Subsidiary of the Other)**

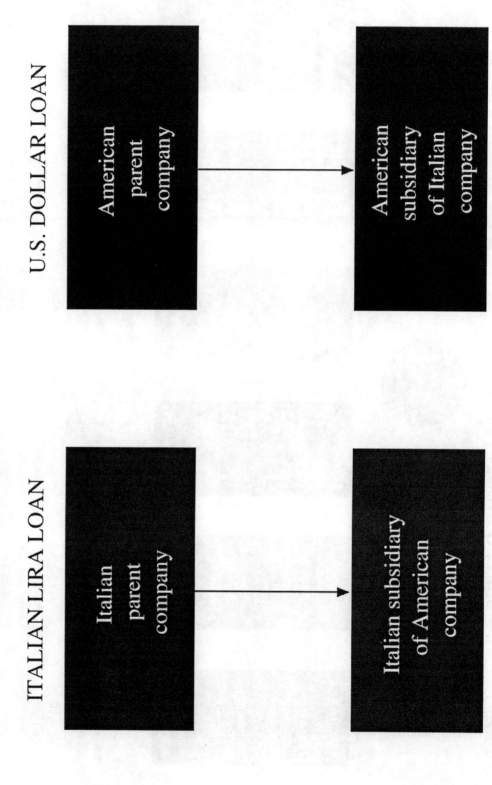

ITALIAN LIRA LOAN

U.S. DOLLAR LOAN

Italian parent company

Italian subsidiary of American company

American parent company

American subsidiary of Italian company

TM 19.4
Figure 19.4

Parallel Swap (Where a Soft Currency is Involved)

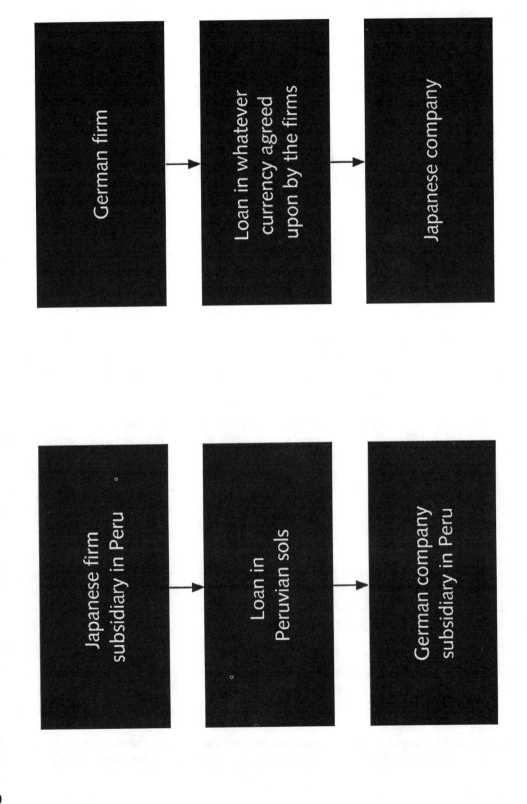

McGraw-Hill/Irwin

CHAPTER 20
GLOBAL OPERATIONS MANAGEMENT

Learning Objectives

1. To show Japanese, American and European efforts to improve quality and lower costs.

2. Explain why multinational firms wish to standardize production processes and procedures.

3. To examine some of the reasons why standardization may be difficult to achieve.

4. To discuss problems with just-in-time and describe synchronous manufacturing, the American solution.

5. To study the four principal factors involved in the efficient operation of the production system

6. To examine global sourcing and the increasing role of electronic purchasing for global sourcing.

Overview

As firms continue to enter global markets, global competition increases, which forces managements of international and domestic firms to search for ways to lower costs and improve their products to remain competitive. Often, the solution is outsourcing of non-core activities. The emergence of electronic purchasing has the potential to significantly influence the nature and extent of global outsourcing activities.

Because General McArthur could not find reliable radios in Japan after World War II, he brought two American engineers to Japan to lecture Japanese executives on the use of statistics to get the production system under control to produce quality products. W. Edwards Deming was brought over to teach the course in statistical control of quality.

After WW II, Japanese manufacturers created a production system, just-in-time, based primarily on American production concepts, to improve product quality and lower production costs. The system required coordinated management of materials, people and suppliers. There are some problems with JIT, however, and American production experts developed synchronous production, whose goal is unbalanced production scheduling instead of the balanced scheduling of JIT. Attention is focused on the bottleneck of the production system and scheduling for the entire system is controlled by the output of the bottleneck operation.

Multinational managements prefer to standardize production processes worldwide, but environmental differences may require some to be altered or discarded. Governments in developing nations, preoccupied with high unemployment and rising capital costs, are urging investors to use an intermediate technology instead of the highly automated process of industrialized nations. The multinationals' response has been, in some instances, to search for the appropriate technology, which may range from the most advanced to the most primitive.

The factors involved in the efficient operation of a production system are (1) plant location, (2) plant layout, (3) materials handling and (4) the human element. Once the system is in operation, two general classes of activities must be performed: (1) productive and (2) supportive. The line organization which is responsible for the productive activities must produce on time the required amount of product with the desired quality at the budgeted cost. Low output, inferior quality and excessive manufacturing costs are obstacles to meeting production standards. The supportive activities which are essential to the operation of the system include quality control, inventory control and purchasing, maintenance and technical functions.

Suggestions and Comments

1. We find that business students are generally interested in this material much of which has not been covered in other classes. In fact, we included in our AACSB self study the hours spent on covering production in this course as part of our general coverage of the production area.

2. Our experience with this chapter has shown us that the material is fairly easy to cover because by now the students are familiar with our approach of examining the environmental forces which require exceptions to be made to management's desire for worldwide standardization.

3. There is new material here even for the students who have taken a production course–the discussion of electronic purchasing and the discussion of intermediate and appropriate technologies, for example.

Student Involvement Exercises

1. Point 5 in the section, Japanese Efforts to Lower Costs and Improve Quality, points out a problem that a marketing manager might have with the Japanese JIT. Ask the class what objections a marketing manager and customers might have to the Japanese JIT production system.

2. "There's no free lunch." What do the Japanese give up when they eliminate inventory?

3. Overby Manufacturing of Boston has begun to build a plant in Bangkok and management is choosing American personnel who will be sent to fill the top administrative positions. The Vice President for Procurement wants to send a promising young buyer to head up the purchasing department of the new operation, but the Personnel Manager in the home office insists that someone from Bangkok should be hired for the position. What do you suppose are the arguments that each is using to convince the other? What would you recommend?

Guest Lecturers

1. The material in this chapter opens up a whole new area of experts which have not been called upon in previous chapters. You can invite someone from a multinational who has been a purchasing agent in an overseas plant, for example, or someone from purchasing who has been involved in designing or implementing electronic purchasing system.

2. Someone from the Technical Department of the international operations of a multinational can relate some interesting experiences about getting along with local inputs while trying to maintain company quality standards.

3. Someone who has had overseas production experience (many in the technical department of the local multinational have been factory managers) can tell the class about production problems and difficulties in motivating workers, etc.

4. The Industrial Relations Department of a local multinational may have people who have held this job in an overseas plant. If so, they can give accounts of what they did to reduce absenteeism and what special kinds of facilities had to be furnished the workers. This speaker can also discuss points covered in the next chapter.

Lecture Outline

I.   Opening Section
      Originally, as the name indicates, Johnson Controls was known for producing heating controls. It

also manufactured plastic containers, but not automotive products. Until 1985, carmakers made their own car seats, but then Johnson and another firm, Lear, thought of supplying these essential parts for them.

Now, the company estimates that 80 percent of the seating in American-made cars is outsourced. As their customers move overseas, they expect Johnson to supply them from local production. In response, the company has established over 130 seatmaking plants. Johnson is increasing the input of its engineers to the seating design so that it can use the results in seats of other car manufacturers. Another strategy has been to increase its sales by supplying more of the interior than just seats. To manage the complexity of a global production system, the company is creating a standardized business operating system and a single, global infrastructure, thus helping to eliminate variation and inefficiencies across factories.

Johnson is building on its experience that existing customers are its largest source of growth by offering them opportunities to outsource more to them, such as the operation and maintenance of commercial buildings for whom they once were the source of just heating and ventilation controls.

II. Sourcing Globally

To improve competitiveness in the face of increasing global competition, both international and domestic companies seek ways to lower costs while improving their products. A common solution is outsourcing (hiring others to do noncore activities instead of doing them inhouse), and any activity in the value chain can be outsourced. The examples of Johnson Controls and Walkerhut provide illustrations of firms trying to exploit this trend toward outsourcing, and they topsy-turvy example shows a company based on outsourcing most of its activities.

A. Reasons for Sourcing Globally

The primary reason for sourcing globally is to obtain lower prices. In addition, certain products may not be available locally. Also, the firms; competitors may be using components of better quality or better design. Table 20.1, p. 675 presents the reasons given and the percentages of the respondents for each reason in a survey of 149 American firms doing foreign sourcing.

B. Global Sourcing Arrangements

1. Wholly owned subsidiaries–established in a country with low cost labor.

2. Overseas joint venture–established where labor costs are lower to supply components to the home country.

3. In-bond plant contractor–home country plant sends components to be machined and assembled or just assembled by an independent contractor in an in-bond plant.

4. Overseas independent contractor–common in the clothes industry in which firms with no production facilities such as DKNY, Liz Claiborne, and Nike, contract foreign manufacturers to make clothing to their specifications with their label.

5. Independent overseas manufacturer.

C. Importance of Global Sourcing

In 1998, U.S. parent companies imported $158.1 billion (44% of all American imports) from their overseas subsidiaries and foreign firms imported from the U. S. affiliates $185.4 billion (42% of total American exports). In U.S. industry, the proportion of purchased materials in the overall cost of goods sold has been increasing for several decades, from an average of 40% in 1945 to 40% in 1960 and 55% to 79% today. The Cognizant Technology Solutions example on page 689 illustrates a small or medium sized firm taking advantage of global sourcing developments.

D. Finding Global Sources and the increasing use of electronic purchasing for global sourcing. The import sources in Chapter 17 are the ones a professional purchasing agent would investigate. Entering exporter and the product name in a search engine will bring up Web sites of exporters around the world that have on-line catalogs and information on how to order their products. Some buyers use the Internet to look for suppliers. See the text for examples of electronic procurement exchanges, such as Exostar, Covisint, Chem Connect, and Elitex, which instructors could use as Internet exercises to have students examine the nature of these exchanges.

The purchasing function has been neglected for many years in many companies. However, purchasing is increasingly being viewed as a strategic function, a trend encouraged by rapid development of electronic procurement. Along with this trend is the increasing level of attention being given to indirect procurement, or the purchasing of goods and services that are not part of finished goods.

Options for Global Electronic Procurement

Among the most basic transactions that can occur over electronic purchasing exchanges are catalog purchases. Suppliers provide a catalog of available products, and the offerings and prices can be adjusted in real time according to availability and the need to move particular products.

Electronic exchanges can permit buyers and sellers to interact through a standard bid/quote system in which buyers can post their purchasing needs online for all prospective suppliers to view, and suppliers can then submit private quotes to the buyer.

Benefits of Global Electronic Procurement Systems

The use of electronic purchasing systems results in substantial benefits. Oracle Corporation announced it would save $2 billion in 2000 due to company wide ebusiness initiatives. Hewlett-Packard estimated that business-to-business exchanges could reduce purchasing costs for high-technology industries by at least 40%.

Electronic procurement systems can also benefit smaller companies in their purchasing or sales effects. These systems might enable smaller, resource-constrained suppliers to establish and maintain competitively viable electronic sourcing or purchasing systems of their own or exploit potential benefits of global supplier or buyer markets.

Overall, development in electronic procurement systems can help to optimize the management of supply chains not only within a single company, but across entire networks of organizations.

E. Problems with Global Sourcing
Companies making foreign purchases may be surprised to find that the supposedly low price of the import is not low when all costs are considered. Following are the costs of importing with an estimated percentage of the quoted price that each adds:

1. International freight, insurance, and packing (10-12%)
2. Import duties (0-50%)
3. Customhouse broker fees (3-5%)
4. Inventory in the pipeline (5-15%)
5. Cost of letter of credit (1%)
6. International travel and communications (2-8%)
7. Company import specialists (5%)
8. Rework of products out of specifications (0-15%)
   Boeing decided to buy a subassembly from a Japanese manufacturer after buying from an American supplier for years. It soon found the Japanese firm's quality and delivery

performance so poor, Boeing's engineers wished they had stayed with the American supplier.

Many firms have brought their overseas manufacturing facilities back from overseas. The labor content is down in many instances to 5%. The time value of fast service is worth more than that.

Other disadvantages of Global sourcing

Importers can face an increase in price because the home currency has lost value as a result of exchange rate fluctuation. To address this risk, as discussed in Chapter 19, hedging has been used for many years by companies that operate internationally, particularly if their raw materials include one or more of the commodities traded or established commodities markets.

The emergence of electronic procurement has also been accompanied by problems. Many early efforts at developing e-procurement systems have been done in isolation from the company's overall business systems and have subsequently failed to achieve their potential benefits. Security can also be a significant concern for e-procurement, including allowing competitors or customers to see proprietary details of their business. Different country standards are also a concern when attempting to implement international e-procurement systems.

III.   Production Systems

    A. Advanced Production Technology–Japan
        The Japanese realized after WW II that they would have to produce high quality products at low prices to be able to compete in world markets. Japanese goods were known to be of poor quality. They brought in American experts such as Duran and Deming who showed them how to improve quality and productivity.

    B. Japanese Efforts to Lower Costs and Improve Quality

       1. Lower Costs
           In examining costs, they realized that inventory costs are a major factor. They would have to operate without inventory, but certain requirements would have to be met;

          a. Components had to be defect-free.

          b. Components had to be delivered at each point in the production process when they were needed.

          c. If they were to eliminate inventory and still satisfy customers' delivery time demands, they would have to set up flexible production units which necessitated rapid setup times.

          d. They also had to reduce process time.

          e. They simplified product lines to decrease need for production changeovers.

          f. They had to have the cooperation of their suppliers.

          g. Marketers, production people, designers, and suppliers had to work as a team before the first product was produced.

          h. This enabled any of the members to suggest changes before the first product was produced.

       2. Improve Quality

          a. Everyone in the company had to be committed to quality-total quality control.

          b. Quality circles with worker participation were started.

       3. Problems with Implementing the Japanese Just-In-Time system

          a. American manufacturers copied parts of JIT without realizing it was a total system.

     b. Difference in attitudes between Japanese and American managers–Americans valued the specialization of the worker.

     c. Difficult to get worker loyalty in American plants–no guarantee of employment.

     d. Failure to train and integrate suppliers into the system. Example, an auto company in Michigan receiving parts from a supplier in Canada.

C. Advanced Production Technology

  1. Problems with JIT

     a. JIT is restricted to operations that product the same parts repeatedly–balanced system.

     b. If one operation stops, the whole line stops.

     c. Difficult to achieve a balanced system because production capacities differ among the different classes of machines.

     d. JIT makes no allowances for contingencies so every piece must be defect-free or line stops.

     e. JIT is a slow process to put into effect because it is a process of trial and error.

  2. Synchronous Manufacturing

     a. Because of these problems, Americans turned to synchronous manufacturing, a manufacturing system whose output is set at the output of the operation that is working at full capacity (bottleneck). Output levels are *unbalanced,* instead of balanced as in JIT. Attention is focused on the bottleneck. a defective part won't shut down the system.

  3. Soft Manufacturing
    In the new American factory, software and labor are more important than production machines. IBM found that hand labor with software networks to be more efficient than robots. Soft manufacturing has made plants more agile. A firm can customize products one at a time while producing them at mass production speeds. Example: Motorola pagers factory in Florida.

  4. European Production Technology
    Knowledge sources say Europeans are two year behind Americans. However, Germans are reengineering, delayering, and outsourcing to regain competitiveness. Europeans are consolidating operation to reduce costs. IBM France produces all mainframes for Europe.

  5. Europe has Fallen Farther Behind
    Two recent studies claim that Europe has fallen farther behind in world competitiveness. The McKinsey study described in Chapter 13 claims there is a large and growing age between the performances of six industries in Germany and France compared to those in the world's leaders. Another study done in 1998 blamed the European nations for failing to restructure their economies to face growing competition. The report criticized France's strategy of trying to reduce unemployment by imposing shorter working hours.

D. International Effort to Improve Quality and Lower Costs
  Western firms that are succeeding–G.M., G.E., IBM, Ford, and Motorola are examples of American firms that have synchronous production and a TQM system. Corning has increased productivity 25% annually. Its integration of employees and technology has attracted so many visitors from European, Japanese, and American firms, it conducts a tour of the plant for a fee. Corning brings together under one roof representatives from product design, engineering, manufacturing, procurement, marketing, and suppliers to work on new products, a technique called concurrent engineering.

E. Reasons for Global Standardization of Manufacturing Systems

1. Standards are documented agreements containing technical specifications or other precise criteria that will be used consistently as guidelines, risks, or definitions of the characteristics of a product, process or service. Standards help ensure that materials, products, processes, and services are appropriate for their purpose. Examples include credit cards and phone cards. In most countries, standards have been developed across product lines and for various functions. Examples discussed include ASTM in the United States and the most-used standard in Europe, ISO 9000. The ISO 9000 and ISO 9001 sets of standards are for products and services, while the ISO 14000 series provides a framework for quality assurance in the area of environmental management.

2. Organization and Staffing
   Standardization of production processes simplifies production organization at headquarters because it permits work to be accomplished with a smaller staff. Fewer different specialists are needed.

3. Logistics of supply-standardization of processes and machinery should make parts produced in all plants interchangeable so that the production of components can be divided among them (called rationalization). See Figure 20.1, page 691 for the many sources of components of the Ford Escort.

4. Purchasing, control, and planning–all are easier with standardization production systems.

F. Impediments of Globalization of Production Facilities
   1. Environmental Forces
      The foreign environmental forces, especially the economic, cultural and political, often intervene to cause diversity in the units of a multiplant operation.
      a. Economic Forces
         (1) Production requirements vary among plants because of differences in market size.
         (2) Plant designer has option of selecting capital-intensive processes incorporating automated, high-output machinery or labor-intensive methods which employ more people operating semi-manual, general-purpose machinery. A third alternative, CIM, is becoming available but its high cost and high technological content limits its application to industrialized nations.
         (3) Automatic machines are high output but are inflexible as to range of work they will do.
         (4) Automation increases the productivity per worker, but output may be so high that machine is used only part of time. Labor costs may be lower, but capital costs can be higher.
         (5) Lack of floor space may require a few high capacity machines.
         (6) This specialized machinery does require process materials to be supplied that are within narrow limits as to size and quality. Local suppliers may be unable to furnish them within such tight specifications. Firm may overcome this problem by backward vertical integration even when it would be preferable economically to purchase the materials from local vendors.
      b. Cultural Forces
         (1) The lack of trained operators for the semi-manual general purpose machinery may be sufficient reason to install highly automated equipment.
         (2) Absenteeism–if the few highly skilled people necessary to operate the automated machinery do not come to work, the entire plant may be shut down. Some plants maintain an extra backup crew to overcome this problem.

318

c. Political Forces
    (1) Government officials often insist that the most modern equipment be installed even when there is high unemployment which would favor using labor-intensive processes.
    (2) The reasons may be local pride or the fear that "old fashioned" processes will not produce goods of export quality.
2. Some Design Solutions
    a. Hybrid Design
       The plant may incorporate capital-intensive processes where they are considered essential for product quality and labor-intensive procedures to take advantage of low cost labor.
    b. Intermediate Technology
       (1) Many LDC governments are searching for something between the capital-intensive and the labor-intensive processes.
       (2) This requires companies to develop manufacturing methods with which they have no experience.
3. Appropriate Technology
    a. Some firms are studying all possibilities for manufacturing a product to come up with the appropriate technology.
    b. In some instances, the newest, most automated processes will be installed, whereas in other situations, the processes may be quite primitive.
    c. See Table 20.2, page 697 for comparisons of appropriate and capital intensive technologies.
G. The Local Production System
1. The local production organization is commonly a scaled-down version of the parent company's organization.
2. Horizontal and Vertical Integration
    a. The overseas affiliate is rarely as integrated as is the parent.
    b. Additional investment is required and the parent does not want to lose sales to its captive customers, the foreign affiliates, of the inputs which the more highly integrated parent frequently produces.
3. Design of Manufacturing System
    A manufacturing system is essentially a functionally related groups of activities for creating value. Factors involved in the efficient operation of the system are: (1) plant location, (2) plant layout, (3) materials handling, and (4) the human element
    a. Plant Location
       (1) Plant location is significant because of its effect on production and distribution costs which may be in conflict.
       (2) The gain in lower land and labor costs obtained by locating away from cities may be offset by the increased expense of warehousing and transportation of the finished products to serve these markets.
    b. Plant Layout
       (1) The designer must try to obtain the maximum utility from the building space while providing room for future expansion of each department.

319

(2) Sometimes, management in developing countries will stint on space for employees' facilities believing that employees will accept less because they are used to less. Labor laws, however, may require more than the home country does.

c. Materials Handling

(1) Careful planning of materials handling systems is a major consideration in synchronous manufacturing

(2) In countries with an abundance of labor, this fact frequently is overlooked. Poor materials handling methods can result in idle machinery, damaged products and late deliveries.

d. Human Element

(1) The effectiveness of manufacturing system depends on people who are affected by the system.

(2) Lower production results from excessive noise, poor illumination and extreme heat or cold.

(3) In nations where workers are smaller, machinery controls may need to be altered or extra lifting devices added.

4. Operation of the Manufacturing System
Two general classes of activities must be performed: (1) productive and (2) supportive.

a. Productive Activities
The line organization must work with labor, raw materials and machinery to produce on time the required amount of product with the desired quality at the budgeted cost.

b. Obstacles to Meeting Production Standards

(1) Low Output

(a) Suppliers either fail to meet delivery date of deliver out-of-spec materials.

(b) Poor coordination of production scheduling

(c) Absenteeism

(2) Inferior Product Quality

(a) Excessively high quality standards may be set by headquarters

(b) If local plant parts of worldwide logistics system, it may have to product a special export quality as well as something of lower quality for its domestic market.

(3) Excessive Manufacturing Costs

(a) Budget assumptions may be incorrect.

(b) Production and Maintenance may overstock raw materials and spare parts.

(c) Just-in-time minimum inventory of component parts.

c. Supportive Activities

(1) Purchasing

(a) Production depends on the purchasing department to buy raw materials, components parts, supplies and machinery at prices which are comparable to what competitors are paying.

(b) Purchasing agents must be able to develop sources of supply.

(c) Where firms depends heavily on imports, purchasing agent needs to know import procedures and have good relations with government officials.

(d) There is frequently considerable debate at headquarters over whether a local citizen should be in charge of purchasing because he or she is familiar with local suppliers and government officials or should home office employees be in charge because of their knowledge of company purchasing procedures and because they have no family or friends to favor when awarding contracts.

(2) Maintenance

(a) The maintenance department is responsible for preventing the occurrence of unscheduled work stoppages caused by equipment failure.

(b) Preventive maintenance programs, common in developed nations, are difficult to install in developing countries where there often is a fatalistic attitude towards equipment.

(c) Furthermore, managements dislike stopping production for maintenance when they need the output to fill orders.

(3) Technical Function

(a) The technical department provides production with manufacturing specifications.

(b) The technical manager is a key figure in the maintenance of product quality and is influential in the choice of suppliers.

(c) Globals and multinationals strive to place their own people in this position so that the affiliate will be sure to purchase all possible inputs from the parent.

Answers to Questions

1. Operations are designed to produce the same quantity of parts but when one operation stops because of a machine breakdown, the entire production line stops. Achieving a balanced line is difficult because production differs for different classes of machines. Every piece must be defect-free so there is no provision for any sudden output of defective parts. JIT is a slow process to put into effect because it is the result of trial and error. These are the tradeoffs or disadvantages of JIT.

2. The reasons for a large and increasing proportion of purchased materials in the overall cost of goods sold for U.S. industry include greater complexity of products and increasing pressure for firms to focus on their core business and outsource other activities in which they lack strong competitive ability. In addition, competitive pressures and an emphasis on reduced concept-to-market cycle times in many product and service sectors have resulted in a rapid increase in the number of new products that are made available to the market. It has been estimated that at least 50% of products currently on the market were not available 5 years ago. This development creates additional pressure to locate suppliers worldwide that can provide inputs at competitive prices and quality and with quick responsiveness to market changes.

3. a. Who is responsible for inventory? Responsibility must be shared among suppliers, customers and the company. Suppliers have a key role in inventory, since defects in components affect such factors as the levels of work-in-progress and the level of finished goods inventory (e.g., for safety stock). The ability of supplier to deliver the proper quantity and quality of parts and components, and at the proper time, also influence inventory levels. Customers have a role in inventory since the level of product they hold (e.g., inventory held by distributors and retailers), the urgency with which they require replenishment inventory, and the distribution infrastructure (e.g., delivery times and costs) influence the level of inventory, of course. Decisions regarding general purpose versus specialized machinery can influence changes over times and costs, and thus influence the size and timing of production runs (and thus the level of inventory to hold). The internal systems (e.g., regarding the ability of a worker to shut down the production line if a defect or problem is discovered) also affect inventory.

Overall, systems such as just-in-time require balance within and among the company's parts (and with suppliers and customers in order to effectively manage inventory.

    b.   Inventory is carried as an asset on the balance sheet, but the costs associated with financing inventory (including costs for product obsolescence) end up on the income statement (and correspondingly can influence levels of retained earnings and shareholder equity on the balance sheets).

4.   Traditionally the costs to carry inventory include: storage, handling, taxes, insurance, shrinkage (pilferage), shelf life (obsolescence, spoilage), interest (usually some cost of capital based on one of several methods of determining the firm's cost to acquire capital, but not the opportunity cost of capital), and stockouts (admitted as a problem, but seldom formally incorporated by managers as part of the calculation of costs of carrying inventory, due to the difficulty of determining an appropriate value).

In the past a major problem with inventory carrying or holding costs has been that, while these costs have been acknowledged in the classroom, in the "real world" there was no such category on the firm's accounting statements nor did any particular person usually have an explicit responsibility for them. (For example, the instructor can have students look at the balance sheet and income statement of essentially any company - ask if they see any mention of "the cost to carry inventory for the last accounting period?" Of course, there will not be such an item listed). So the costs of carrying inventory have basically been ignored unless managers (or teachers) needed a value to plug into the old "economic lot size" ordering rule (i.e., Economic Order Quantity calculations). This figure was usually something around 20% of the value of the inventory (this figure was probably used because it was easier to calculate the square root of 20!).

Finally, managers (particularly in Japan) came to the conclusion that the cost to carry inventory was indeed a real cost and that it should include the opportunity cost of capital. Although the actual value is difficult to determine in any particular firm, the Japanese estimates have often been about 40 to 50% of the value of the inventory as the annual cost of carrying the inventory. That is, if a company has inventory valued at $8 million, then it would be estimated to cost from $3.4 to $4 million a year to carry it! This has fundamental implications for the adoption of just-in-time scheduling (JIT), popularized by practices in Toyota (for example, see article by Y. Monden, Journal of Industrial Engineering, January, 198 1, pages 36-46). By managing the quantity and timing of inventory delivered to a plant, as well as carefully managing the amount of inventory carried in work- in-progress and finished goods, the overall level of inventory (and the associated costs of carrying this inventory) can be substantially reduced.

5.   Instead of trying to balance the manufacturing system, synchronous manufacturing's output is set at the output of the operation that is working at full capacity. Work is assigned to each operation rather than to the entire system. Other operations work at less than full capacity. Because capacities of each operation are known, production scheduling can be simulated instead of having to arrive at solutions by trial and error. Instead of having the production stop in case of a shutdown of the machine at the bottleneck operation, inventory can be placed there. If necessary, a quality control inspector can be placed at the bottleneck operation to check output. Note that management's attention is focused on the bottleneck operation rather than on all operations whose output can be increased for a period if any problem occurs.

6.   For a person in a developed country, a good quality pickup may be one that can travel at high speeds over paved highways for hours without problems. As long as the owner maintains it according to the manufacturer's specifications, the ride is smooth and quiet. To a farmer in Africa, a quality pickup may be one that can carry heavy overloads at slow speeds over bad dirt roads with little maintenance. Noise of operation and high speed capability are of little importance.

7. Synchronous manufacturing requires participative management which runs counter to the cultures of some developing nations. Although synchronous manufacturing will permit some tardiness in the arrival of supplier deliveries, its delivery requirements are much stricter than those to which many suppliers in developing nations are accustomed. Absenteeism will create problems with synchronous manufacturing as it will with JIT and this is a problem in developing nations. Maintenance to avoid unscheduled breakdowns is less critical with synchronous manufacturing than it is for JIT (except at the bottleneck operations) but it is important nevertheless. Getting people to practice preventive maintenance is still not easy in developing nations. Synchronous manufacturing requires a high degree of planning, which is still difficult to achieve in developing nations.

8. Benefits of standards to a buyer company include assurance that materials, products, processes, and services are appropriate for their purpose, which helps to reduce uncertainty for the buyer company, as well as customers of the buyer company.
Benefits of standards to a vendor company include 1) the ability to qualify as a supplier by providing assurance that the vendor's materials, products, processes, and services are appropriate for the intended purpose of the buyer, (2) avoidance of unexpected technical barriers due to the existence of unknown, non-harmonized standards and thus facilitating international exchange of goods and services, and (3) reductions in customer complaints as well as reduced operating costs and increased demand for the vendor's products and services.

9. A JIT manufacturing system must have components delivered exactly when they are needed and they must all be useable or the system stops. There is no inventory that production can call on if parts are defective.

10. The worldwide standardization of manufacturing systems simplifies both their organization and their control from headquarters. Because the planning and design work is essentially a duplication of what has already been done, there is a saving in both time and money. Product specifications are easier to change and parts manufactured by the various plants are interchangeable–important if company wants to rationalize the manufacturing process worldwide.

11. a. Economic force–the wide range of market sizes makes standardization difficult. The domestic plant whose daily output may be greater than the year's production of a small foreign affiliate, will have a special purpose machines set up to product continuously one size of one product. The subsidiary may require a general purpose machine capable of producing many sizes of a multiplicity of products. Machine setups to produce different products may have to be made two or three times a shift.
Because of labor and capital cost differences, the mix of labor and capital-intensive machinery generally will differ among markets more than the home office would like.

   b. Cultural force–Elements of the cultural force may override the decisions taken on the basis of economic reasoning and tend to favor worldwide standardization. Pressures from the political force, however, can require management to deviate from its plan to standardize production.

   c. Political force–Government officials, when pressured to provide jobs, will exert tremendous pressure on the multinational to install labor-intensive processes. Production costs are of secondary importance unless they wish the affiliate to export. In addition, pride in having a plant with the latest equipment is strong among government administrators. Just read an LDCs newspaper account of a new plant's inauguration. The account is complete with pictures of the president accompanied by dignitaries from nearby with pictures of the president accompanied by dignitaries from nearby countries to watch him cut the ribbon at the dedication. (You have to see it to believe it.)

12. Inasmuch as production costs are considered to be excessive when they are higher than budgeted (standard) costs, either the actual or the standard cost may be at fault. A lower than normal rate of output or the carrying costs of inventories (raw materials and finished goods) could be responsible for higher actual costs. A high rate of product rejects or a large amount of scrap are other possibilities.

    Standard costs which are set for a given rate of production will be low relative to actual costs when less than the amount forecast is being manufactured. This is because fixed overheads are being allocated among smaller quantities. Overly optimistic sales forecasts, excessive standard production rates (based perhaps on the domestic experience) and unforeseen shutdowns are some of the reasons why the standard costs will be too low.

13. This question usually creates a good discussion.
    Advantages of hiring a local citizen:

    a. The citizen is better acquainted with local supply sources.

    b. The citizen's knowledge of government procedures and officials is invaluable when the subsidiary depends heavily on imports.

    c. The citizen is familiar with the local way of doing business.

    Advantages of employing someone from the home office:

    a. The home employee is familiar with company purchasing procedures and the requirements for raw materials, machinery and supplies.

    b. The home employee will not be concerned with giving business to members of the extended family.

    c. Perhaps the home employee will be less susceptible to taking bribes. At least the home employee is likely to be fearful of jeopardizing future employment with the company by committing unethical practices.

14. Production machinery must not stop unexpectedly in either a JIT or a synchronous production system, but unforeseen stoppages create problems for any system. When a company can sell everything it produces and has large backorders, management is reluctant to stop production while maintenance personnel inspect and replace worn parts. A fatalistic attitude that is common in some cultures is a deterrent to planning, the basis of preventive maintenance.

15. Breakdown maintenance refers to the situation in which the company chooses to wait until a machine or another element in the production process fails, and then the failed machine or other element is repaired. Breakdown maintenance may be a viable alternative for situations in which breakdowns cannot be readily predicted or for which maintenance cannot be easily and cost-effectively applied in a preventive manner. In addition, if the costs of breakdown are low (e.g., there is adequate inventory to allow the company to respond to the breakdown; the implications of breakdown are not significant for employment, customer satisfaction, etc.), then the implications of a breakdown maintenance approach may be mitigated. In some cases, preventive maintenance may also require a greater degree of skill and knowledge than does breakdown maintenance, and indeed a level of skill or knowledge that is scarce in the company or country of operation. As discussed in the text (page 703), however, there are many potential drawbacks of a breakdown maintenance approach and these must be considered by management.

Answers to Internet Problems

1. The students will find information on investing in Mexico at the Mexico Connect Business Web site (among others). The address is www.mexconnect.com/mex_/buisness.html. Click on "General Info" and then on "Trade and NAFTA" and then on "Doing Business."

a. For most activities, it is 100 percent. There are a few activities where 100 percent ownership by foreign investors is not permitted.

b. There is no maximum limit in Mexico as there is in some countries.

c. 48 hours

d. interestingly, it's 125 percent

e. A company can import raw materials, packaging materials, machinery, fuel, and spare parts without paying import duty or value added tax to manufacture their goods.

Discussion of Minicase 20–1: Maquinas para el Hogar Penwick

a. You will have to show the local managers how synchronous production has reduced costs and improved quality at other Penwick plants.

b. The home office is proud of the fact that Penwick-El Pais is the country's market leader and wants to help them remain the market leader.

c. Top management wants the local company to grow and possibly produce for export as soon as it can compete on price and quality in world markets.

d. Furthermore, by manufacturing world class products, foreign competitors will be reluctant to set up plants in El Pais which could create competition that could lead to cutbacks in the Penwick-El Pais plant.

e. Synchronous manufacturing has made Penwick plants in the U. S. more profitable, which has resulted in larger year-end bonuses for managers. You expect that similar improvement in Penwick-El Pais will enable local managers to receive similar increases in their bonuses.

f. Another advantage is the fact that after installing synchronous manufacturing in the U. S. production has run more smoothly–less headaches for managers. For example, now, regular meetings of the production manager, purchasing manager, design manager and the marketing are followed without much worker input. The local plant may have trouble initially in educating workers to participate in quality circles and take responsibility for quality control. But this was also a problem in Penwick-US so the company has experience in training workers on these points.

g. The purchasing department will have a lot of work to do in persuading suppliers in a sellers market to deliver defect-free components on time. It requires suppliers to adopt statistical control of production (the Deming process) so that they know how free of defects their output will be before it is produced. This is a significant change and some suppliers who sell everything they make, may be reluctant to do it. Suppliers may have to have their own transportation system if they can't find truckers to provide the service they require. One way out may be for Penwick-El Pais to work with the cottage industry as the Japanese do. In any developing country, there are families of artisans that have "factories" in their homes. Penwick-El Pais may have to build a network of these people–lend them capital to buy a machine or two and train them. Singer Sewing Machine has sold many industrial sewing machines on credit in developing nations to women who have their own businesses in their homes.

h. Preventive maintenance is crucial. Cultural forces may make it difficult to establish preventive maintenance.

i. Managers have to plan in synchronous manufacturing and they do have time to plan because supervisors and workers run much of the production system by themselves. Because of the culture, is there an aversion to planning in El Pais?

Note that these are all problems that Penwick-US has had to face so the company has experience in educating workers and managers. Because of cultural differences, the training probably will take longer in El Pais, however.

TM 20.1
Figure 20.1

UNITED KINGDOM
Carburetor, rocker arm, clutch, ignition, exhaust, oil pump, distributor, cylinder bolt, cylinder head, flywheel ring gear, heater, speedometer, battery, rear wheel spindle, intake manifold, fuel tank, switches, lamps, front disc steering wheel, steering column, glass, weatherstrips, locks, mirrors, starter, alternator

FRANCE
Cylinder head, master cylinder, brakes, underbody coating, weatherstrips, clutch release bearings, seat pads and frames, transmission cases, clutch cases, tires, suspension bushes, ventilation units, heater, hose clamps, sealers, hardware

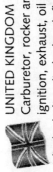

CANADA
Glass, radio

UNITED STATES
EGR valves, hydraulic tappet, glass

ITALY
Carburetor, lamps, defroster grills

SWEDEN
Hose clamps, cylinder bolt, exhaust down pipes, pressings, hardware

NETHERLANDS
Tires, paints, hardware

BELGIUM
Tires, tubes, seat pads, brakes, trim

SPAIN
Wiring harness, radiator and heater hoses, fork clutch release, air filter, battery, mirrors

SWITZERLAND
Underbody coating, speedometer gears

GERMANY
Locks, pistons, exhaust, ignition, switches, front disc, distributer, weatherstrips, rocker arm, speedometer, fuel tank, cylinder bolt, cylinder head gasket, front wheel knuckles, rear wheel spindle, transmission cases, clutch cases, clutch, steering column, glass, mirrors, starter, alternator

NORWAY
Exhaust flanges, tires

DENMARK
Fan belt

AUSTRIA
Tires, radiator and heater hoses

JAPAN
Starter, alternator, cone and roller bearings, windscreen washer pump

McGraw-Hill/Irwin

VIDEO CASES

Chapter 2

American Companies Invest in South Africa

Historically, American companies' investments in Africa have been rather modest. However, the level of U.S. investment has been increasing in recent years. This investment trend has been promoted by the emergence of democracy in the Republic of South Africa and other nations, which promotes political stability and the attractiveness of this region as a source for investment.

Levi Strauss opened a jeans manufacturing factory in the Republic of South Africa two years before the video was made. This was the company's first major investment in Africa, and served as a springboard for business in other African nations. The company reports that American companies have been welcomed by the government and by local consumers.

Business in Africa as a whole is growing rapidly for American firms. Sub-Saharan Africa now has about $5 billion in investment by American firms, including $160 million in Zimbabwe and $190 million in Kenya. At the time of the video, U.S. firms were opening offices in Africa at the rate of one company per week. Andrew Young, former U.S. representative to the United Nations, reports that the use of multinational delegations by U.S. companies makes them similar to the multiracial population in South Africa and helps to promote good relationships.

Chapter 4

World Bank/IMF

This video, which is from a news report, discusses a meeting of the World Bank and IMF held in Prague, Czech Republic. The video talks about those questioning international organizations and whether the international organizations help people. The video discusses debt relief for the heavily indebted poor countries (HIPCs). This video should encourage debate about international organizations and protests surrounding them such as what happened in Seattle in 1999 and Quebec City in 2001.

1. Should the World Bank and the IMF cancel debts of the HIPCs? What issues are involved in doing so? Answers will vary.
2. Are there other steps that the World Bank and the IMF should take to relive debt? Answers will vary.
3. Do international organizations assist people more in developing countries than in developed countries? Answers will vary.
4. Should other international organizations be concerned with this issue? Answers will vary.
5. How does this affect international business? Answers will vary, but it is important to understand that stability is necessary for business to success and it is difficult for a government to maintain stability when it is heavily in debt.

Chapter 5

Relative currency strengths help determine what country tourists come from and where they go. The video illustrates some results of the growth in strength of the US dollar in terms of the euro. When the euro was introduced in January 1999, it cost $1.17 for one euro, and the euro was forecast to strengthen and therefore to cost more in the future.

In fact, to the consternation of the "expert" forecasters, the euro weakened and by mid 2001 it cost around $.89, a 24 percent loss of value. Thus, unless European sellers raised their prices, buyers with US dollars enjoyed prices in dollar terms about a quarter lower in 2001 than in 1999. You can understand why American tourists were happily buying their ways through Europe.

Of course, as they spend dollars and buy euros to travel and shop, the increased demand for the euro tends to strengthen it. As the demand continues not only by tourists, but also by non-European businesses taking advantage of low European prices, the euro may move up in value as originally forecast.

1.   Why did US dollar holding tourists get lower prices in Europe in 2001 than in 1999?
2.   Are tourists the only ones taking advantage of lower euro prices?
3.   What changes in relative currency values are likely to occur due to increased demand for the euro?
4.   How does this video illustrate the importance of changes in relative currency values?

Chapter 6

Introduction of the euro

This video, which is from a news report on December 31, 1998, discusses the introduction of the euro as the currency in twelve of the EU member nations. (It was 11 countries at the time of the video, but Greece has since adopted the euro.) The video discusses the impact of the euro on U.S. businesses in Europe. The video can be used to start a discussion of the impact of the euro.

Discussion Questions:

1.   What is the euro? The currency of 12 EU member nations.
2.   What made it necessary for U.S. banks to spend money at the time of the introduction of the euro? It was necessary to convert software to accommodate the euro.
3.   Why will the euro make it easier for U.S. companies to do business in Europe? Instead of dealing with 12 separate currencies, companies now only need to deal with one.
4.   Why would U.S. companies welcome a euro that is stronger than the dollar? It would make U.S. exports more attractive in Europe.
5.   Will the euro replace the dollar in importance in the international monetary system? Answers will vary.

Chapter 7

Economic and Socioeconomic Forces

What do Global Exchange and The Rainforest Action Network have in common? When the World Trade Organization holds meetings, an opportunity presents itself for these and other groups to try to make their viewpoints known to a number of world leaders. At the last World Trade Organization meetings in Seattle, Washington, demonstrators at an outdoor pro-labor demonstration were seen carrying signs such as "Labor Says? Globalize Workers Rights!" "Tell The WTO No Child Labor! Would You Want Your

Child Working To Death?" At night, demonstrators staged sit-ins outside the Westin Hotel where WTO delegates were staying.

The protests at the WTO meetings help to illustrate socioeconomic differences between countries. Producers in the richer countries want to employ workers in developing countries who are willing to work for lower wages. But from the point of view of workers in richer countries, these workers in poorer countries are taking jobs away. At the same time, preferences in terms of child labor and environmental standards are different.

In this video, former President Bill Clinton is seen as well as United States Trade Representative Charlene Barshefsky. President Bush and Robert B. Zoellick, a former State and Treasury department official who is the new USTR, have these and other new trade issues before them. A new battleground for these groups as well as the next major international managed trade negotiations is the movement to negotiate the free trade area of the Americas (FTAA), an expansion of free trade to all 34 countries in the Americas except for Cuba.

Discussion Questions:

1.   What was the point of the protests in Seattle?

2.   With whom do low-wage workers compete in the richer countries?

3.   Why might it be difficult to harmonize child-labor laws around the world?

4.   What advantages might there be for poorer countries to belong to international organizations like the WTO?

Chapter 9

Feng Shui

Feng Shui is an ancient Asian art of harmonizing people and their environment, and virtually all high-rises in Hong Kong were built after consultation with a feng shui expert. This practice has spread, and a Trump hotel tower is shown as an example in the West of adoption of these principles here. Examples of bad feng shui are the front entrance to the Hong Kong legislative building and the governor's residence. An interesting example shown is the hotel with a large hole in its side, to allow the dragon in the mountain behind the hotel to come down and drink from Hong Kong Harbor.

Despite what the anchor says in the introduction to this report, I find no evidence that feng shui originated in Japan. In fact it is first seen in ancient China. Although seen earlier, the first textual references are from the Zhou dynasty (1046- 256 BC). An historical discussion is available at www.fengshuigate.com/qimancy.html.

Feng Shui is based on a a set of relationships between the "five elements" (wood, metal, fire, earth, water) and the "12 earthly branches" (rat, ox, tiger, rabbit, dragon, snake, horse, ram monkey, rooster, dog, pig). In addition to harmony with physical objects, feng shui provides principles concerning appropriate colors and the meaning of colors.

The pronunciation of this art is feng "schhhway," in one syllable, not a two-syllable "shoo-ey." A Chinese student would be happy to help with this pronunciation.

An example of the principles of feng shui: Ch'i (dragon's breath) can be good or bad. Bad ch'i flows in a straight line. Therefore you don't want to have a house where there is a direct path for wind entering the front door to leave through the back. Rather, a wall or other partition should break up the flow from front to back, allowing the air to circulate through the house. You might even be able to use a mirror to break up the straight line from front to back..

A second example is as follows. In an office, a manager's desk should not be close to the entry door, nor face the back wall, nor be free-standing in the middle. It needs to "lean"on a wall for support. The best wall is the one opposite the entry door, or a short side of the desk can lean against the back wall. (This is difficult to visualize, and are diagrams at my.geomancy.net/fs/office.htm).

Students may wonder about the complicated "compass" shown in the video. This is a *luopan* (see www.fengshuigate.com/qimancy.html).

Discussion Questions:

1.   Feng shui is intended to ensure harmony between what elements?
2.   What's wrong with the main entrance to Hong Kong's legislative building?
3.   Assume that you are planning to build a factory on Hong Kong. How could you use the information contained in this video case to illustrate that you are sensitive to the local environment?
4.   The next time you are in an office, examine the position of the desk. Is it in a good location or not?

Chapter 11

U.S. Apprehension of Suspected Criminal

This video, which is from a news report, discusses a decision of the United States Supreme Court authorizing the apprehension of a suspected criminal in Mexico. The decision caused public outcry in Latin America and other places because it raised questions about how much the United States actually respected the sovereignty of other nations. The United States defended its actions, which it called extraterritorial criminal apprehension. This video should engender debate about how far the United States should go in apprehending suspected criminals.

Discussion Questions:

1.   Why did the United States believe it was justified in entering another country and apprehending a suspected criminal? The U.S. felt it was within the law (citing a treaty with Mexico).
2.   What other steps should the U.S. have taken in order not to offend a neighboring sovereign nation? Answers will vary.
3.   What is the significance of the treaty that allowed the Supreme Court to make this decision? Answers will vary.
4.   Should Mexico and U.S. cooperate in other ways to prevent drug trafficking? Answers will vary.
5.   Did it matter that this was a criminal case and not a civil case? It probably could not have been done if it were a civil matter.

Chapter 12

Reports on Labor Abuses in Chinese Factories

This video, which is from a news report, discusses claims of labor abuses in Chinese factories, factories that produce goods for many large United States companies including Wal-Mart and Nike. The video discusses findings of the National Labor Committee for Human Rights, which investigated conditions in Chinese factories. The investigation found many workers were exposed to toxins and paid very low wages. Industry officials dispute the claims. The video should engender debate about whether labor conditions and human rights issues should be tied to trade issues.

Discussion Questions:

1. What conditions did the National Labor Committee for Human Rights find in Chinese factories? Low wages and poor working conditions

2. What is the National Labor Committee for Human Rights? An organization investigating potential working abuses in China.

3. Should foreign aid decisions or decisions on international trade and investment be tied to labor? Answers will vary.

4. Should the United States government and United States companies be concerned about labor conditions in other countries? Answers will vary.

Should United States companies continue to buy products produced in factories guilty of labor abuses? Answers will vary.

Chapter 13

Copy Right: Russia's Black Marketing of American Movies

Black market copying and sale of American movies has become a major business in Moscow. According to the video, the sale of pirated videos in Russia has cost Hollywood and other movie studios worldwide approximately $600 million. Russia is viewed as perhaps the most severely pirated market in the world by Jack Valenti, the President of the Motion Picture Association. New releases from American and other studios are quickly pirated, duplicated, and sold in the black market by pirate firms.

In Moscow, there are entire open-air markets that sell pirated videotapes, and these illicit tapes are also sold in neighborhood kiosks. The bootleg videos are quite popular, as they are cheaper than legitimate tapes and a consumer reports that there are not any video stores around anyway. The extent of piracy not only upsets the studios, which are losing revenues, but also the Russian government, which is upset because the video pirates are also cheating on their taxes.

Fighting the video pirates is a difficult challenge. The industry has attempted such efforts as "Video Amnesty Night," in which consumers can turn in their bootleg videotapes for legitimate tapes and also receive a t-shirt. The Russian government is trying to reduce the extent of piracy by establishing stiff fines and jail terms if the pirates are caught. However, the problem is still large and may be difficult to eradicate.

Chapter 15

Assessing and Analyzing Markets

As this segment opens, bank customers are shown waiting in line in Russia. Here the problem isn't poor customer service, but an example of the status of the Russia economy. In the late 1990s, the value of the ruble plummeted, while consumer prices skyrocketed. Banks in Russia had to close their doors to depositors.

Meanwhile, the report says things are bad in Japan as well. There, stock prices slid by $4240 billion in one week, the equivalent of the size of the entire Russian economy. Nor was the late-1990s malaise confined to two countries—in several nations, among them Mexico, Brazil, the Philippines and Australia, the stock market lost between 7 and 13%. The U.S. economy enjoyed a very strong economy for virtually the entire decade, helping to act as an economic boost to the rest of the world. However, by 2000 a considerable slowdown was in effect there.

This story gives a good snapshot of what is called the "domino effect—economies are to a large extent interdependent. Although we may want to evaluate countries on an individual basis, the forces that move an economy are only partially contained within that country.

Like changes in fashion which move across the world from one continent to another, "infecting" new populations along the way, economic "illness" also is not aware of political borders. Sometimes we can pick countries or markets which are the lucky recipients of economic good fortune sweeping a region, if not the global economy in general. At other times, we will not be so lucky.

Discussion Questions:

1. What is the "domino effect' described in this story?
2. Is a strong economy in one country—even if very large—likely to be sufficiently stimulating to prevent economic malaise everywhere?
3. In recent years we have seen several illnesses, such as AIDS, move from a limited area to affect much of the world. Is the analogy of the spread of a medical contaigon useful when considering the movement of consumer preferences, fads, and economic malaise across borders?
4. Japan and Russia are described as suffering from economic malaise. What, if anything, should this indicate for the potential of foreign direct investments made in either economy?

Chapter 16

Cannondale in Japan

Cannondale Japan has made a successful effort to market their all-terrain bikes to the Japanese. Their effort has required complete adaptation to the local culture on two levels. First, they adapted to local methods of approaching Japanese retailers who would carry their products. This required personal visits and small gifts to individual retailers. This had to be supported by further adaptations, in such areas as payments, marketing, advertising, and sponsorship of athletes. As one of the founders says, each of these elements is part of a "package—they all work together."

Of course even the goodwill of their retailers was necessary but not sufficient - they had to provide a product of interest to the Japanese consumer. Again, adaptation was necessary. Small changes such increasing the standover height to accommodate Japanese sizes and providing colors for local tastes - periwinkle purple proved to be popular—were required. It also helped that the Cannondale was able to provide a product that appeals to the growing Japanese taste for leisure activities. As the video aptly put it, the Japanese "want something exciting in their lives." The bikes are selling, even at twice their U.S. cost, because they appeal to Japanese tastes.

It is this need to adapt to local tastes that seems to be the key to success, since American products are actually very popular. Again, quoting one of the founders, few American companies seem willing to do so.

Discussion Questions:

1. If expensive, specialized bicycles can be sold to Japanese retailers by Americans, is there any trendy, updated American or European product that could not be sold in Japan?

2. You might ask your class whether there are any providers of unusual products or services in your local community that could be adapted to appeal to the Japanese (or any other foreign) market.

3. Does the experience of Cannondale Japan suggest that a strategy of standardization would work in Japan?

4. Cannondale Japan had to make modifications in both the product and the way it was marketed to succeed in Japan. But did those modifications seem to affect the core product, all terrain bicycles, very much?